GUN CONTROL IN THE UNITED STATES

A Reference Handbook

Other Titles in ABC-CLIO's
CONTEMPORARY
WORLD ISSUES
Series

Books in the Contemporary World Issues series address vital issues in today's society such as genetic engineering, pollution, and biodiversity. Written by professional writers, scholars, and nonacademic experts, these books are authoritative, clearly written, up-to-date, and objective. They provide a good starting point for research by high school and college students, scholars, and general readers as well as by legislators, businesspeople, activists, and others.

Each book, carefully organized and easy to use, contains an overview of the subject, a detailed chronology, biographical sketches, facts and data and/or documents and other primary-source material, a directory of organizations and agencies, annotated lists of print and nonprint resources, and an index.

Readers of books in the Contemporary World Issues series will find the information they need in order to have a better understanding of the social, political, environmental, and economic issues facing the world today.

GUN CONTROL IN THE UNITED STATES

A Reference Handbook

Gregg Lee Carter

CONTEMPORARY WORLD ISSUES

A B C CLIO

Santa Barbara, California
Denver, Colorado
Oxford, England

Copyright © 2006 by ABC-CLIO, Inc.

Library of Congress Cataloging-in-Publication Data

Carter, Gregg Lee, 1951-
  Gun control in the United States : a reference handbook / Gregg Lee Carter.
    p. cm. — (Contemporary world issues)
  Includes bibliographical references and index.
  ISBN 1-85109-760-0 (hardcover : alk. paper) — ISBN 1-85109-765-1 (ebook) 1. Gun control—United States. 2. Firearms—Law and legislation—United States. 3. Firearms—Social aspects—United States. 4. Violent crimes—United States. I. Title. II. Series.

  HV7436.C36 2006
  363.330973--dc22

                                    2006010884

ISBN 1-85109-760-0
E-book ISBN 1-85109-765-1

09 08 07 06 10 9 8 7 6 5 4 3 2 1

This book is also available on the World Wide Web as an e-book.
Visit www.abc-clio.com for details.

ABC-CLIO, Inc.
130 Cremona Drive, P.O. Box 1911
Santa Barbara, California 93116-1911

This book is printed on acid-free paper ∞.
Manufactured in the United States of America

Contents

Preface

Gun Control in the United States: A Reference Handbook is the result of a decade of research on the controversial topic of gun control. My goal is to provide a well-organized and readable reference that makes this complex subject more accessible to a variety of audiences: researchers, teachers, students, public officials, law-enforcement personnel, journalists, and interested members of the general public. To enhance accessibility, I have broken down gun control in the United States along its key dimensions: its current and proposed regulations, its effectiveness, its chronology, its similarities and differences to gun control in other industrialized democracies, important legislation and court rulings, individuals that have had a notable impact on it through political action or academic research, prominent organizations and agencies involved on both sides of the gun control debate, and those print and electronic resources that use valid data and skilled analysis to pursue each of these areas in more depth.

I propose no easy solutions to the problem of gun violence, and I take seriously the arguments and data supporting both sides of the gun debate. This is unusual. The vast literature on gun control is biased—strongly so. Popular writers and academics alike generally begin their books and essays with either a pro- or anti-gun slant and then proceed to line up the evidence to correspond with it—ignoring or discounting or misinterpreting any studies that do not fit. In contrast, I try to present enough information and logical reasoning, based on the best scholarly research to date, for each reader to make up his or her own mind on the benefits or harms that the strict control of guns might incur, as well as the obstacles facing those who would like to strengthen or weaken the current level of control. Everyone agrees that some control is necessary; the debate is over how much and what kind. All of this said, I must admit that over the years I have come to change my outlook from a fairly strong "gun rights" to a fairly strong "gun control" inclination. At heart, I am an empiricist, and though the logical reasoning of both sides of the gun debate have their strengths and moments of shining glory, in the end I find the scientific data to favor gun control. These data and their interpretations are complex, but I have struggled with them long enough to realize that comprehensive gun control can both reduce the economic costs and human suffering involved in the enormous amount of gun violence that the United States presently endures on a daily basis, while still protecting the right of individuals to own and use guns for lawful purposes, including hunting, target shooting, and self defense.

I am grateful to the following scholars for the assistance noted: Stephen P. Halbrook, for clarification of federal gun control laws relating to domestic violence; David Hemenway (Harvard University), for sharing some of the unpublished data that have been amassed in recent years by the National Violent Injury Statistics System Workgroup; David B. Kopel (Independence Institute) for his review of the Neal Knox biography and of selected other biographies in Chapter 7; Glenn L. Pierce (Northeastern University) for his thoughtful conversations with me on ways to curb illegal gun trafficking, which is high on the agenda of gun control advocates; Robert J. Spitzer (State University of New York, Cortland), for his review of the topics covered in the *Handbook*—to make sure that they fairly represent the range and complexity of the gun control issue; and Garen J. Wintemute (University of California, Davis) for updating me on California's attempts to control the manufacture of cheap handguns.

My research benefited greatly from the library staff at Bryant University; reference librarian Colleen Anderson was particularly helpful. Administrative assistant Joanne Socci performed many valued clerical services, as did my research assistants Theresa Gomes and Travis Carter. Mr. Carter was especially helpful in preparing Chapters 6 and 7 (the court cases and biographies), and he wrote fine first drafts of them. The Bryant University administration supported my research with course releases, summer stipends, and a sabbatical, and I especially thank David Lux, Ronald Machtley, and V. K. Unni. My acquisition editor at ABC-CLIO, Mim Vasan, was encouraging and helpful from the start to the end of this endeavor. ABC-CLIO project editor Dayle Dermatis and senior production editor Vicki Moran were similarly enthusiastic and helpful. Finally, on a personal note, I want to thank my wife, Lisa, for her constant encouragement, and my children—Travis, Kurtis, Alexis, and Davis—for their love and forbearance.

—*Gregg Lee Carter*
North Smithfield, Rhode Island

1

Gun Control in the United States: The Social and Political Landscape

Few topics engender more controversy than "gun control."
Large segments of the population express contradictory
opinions and assert contradictory facts when they discuss the
role of firearms in violence and especially how to reduce
violent injuries and deaths that involve firearms.

—National Research Council
Firearms and Violence (2005)

It is shameful that tens of thousands of Americans die
needlessly from guns each year, while our gun policy is driven
more by rhetoric than scientific information.

—David Hemenway
Private Guns, Public Health (2004a)

Public and private debate on gun control is generally only minimally informed by the relevant social science research. Based on personal experiences—such as being introduced to hunting at a young age, or being revolted by the television images of an act of gun violence—individuals talk themselves into either a pro– or anti–gun control position. There is good reason why most people sidestep the research—as much of it relies on complex, arcane statistical analyses, and it is generally not well organized into a coherent whole.[1]

The primary aim of *Gun Control in the United States: A Reference Handbook* is to rectify this situation—to help policymakers, academics, and average citizens understand the research and to reach the point where each one can make an informed decision on whether to support stricter or more lenient gun control, as well as on which types of control have the best chances for success. The *Handbook* draws on the most recent and scientifically sound research on the various aspects of gun control. It illuminates gun control efforts in the United States by putting them into both cross-national and historical contexts.

Gun Prevalence, Gun Control, and Violence

Of the many aspects surrounding the issue of gun control, none is more important than whether there exists a causal link between gun prevalence and violence; and if it exists, what its nature is. Many people assume that such a link exists: that gun prevalence is the independent variable (cause), that violence is the dependent variable (effect), and that the relationship is linear and strongly positive (more guns yields more violence). The social policy implication is that if we reduce the number of guns in our society, we will reduce the amount of violence. Yet establishing the validity of the guns-lead-to-violence link is much more difficult to confirm than the ordinary person might think. The same can be said for the supposed effects of gun control in reducing violence. This chapter will review the social science research that speaks to these issues. To anticipate its conclusion, there *is* a causal link between gun prevalence and several kinds of violence (robbery-related; deaths resulting from murder, suicide, and accidents), but it is complex and modified by a number of social contexts. Furthermore, even though gun control in the United States has produced few of the benefits its proponents have alleged, lessons from the experiences of some U.S. states, as well as from our peer nations (economically developed, industrialized democracies), reveal that this needn't be the case—that there are indeed some approaches to gun control cohering with both the cultural unwillingness in the United States to give up guns and the laudable societal goal of reducing gun-related violence.

The United States has a huge number of guns, perhaps as many guns as there are adults (well over 200,000,000). It also has weak national gun laws in comparison with almost all other economically developed, democratic nations. And compared with these countries, U.S. gun violence is very high. For example, Krug's analysis of firearm-related deaths in the United States and twenty-five other high-income countries found that the age-adjusted rate of firearm death (homicide, suicide, accident) "in the U.S. (14.24 per 100,000) is eight times the pooled rate for the other H[igh]-I[ncome] countries (1.76)" (Krug, et al., 1998; data are from the 1990s). In the same article, Krug reports that the U.S. crude homicide rate is six times higher than that for the typical economically developed country.

To gun control advocates these social facts are causally connected: The more firearms circulating in a society, and the weaker the regulations governing their possession and use, the greater the likelihood of the occurrence of violent crime, suicide, and accidental firearm-related death. Guns are not just another weapon: Assault with a gun, whether inflicted by another or self-inflicted, is many times more likely to result in death or serious injury than with any other weapon (Lindgren and Zimring, 1983). However, gun control opponents argue that the United States would be a violent and bloody society with or without the 200,000,000 or so rifles, shotguns, and pistols currently in circulation. This argument is not groundless: Krug's cross-national analyses reveal that when all of the firearm-related homicides for the United States are eliminated, its rate is still one and three-quarters times greater than the entire murder rate (gun- and nongun-related) of the typical high-income country. Moreover, even if all guns were removed, some of the murders committed by guns would undoubtedly be committed by other means, so the net effect is that the U.S. murder rate would still actually be at least two to three times higher than that of its typical peer nation. Finally, the suicide rate in the United States is not particularly high compared with its peers—much higher than Italy, Spain, and England, but much lower than Finland, Switzerland, and Austria. Overall, the United States ranks sixteenth out of the twenty-six nations in the Krug data set. In short, at first wash it appears that persuasive data can be marshaled to fit either side of the gun control debate. Ironically, as observed by criminologists James Lindgren and Franklin E. Zimring (1983, 837), the debate over gun control is a war of statistics—but "both sides in the debate often invoke the same statistics."

In actuality, the data do tell a more coherent story when examined more carefully, the process of which will begin in the next section and continue in Chapter 2. But the first point to be made is that even though it might be hard to ascertain which side has the upper hand in the assessment of the guns-lead-to-violence data, it is clear that these varying assessments are at the heart of the gun control debate. Those working for stronger national gun laws, akin to the laws existing in most economically developed democracies, assume that such laws will reduce violence and save lives. As the Brady Campaign to Prevent Gun Violence (formerly known as Handgun Control Inc.) states in many of its advertisements and communications with its supporters: "Our goal is to enact a comprehensive federal gun control policy to reduce gun violence." (The Brady Campaign is the largest and most important organization sustaining the movement to control guns; see its Web site at http://bradycampaign.org/). Indeed, the organization argues that gun control works. In the fall of 2000, for example, it sent a letter to its supporters contending that the 1993 Brady Handgun Violence Prevention Act resulted in gun deaths dropping from 37,776 in 1992 to 32,436 in 1997 (Brady, 2000). On the other hand, pro-gun groups challenge the premise that a comprehensive federal gun control policy will reduce gun violence. In the words of the National Rifle Association (NRA), "Guns don't kill; people do." In its flyers and on its Web page (http://www .nra.org/), the NRA repeatedly stresses that strict national gun laws, especially "registration and licensing," would have no effect on criminal violence, "as criminals, by definition, do not obey laws."

Cross-National Comparisons

As noted previously, the United States has an overall murder rate that is six times higher than the average economically developed nation. Comparisons of murder-by-gun rates reveal an even more dramatic ratio: The U.S. rate of 7.07 is more than twelve times higher than the 0.58 average rate of its peer nations (Krug, et al., 1998, 216). Concomitantly, this huge murder-rates disparity is accompanied by generally huge differences in gun prevalence: Killias (1993) reports that in the United States the percentage of households in the early 1990s with any type of gun was 48.0, which is three times greater than that for the typical European country (16.2 percent), and twice as high as the rate of Australia and Canada (24.3 percent). (Note that the percentage of U.S. households with a firearm on the premises has dropped significantly in recent years—to about 38 percent, according to the Gallup poll, and 34 percent, according to the General Social Survey. Why? Hunting has dropped in popularity, and millions of immigrants, relatively few of whom possess guns, have established households in the past decade. We've also become more urban, and city dwellers are much less likely than their counterparts in rural areas and small towns to own guns [see Carlson, 2005, and General Social Survey, 2002a]). Killias's data reveal a strong positive correlation between gun prevalence and homicide. Hemenway and Miller (2000) confirm this correlation, using the twenty-six high-income countries in the Krug data set. On the other hand, Gary Kleck's (1997, 254) analysis of all thirty-six nations (both high- and low-income) in the Krug data set reveals a much more modest correlation. Kleck believes that the entire Krug data set is a better indication of the truth, because a careful review of gun-prevalence/violent-crime studies in U.S. cities and counties shows no consistent relationship (see Kleck, 1991, 185–215). However, Mark Duggan (2001, 1086) believes that "previous research has suffered from a lack of reliable data on gun ownership." Using the level of sales of the magazine *Guns & Ammo* as an indicator of the level of gun ownership, he finds that "changes in gun ownership are significantly positively related to changes in the homicide rate, with this relationship driven almost entirely by an impact of gun ownership on murders in which a gun is used" (Duggan, 2001, 1086).

Canada, Australia, New Zealand, Japan, and most European countries have much stricter gun regulations than the United States. Most importantly, these countries require that guns be registered, that gun owners be licensed, and that guns be stored with utmost security. To get a license, a potential gun owner must typically pass an exam on gun safety. Also required are comprehensive background checks of individuals seeking to purchase guns, including any histories of criminality or mental incapacity. Although in the United States background checks are required by federally licensed firearms dealers when selling guns to their customers, sales between private individuals (including those at gun shows and flea markets) are not regulated by federal law, like they are in its peer nations. Of special interest to countries that advocate gun control, *handguns* (because they are considered the most blameworthy weapons of violence) are either outlawed or restricted so severely that ownership of them is extremely rare. This is reflected in the comparatively high percentage of households with a handgun present in the United States (about 22 percent) and the relatively tiny percentages elsewhere: 0.1 percent in the United Kingdom, 0.2 percent in the Netherlands, 2 percent in Australia, 2.5 percent in Spain, and 7 percent or less in Belgium, Canada, Finland, France, and Norway. The striking exception in Europe is Switzerland, which has a laxity in its gun laws comparable to that of the United States and a relatively high percentage of households where guns are present. Switzerland is the NRA's favorite example of the maxim "guns don't kill, people do," because it has low murder rates (both overall and by gun). However, gun control advocates are quick to point out that Switzerland's population is generally better trained in the safe use of firearms than the population of the United States, because most adult Swiss men are members of the national militia.

The case of Switzerland warns us not to oversimplify when making cross-national comparisons. Pro-gun writers and groups have other favorite examples—Finland and Norway have high numbers of firearms but low rates of violence. On the other hand, Mexico and Russia have low numbers of firearms but high rates of violence. In short, there are forces beyond gun availability that influence the level of violence in any particular country. Most importantly, varying combinations of social heterogeneity and economic development have been linked to violence. For this reason, when countries are compared, they should be socioeconomically similar. Simplistic pair-wise comparisons are rarely useful, because as Kleck (1991, 188–189) correctly argues, "out of any large number of possible pairings, it is safe to say that at least a few pairs can be found to appear to support either side" of the gun control debate. For example, in recent years pro-gun writers have liked to point out that Russia is extremely violent, yet has strict gun control and a relatively low percentage of households with guns, whereas in Switzerland, gun prevalence is high but gun violence tends to be low (notwithstanding the massacre in the Swiss Canton of Zug in September 2001, when a gunman broke into a government building and shot fourteen people to death).

The Nature of Gun Violence in the United States

Victimization

Gun violence in the United States does not affect all segments of the population equally. For example, African American males in and near their twenties are the most likely to suffer such violence in its criminal form, whereas older white males are most likely to commit suicide with a firearm.

Homicide

In 2003, 14,408 people were murdered in the United States, with 2 out of 3 of these (9,638, or 66.9 percent) having been killed with a firearm. Seventy-nine percent of these victims were under the age of forty-five. And even though African Americans represent only about 12 percent of the population, 48 percent of the victims were African American (Federal Bureau of Investigation, 2004, Tables 2.3 and 2.10).

In the 1990s, the rate of homicide due to firearms for African American males in their early twenties (ages twenty through twenty-four) was 140.7 per 100,000; the rate for all individuals in their early twenties was 17.1 per 100,000. Similarly, the rate of homicide due to firearms for African American teenagers (ages fifteen through nineteen) was 105.3 per 100,000, whereas it was 14.0 per 100,000 for teenagers taken as a whole. Although the absolute numbers of victims involved has fallen in recent years, the racial slants in the data have not (see Table 1.1; also see Carter, 1997, 2001; Fox, 2000).

Table 1.1 shows that the most common age range for gun homicide victimization is the early twenties, followed by the late twenties and early thirties. Figures 1.1 and 1.2 graphically display the rates for these age groups, thereby more starkly revealing the hugely disproportionate rates suffered by African American men—and to a somewhat lesser degree by Hispanic men—in their twenties and early thirties.

These slants stand in stark contrast to the high-media coverage shootings involving teenage boys in the late 1990s and early 2000s. All but one of these high-profile incidents involved white, male teenagers from small towns and suburbia (Springfield, Oregon; Pearl, Mississippi; West Paducah, Kentucky; Jonesboro,

TABLE 1.1
U.S. Firearm Homicide Rate in 2002 by Age, Race, Ethnicity, and Sex

Ages	ALL		WHITE*				BLACK*				HISPANIC				ASIAN			
			Male		Female		Male		Female		Male		Female		Male		Female	
	N	Rate	N	Rate	N	Rate	N	Rate	N	Rate	N	Rate	N	Rate	N	Rate	N	Rate
ALL**	11829	4.1	2139	2.2	913	0.9	5482	29.5	699	3.6	1942	8.1	226	1.2	189	2.8	53	0.8
0–14	263	0.4	47	0.3	42	0.2	65	1.4	35	0.8	37	0.6	17	0.3	8	0.6	4	0.3
15–19	1567	7.7	191	2.9	62	1.0	768	49.9	83	5.6	371	22.2	31	2.0	32	7.1	1	0.2
20–24	2750	13.5	297	4.7	92	1.5	1557	109.5	139	9.5	538	26.4	36	2.2	43	8.4	8	1.6
25–34	3465	8.7	465	3.7	171	1.4	1854	75.6	194	7.2	619	16.1	60	1.8	40	3.4	13	1.1
35–44	2042	4.6	531	3.4	204	1.3	784	30.0	147	5.0	245	8.3	49	1.8	35	3.4	13	1.2
45–54	1025	2.6	321	2.2	162	1.1	317	15.3	68	2.8	91	5.1	25	1.4	18	2.3	7	0.8
55–64	409	1.5	174	1.7	79	0.7	88	7.7	19	1.3	26	2.8	5	0.5	10	2.2	4	0.8
65–74	161	0.9	58	0.9	49	0.6	32	4.7	7	0.7	7	1.3	2	0.3	2	0.8	1	0.3
75+	134	0.8	52	0.9	51	0.6	15	3.5	7	0.8	4	1.3	1	0.2	1	0.6	2	0.9

Source: Centers for Disease Control and Prevention (2003a).

* Non-Hispanic

** Rates on this row are age adjusted. (Some events occur more often among certain age groups than others. For instance, gun homicide is more common among those in their twenties than among any other age group. Age adjustment enables the comparison of injury rates without concern that the differences uncovered are because of differences in the age distributions among different populations.)

FIGURE 1.1
U.S. Firearm Homicide Rate in 2002 for Ages 20–24

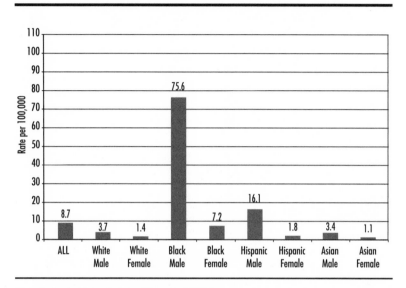

Source: Centers for Disease Control and Prevention (2003a).

Arkansas; Edinboro, Pennsylvania; Raleigh, Virginia; Santee, California; and most tragically, Littleton, Colorado). Except for the bloodbath at Columbine High School in Littleton, shootings of young people in the neighborhoods surrounding our inner-city schools are on par with these high-profile cases—though little publicized except in the local media. In short, white and minority gun violence are treated differently in the national media.

Suicide

In 2001, there were 30,622 reported suicides in the United States, with 55 percent of these being classified as firearm-related. Males were four times more likely than females to kill themselves, using a gun in 60 percent of the cases (Centers for Disease Control and Prevention [CDC], 2005).

As shown in Table 1.2, gun-related suicides are associated with white males much more than any other racial-ethnic-gender combinations listed. The rate rises with age for men of all racial and ethnic backgrounds, though not for women. The higher rates

FIGURE 1.2
U.S. Firearm Homicide Rates in 2002 for Ages 25–34

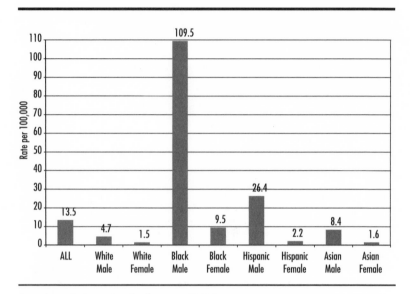

Source: Centers for Disease Control and Prevention (2003a).

for older men, however, mask the fact that suicide disproportionately affects younger people. For example, in 2002, as shown in
Table 1.2, nearly two in three suicides were committed by individuals under the age of fifty-five (10,866÷17,108=0.64). Furthermore, as other Centers for Disease Control and Prevention
(2003b) data reveal, suicide does not even make the Top 10 list for
those over sixty-five, whereas it is a leading cause of death of adolescents and younger and middle-aged adults; more specifically,
it is the number 3 cause of death for those ten to twenty-four, the
number 2 cause for those twenty-five to thirty-four, the number 4
cause for those thirty-five to forty-four, the number 5 cause for
those forty-five to fifty-four, and the number 8 cause for those
fifty-five to sixty-four (accidents are the number 1 cause of death
for those under forty-five, whereas cancer and heart disease top
the list for those forty-five and older).

As noted earlier, the overall U.S. firearm suicide rate is not
especially high compared with our peer nations, but this conceals
that U.S. youth and young adult firearm-related suicide rates are
far out of line with those of its peer nations. More particularly,

TABLE 1.2
U.S. Firearm Suicide Rate in 2002 by Age, Race, Ethnicity, and Sex

Ages	ALL		WHITE* Male		WHITE* Female		BLACK* Male		BLACK* Female		HISPANIC Male		HISPANIC Female		ASIAN Male		ASIAN Female	
	N	Rate	N	Rate	N	Rate	N	Rate	N	Rate	N	Rate	N	Rate	N	Rate	N	Rate
ALL**	17108	5.9	13014	13.0	1851	1.8	945	6.1	96	0.5	763	4.8	71	0.4	146	2.4	24	0.3
0–14	86	0.1	53	0.3	10	0.1	8	0.2	1	0.0	5	0.1	5	0.1	2	0.2	1	0.1
15–19	742	3.7	485	7.2	55	0.9	68	4.4	9	0.6	81	4.9	7	0.5	13	2.9	2	0.5
20–24	1346	6.6	890	14.0	91	1.5	161	11.3	12	0.8	127	6.2	9	0.6	18	3.5	0	0.0
25–34	2399	6.0	1573	12.6	280	2.3	258	10.5	14	0.5	183	4.8	15	0.5	32	2.7	9	0.7
35–44	3157	7.1	2319	14.9	430	2.8	170	6.5	29	1.0	128	4.3	17	0.6	24	2.3	5	0.5
45–54	3136	7.8	2423	16.3	423	2.8	115	5.5	15	0.6	88	4.9	10	0.6	23	2.9	6	0.7
55–64	2234	8.4	1774	17.5	289	2.7	63	5.5	8	0.6	62	6.7	5	0.5	19	4.1	0	0.0
65–74	1776	9.7	1507	22.2	146	1.8	48	7.0	6	0.6	49	9.4	3	0.5	6	2.3	1	0.3
75+	2230	12.9	1989	35.9	127	1.4	54	12.5	2	0.2	40	13.2	0	0.0	9	5.5	0	0.0

Source: Centers for Disease Control and Prevention (2003a).

* Non-Hispanic

** Rates on this row are age adjusted. (Some events occur more often among certain age groups than others. For instance, gun homicide is more common among those in their twenties than among any other age group. Age adjustment enables the comparison of injury rates without concern that the differences uncovered are because of differences in the age distributions among different populations.)

Johnson, Krug, and Potter (2000) found in a study of thirty-four economically developed nations—including those in Western Europe, Canada, and Australia—that only Finland (11.4 per 100,000) had a suicide-by-firearm rate higher than that in the United States (9.3 per 100,000), and that the U.S. rate positively dwarfed those of most of these nations. For example, the rate per 100,000 in Canada was 5.9, in Australia 3.9, in New Zealand 2.7, and less than 1.0 in France, Germany, the Netherlands, the United Kingdom, Spain, Italy, and Portugal. The human tragedy here is that adolescents tend to be more impulsive than adults, and scientific study reveals that many suicides are impulsive acts; moreover, many survivors of attempted suicide are glad to be alive when interviewed months and even years later (see Hemenway's [2004a, 38–39] review of these studies). Research also reveals that there is more myth than truth in the common assumption that those intent on killing themselves will use whatever means necessary: Estimates are that only 10 to 15 percent of individuals who commit suicide have an "unbreakable determination" to kill themselves. The implication of this finding is that there should be a positive correlation between gun availability and suicide, and indeed there is (where guns are less available—in the home, in the neighborhood, in the community—suicide rates are significantly lower; see Azrael, 2004, for a review of these studies).[2] The implication would seem obvious to many: With the risk period being transient for most potential suicide victims, "reducing the availability of firearms—the most common, lethal, and symbolically resonant instruments—during this period may prevent suicide attempts and would certainly reduce the rate of suicide completions" (Hemenway, 2004a, 38–39)—especially for adolescents and younger adults, who are more likely to act impulsively and less likely than their older counterparts to comprehend the absolute finality of death.

Accidental Death and Injury

In 2003, emergency rooms in the United States reported a total of 18,941 individuals having been unintentionally shot. The Centers for Disease Control and Prevention reported that 762 individuals were accidentally killed with a firearm the year before (CDC injury statistics are a year more current than death statistics). As indicated in Table 1.3, males between the ages of fifteen and thirty-four are most likely to die or suffer injury from an accidentally fired gun.

TABLE 1.3
Firearm-Related Unintentional Death and Unintentional Injury Rates by Age and Sex

| | ALL | | | MALES | | | FEMALES | | |
| | Deaths | | Injuries | Death | | Injuries | | Death | | Injuries |
Ages	N	Rate	N	Rate	N	Rate	N	Rate	N	Rate	N	Rate
ALL*	762	0.27	18941	6.43	667	0.47	17038	11.51	95	0.06	1902	1.32
0–14	60	0.10	231	0.38	47	0.15	221	0.71	13	0.04	10	0.03
15–19	107	0.53	3380	16.51	101	0.96	2996	28.48	6	0.06	384	3.86
20–24	103	0.51	4102	19.79	94	0.90	3991	37.42	9	0.09	111	1.10
25–34	143	0.36	5168	12.96	129	0.64	4596	22.73	14	0.07	572	2.91
35–44	123	0.27	2562	5.77	98	0.44	2165	9.78	25	0.11	397	1.78
45–54	95	0.24	1984	4.86	84	0.43	1727	8.62	11	0.05	257	1.24
55–64	56	0.21	824	2.95	50	0.39	678	5.05	6	0.04	146	1.01
65–74	36	0.20	415	2.26	32	0.39	390	4.67	4	0.04	25	0.25
75+	39	0.23	250	1.42	32	0.50	250	3.78	7	0.06	0	0.00

Source: Centers for Disease Control and Prevention (2003a).
*Rates on this row are age adjusted.
Note: Injury data are for the year 2002, whereas death data are for 2003.

As observed by Hemenway (2002), about one-third of the individuals involved in nonfatal gun accidents require hospitalization. Most of their injuries are self-inflicted while cleaning or loading a gun, hunting, or target shooting. Injury rates in the United States and most other economically developed countries have fallen over the past three decades—mainly owing to the decreasing popularity of hunting and the decreasing proportion of households having a gun. Between the early 1970s and the early 2000s, the ratio of U.S. adults who reported keeping a gun at home dropped from 1 in 2 to 1 in 3, while the ratio having at least one hunter in the house (the respondent or the respondent's spouse) fell from 1 in 3 to 1 in 6 according to the General Social Survey (2002a, 2002b).

Implied in these social survey facts is a positive correlation between gun prevalence and gun-related accidents, and, indeed, Miller, Azrael, and Hemenway (2001) found this correlation to be substantial at the state level of analysis: For example, a resident of Alabama, Arkansas, Louisiana, or Mississippi has an eightfold greater chance of being killed in a gun accident than his or her counterpart living in Hawaii, Massachusetts, Rhode Island, or New Jersey. The same relationship holds at the household level: Merrill (2002) and Wiebe (2003a, 2003b), using large-scale national surveys, found that the probability of suffering a gun death was significantly related to having a gun in the house—and, moreover, this relationship holds up under a variety of controls, including race, sex, region, age, marital status, education, family income, military service (veteran vs. nonveteran), and city size.[3] Considering this and related evidence, epidemiologist David Hemenway (2004a, 35) reaches the inexorable conclusion that "reduced exposure to firearms should reduce unintentional firearm injuries, all other things being equal. At the extreme, if there are no guns, there certainly can be no gun accidents. States with more guns per capita and less strict handgun control laws appear to have more accident gun fatalities; similarly, high-income nations with more guns seem to have more accidents."

Crime-Related Injury and Assault

In 2003, 42,505 people were treated in emergency rooms after being wounded by a gunshot in a criminal assault (robbery or aggravated assault) in the United States. Ninety-one percent of these victims were males, and 91 percent were also under the age of forty-five (Table 1.4).[4] An additional 336,665 individuals were criminally assaulted with a firearm (41.8 percent of the 413,402 total reported robberies in 2003; 19.1 percent of the total 857,921 reported aggravated assaults) according to the Federal Bureau of Investigation's 2003 *Uniform Crime Report*.[5]

The Bureau of Justice Statistics' (2003) National Crime Victimization Survey (see endnote 4) reveals that victims of a robbery in which a gun is used are less likely to be non-fatally injured than when no weapon is used. This is because they are less likely to resist when confronted with a gun. However, victims of gun robberies and gun-related aggravated assaults are much more likely to be killed—40 times more likely than when no weapon is used (see Alba and Messner, 1995; also see the discussion that follows in the Magnification Hypothesis).

TABLE 1.4
Firearm-Related Injuries Due to Violent Assault by Age and Sex, 2003

Ages	ALL		MALES		FEMALES	
	N	Rate	N	Rate	N	Rate
ALL*	42505	14.3	38756	25.7	3749	2.6
0–14	760	1.3	590	1.9	170	0.6
15–19	7453	36.4	6721	63.9	732	7.3
20–24	11545	55.7	10904	102.3	641	6.4
25–34	13326	33.4	12270	60.7	1055	5.4
35–44	5605	12.6	4996	22.6	608	2.7
45–54	2515	6.2	2151	10.7	364	1.8
55–64	637	2.3	586	4.4	50	0.4
65–74	111	0.6	111	1.3	0	0.0
75+	228	1.3	125	1.9	103	0.9

Source: Centers for Disease Control and Prevention (2003a).
*Rates on this row are age adjusted.

The nature of the relationship between gun prevalence and violent crime is currently a hotly debated issue in academic circles, as well as in organizations involved in gun control. Indeed, a prestigious panel of social scientists reviewed the empirical studies relating gun ownership and prevalence to criminal violence and suicide and concluded that the data "do not credibly demonstrate" any fundamental causal relationships (National Research Council, 2005, 6). Among the major reasons the panel arrived at this conclusion was the lack of data on gun ownership and the lack of access to the Bureau of Alcohol, Tobacco, Firearms and Explosives' database that tracks guns used in crimes. However, other scholars believe this is an overly conservative conclusion (for example, see Cook and Ludwig, 2004; Hemenway, 2004a). The next section explores more of the contours of this debate and some of its implications for present and future gun control policies.

Establishing Causality—Not an Easy Task

Whether a causal link exists between the high number of firearms in the United States and its relatively lax federal gun laws, on the one hand, and its high rates of violence, on the other hand, represents the heart of the gun control debate. From the mid-1980s through early 1990s, guns spread throughout the inner cities and many suburban communities of the United States. At the same time, these areas experienced growing rates of violence. Between 1984 and 1992, the FBI's *Uniform Crime Reports* revealed that property crime was leveling off; yet violent crime continued to rise—steeply so between 1987 and 1993; and, most significantly, handgun violence catapulted from 589,000 murders, rapes, robberies, and assaults committed with handguns in 1988, to 1.1 million in 1993 (see Bastian and Taylor, 1994; Mackellar and Yanagishita, 1995). That crime rates—property, violent, gun-related—have fallen in the past decade to roughly those levels of the early 1980s does not negate the argument that the influx of guns was connected to the steep rise in violence in the late 1980s and early 1990s. Just as the riots of the 1960s in African American neighborhoods were self-limiting (one can only burn down a neighborhood so many times), so too was much of the inner-city youth violence in the 1980s and early 1990s. More specifically, the most violence-prone were the first to be cut down; those succeeding them were more mindful of the destructiveness of firearms; they also realized the benefits of a stabilized drug market. Alfred Blumstein (1995a, 30–31) offers the following interpretation:

> [Beginning in 1985,] in order to accommodate the increased demand, the drug sellers had to recruit a large number of new sellers. . . . The economic plight of many young urban African-American juveniles, many of whom see no other comparably satisfactory route to economic success or even sustenance, makes them particularly amenable to the lure of the drug markets. These juveniles, like many other participants in the illicit-drug industry, are likely to carry guns for self-protection, largely because that industry uses guns as an important instrument for dispute resolution. . . . Since the drug

markets are pervasive in many inner-city neighborhoods, and the young people recruited into them are fairly tightly networked with other young people in their neighborhoods, it became easy for the guns to be "diffused" to other teenagers who go to the same school or who walk the same streets. . . .

In view of both the recklessness and bravado that is often characteristic of teenagers, and their low level of skill in settling disputes other than through the use of physical force, many of the fights that would otherwise have taken place and resulted in nothing more serious than a bloody nose can now turn into shootings as a result of the presence of guns. This may be exacerbated by the problems of socialization associated with high levels of poverty, high rates of single-parent households, educational failures, and a widespread sense of economic hopelessness. But those factors have been changing gradually over the years, and so they cannot readily provide the explanation for the sharp changes that began to take place in the mid-1980s.

Blumstein also contends that *white* juvenile homicide rates increased during the same era because of a "gun diffusion process" into suburbia (as guns crossed over into suburbia, guns begat guns in close-knit teenage circles). However, because national data, most importantly from the General Social Survey (GSS), reveal no increase in the percentages of individuals (including blacks and urban dwellers) or households possessing a gun, some analysts reject the notion that guns spread throughout the inner city and parts of suburbia during this period and accept the simpler "rise-in-gang-activity" interpretation (for example, see Kleck, 1997, 72–74 and 256–258). Respondents to the GSS are noninstitutionalized adults willing to take the survey. Not a very social scientific statement—but to those living in the streets of Boston, Chicago, Las Vegas, Los Angeles, Miami, New York, and other urban areas during the 1980s, the GSS data seem unable to detect or speak to the diffusion of guns they witnessed. Indeed, in line with the basic contours of the Blumenstein thesis (that guns generate violence), Duggan's (2001) research reveals that part of the drop in violent crime and murder over the past decade in the United States reflects a falling proportion of gun-owning households.

The Knotty Problems of Causal Direction and Defensive Gun Use

Even if we find intuitive appeal in the Blumstein and Duggan line of reasoning and the correlations contained in Killias's cross-national data cited earlier, correlation itself does not prove causality. Pro-gun researchers and writers argue that the causal arrow might very well run the other way—in other words, that rising rates of violence prompt citizens to arm themselves. Indeed, this is the argument of John R. Lott Jr. (1998, 2000; also see Lott and Mustard, 1997): that rising criminal violence motivates people to acquire guns for defensive purposes, and that when a sufficient number of such people are armed, crime rates actually begin to fall.

Lott's thesis—made popular with the catchy title of his 1998 book, *More Guns, Less Crime*—fueled one of the greatest debates on the effectiveness of gun control, and it is closely linked to Gary Kleck and Marc Gertz's (1995) controversial research on the "good" effects of gun possession—that is, its usefulness in defending against criminal attack. Meta-analyses conducted by Kleck and Lott of both area-level (e.g., cities or counties) and individual-level data reveal no consistent relationship between gun prevalence/ownership and violent crime. Indeed, according to their research, when individuals are freely allowed to carry concealed weapons, rates of violent crime drop. Their interpretation is straightforward and has intuitive appeal: Criminals are rational, and they are less likely to rape, rob, or assault when they are fearful that a potential victim might be armed. For example, "in Canada and Britain, both with tough gun-control laws, almost half of all burglaries are 'hot burglaries' [where a resident is at home when a criminal strikes]. In contrast, the United States, with fewer restrictions, has a 'hot burglary' rate of only 13 percent. Criminals are not just behaving differently by accident. . . . The fear of potentially armed victims causes American burglars to spend more time than their foreign counterparts 'casing' a house to ensure that nobody is home" (Lott, 1998, 5).

However appealing, the research of Lott/Mustard and Kleck/Gertz has been assailed on a number of accounts, mainly methodological. Kleck and Gertz's data, based on a 1993 national probability-sample telephone survey, led them to estimate some 2,500,000 defensive uses of guns per year. However, criminologists Philip J. Cook and Jens Ludwig (2000, 37) question this estimate (as do Hemenway, 2004a, Spitzer, 2004, and many other social scientists skilled in quantitative analysis). They do so because it is so far out of line with the estimate of 100,000 defensive gun uses suggested by the *National Crime Victimization Survey* (NCVS), considered the "most reliable source of information on predatory crime because it has been in the field continuously since 1973 and incorporates the best thinking of survey methodologists." And even though the 1994 National Institute of Justice survey on the "Private Ownership of Firearms" (National Survey of the Private Ownership of Firearms, NSPOF) revealed a very high estimate for defensive gun use, 1.5 million uses (more in line with the Kleck and Gertz's data than with the NCVS estimate), Cook and Ludwig (1997, 9) still contend the NCVS data are much more reasonable.

> *National Crime Victimization Survey* (NCVS) }*Some troubling comparisons:* If the DGU [defensive gun use] numbers are in the right ballpark, millions of attempted assaults, thefts, and break-ins were foiled by armed citizens during the 12-month period. According to these results, guns are used far more often to defend against crime than to perpetuate crime. (Firearms were used by perpetrators in 1.07 million incidents of violent crime in 1994, according to NCVS data.) Thus, it is of considerable interest and importance to check the reasonableness of the NSPOF estimates before embracing them. Because respondents were asked to describe only their most recent defensive gun use, our comparisons are conservative, as they assume only one defensive gun use per defender. The results still suggest that DGU estimates are far too high.
>
> For example, in only a small fraction of rape and robbery attempts do victims use guns in self-defense. It does not make sense, then, that the NSPOF estimate of the number of rapes in which a woman defended herself with a gun was more than the total number of rapes estimated from NCVS. For other crimes . . . the results are almost as absurd.

In the appendix to his *Private Guns, Public Health* (2004a, 239–240), David Hemenway zeroes in on why Kleck and Gertz were led so far astray in their survey estimating the frequency of defensive gun use:

> Two aspects of [Kleck and Gertz's] survey combine to create a severe false-positive problem. The first is the likelihood of "social desirability" responses. . . . For example, an individual who acquires a gun for protection and then uses it successfully to ward off a criminal is displaying the wisdom of his precautions and his capacity to protect himself. His action is to be commended and admired. . . .
>
> Some positive social-desirability bias might not by itself lead to serious overestimation. However, combined with a second aspect of the survey—the attempt to estimate a rare event—it does. . . . Because the survey is trying to estimate the incident of a rare event, a small percentage bias can lead to extreme overestimation. . . . In Kleck and Gertz's (1995) self-defense gun survey, if as few as 1.3 percent of respondents were randomly misclassified, the 2.5 million figure would be thirty-three times higher than the true figure. [In short,] using surveys to estimate rare occurrences with some positive social-desirability bias, will lead to large overestimates.

As for Lott's findings that the legalization of the carrying of concealed weapons has a significant marginal effect on the deterrence of violence crime, his complex data set and arcane statistical analyses were far beyond the ken of most policymakers and others interested in the issue of gun control when first published in 1997 and 1998. But of those scholars who understood such complicated quantitative analysis, many soon poked holes in his findings (see, for example, Bartley and Cohen, 1998; Black and Nagin, 1998; Dezhbakhas and Rubin, 1998; Duggan, 2001; and Ludwig, 1998, 2000), and the coup de grace was struck in 2003, when a rigorous reassessment of Lott's data revealed that he had committed fundamental errors in specifying his model and conducting his analyses. When these errors were corrected, Ayres and Donohue (2003) found no support for the "more guns, less crime" thesis; instead, they actually found the data were more in line with a "more guns, more crime" thesis (also see Lambert, 2005, for an even more complete dismantling of Lott's thesis).

The Magnification Hypothesis

Simple correlations do not take into consideration other variables that might be determinative of both gun prevalence and violence (implying that the guns/violence correlation is spurious). For example, rising immigration rates and subsequent rises in violence based on cultural conflict could account for the 1980s rise in gun violence. Or, more likely, it might have been the growing presence of violent youth gangs—springing from low to high levels of salience with the introduction of crack cocaine in many urban areas—that produced the surge in violent crime. In short, dealt with at a simplistic level of analysis, the data do not fit neatly either the pro- or anti-gun control side of the debate. However, it is not unreasonable to hypothesize that the easy availability of guns, both legally and illegally, and their diffusion in urban areas during the 1980s greatly *magnified* the problems of violence associated with culture conflict and street gangs—even though some would argue that these forces would produce the same levels of violence even if guns were not on the scene.

The magnification hypothesis is supported when one considers that property crime (larceny, burglary, and auto theft) rates were flattening out in the United States during the late 1980s and early 1990s. Having ascertained that much of the rising crime rate in the 1960s and 1970s was due to the youthfulness of the population, demographers and criminologists had long ago predicted this flattening out. They predicted that as the post–World War II baby-boom generation aged, crime rates would fall (because crime is strongly correlated with youth: More than half of all street crime is committed by individuals under twenty-five, with arrests peaking at age eighteen). If property crime was flattening out between 1984 and 1994, why wasn't violent crime (robbery, murder, aggravated assault) following a similar pattern? The diffusion of guns into urban areas—their availability, possession, and use—could account for the divergent trends in property crime and violent crime.

At the cross-national level, as noted earlier, one must also consider that the correlation between gun prevalence and violence can be accounted for by other factors, throwing suspicion on its causal nature. The two most important factors that must be taken into account are social homogeneity and economic inequality. Were the United States more socially and economically homogeneous, would its much greater prevalence of guns really matter that much? "A culture in which the citizens are very similar—sharing similar ethnicity, religious beliefs, income levels and values, such as Denmark—is more likely to have laws that represent the wishes and desires of a large majority of its people than is a culture where citizens come from diverse backgrounds and have widely disparate income levels and lifestyles, as in the United States" (Stephens, 1994, 23). For this reason, countries with a good deal of homogeneity normally have lower levels of law violation and violence than their heterogeneous counterparts. Kleck (1991, 393–394) presents data in support of the notion that culture and not gun availability is what best distinguishes the United States from other developed countries that have much lower rates of violent crime. For example, Great Britain and Canada—two countries with low gun availability and low homicide rates—are often contrasted with the United States. In those societies, guns were not restricted in the early part of the twentieth century, yet their homicide rates were still extremely low (12 to 14 times lower than that of the United States).

It is difficult to rule out these alternative explanations for much greater levels of violence in the United States compared with other economically developed countries, though there is little doubt that heterogeneity plays a huge role in explaining the level of violence and crime in a nation. However, it is not unreasonable to hypothesize that the easy availability of guns greatly magnifies the problems of crime and violence encouraged by the high levels of social/cultural heterogeneity and economic inequality in the United States.

The magnification hypothesis is further supported when one considers the *lethality effect* that assault by guns produces. Numerous studies confirm that gunshot wounds are much more likely to result in death than wounds inflicted by a knife (the weapon generally assumed to be the next most lethal; see Cook and Ludwig, 2000, 34–36). In comparing U.S. violence rates to those of its peer nations, gun control advocates observe that assaults in the United States are more likely to involve guns and that "guns kill." There is support for this position. A major international crime survey—that asked the same questions in each country to obviate the problem of varying official national definitions of "assault"—revealed that the U.S. assault rate (5.4 percent of respondents reporting having been assaulted) was two and a third times greater than that in other developed countries (average=2.9 percent), but the U.S. homicide rate was six times greater. Moreover, although several nations have assault-with-weapon rates on par with that of the United States—of those assaulted, 15 percent were attacked with weapons in the Netherlands and France, 14 percent in Northern Ireland and the United States, and 12 percent in Canada—the homicide rates of those same nations, where the weapon is much less often a gun, are many magnitudes smaller than that of the United States (see Carter, 1997, 19). Such data support the argument that guns transform violent situations into lethal events. As epidemiologist David Hemenway phrases this notion, it is "the presence of a firearm [that] allows a petty argument to end tragically" (see Henigan, Nicholson, and Hemenway, 1995, 57). In short, compared with the rest of the economically developed world, what distinguishes the United States is not so much its overall crime rate, but its "extremely high rates of lethal violence," which is "a distinct social problem that is the real source of fear and anger in American life" (to quote Zimring and Hawkins in their highly praised book *Crime Is Not the Problem: Lethal Violence in America*, 1997, 3).

The complex data arguments regarding gun prevalence/violence have prompted some on the pro-control side to adopt a new view. They see the relevant data as not fitting either side neatly; moreover, they believe that it will be a long time before the question of whether gun prevalence/ownership/possession foments or thwarts violent crime is convincingly answered. They know that the elimination of guns can and does reduce violence: Put metal-detectors in airports, and hijackings are reduced; put metal detectors in high schools, and shootings on school grounds disappear. However, with more than 200 million guns currently in private hands in the United States, we are not going to eliminate our guns—not soon, not ever. Neither, given our great levels of heterogeneity and inequality, are we going to eliminate crime. But, by keeping guns out of our streets as much as possible—that is, by strictly controlling them—we can reduce the harm that they cause. This view is becoming increasingly popular among those examining the medical and other costs of gun violence. Philip J. Cook and Jens Ludwig (2000, 36) express this best when they observe that "guns don't kill people, but they make it real easy"; that is, controlling guns might not reduce violent crime but it can reduce the harm done in the commission of such crimes. Their analyses of the medical, job-related/productivity, criminal-justice, school, and other expenses produced by gun violence indicate that it costs the U.S. public "on the order of $100 billion per year, and affect[s] all of our lives in countless ways" (Cook and Ludwig, 2000, 117).

The Second Amendment

A well regulated Militia, being necessary to the security of a free State, the right of the people to keep and bear Arms, shall not be infringed.

—Second Amendment to the U.S. Constitution

For many individuals involved in the debate over gun control in the United States—including scholars, lawyers, judges, journalists, politicians, and everyday citizens concerned about public policy and law—the Second Amendment, and how they interpret it, forms the foundation of their position. The proponents of "gun rights"—archetypically vocalized by the National Rifle Association (NRA)—would have the public, lawmakers, and judges believe that the amendment guarantees the *individual* the right to own and use arms for protection—protection of one's person, home, or property, as well as against a government that might descend from democracy into tyranny. On the other hand, the proponents of gun control—most strongly articulated by the Brady Campaign to Prevent Gun Violence—would have everyone believe that the Second Amendment is a *collective* right that guaranteed *states*, not individuals, the right to form armed militias for protection in case the democracy of the fledgling nation failed. Some scholars believe that *both* the individual rights theory and the collective rights theory miss the boat—that is, both demonstrate a lack of "understanding [of] the eighteenth-century world in which the Second Amendment was drafted and adopted" (Cornell, 2004, 161). What is the average citizen to make of these differing points of view on the Second Amendment and how the amendment does or should influence the nature of gun control in the contemporary United States?

How the Proponents of Gun Control View the Second Amendment

The Brady Campaign and similarly minded organizations promoting gun control prominently advertise the fact that no federal court has ever struck down a gun-control law as unconstitutional based on the Second Amendment. The U.S. Supreme Court has given at least five judgments bearing on this amendment, and lower federal courts have made dozens more. In all but one of these decisions,[6] the courts have failed to rule that the Constitution guarantees the unfettered right of an individual to own or bear their own firearms. On the contrary, the courts have consistently decreed that both federal and state governments can restrict who may and may not own a gun, and can also regulate the sale, transfer, receipt, possession, and use of specific categories of firearms.

Advocates of gun control like to take the short view of history regarding the Second Amendment. Their favorite starting point is sometimes 1876 (*U.S. v. Cruikshank*) or 1886 (*Presser v. Illinois*), but they are on firmer and more morally comfortable ground when they begin with 1939 (*United States v. Miller*).

In *U.S. v. Cruikshank* (92 U.S. 542, 1876), Louisiana state officials—who happened to be members of the Ku Klux Klan—were challenged for conspiring to disarm a meeting of African-Americans. Attorneys for the African-Americans argued that the Second Amendment protected the right of all citizens to keep and bear arms. However, the Supreme Court held that the officials had the legal prerogative to disarm them in protection of the common weal. More particularly, the court held that "bearing arms for a lawful purpose . . . is not a right granted by the Constitution." More specifically, the Court ruled that the Second Amendment was not "incorporated," meaning that it only applied to the federal government, not to state governments. The states did not have to honor it, except that they could not prevent citizens belonging to the militia from possessing their own firearms—as long as the firearms were appropriate for use in the militia.

Although this ruling supports their contention that the Second Amendment should pose no barrier to the enactment of strict gun control laws, at least at the state level, many advocates of the gun control movement are not particularly eager to tout *U.S. v. Cruikshank*. First, the ruling is based on an increasingly outdated legal philosophy. The notion that the First Amendment, for example, does not apply to the states is long gone, and no one would argue this today (nevertheless, the Supreme Court has yet to "incorporate" the Second Amendment). More importantly, the ruling was racist—providing a justification for keeping former slaves unarmed and in a position of vassalage in the South, thereby partly counteracting the effect of the Emancipation Proclamation. This fact is not lost on many African-American and Jewish jurists, or on interest groups opposed to gun regulation such as the National Rifle Association. Even though African-Americans and Jews generally tend to support strict gun control, some such jurists have contended that regulations on gun possession are a means of suppressing a society's minorities and of allowing unjust rulers to hold sway because they control all weaponry (see Cottrol and Diamond, 1995).

There is no denying that totalitarian regimes in the modern era, from Fascist to Communist, have routinely denied ordinary citizens the right to keep and bear arms. Only the political elite could keep arms in Fascist Spain or in Communist East Germany and other countries behind the Iron Curtain. And closer to home, so-called Black Codes in the post–Civil War South routinely contained statutes such as Mississippi's code that "no freedman, free Negro, or mulatto not in the military service of the United States government, and not licensed so to do by the board of police of his or her county, shall keep or carry firearms of any kind, or ammunition, dirk, or Bowie knife" (as quoted in Cramer, 1994, Chapter 6). However, as democracy has entrenched itself in the political system and the culture of the United States over the course of two centuries, it is highly unlikely that the country will witness abuses of its citizens comparable to what occurred in the South after the Civil War and in totalitarian regimes elsewhere in the world. In the present-day United States, advocates of strict gun control emphasize there are authentic institutionalized means for changing the political system and getting one's concerns aired and remedied. Gun control advocates also argue that even if the fantastically improbable did occur—even if the United States went totalitarian—ordinary citizens armed with shotguns, deer rifles, 22s, and pistols could not do much in the face of a massive, well-trained, high-tech military.

Presser v. Illinois (116 U.S. 252, 1886) involved the case of Herman Presser, the leader of a German-American labor group called the *Lehr und Wehr Verein* (the Learning and Defense Club), who was arrested for parading the group through downtown Chicago while carrying a sword. More specifically, he was arrested for conducting an "armed military drill," which could legally be done only with a license, under Illinois statutes in force at the time. Presser appealed, invoking the Second Amendment in his defense. The Supreme Court judged against him, citing the *U.S. v.*

Cruikshank ruling discussed earlier. Again, the Court contended that the Second Amendment had not been "incorporated" and thus did not apply to the individual states. As was the case with *Cruikshank*, the Supreme Court's decision smacked of bigotry—in this instance, in the repression of exploited immigrant laborers trying to improve their collective lot via unionization.

A more morally and legally defensible starting point for gun control advocates contending that there is no constitutional or other legal basis for disallowing the strict regulation of firearms is *United States v. Miller* (307 U.S. 174, 1939). In that case, the Supreme Court ruled that the federal government had the right, which it exercised in the 1934 National Firearms Act, to control the transfer of (and in effect, to require the registration of) certain firearms. More particularly, the sawed-off shotgun, a favorite weapon of gangsters, was deemed unprotected by the Second Amendment. The ruling reads, in part, "In the absence of any evidence tending to show that possession or use of [a] 'shotgun having a barrel of less than eighteen inches in length' at this time has some reasonable relationship to the preservation or efficiency of a well regulated militia, we cannot say that the second amendment guarantees the right to keep and bear such an instrument." Lower court decisions involving the National Firearms Act and the kindred 1938 Federal Firearms Act used even more direct language. In upholding the National Firearms Act, the district court held in *United States v. Adams* that the Second Amendment "refers to the Militia, a protective force of government; to the collective body and not individual rights." Another district court decision in *United States v. Tot* referred to this ruling in upholding the Federal Firearms Act. Both court decisions made clear that no personal right to own arms existed under the federal Constitution.

However, in its *Miller* ruling, the Supreme Court noted that the writers of the Constitution clearly intended that the states had both the right and the duty to maintain militias and that a "militia comprised all males physically capable of acting in concert for the common defense. . . . And, further, that ordinarily when called for service, these men were expected to appear bearing arms supplied by themselves and of the kind in common use at the time. . . . This implied the general obligation of all adult male inhabitants to possess arms, and with certain exceptions, to cooperate in the work of defense. The possession of arms also implied the possession of ammunition, and authorities paid quite as much attention to the latter as to the former." Thus, the full text of the

Supreme Court decision mitigates the impact of its decision on sawed-off shotguns. Such weapons had no place in a militia and were thus not protected, but the general principle of ordinary citizens owning arms and ammunition was clearly preserved.

Gun control advocates are on their strongest ground with more recent Supreme Court decisions. In *Lewis v. United States* (445 U.S. 95, 1980), the Court ruled that the 1968 Gun Control Act's prohibition of felons owning firearms was constitutional. The Court held that "legislative restrictions on the use of firearms do not entrench upon any constitutionally protected liberties." Since then, the Supreme Court has on six occasions made its interpretation of the Second Amendment known by letting stand lower court decisions regarding the regulation of firearms. One of these was *Farmer v. Higgens*, wherein the Eleventh Circuit Court of Appeals denied the plaintiff a license to manufacture a new machine gun, based on the 1986 Firearms Owners' Protection Act, which put an outright ban on new sales of machine guns and automatic weapons. Another was the Seventh Circuit Court of Appeals ruling that the Morton Grove (Illinois) ban on the possession and sale of handguns was within the legal bounds of the Second Amendment. More particularly, the Circuit Court affirmed that "possession of handguns by individuals is not part of the right to keep and bear arms." The Supreme Court refused to hear an appeal of this ruling.

Taking into consideration the entirety of federal court decisions in support of laws regulating firearms, political scientist Robert J. Spitzer (1995, 49) concludes that "the desire to treat the Second Amendment as a constitutional touchstone is . . . without historical, constitutional, or legal foundation. More problematic, this constant and misplaced invocation of rights only serves to heighten social conflict, cultivate ideological rigidity, and stifle rational policy debate." Similarly, former Supreme Court Chief Justice Warren Burger (1991) observes that:

> The very language of the Second Amendment refutes any argument that it was intended to guarantee every citizen an unfettered right to any kind of weapon he or she desires. In referring to "a well regulated militia," the Framers clearly intended to secure the right to bear arms essentially for military purposes. In the late 18th century, the "militia" was the aggregate of all able-bodied men, and the word "militia" was defined as "a body of troops; soldiers collectively." Moreover, even

where the militia was concerned, it is clear that the Framers contemplated that the use of arms could be "well regulated." If an 18th-century militia was intended to be "well regulated," surely the Second Amendment does not remotely guarantee every person the constitutional right to have a "Saturday Night Special" or a machine gun without any regulation whatever.

The Gun Rights View of the Second Amendment

The National Rifle Association and other organizations similarly opposed to gun control prefer to take the long view of history with regard to the Second Amendment. As already noted, Supreme Court decisions between 1876 and 1938 contained language that supported the notion that the framers of the Constitution clearly intended ordinary citizens to possess arms and to be prepared to carry these arms into battle in defense of the state. However, the favorite starting point of gun control opponents is pre-Revolutionary America and even earlier—as far back as Saxon England in the seventh century. For then and thereafter, up through the ratification of the Second Amendment in 1791, various governments clearly intended that individual citizens have both the right *and the duty* to keep and bear firearms.

The Anglo-Saxon tradition of all free men having the right, and even the duty, to keep and bear arms was transferred to Colonial America, where all the colonies individually passed militia laws that required universal gun ownership. Hunting was essential to many families, and in light of immediate threats from the French, Dutch, Spanish, and Native Americans, it is not surprising that colonial militia statutes required that all able-bodied males be armed and trained (see Hardy, 1986, 41; also see Halbrook, 1989). Intellectually, the colonial elite imbibed the writings of Whig political philosophers, who emphasized decentralized government, fear of a standing army, and the right of the common people to keep and bear arms in defense of themselves—against criminals, foreign powers, and especially the state itself (Colburn, 1965).

Critical in setting the stage for the beginning of the Revolutionary War were British attempts to disarm the local populations of Massachusetts. Indeed, the first battle at Lexington in April 1776 was touched off when British soldiers approached a group of local militiamen in an attempt to enforce the new disarm-the-people policy. Colonialists bent on independence feared that the British would soon try to disarm not only the residents of Massachusetts, but also residents of the other twelve colonies. Indeed, their fears received confirmation when Britain's Colonial Undersecretary William Knox circulated to Crown officials the tract "What Is Fit to be Done with America?," which, among other things, advised that "The Militia Laws should be repealed and none suffered to be re-enacted, & the Arms of all the People should be taken away, . . . nor should any Foundery or manufactuary of Arms, Gunpowder, or Warlike Stores, be ever suffered in America, nor should any Gunpowder, Lead, Arms or Ordnance be imported into it without License" (as quoted in Peckman, 1978, 176). As the Revolutionary War got under way, the individual states began to adopt constitutions and bills of rights that were partly shaped by perceived and actual British attempts to disarm Americans (Halbrook, 1989, 17). Four states (Pennsylvania, North Carolina, Vermont, and Massachusetts) included the right to bear arms in their formal declaration of rights.

The core issues involved in constitutional debates on the right to bear arms in these four states resurfaced during the U.S. Constitutional Convention's deliberations in 1787 on the need for such a provision, as well as during the First U.S. Congress's debates that eventually led to the Second Amendment in 1789. These issues were fear of a standing army and federalism versus states' rights. States' rights advocates, such as Edmund Randolph, emphasized that citizens in new republics should fear standing armies at all costs; these advocates were quick to invoke the historical record in 1767–1776 Massachusetts, where the British army's presence inflamed and abused the local population—and where the standing army tried to weaken the people by disarming them. States' rights advocates were also quick to point to the sorry records of Charles I, Oliver Cromwell, and James II, who used their armies to disarm and tyrannize much of the English populace between 1639 and 1688. The states' rights advocates—also known as the Antifederalists—comprised the overwhelming majority of delegates, but their zeal was tempered by the ineffective governance that existed under the Articles of Confederation (1778–1789), which kept the federal government very weak and state governments very strong.

Federalists, such as Alexander Hamilton, were also fearful of standing armies, but believed the survival of the United States depended on a strong national government—a government that, among many other things, had its own army and navy. The great compromises between proponents and opponents of federalism were Article I, Section 8 of the Constitution and the Second Amendment of the Bill of Rights. In Article I, Section 8, Congress is granted the power to

- raise and support an army (8.12);
- provide and maintain a navy (8.13);
- call forth the militia to execute the laws of the Union, suppress insurrections, and repel invasions (8.15);
- provide for organizing, arming, and disciplining the militia, and for governing such part of them as may be employed in the Service of the United States (8.16).

Concessions to satisfy the Antifederalists included the right of the states to appoint officers to the militia and to train militiamen (according to standards set by Congress). State militias were seen as counteracting forces to the potential might of a standing federal army. Fears of a standing army were further assuaged by giving the civilian Congress control over the military's purse strings and by requiring that the Secretary of War (Defense) be a civilian (Heathcock, 1963, 81–83).

Nagging doubts over the power of the states to maintain and control militias were addressed in the First Congress and eventually alleviated with the passage of the Second Amendment. States' rights advocates wanted to be certain that federal power could not be used to annul state sovereignty. "The aim was to ensure the continued existence of state militias as a military and political counterbalance to the national army, and more broadly to national power (the federalism question; see Spitzer, 1995, 36)."

However, this was not the only intent of Congress regarding the Second Amendment—which in recent times is difficult to tell because the amendment is so sparsely worded. The spare language was doubtlessly due to the framers' shared understanding of the institutions and convictions behind it. But, in the long run, "these understandings have vanished as brevity and elegance have been achieved at the cost of clarity" (Malcolm, 1994, 161). Historian Joyce Malcolm's analysis of the First Congress's debate over the amendment resulted in her conclusion that its framers clearly intended the amendment to guarantee the *individual's* right to have arms for self-defense and self-preservation. For example, the First Congress, like its English predecessors, rejected language restricting the people's right only to "the common defence" (163).

How early Americans understood the Second Amendment is captured not only in the historical records of the First Congress, but also in how the amendment was announced and interpreted to the citizenry. The *Philadelphia Federal Gazette* and the *Philadelphia Evening Post* of June 18, 1789, in an article reprinted in New York and Boston, explained the Second Amendment as follows: "As civil rulers, not having their duty to the people duly before them, may attempt to tyrannize, and as the military forces which must be occasionally raised to defend our country, might pervert their power to the injury of their fellow-citizens, the people are confirmed . . . in their right to keep and bear their private arms" (as quoted in Malcolm, 1994, 164).

Finally, the meaning that the First Congress intended for the Second Amendment is revealed in its passage of the Militia Act of 1792. The act required all able-bodied men between the ages of eighteen and forty-five to own a firearm and ammunition and to be willing to put their weapons to use when called upon by the federal government. Each man within the specified age range was to

> provide himself with a good musket or firelock, a sufficient bayonet and belt, two spare flints, and a knapsack, a pouch with a box therein to contain not less than twenty-four cartridges, suited to the bore of his musket or firelock, each cartridge to contain a proper quantity of powder and ball: or with a good rifle, knapsack, shot-pouch and powder-horn, twenty balls suited to the bore of his rifle, and a quarter of a pound of powder, and shall appear, so armed, accoutred and provided, when called out to exercise, or into service, except, that when called out on company days to exercise only, he may appear without a knapsack. (*Militia Act*, Ch. 33, 1 Stat. 271–274, 1792; as quoted in Reynolds, 1995, 487).

A perusal of the deliberations of the First Congress on the Militia Act discloses no instance of any representative questioning whether individual citizens had the right to possess a firearm.

Rather, the representatives agonized over how well citizens should be armed—fearing that the average citizen could not bear too much cost. One congressman asserted, "as far as the whole body of the people are necessary to the general defence, they ought to be armed; but the law ought not to require more than is necessary; for that would be a just cause of complaint." In response, other legislators argued that those Americans who did not possess arms should have them supplied by the states. Such discussions clearly indicated that the problem perceived by the representatives was how to get arms into the hands of the people, not how to restrict their possession (see Shalhope, 1982).

A Limited Individual Right

In sum, a dispassionate examination of history and of federal court decisions reveals that there is undeniable constitutional and historical support for the contention that the Second Amendment protects the right of *selected individuals* to keep and bear arms—those individuals being able-bodied men capable of serving in a state militia. This is a fundamental claim of the National Rifle Association and others who are opposed to the strict regulation of firearms; indeed, such groups and individuals would contend that, with the exception of convicted felons, the right goes beyond selected individuals to include all individuals, including women, people of color, resident aliens, and many others that the Founding Fathers would have excluded from the keeping and bearing of arms. However, the same examination also leads to the conclusion that this is a *limited right*—which is to say that both state and federal governments[7] can "infringe" upon the possession ("keeping") and carrying ("bearing") of arms, and that many contemporary legislators and judges have not felt the need to be in lockstep with the full intentions of the framers of the Second Amendment.

More generally, these legislators and judges recognize the significant changes that have occurred in the United States since 1776, when an armed population was critical to the defense of the new nation. As pointed out by Spitzer (2004) and Edel (1995, 28–36), in the past 230 years, the standing army has become entrenched in U.S. life, and notions that it is a threat to personal liberty have long ago been dispelled. The concept of defense being limited to fighting at the borders of one's homeland repelling foreign invaders has been greatly broadened to the point where the defense business of the United States includes sending soldiers to Europe, Asia, Central America, Africa, and the Middle East; in short, the place of the United States in world affairs has changed dramatically. In the eighteenth century, the protection of the home, the farm, the village, the town, the city were left to the individual or to the militia; but by the middle of the nineteenth century, local police forces were the norm, and by the middle of the twentieth century, national law enforcement agencies (the FBI, Secret Service, Customs Service, Drug Enforcement Administration, Immigration and Naturalization Service) were well established. In sum, eighteenth-century notions of the purpose and place of the militia in the community are out of step with the realities of the twenty-first century, and so too, consequently, is the need to ensure the keeping and bearing of arms in private hands.

More particularly, the states and the federal government can and do (1) outlaw the possession and transfer of certain categories of firearms (as they have done with machine guns, and as many gun control advocates would like to see done with handguns); (2) outlaw the right of certain categories of individuals to own firearms (most notably convicted felons and the mentally incompetent); (3) require shooters to be licensed and to have passed a firearms safety examination; and (4) require that the purchasers of certain classes of guns obtain special permits (most notably, handguns, as is now the case in twelve states and the District of Columbia[8]). In short, "the Second Amendment poses no obstacle to gun control as it is debated in modern America" (Spitzer, 1995, 49), and it cannot account for the difficulties and defeats the modern gun control movement has thus far encountered. The courts have been consistently unwilling to strike down local, state, and federal gun control laws on the basis of the amendment. Indeed, the courts have seldom veered from the decision handed down by the New Jersey Supreme Court that "The Second Amendment, concerning the right of the people to keep and bear arms, was framed in contemplation not of individual rights but of the maintenance of the states' active, organized militias" (as quoted in Cress, 1984, 42). Furthermore, the courts have ruled that state militias are, for all intents and purposes in the modern era, tantamount to their respective National Guard units.[9] Finally, it should be noted that public opinion favors the limited individual rights interpretation of the Second Amendment: When a 2003 Gallup poll asked a national probability sample of U.S. adults if the amendment "was intended to give Americans the right to keep and bear arms for their own defense, (or) was only intended to preserve the existence of citizen-militias," 68 percent responded that it "gives the right to keep and bear arms"; however, of those respondents saying that the Second Amendment was so intended, 82 percent responded that "the government can impose some restrictions on gun ownership without violating the [amendment]" (Gallup Organization, 2004).

Public Opinion and Gun Control

Do Americans Want Strict Gun Control?

Overall, via local, state, regional, and national surveys, Americans are polled on their attitudes toward guns and gun control several dozen times per year. Variations in the wordings of questions concerning particular sub-issues can significantly affect the findings, as many researchers have demonstrated (see for example, Kleck, 1997, Chapter 10; Kopel, 2000). However, the overall pattern in the polling data is so consistent and so strong that the inescapable conclusion is that the U.S. public supports the strong control of firearms. However, Americans are opposed to restricting guns to the degree to which they are in many other industrialized countries—most importantly, they do not think handguns should be banned from private ownership.

Since 1972, the National Opinion Research Center (NORC) has polled a random sample of adult Americans on a variety of social issues (almost annually until 1994, with samples of approximately 1,600; and biannually since then, with samples of approximately 3,000). NORC's *General Social Survey* (GSS) provides one of the best data sources currently available on U.S. social structure, as well as on the attitudes and self-reported behaviors of the population. Because it asks the same question concerning gun control on all of its surveys, the GSS provides one of the most important over-time data sources available on this issue: *Would you favor or oppose a law which would require a person to obtain a police permit before he or she could buy a gun?* Over the past three decades, survey results reveal a strong and generally increasing tendency toward favoring police permits (see Figure 1.3). This implies support for the Brady Handgun Violence Prevention Act, which requires a background check for handgun purchases from licensed gun dealers, manufacturers, or importers. The background check is conducted through information provided by the

FIGURE 1.3
Trends in Support for Police Permits to Buy a Gun

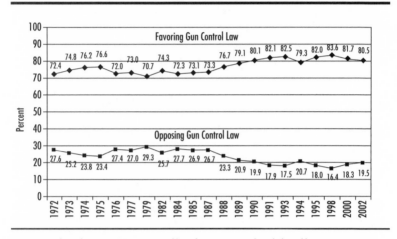

Source: General Social Survey 1972–2002. "Would you favor or oppose a law which would require a person to obtain a police permit before he or she could buy a gun?"

FBI's National Instant Criminal Background Check System, and it is intended to prevent individuals convicted of a serious crime (carrying a sentence of at least a year), under a violence-based restraining order, having a drug-related arrest, classified as a fugitive from justice, deemed an illegal alien, or certified as mentally unstable from purchasing a handgun. Indeed, Gallup, Harris, and other national surveys consistently reveal strong support (85–90 percent) for the Brady law, even among gun owners (75–80 percent). Enacted in November 1993, after overcoming vehement opposition from the NRA, it is one of the very few national gun control laws in the United States today.

In their quest to reduce gun violence, proponents of strict gun control would like to see the enactment of *national* regulations on par with those in most other industrialized democracies. Among these regulations are required safety classes (which implies requiring all shooters to be licensed), a ban on all types of assault weapons, a ban on cheap handguns, a ban on the importation of high-capacity ammunition clips, reducing the number of guns individuals can buy during a specified period of time (e.g., limiting gun purchases to one per month to prevent gun trafficking), prohibiting minors and violent criminals from buying guns,

FIGURE 1.4
Percentage of U.S. Adults Favoring Selected Gun Control Measures

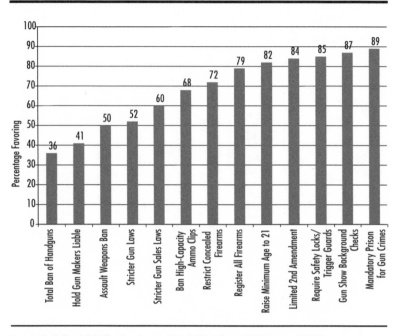

Sources: The Gallup Poll (Gallup Organization, 2004, 2005a; Gillespie, 1999; Newport, 1999b)

allowing concealed weapons to be carried only by law enforcement officers or a few select individuals who might have the need
(e.g., those transporting large amounts of cash), requiring all guns
to be registered, and requiring background checks on the purchasers of guns—whether the seller is a licensed firearms dealer,
a private individual, or a flea market or gun show vendor. According to a series of Gallup polls conducted over the past two
decades, the general population strongly supports *all* such regulations. For a presentation of the various findings of these polls,
see Carter, 1997, Chapter 4; Gallup Organization, 1993, 2004,
2005a; Gillespie, 1999; Kleck, 1997, Chapter 10; and Newport,
1999a, 1999b. (See Figure 1.4).

An especially interesting poll was conducted in 1993 when
Gallup compared the responses of the general population to
those of gun owners; importantly, the poll found gun owners to

FIGURE 1.5
Percentage of General Population vs. Gun Owners Favoring Selected Gun
Control Measures

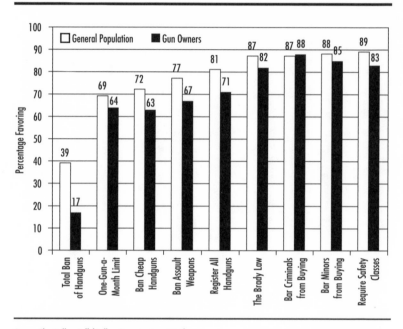

Source: The Gallup Poll (Gallup Organization, 1993)

be nearly as supportive as everyone else for strong national gun
control laws (see Figure 1.5). Only a total ban on handguns and
holding gun manufacturers liable for crimes committed with
their guns lack majority support (Figures 1.4 and 1.5). As with
the Brady legislation, the NRA and its allies strongly oppose all
of these gun control measures—except for banning sales to criminals (the NRA's views on these measures are available online at
http://www.nraila.org/).

Social and Economic Correlates of Support for Gun Control

Regardless of social or economic background, most U.S. adults
favor gun control—at least in terms of the GSS question concerning

TABLE 1.5
Social and Economic Correlates of Support for Gun Control

Attribute	Percent In Favor	Attribute	Percent In Favor
Gender		**Region**	
Male	72.3	Northeast	85.4
Female	86.1	Midwest	78.0
Race		South	80.2
White	77.8	West	74.2
Black	86.2	**Urbanization**	
Native American	80.0	City	81.9
Asian	88.9	Suburb	80.9
Other/Mixed	82.8	Small Town	74.5
Age		Rural	74.7
18–39	81.4	**Political Affiliation**	
40–64	77.6	Democrat	85.1
65+	80.5	Independent	81.8
Family Income		Republican	71.7
Less than $25,000	81.7	**Foreign Born?**	
$25,000–$74,999	77.6	No	78.8
$75,000+	77.7	Yes	86.8
Years of Schooling		**Hunter in the Household?**	
Less than 12 years	81.3	No	83.5
12 years	80.7	Yes	61.3
13–15 years	77.7	**Gun in the Household?**	
16+ years	79.0	No	86.3
		Yes	67.3

Source: Cumulated 2000–2002 General Social Survey (N=2,785). "Would you favor or oppose a law which would require a person to obtain a police permit before he or she could buy a gun?"

the requirement of a police permit to buy a gun. Only hunters (who constitute only about 18 percent of the U.S. adult population) do not have an overwhelming majority in support of this gun control measure. But what kinds of people are *especially* likely to favor gun control? The General Social Survey allows us to investigate respondents' social and economic attributes. Most notably, women, people of color, city-dwellers, Northeasterners, foreign-born individuals, Democrats, nonhunters, and non-gun owners are significantly more likely to favor gun control than their counterparts (men, whites, small-town/rural dwellers, Westerners, native-born individuals, Republicans, hunters, and gun owners; see Table 1.5).

None of these findings is particularly surprising—save perhaps for the fact that more than two-thirds of Republicans express support for the GSS gun control item (as observed later in this chapter, the combination of a Republican president and a Republican Congress effectively eliminates the possibility for the passage of strong national gun control legislation). Hunters and gun owners are predictably less likely to favor restricting an essential part of their recreational lifestyles (whether hunting in the field or participating in gun-club and range shooting) and personal philosophies (the right to use firearms in self-defense). Although a purchase permit by itself is a moderate measure, some gun owners "may fear that passing a moderate measure now would make it easier to pass more objectionable and restrictive measures later" (Kleck, 1991, 375). In addition, hunters and gun owners are much more likely than their nonhunting/non-gun owning counterparts to read gun magazines, where "gun rights" essays abound. Every issue of *The American Rifleman, The American Hunter, Guns and Ammo,* and *Handguns,* for example, contains at least one anti-gun control article.

Men are more likely to have a machismo attraction to weapons. In the words of psychologist Leonard Berkowitz, "for many, guns signify manliness" (as quoted in Gest, 1982, 38). Men are also much more likely to be hunters and gun owners. The latter applies also to small town- and rural-dwellers. City-dwellers, on the other hand, are less likely to be gun owners and hunters; moreover, they are more likely to read about gun violence and to experience it personally, as well as to have heightened fears that guns can fall too easily into the wrong hands (e.g., those of gang members). Foreign-born individuals are more likely to have been raised in cultures where firearms are highly regulated and, in turn, are less likely to own guns.

FIGURE 1.6
Percentage Favoring GSS Gun Control Item by Combinations of Gun Ownership,
Hunter, and Gender

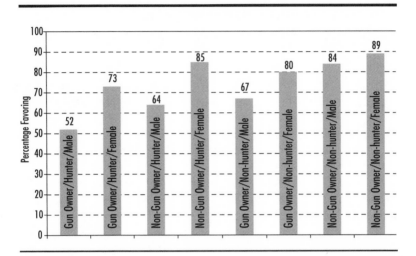

Source: Cumulated 2000–2002 General Social Survey (N=2.785). "Would you favor or oppose a law which would require a person to obtain a police permit before he or she could buy a gun?"

While attitudes toward gun control tend to vary somewhat with the previously mentioned social-background characteristics, they do *not* vary significantly with age, education (years of schooling), or income. The GSS finds essentially equal support for gun control among all ages, educational levels, and income groups. Sociologist Erich Goode (1984, 230) observes that "just about all aspects of our lives—from the newspapers we read to the ways we make love, from the food we eat to our political ideology and behavior—are either correlated or causally connected with socioeconomic statuses." But not here. Goode (1984, 321) also observes that "aging generates attitudes." But again not here. That support for gun control cuts across the lines of both social class and age bodes well for those wanting to strengthen gun control laws in the United States.[10]

Interestingly, combinations of the attributes displayed in Table 1.5 cannot be created that would push support for the GSS gun control item below the fifty percent level. The various combinations of the three strongest predictors of responses to the gun control question (gun ownership, hunting, and sex) are displayed in Figure 1.6. Although non-gun owning, nonhunting women are much more likely to respond that they favor police permits (the GSS gun-control question), more than half of gun owning men who hunt are also in favor of permits.

How Strong Are Attitudes Regarding Gun Control?

Because the NRA's position is generally not supported by public opinion polls, the organization has a tendency to repudiate them: "Polls can be slanted by carefully worded questions to achieve any desired outcome. It is a fact that most people do not know what laws currently exist; thus, it is meaningless to assert that people favor 'stricter' laws when they do not know how 'strict' the laws are in the first place" (National Rifle Association, 1994, 2). Indeed, instead of looking to polls to gauge the feelings of the general population, the NRA argues that "a more direct measure of the public's attitude on 'gun control' comes when the electorate has a chance to speak on the issue. Public opinion polls do not form public policy, but individual actions by hundreds of thousands of citizens do" (via voting down gun regulation proposals, as has happened in some states and localities during the past two decades; or loosening restrictions on the carrying of concealed weapons by ordinary citizens, as has happened in two dozen states during the same time period; see National Rifle Association, 1994, 3). Similarly, criminologist Gary Kleck (1991, 365–366), a scholar the NRA favors highly, argues that: "The survey-based support for gun control may be less substantial than it appears. . . . Sometimes, a survey 'opinion' is little more than a response given on the spur-of-the-moment to a stranger who calls unannounced at the respondent's door or on the telephone, and asks a question about a topic to which the R[espondent] has given little thought. [In short,] . . . the appearance of support for [gun control] can be created by the simple fact that most people will provide an opinion if asked, regardless of whether or not they had a well-formed, stable, or strongly held opinion on the issue before they were interviewed."

Kleck overstates his case, however, for according to data from the 1984 General Social Survey (the last GSS to investigate this), the public is actually better informed and much more concerned about gun control than he suggests. When asked, "How much information do you have about the gun control issue?" only one in five respondents (23 percent) answered "very little." Two in five respondents (41 percent) claimed to have at least "some" information, and more than a third (36 percent) reported having "most" or "all" information. When asked, "How important is the gun control issue to you?" most respondents (70 percent) said that it was either an "important" issue or "one of the most important" issues to them. This finding is consistent with that of Schuman and Presser (1981), who asked a random sample of adult Americans, "Compared with how you feel on other public issues, are your feelings about permits for guns: extremely strong, very strong, fairly strong, or not strong at all?" More than 80 percent responded between "fairly strong" and "extremely strong," leaving fewer than 20 percent responding "not strong at all."

Of critical importance to the ultimate success of those favoring stronger gun control is whether they hold their beliefs as strongly as those opposed to gun control do. One of Schuman and Presser's findings could be interpreted as showing that gun control advocates do not hold their beliefs as strongly as gun control opponents. Asked if they have done anything tangible in support of their beliefs, opponents were three times more likely than proponents of control to report writing letters to public officials or donating money to a group representing their interests. However, Schuman and Presser (1981, 46) do not interpret this finding as evidence that gun control opponents hold their beliefs more solidly than gun control supporters. Rather, they hypothesize that opponents were more likely to act on their beliefs because of "the efficiency of the National Rifle Association in mobilizing supporters" (an issue discussed in the next section). Kleck (1991, 365) rejects this conclusion because only a fraction of the respondents could possibly belong to the NRA. Whatever the exact explanation of gun control opponents' greater activism, however, Schuman and Presser's idea that opponents do not hold their beliefs more strongly than supporters is corroborated by the GSS data, for those who favor gun control are significantly more likely to report that the issue is either "important" or "one of the most important" to them (74 percent of those favoring gun control versus 64 percent of those opposing it).

Is the Will of the People Being Thwarted?

Do U.S. adults want strict gun control? On balance, the answer is yes. As public opinion polls have repeatedly shown, most adults strongly believe in required safety classes, required safety locks and trigger guards, restricting the carrying of concealed firearms, limiting gun purchases to one per month to hinder gun trafficking, police permits, the registration of firearms, keeping guns out of the hands of criminals and minors, and background checks—even when sales are between private individuals. Proponents of gun control see the nation's lack of strict gun control regulations as evidence that the will of the people is being thwarted.

The near past offers us many instances of the government being disconnected with popular sentiment. For example, the 1994 U.S. invasion of Haiti was preceded by a national opinion poll showing that only 18 percent of the population would support this action (Dickstein and Farley, 1994, 16). Similarly, the 1995–1996 deployment of U.S. troops in Bosnia-Herzegovina was preceded by a national poll showing only 30 percent of the population favoring the deployment (*Providence Journal-Bulletin,* 1995, A14). More recently, just under half of U.S. adults sampled by the Gallup poll in the fall of 2004 agreed with the statement, "the Bush administration deliberately misled the American public about whether Iraq ha[d] weapons of mass destruction" (Gallup Organization, 2005b).

What can explain the people's will not being acted upon with regard to gun control? This question is magnified by the preceding analysis of the Second Amendment, which revealed that strong gun control legislation is not being impeded by the amendment.

The Role of Politics

Outside interests, particularly the president and pressure groups, exercise excessive influence over Congress, preventing the legislators from applying independent judgment about the programs that the national interest seems to require.

—Leroy N. Rieselbach
Congressional Politics (1995, 5)

The existence of the National Rifle Association is the greatest single reason why the United States has not adopted the types of firearms restrictions which are common in many countries.

—Edward F. Leddy
Magnum Force (1987, 1)

Ultimately, the informed citizen must make up his or her own mind about the issue of gun control on the basis of his or her fundamental values and view of human nature. For many, this choice will be manifested in their voting—as, politically speaking, several features of U.S. society ensure that the gun debate will continue to be salient, and often heated, in the decades to come. First, the United States is awash in guns—with more than 200 million rifles, shotguns, and handguns as of 2005, with two to three million new firearms—a third of them handguns—being added to the total each year (Bureau of Alcohol, Tobacco and Firearms, 2001, 2002). Because guns don't wear out, the total number of firearms in the United States will exceed the size of its population within the next few decades. Easy availability of firearms—through both legal and illegal means—is a fact of life in contemporary U.S. society.

Second, crime rates in the United States have been falling for the past decade, partly in response to the baby boom generation growing up (youth and crime are significantly correlated). However, the children of the baby boom produced a baby boomlet, and individuals in this cohort—40 million strong—are now hitting their teens and early twenties, and the ten-year decline in street crime is expected to taper off, if not rise, in response. These two forces, youth and easy firearm availability, will keep gun violence alive and well.

Such violence will undoubtedly receive heavy media coverage, which will almost assuredly be slanted toward the pro-control side of the gun debate (those in the media overwhelmingly support gun control). Sympathetic media coverage will keep the Brady Campaign to Prevent Gun Violence and its agenda for strict gun control in the limelight, and it should therefore be expected that membership rates and donations will remain high, if not grow outright. On the other side, the NRA's head start in membership and resources (in the late 1990s about an 8 to 1 advantage in membership and at least a 10 to 1 advantage in financial assets) will allow it to maintain a powerful presence on Capitol Hill no matter how much the Brady Campaign expands over the coming decade.

The trump card in this war over gun regulation will be the political makeup of Congress and the presidency. Each side of the debate makes its greatest gains when political opportunity favors it. History has demonstrated that a conservative president and one conservative house of Congress favor the NRA and the "gun rights" side. In contrast, a liberal president and a liberal majority in at least one house favor the Brady Campaign and the "gun control" side. Any other combination—liberal president/conservative Congress or conservative president/liberal Congress—produces a standoff. With Republicans controlling both the presidency and the Congress (at least through the beginning of 2009), we can expect more of what occurred in September 2004, when the federal assault-weapons ban was allowed to expire. This occurred despite a Gallup poll revealing more adults supporting (50 percent) than opposing (46 percent) a complete ban on the manufacture, sale, or possession of assault rifles (Gallup Organization, 2005a).

The key political trend for most of the past three decades has been toward conservatism. If it continues, which is more likely than not, then we might well find another conservative Republican in the White House after the election of 2008 and another Republican majority in the Congress. If this scenario unfolds, success for those wanting stricter gun control measures will be defined by what they do not lose (e.g., more states approving laws allowing ordinary citizens to carry concealed firearms) rather than by what they gain.

On the other hand, if by some series of quirks the presidency lands in the hands of the Democrats in 2008, and if this is accompanied by the election of a more liberal (Democratic) Congress, then it would not be surprising to see a series of gun regulations enacted that would put the United States more in line with those of its peer nations in Western Europe. There would be a convergence of forces that has never occurred in U.S. history: a liberal Congress, a liberal president, public opinion strongly favoring gun control, and a powerful and well-organized gun control movement, spearheaded by the Brady Campaign, to counteract the NRA and others that prefer the status quo.

The serious gun control measures that organizations like the Brady Campaign would like to see enacted on a national level are identified and assessed in detail in the next chapter.

Notes

1. Portions of this and subsequent chapters have been updated from the "Introduction" and various entries in *Guns in American Society: An Encyclopedia of History, Politics, Culture, and the Law*, Volume 1 (Santa Barbara, CA: ABC-CLIO, 2002), pp. xxv–xxxiv. © 2002 by Gregg Lee Carter; used by permission from the publisher.

2. For a review of the research that reaches a much weaker conclusion than that of Azrael (2004), see Kleck (1997, Chapter 8): "At best, one can say . . . that gun control measures that reduced gun availability among suicide-prone persons might save at least a few lives" (275). For a scholarly rebuttal to this much weaker conclusion, see Hemenway (2004a, Chapter 3; 2004b).

3. The use of control variables in nonexperimental studies is critically important if one is to trust any fundamental conclusions drawn about a causal relationship between gun prevalence and gun violence (homicides, suicides, accidental shootings, or crime-related injuries). Kleck (1997, 2001) severely criticizes earlier research (e.g., by Kellermann, 1992, 1993) that lacked such controls.

4. The *National Crime Victimization Survey* (NCVS) is the primary source of information on criminal victimization in the United States. Each year, data are obtained from a nationally representative sample of 42,000 households, comprising nearly 76,000 persons, on the frequency, characteristics, and consequences of criminal victimization. According to the NCVS, 60,108 individuals were injured with a gun during a criminal assault in 2002 (see Bureau of Justice Statistics, 2003; this number fell slightly in 2003, though the final tally was not available at the time of this writing in January 2005). It should be noted that not all of gun-related injuries recorded by the NCVS involved treatment in an emergency room.

5. The number of robberies and aggravated assaults is somewhat higher according to the NCVS data (Bureau of Justice Statistics, 2003): For example, in 2002 there were 458,460 robberies (25.6 percent involving a firearm) and 848,030 aggravated assaults (26.5 percent involving a firearm).

6. The single exception was *United States v. Emerson* (No. 99–10331, 5th Cir.), wherein the United States Court of Appeals for the Fifth Circuit in New Orleans ruled that the U.S. Constitution guarantees individuals, as opposed to state-mustered militias, the right to "privately possess and bear their own firearms . . . whether or not they are a member of a select militia" (132–133). The case involved the indictment of Dr. Timothy Joe Johnson for violating a statute forbidding a person under a restraining order from possessing a firearm (the 1994 Violence against Women Act). A federal judge in Lubbock, Texas, agreed with Johnson's contention that his constitutional right to possess a firearm had been violated and dismissed the indictment. Despite the Fifth Circuit appellate court's declaration on the right of the individual to own a firearm, the court ruled in the same decision that the government could regulate guns and thus reinstated Emerson's indictment. The *Emerson* decision applies only to the fifth circuit (Texas, Mississippi, and Louisiana), and the U.S. Supreme Court has refused to hear an appeal.

7. However, in forty-two states *local* governments are "preempted" from passing their own gun control laws. The NRA, which has fought strongly for preemption laws, argues that the state laws overcome a fundamental problem associated with local firearm ordinances—their ". . . sheer variety. Where no uniform state laws are in place, the result can be a complex patchwork of restrictions that change from one local jurisdiction to the next. But it is unreasonable to require citizens, whether residents of a given state or persons passing through or visiting a state, to memorize a myriad of laws. Where so many ordinances exist, citizens with no criminal intent are placed in jeopardy of running afoul of restrictions they don't even know exist" (National Rifle Association, 2003). Alaska, Hawaii, Illinois, Kansas, Nebraska, New Hampshire, and Ohio do not have statewide firearm preemption of local ordinances. Connecticut, Massachusetts, New Jersey, and New York have preemption through judicial ruling, not statute. In Massachusetts, local ordinances may be imposed if approved by the state legislature. The NRA was prompted into fervent support of preemption laws after Morton Grove (Illinois) passed a local law banning all handguns, a law that was subsequently upheld through appeals all the way to the U.S. Supreme Court.

8. The twelve states are Connecticut, Hawaii, Illinois, Iowa, Massachusetts, Michigan, Minnesota, Missouri, Nebraska, New Jersey, New York, and North Carolina.

9. Congress created the National Guard in 1903 and put it under close federal control with the National Defense Act of 1916. As private "militia movement" groups increasingly come face-to-face with the law, we can expect to see more court rulings on what constitutes the "militia" described in Second Amendment. According to legal historian Glenn Harlan Reynolds (1995, 509), private militia groups that argue that *they* are the militia described by the Constitution have it wrong: "Although the militia was a body that was, in a way, external to the state in the sense of being an institution of the people, the expectation was that the state, not private groups, would provide the foundation upon which the structure of the militia would be erected." Private militias have received considerable press since militia members were implicated in the bombing of the Alfred P. Murrah Federal Building in Oklahoma City that took 167 lives in April 1995 (see, for example, Coates, 1995).

10. The lack of significant relationships between attitudes on gun control and social class or age has been consistent across time. Smith's (1980, 302–304) analyses of Harris, NORC, and University of Michigan survey data collected in the 1950s, 1960s, and 1970s led him to conclude that there is "no relationship between age and gun control

over the period," and, moreover, that the "stratification variables [of] education and income . . . show no relationship to attitudes on gun control . . . which has not changed over time."

References

Alba, Richard D., and Steven F. Messner. 1995. "'Point Blank' against Itself: Evidence and Inference about Guns, Crime, and Gun Control." *Journal of Quantitative Criminology* 11: 391–410.

Ayres, Ian, and John D. Donohue III. 2003. "Shooting Down the More Guns, Less Crime Hypothesis." *Stanford Law Review* 55 (April): 1193–1312.

Azrael, Deborah. 2004. "Cook and Ludwig's *Principles for Effective Gun Policy:* An Extension to Suicide Prevention." *Fordham Law Review* 73 (November): 615–621.

Bartley, William Alan, and Mark A. Cohen. 1998. "The Effect of Concealed Weapons Laws: An Extreme Bound Analysis." *Economic Inquiry* 36: 258–265.

Bastian, Lisa D., and Bruce M. Taylor. 1994. "Young Black Male Victims." *Bureau of Justice Statistics Crime Data Brief, National Crime Victimization Survey, NCJ-147004.* Washington, DC: Bureau of Justice Statistics, U.S. Department of Justice. December.

Black, Dan A., and Daniel S. Nagin. 1998. "Do Right-to-Carry Laws Deter Violent Crime?" *Journal of Legal Studies* 27 (January): 209–219.

Blumstein, Alfred. 1995a. "Youth, Violence, Guns, and the Illicit-Drug Industry." *Journal of Criminal Law and Criminology* 86 (Fall): 10–36.

Brady, Sarah. 2000. *Letter to the HCI Membership.* Washington, DC: Handgun Control Inc. November 7.

Bureau of Alcohol, Tobacco and Firearms. 2001. *Annual Firearms Manufacturers and Export Report, 2000.* http://www.atf.treas.gov/firearms /stats/afmer/afmer2000.pdf. Accessed January 29, 2005.

———. 2002. "AFT Speech: National HIDTA Conference." http://www .atf.treas.gov/press/speech/fy01/120500hidtaconf.htm. Accessed January 29, 2005.

Bureau of Justice Statistics. 2003. *National Crime Victimization Survey, 2002.* http://www.ojp.usdoj.gov/bjs/abstract/cvusst.htm. Accessed January 28, 2005.

Burger, Warren E. 1991. "The Meaning, and Distortion of the Second Amendment." *The Keene Sentinel*, November 26, 1991.

Carlson, Darren K. 2005. *Americans and Guns: Danger or Defense?* Princeton, NJ: The Gallup Organization.

Carter, Gregg Lee. 1997. *The Gun Control Movement*. New York: Twayne Publishers.

———. 2001. "Guns." In *Boyhood in America: An Encyclopedia*, ed. Priscilla Ferguson Clement and Jacqueline S. Reinier, 330–335. Santa Barbara, CA: ABC-CLIO.

———. 2002. *Guns in American Society: An Encyclopedia of History, Politics, Culture, and the Law*, Vols. 1 and 2. Santa Barbara, CA: ABC-CLIO.

Centers for Disease Control and Prevention. 2003a. *Web-based Injury Statistics Query and Reporting System (WISQARS) [Online]*. National Center for Injury Prevention and Control. Available from: URL http://webappa .cdc.gov/sasweb/ncipc/mortrate10_sy.html. Accessed January 8, 2005.

———. 2003b. "10 Leading Causes of Death, United States 2002, All Races, Both Sexes." National Center for Injury Prevention and Control. Available from URL: http://webappa.cdc.gov/sasweb/ncipc/ leadcaus10.html. Accessed January 10, 2005.

———. 2005. *Suicide Fact Sheet*. http://www.cdc.gov/ncipc/factsheets /suifacts.htm. Accessed January 25, 2005.

Coates, James. 1995. *Armed and Dangerous: The Rise of the Survivalist Right*. New York: Hill and Wang.

Colburn, Treavor. 1965. *The Lamp of Experience: Whig History and the Intellectual Origins of the American Revolution*. Chapel Hill: University of North Carolina Press.

Cook, Philip J., and Jens Ludwig. 1997. *Guns in America: National Survey on Private Ownership and Use of Firearms*. Research in Brief Report No. NCJ165476. Washington, DC: National Institute of Justice, Office of Justice Programs, U.S. Department of Justice. May.

———. 2000. *Gun Violence: The Real Cost*. New York: Oxford University Press.

———. 2004. "Principles for Effective Gun Policy." *Fordham Law Review* 73: 589–613.

Cornell, Saul. 2004. "A New Paradigm for the Second Amendment." *Law and History Review* 22 (Spring): 161–167.

Cottrol, Robert J., and Raymond T. Diamond. 1995. "The Second Amendment: Toward an Afro-Americanist Reconsideration." *Guns: Who Should Have Them*, ed. David B. Kopel, 127–157. Amherst, NY: Prometheus.

Cramer, Clayton E. 1994. *For the Defense of Themselves and the State: The Original Intent and Judicial Interpretation of the Right to Keep and Bear Arms*. Westport, CT: Praeger.

Cress, Lawrence Delbert. 1984. "An Armed Community: The Origins and Meaning of the Right to Bear Arms." *Journal of American History* 71: 22–44.

Dezhbakhas, Hashem, and Paul H. Rubin. 1998. "Lives Saved or Lives Lost? The Effects of Concealed-Handgun Laws on Crime." *American Economic Review Papers and Proceedings* 88 (2): 468–474.

Dickstein, Leslie, and Christopher John Farley. 1994. "Vox Pop." *Time* May 10: 16.

Duggan, Mark. 2001. "More Guns More Crime." *Journal of Political Economy* 99 (October): 1086–1114.

Edel, Wilbur. 1995. *Gun Control: Threat to Liberty or Defense against Anarchy.* Westport, CT: Praeger.

Federal Bureau of Investigation. 2004. *Uniform Crime Reports: Crime in the United States, 2003.* http://www.fbi.gov/ucr/03cius.htm. Accessed January 25, 2005.

Fox, James Alan. 2000. "Demographics and U.S. Homicide."In *The Crime Drop in America,* eds. Alfred Blumstein and Joel Wallman, 288–317. New York: Cambridge University Press.

Gallup Organization. 1993. "Gun Control." Princeton, NJ: The Gallup Organization.

———. 2004. "Guns." January. Available online for Gallup poll subscribers at http://www.gallup.com/poll/. Accessed January 28, 2005.

———. 2005a. "Guns." January. Available online for Gallup poll subscribers at http://www.gallup.com/poll/. Accessed January 28, 2005.

———. 2005b. "Iraq." February. Available online for Gallup poll subscribers at http://www.gallup.com/poll/. Accessed January 28, 2005.

General Social Survey. 2002a. "Do you happen to have in your home (or garage) any guns or revolvers? If yes, is it a pistol, shotgun, rifle, or what?" Inter-University Consortium for Political and Social Research: http://webapp.icpsr.umich.edu/GSS/. Accessed January 10, 2005.

———. 2002b. "Do you or your (husband/wife) go hunting?" Inter-University Consortium for Political and Social Research: http://webapp.icpsr.umich.edu/GSS/. Accessed January 26, 2005.

Gest, Ted. 1982. "Battle Over Gun Control Heats Up Across the U.S." *U.S. News and World Report* (May 31): 38.

Gillespie, Mark. 1999. "New Gun Control Efforts Draw Mixed Support from Americans." July 13. Available online for Gallup poll subscribers at http://www.gallup.com/poll/. Accessed January 31, 2005

Goode, Erich. 1984. *Sociology.* Englewood Cliffs, NJ: Prentice Hall.

Halbrook, Stephen P. 1989. *A Right to Bear Arms: State and Federal Bills of Rights and Constitutional Guarantees.* Westport, CT: Greenwood Press.

Hardy, David T. 1986. *Origins and Development of the Second Amendment.* Chino Valley, AZ: Blacksmith Publishers.

Heathcock, Claude L. 1963. *The United States Constitution in Perspective.* Boston: Allyn and Bacon.

Hemenway, David. 2002. "Accidents, Gun." In *Guns in American Society: An Encyclopedia of History, Politics, Culture, and the Law,* ed. Gregg Lee Carter, Vol. 1, 2–3. Santa Barbara, CA: ABC-CLIO.

———. 2004a. *Private Guns, Public Health.* Ann Arbor: University of Michigan Press.

———. 2004b. "Article Review of Gary Kleck, 2004." http://www .hsph.harvard.edu/ announcements/kleck.html. Accessed January 25, 2005.

Hemenway, David, and Matthew Miller. 2000. "Firearm Availability and Homicide Rates across 26 High-Income Countries." *Journal of Trauma* 49 (6): 985–988.

Henigan, Dennis A., E. Bruce Nicholson, and David Hemenway. 1995. *Guns and the Constitution: The Myth of Second Amendment Protection for Firearms in America.* Northampton, MA: Aletheia Press.

Johnson, G. R., E. G. Krug, and L. B. Potter. 2000. "Suicides among Adolescents and Young Adults: A Cross-National Comparison of Thirty-Four Countries." *Suicide and Life Threatening Behavior* 20: 74–82.

Kellerman, Arthur L., et al. 1992. "Suicide in the Home in Relationship to Gun Ownership." *New England Journal of Medicine* 327: 467–472.

———. 1993. "Gun Ownership as a Risk Factor for Homicide in the Home." *New England Journal of Medicine* 329: 1084–1091.

Killias, Martin. 1993. "International Correlations between Gun Ownership and Rates of Homicide and Suicide." *Canadian Medical Association Journal* 148 (10): 1721–1725.

Kleck, Gary. 1991. *Point Blank: Guns and Violence in America.* New York: Aldine de Gruyter.

———. 1997. *Targeting Guns: Firearms and Their Control.* New York: Aldine de Gruyter.

———. 2001. "Can Owning a Gun Really Triple the Owner's Chances of Being Murdered? The Anatomy of an Implausible Causal Mechanism." *Homicide Studies* 5: 64–77.

Kleck, Gary, and Marc Gertz. 1995. "Armed Resistance to Crime: The Prevalence and Nature of Self-Defense with a Gun." *Journal of Criminal Law and Criminology* 86 (1): 150–187.

Kopel, David. 2000. "Polls: Antigun Propaganda." Fairfax, VA: NRA Institute for Legislative Action. http://www.nraila.org/Issues/Articles/Read.aspx?ID=40. Accessed February 22, 2005.

Krug, E. G., K. E. Powell, and L. L. Dahlberg. 1998. "Firearm-Related Deaths in the United States and 35 Other High- and Upper-Middle-Income Countries." *International Journal of Epidemiology* 27 (2): 214–221.

Lambert, Tim. 2005. *Do More Guns Cause Less Crime?* http://www.cse.unsw.edu.au/ ~lambert/guns/lott/onepage.html. Accessed January 30, 2005.

Leddy, Edward F. 1987. *Magnum Force: The National Rifle Association Fights Gun Control.* New York: University Press of America.

Lindgren, James, and Franklin E. Zimring. 1983. "Regulation of Guns." In *Encyclopedia of Crime and Justice,* ed. Sanford H. Kadish, 836–841. New York: Free Press.

Lott, John R., Jr. 1998. *More Guns, Less Crime: Understanding Crime and Gun-Control Laws.* Chicago: University of Chicago Press.

———. 2000. *More Guns, Less Crime: Understanding Crime and Gun-Control Law, 2nd Edition.* Chicago: University of Chicago Press.

Lott, John R., Jr., and David B. Mustard. 1997. "Crime, Deterrence, and Right-to-Carry Concealed Handguns." *Journal of Legal Studies* 261 (January): 1–68.

Ludwig, Jens. 1998. "Concealed-Gun-Carrying Laws and Violent Crime: Evidence from State Panel Data." *International Review of Law and Economics* 18: 239–254.

———. 2000. "Gun Self-Defense and Deterrence." *Crime and Justice* 27: 363.

Mackellar, Landis F., and Machikio Yanagishita. 1995. *Homicide in the United States: Who's at Risk?* Washington, DC: Population Reference Bureau.

Malcolm, Joyce. 1994. *To Keep and Bear Arms: The Origins of an Anglo-American Right.* Cambridge, MA: Harvard University Press.

Merrill, Vincent C. 2002. *Gun-in-Home as a Risk Factor in Firearm-Related Mortality: A Historical Prospective Cohort Study of United States Deaths, 1993.* Ph.D. dissertation, Department of Environmental Health Science and Policy, University of California, Irvine.

Miller, Matthew, Deborah Azrael, and David Hemenway. 2001. "Firearm Availability and Unintentional Firearm Deaths." *Accident Analysis and Prevention* 33: 477–484.

National Research Council. 2005. *Firearms and Violence: A Critical Review.* Committee to Improve Research Information and Data on Firearms.

Charles F. Wellford, John V. Pepper, and Carol V. Petrie, editors. Committee on Law and Justice, Division of Behavioral and Social Sciences and Education. Washington, DC: The National Academies Press.

National Rifle Association. 1994. *Ten Myths about Gun Control*. Fairfax, VA: NRA Institute for Legislative Action.

———. 2003. *Firearms Preemption Laws*. Fairfax, VA: NRA Institute for Legislative Action. http://www.nraila.org/Issues/FactSheets/Read .aspx?ID=48. Accessed January 31, 2005.

Newport, Frank. 1999a. "Americans Support Wide Variety of Gun Control Measures." June 16. Available online for Gallup poll subscribers at http://www.gallup.com/poll/. Accessed January 28, 2005.

———. 1999b. "Fort Worth Shootings Again Put Focus on Gun Control." September 17. Available online for Gallup poll subscribers at http://www.gallup.com/poll/. Accessed January 30, 2005.

Peckman, Howard H., ed. 1978. *Sources of American Independence: Selected Manuscripts from the Collection of the William Clements Library, Vol. 1.* Chicago: University of Chicago Press.

Providence Journal-Bulletin. 1995. "Public Opinion Against Deployment." December 6: A-14.

Reynolds, Glenn Harlan. 1995. "Critical Guide to the Second Amendment." *Tennessee Law Review* 62 (Spring): 461–512.

Rieselbach, Leroy N. 1995. *Congressional Politics: The Evolving Legislative System.* 2nd ed. Boulder, CO: Westview Press.

Schuman, Howard, and Stanley Presser. 1981. "The Attitude-Action Connection and the Issue of Gun Control." *Annals of the American Academy of Political and Social Science* 455 (May): 40–47.

Shalhope, Robert E. 1982. "The Ideological Origins of the Second Amendment." *Journal of American History* 69 (December): 599–614.

Smith, Tom. 1980. "The 75% Solution: An Analysis of the Structure of Attitudes on Gun Control, 1959–1977." *Journal of Criminal Law and Criminology* 71 (3): 300–316.

Spitzer, Robert J. 1995. *The Politics of Gun Control.* New York: Chatham House.

———. 2004. *The Politics of Gun Control.* 4th ed. Washington, DC: Congressional Quarterly Inc.

Stephens, Gene. 1994. "The Global Crime Wave." *The Futurist* 28 (4): 22–28.

Wiebe, Douglas J. 2003a. "Homicide and Suicide Risk Associated with Firearms in the Home: A National Case-Control Study." *Annals of Emergency Medicine* 41 (6): 771–782.

————. 2003b. "Firearms in U.S. Homes as a Risk Factor for Unintentional Gunshot Fatality." *Accident Analysis and Prevention* 35: 711–716.

Zimring, Franklin E., and Gordin Hawkins. 1997. *Crime Is Not the Problem: Lethal Violence in America.* New York: Oxford University Press.

2

What Serious Gun Control Means in Practice

Providence—Ten dollars cost a 14-year-old boy his life. For the 14- and 17-year-old brothers charged with his murder, it may cost them their freedom. And in the mixed neighborhood where Jamont Richardson spent his short life, the residents are wondering whether his murder will cost them peace with one another.

The trouble started . . . when a friend of Jamont's did not pay for his hair-braiding session. The angry hairdresser, a 17-year-old girl living on Goddard Street, called her cousins—the two brothers—in another neighborhood and demanded they get her money, according to Deputy Police Chief Paul Kennedy.

The brothers arrived and looked for Jamont and his friend. They and nearly a dozen other teenagers rumbled outside the tenement house at 72 Goddard St. Then the brothers got a gun, the police said, and the 14-year-old pulled the trigger.

At least since 2000, every young teenager murdered in the city has been killed by gunfire. . . . "This is a dispute that happens every day in this country somewhere because of the introduction of a gun," Kennedy said. "Kids don't look that far into the future. . . . They don't think about the repercussions of what they do until it's done. And then it's too late. Two families are devastated by this and destroyed by this," he said.

—Amanda Milkovits,
"Two Arrested in Teen's Killing" (2005, 1)

57

There is no lack of opinions on policies to regulate gun commerce, possession, and use, with most policy proposals engendering intense controversy.

— Philip J. Cook and Jens Ludwig,
"Pragmatic Gun Policy" (2003, 1)

What will improve the gun debate at the top end of the policy community is careful attention to the differences between types and intensities of firearms regulation. If experts start avoiding the silly overgeneralizations that come from assuming that all gun regulations were created equal, there is some hope that a more specific and pragmatic approach to reducing the harms of gun violence might trickle down to the intellectual food chain to the powerful and powerfully confused citizenry who will shape gun policy in the fast-approaching future.

—Franklin E. Zimring,
"Continuity and Change in the
American Gun Debate" (2003, 452)

In this chapter, the most important measures to regulate guns are described and evaluated. The evaluations are incomplete because the majority of the measures are not in effect at the national level. Most action on gun control—public debate, passage of laws, and court decisions—occurs at the state and local levels, yet serious gun control, control that would have discernable and long-term impacts on gun-related violence, must take place at the national level. As most policymakers and analysts realized long ago, local and state laws regulating access to firearms are easily evaded—for example, guns that might be difficult to buy in one state can be bought in another. Moreover, in forty-two states, local governments are preempted by state authority from passing their own gun control laws if they are in conflict with state law. Everyone seriously involved in the gun control debate believes that some level of control over the possession and use of firearms is needed. Even the most ardent proponent of "gun rights" agrees that violent felons should be barred access to firearms. At the other end of the spectrum, ardent proponents of "strict" gun control would like to see the total number of guns in circulation reduced; minors, felons, and the perpetrators of domestic violence denied access to firearms; handgun possession and carrying severely restricted; a coherent national gun policy requiring all gun owners and users to be licensed and trained and all guns and ammunition to be registered; background checks for potential gun buyers to occur no matter where the sale occurs (a retail establishment, a flea market, a living room); and no matter who the buyers or sellers are (licensed gun dealers or private individuals selling or trading their personal firearms); a coherent set of child access protection laws requiring all gun owners to lock up their guns and ammunition—in separate places, whether at home or while in transport; a demand placed on gun manufacturers and distributors to monitor the retailers who sell their guns (ensuring that they are account-able for all guns sold and that guns sold are done so legally); and, finally, the retooling of older guns and the redesigning of new guns with the latest in "smart gun" technologies (e.g., a "gun-is-loaded" indicator light; trigger locks; guns only capable of firing in the owners' hands). Each of the measures proposed by those wanting stricter gun control would in itself likely reduce gun vio-lence by only a small amount, but as the evidence in this chapter will demonstrate, the sum total of enacting many or all such meas-ures would be large and quite discernable.

It is important to note that there are many acts of gun vio-lence for which no set of gun control laws would be preventative. There are so many guns in circulation in the United States today (well over 200 million) that anyone with determination and a modicum of creativity can acquire one. And in a free society, any-one with determination and a modicum of creativity can shoot just about anyone they want. But that is no reason to conclude that gun control doesn't work. Rather, the evidence needed to show whether it works is at the aggregate level of analysis—do rates of gun-related injuries, deaths, and crimes fall or (as a few would hypothesize) rise in response to serious gun control? Demonstrating this correlation, between gun control and gun-related violence, is an extraordinarily difficult undertaking. To date, it has been only partially accomplished, but what part has been accomplished reveals that gun control can work in a manner that preserves the basic right of individuals to own selected kinds of firearms and use them in selected ways—including recre-ational target shooting, hunting, and home defense.

The Public Health Approach

In the United States, gun violence is a modern-day
public health epidemic. Preventing gun violence requires not

> *only individual (e.g., parental) accountability but also*
> *collective responsibility.*
>
> —David Hemenway, *Private Guns, Public Health* (2004, 9)

The most comprehensive and empirically grounded approach to gun control is that of *public health*. As detailed by Hemenway (2004, Chapter 2) and Azrael and her colleagues (2003), the public health approach sets aside the bifurcation of the social world that predominates in the modern gun control debate: Instead of concentrating on *individuals* and looking at the world as divided into criminals and noncriminals, those who commit suicide and those who do not, those who mishandle firearms and those who do not, the public health approach looks at the *social and physical environments* and how these encourage or discourage gun-related harm. The ultimate goal is to change these environments in such ways as to reduce harm. The approach is proactive, not reactive. It has a long history of success, including the great reduction of communicable disease in the nineteenth and early twentieth centuries, the noteworthy reduction of automobile-related injuries and deaths in the middle of the twentieth century, and the significant decline in tobacco use and subsequent decline in tobacco-related diseases in the last third of the twentieth century. In each case, the use of the public health approach began with the marshaling of huge amounts of data on the health problem at hand; these data pointed to the aspects of the physical and social environment that needed to be changed to solve the problem; the data also provided the evidence needed by the advocates for change as they argued for reform in the political and legal systems. In each case, focusing on environmental causes and large-scale, community-based, "public" solutions proved more effective than trying to change individuals. Not that the behavior of individuals is trivial or incapable of being transformed, but it has been found that this transformation is more readily accomplished after the environmental sources of the problem have been addressed.

Hemenway (2004, 9–10) offers the following description of how the public health approach has dramatically reduced the incidence of communicable disease and subsequently increased the overall health of humanity:

[T]he most important public health advance of the nineteenth century was the "great sanitary awakening, . . . which identified filth as both a cause of disease and a vehicle of transmission. Sanitation changed the way society thought about health. Illness came to be seen as an indicator not of poor moral or spiritual conditions but of poor environmental conditions. . . . [M]ost of the improvement in health of the American people (e.g., a rise in life expectancy from forty-seven years in 1900 to seventy-six years in 1990) has been accomplished through public health measures rather than direct medical advances.

National Violent Death Reporting Systems

As public health researcher Deborah Azrael and her colleagues observe, the critical building block of the public health approach to reducing injury and death is comprehensive, over-time data:

> The National Highway Traffic Safety Administration's Fatality Analysis Reporting System (FARS), which became operational in 1975, is the largest and most comprehensive national surveillance system for *injuries* in the United States. The system, which collects information on approximately 37,000 crashes and 40,000 fatalities annually, . . . [documents] more than one hundred variables . . . on each incident, including information on vehicles (for example, make model, safety features, inspection status), crash features (for example, points of impact, speed), environment (for example, type of roadway, weather conditions, visibility, time of day), [and] people (for example, seating, impairment, alcohol use, license status, previous infractions). . . . [FARS] research findings were instrumental in federal legislation that influenced states to establish 21 as the minimum age for [alcohol] purchase. This policy is in effect in all states and is credited with having saved more than 20,000 lives from 1975 through 2000. (Azrael, et al., 2003, 416–417)

Indeed, Hemenway (2002, 412) argues that the improvement in motor vehicle safety in the United States over the past fifty years provides an excellent model for reducing gun violence. Between 1952 and 1999, the death rate per motor vehicle mile dropped 80 percent—not because drivers got any better, rather because comprehensive data collection and analysis revealed the many flaws in the design of cars (e.g., inflexible steering columns, unyielding dashboards, weak passenger compartments) and roadways (lack of shoulders, lack of guardrails) that were eventually corrected. He concludes "that in the firearm field the United States is currently where we were in motor vehicle safety in the 1950s" (413); moreover, "generating support for collective efforts to reduce gun violence is a current challenge for public health" (2004, 9).

From the public health perspective, serious gun control has yet to begin in the United States because we lack the comprehensive data to evaluate present gun control measures, as well as to develop the kinds of measures that might grow out of such data. Thus, the first step in generating the public support for serious gun control is the development of a national, ongoing, comprehensive data-collection surveillance system to monitor violence-related deaths and injuries. Such a system would be modeled on the National Highway Safety Administration's Fatality Analysis Reporting System (FARS). Two such efforts are under way in the form of pilot programs. The first began in 1999 when the Harvard Injury Control Research Center set up a violent reporting system in collaboration with the Medical College of Wisconsin and ten other medical organizations (university medical centers and health departments) around the country. Labeled the National Violent Injury Statistics System (NVISS), it has developed uniform standards for the collection and organization of data related to violent deaths. These standards are based on FARS, and they have the ultimate goal of doing what FARS has for highway fatalities—that is, to reduce deaths by using multivariable analysis to ascertain the complex mix of causes that underlie incidents of firearms violence (though originally intended for firearm-related deaths, the system has been expanded to include all types of violent deaths). Table 2.1 reveals the comprehensiveness of the variables collected for each violent death incident in the NVISS system.

The NVISS data collection system is already uncovering a host of new social facts. For example, preliminary analyses have revealed that women are two and a half times more likely than men to commit suicide at home, and that suicides are twice as likely as homicides to occur at home.[1]

A second surveillance system to monitor violence-related deaths and injuries was started in 2002, when the U.S. Department of Health and Human Service's Centers for Disease Control and Prevention (CDC) received $1.5 million to fund its National Violent Death Reporting System. The system collects data in the same systematic manner developed by NVISS (see Table 2.1). It is

TABLE 2.1
Selected Variables Collected by the Harvard Injury Control Research Center and Its
Collaborators (Violent Death Statistics System)

Incident Information
Incident narrative
Investigating police agency
Death investigation source
Number of nonfatal victims

Person (victim and suspect) Information
Person ID
Person type
Age
Sex
Race
Ethnicity
Incident at person's residence?
Intoxication suspected?

Suspect Characteristics
Attempted suicide?

Victim Information
Weapon type
Incident type
Med. examiner/coroner cause of death
Death cert. underlying cause of death
Victim/suspect relationship
Abuse
Date and time of injury
Date and time of death
Address of incident

Victim Circumstances
Violence circumstances
Accident/unintentional death circumstances
Suicide—mental health
Suicide intent
Suicide circumstances

Supplemental Homicide Report Variable
SHR homicide type and situation
SHR victim/offender relationship
SHR circumstance
SHR justifiable shooting circumstance

Victim Demographics
Residential address
Homeless status
Marital status
Veteran status
Birthplace
Pregnant
Education
Employment status
Usual occupation
Usual industry

Victim Injury Information
Place of death
Number of wounds and location
Death certificate multiple condition codes
Autopsy performed
Alcohol presence
Blood alcohol level
Drug presence
Date and time body specimen collected

Firearm Information
Firearm ID
Type of firearm physical evidence
Firearm type
Firearm make
Firearm model
Firearm caliber/gauge
Firearm victim table
Stolen
Youth access to firearms

Source: Adapted from Azrael et al. (2003, p. 421).

a pilot program now operating in seventeen states (as of late 2005: Alaska, California, Colorado, Georgia, Kentucky, Maryland, Massachusetts, New Jersey, New Mexico, North Carolina, Oklahoma, Oregon, Rhode Island, South Carolina, Utah, Virginia, and Wisconsin). The CDC intends to add states every year and has estimated its full cost at $20 million per year after all fifty states have been incorporated (for more information, see the CDC Web page: http://www.cdc.gov/ncipc/profiles/nvdrs/facts.htm).

Controlling Guns in the Home: Child Access Protection Laws

The most sophisticated studies to date on whether a gun in the home is related to gun violence reveal a clear association between a gun in the home and increased accidental death and suicide, but not homicide (e.g., see Merrill, 2002). The public health approach is particularly concerned with the large number of injuries and deaths suffered by children in their homes by guns their parents own. In the 1980s, Garen J. Wintemute and his colleagues found that half of the incidents in which a child accidentally shot him- or herself or playmate involved loaded, unlocked firearms in the child's home (Wintemute, Teret, and Kraus, 1987). This research led to the passage of "child access protection" (CAP) laws in many states. CAP laws make parents and homeowners ultimately responsible for any firearm injury, including accidental shootings and suicides, occurring with guns stored on their property. The laws require that guns be locked in a cabinet or safe and, in some states, that ammunition be locked in a separate place (for a summary of state CAP laws, see http://www.bradycampaign.org/facts/issues/?page=capstate). The first CAP law was passed in Florida in 1989; nineteen other states passed similar laws during the 1990s. In three states (California, Connecticut, and Florida) CAP law violations are considered felonies, whereas in the other sixteen they are misdemeanors (Delaware, Hawaii, Illinois, Iowa, Kansas, Maine, Maryland, Minnesota, Nevada, New Hampshire, New Jersey, North Carolina, Rhode Island, Texas, Virginia, and Wisconsin).

Several studies have shown CAP laws to have a modest positive effect. For example, Peter Cummings and his colleagues found that there was a 41 percent reduction in accidental youth deaths in states with CAP laws (Cummings, et al., 1997), while Daniel W. Webster and his colleagues found that CAP laws have significantly reduced adolescent suicide rates (preventing more than 300 suicides in youths fourteen to seventeen years old between 1989 and 2001; see Webster, Vernick, Zeoli, and Manganello, 2004). Similarly, David C. Grossman and his colleagues found that youths under the age of twenty were significantly less likely to unintentionally shoot another person or to commit suicide with a gun in households where guns were locked up (Grossman, et al., 2005). This particular study examined four CAP practices and found each one to have a "protective effect": keeping (1) guns locked, (2) guns unloaded, (3) ammunition locked, and (4) ammunition stored in a separate location. Such research has led a national police group, the Commission on Accreditation for Law Enforcement Agencies, to adopt a new guideline for off-duty police officers—that they store their weapons in "locked boxes" (see Join Together, 2004a).

The fear of gun rights advocates, as exemplified by the National Rifle Association (NRA), is that CAP laws will reduce the ability of individuals to protect their homes from invasion by thieves and rapists. Indeed, Lott and Whitley (2002) found the introduction of CAP laws were associated with state-level increases in police-reported rapes (9 percent), robberies (8–10 percent), and burglaries (4–6 percent). However, Webster (2002) argues that these are specious findings and are a result of the inadequacies of their statistical models (much the same way in that Ayres and Donahue [2003] refuted Lott's thesis that "more guns" leads to "less crime," see Chapter 1).

Currently there is no national CAP law, which puts the United States out of step with its peer nations. The United Nations (1999) reports that 82 percent of the economically developed democracies of Western Europe, Australia, Canada, Japan, and New Zealand require gun owners to store their guns in locked cabinets or safes, and 94 percent require that the same be done with ammunition.[2] As noted in Chapter 1, these peer nations suffer a tiny fraction of the per capita gun violence experienced in the United States.

Trigger Locks, Internal Locks, and Personalized "Smart Gun" Technologies

Related to Child Access Protection laws are a set of gun control measures intended to reduce the unauthorized use of guns—for example, by children, thieves, or those not possessing a gun but wanting to use someone else's gun to commit a crime or suicide—by changing gun-firing technology. The simplest of these measures is encouraging the use of mechanical trigger locks, such as a combination or key lock that fits over the trigger area (the so called clamshell lock) or a cable lock that can be strung through the barrel or trigger guard. Since 1999, the U.S. Department of Justice, in conjunction with the National Shooting Sports Foundation, has funded the distribution of millions of cable and related trigger locks through their Project HomeSafe/ChildSafe programs. (In 2001, there was a safety recall of some 400,000 of these locks, which were found to be too easily unlocked without a key; see http://www.cpsc.gov/cpscpub/prerel/prhtml01/01078.html).

At a more sophisticated level are internal locking systems that have been developed in recent years involving an internal block preventing the firing pin from engaging. One version of this lock requires the use of a magnetic ring by the shooter; the ring unlocks a trigger bar so that the gun can be fired. Another version requires a radio-frequency device on the user's clothing or person. The ultimate in this line of technology uses a microchip that biologically identifies the gun's owner or authorized user. For example, Oxford Micro Devices is developing a grip with a microchip that stores the thermal imprint of several different fingerprints. If the user's print matches one stored in memory, the gun can be fired, otherwise it can't. Another biometric technology currently under development at the New Jersey Institute of Technology employs "dynamic grip" technology. A handgun fitted with this technology can recognize the grip pattern and pressure of an authorized user and prevent its firing by anyone else. Dynamic grip technology is expected to be ready for production by the end of 2006.

Other technologies that gun control advocates would like to see mandatory on the manufacturing of all new guns are a *loaded-chamber* indicator light or mechanism (usually a protruding metal tab), which alerts the user that the gun has a bullet in its chamber, and *magazine safeties*—which prevent a gun from firing when its magazine has been removed even if a round is still in the chamber (many gun handlers seeing the ammunition magazine—or "clip"—disconnected from a semiautomatic pistol erroneously assume that the gun is unloaded, ignoring the possibility that there could still be a round in the chamber). A 1991 federal study of accidental firearm deaths in ten cities revealed that nearly a quarter of them could have been prevented had the guns involved been equipped with either loaded-chamber indicators or magazine safeties (see U.S. General Accounting Office, 1991). Despite such findings, only 14 percent of current pistol models are equipped with magazine safeties (Vernick, Meisel, and Teret, 1999). Speaking on behalf of chamber-loaded indicators, public health researcher David Hemenway (2004, 33) wryly observes, "it is difficult to understand why a person using a camera can tell whether it is loaded without opening it up, but a person with a firearm often cannot." It is important to note that current loaded chamber indicators are not standardized in such a way that it would be common knowledge when they were activated—that is, they presently come in a variety of designs and shapes, and thus gun control advocates would like legislation that would require the gun manufacturing industry to develop a uniform style.

California will require new semiautomatic pistol models introduced in 2006 to have either a loaded-chamber indicator or a magazine safety; by 2007, new models must have both features (Join Together, 2003a). In a similar vein, New Jersey will require that all guns sold in the state be "smart guns" within three years after "dynamic grip" technology is perfected (Smothers, 2004). Other states, especially those where CAP laws currently exist, are expected to follow suit—with Massachusetts and Maryland already having enacted laws requiring new handguns sold in their states to be "childproof," that is, have integrated safeties that prevent the gun from being fired until deactivated.

Gun rights advocates are generally opposed to personalized gun technologies. They contend that such technologies will lead to more gun violence for two key reasons: First, many gun owners will become complacent if they have a "smart gun" and leave it around unlocked and loaded; when the smart-gun technology fails, as do all mechanical and electronic devices, an accident will be waiting to happen. Second, a gun owner under attack, whether at home or on the street, will have a delayed reaction if he or she has to put on a magnetic ring, or might find the smart-gun technology failing just when it is needed most.

Transportation of Guns

As noted in Chapter 1, forty-two states now have "preemption" laws that discourage localities from enacting their own gun control laws. A key motivation for preemption is the possibility of providing uniform laws regulating the transportation of firearms. Municipalities across any particular state have a wide variety of restrictions regulating the transport of firearms, making it very difficult for otherwise law-abiding gun owners to conform to the variations in local ordinances. A state-level preemption law generally allows gun owners to transport their firearms anywhere in the state as long as they're unloaded and encased; in addition, these same states allow gun owners from other states to transport their guns through their states as long as the intent of the gun owner is a "peaceable journey." In this regard, the United States is similar to its peer nations. A United Nations (1999) study comparing cross-national gun laws reveals that the United States, like 88 percent of its peers (the economically developed democracies of Western Europe, plus Australia, Canada, Japan, and New Zealand) has strict laws governing the transporting of firearms.[3]

The Gun Control Act of 1968 allows the legal possessor of a gun to transport it in a vehicle across state lines as long as the gun is unloaded and neither the gun nor its ammunition is readily accessible to the driver or the passengers (in general, this would mean locking the gun in the trunk of a car). If there is no trunk or area that is apart from the driver and passengers, then the gun and its ammunition must be stored in a locked container other than the glove compartment (Section 926A; see Bureau of Alcohol, Tobacco and Firearms, 2000, 56). Gun owners may transport their firearms and ammunition on commercial airlines as long as the guns are unloaded, securely packed, and not taken aboard as carry-on luggage but declared at the check-in counter (see http://www.atf.treas.gov/firearms/100804tsaeducation.htm).

Cheap Handgun Control

The Gun Control Act of 1968 not only put tough restrictions on transporting guns but also sought to reduce the nation's stock of cheap handguns by banning the importation of these so-called Saturday night specials. The argument for trying to reduce this stock builds from three social facts: First, cheap handguns are most often bought by the poor and by the young, and there are strong correlations between poverty and violence and between youth and violence in the United States; second, to be priced so cheaply, these guns are often of poor quality and thus prone to malfunction; finally, these guns are often small and thus easily concealable. Unfortunately, from the perspective of those who favor stricter gun control, the banning of the importation of cheap handguns simply created a windfall for domestic manufacturers. Beginning in the 1970s, many of these manufacturers developed in southern California in an area that public health researcher Garen Wintemute (1994) has dubbed the "Ring of Fire." They include Accu-Tek, Arcadia Machine & Tool (no longer in business), Bryco Arms (now Jimenez Arms of Henderson, Nevada), Davis Engineering (now Cobra Enterprises of Salt Lake City, Utah), Lorcin Industries (no longer in business), Phoenix Arms, and Sundance Industries (no longer in business). These manufacturers mainly produce small and medium caliber handguns (e.g., .22s, .25s, and .380s) with retail prices ranging between $85 and $300—hundreds of dollars cheaper than the higher quality handguns manufactured by Smith & Wesson, Sturm Ruger, Glock, or Beretta (see Southwick, 2002a). The production of these cheap handguns is strongly correlated with street crime and the handgun murder rate, as so many of them end up in the hands of poor, inner-city youth. As demonstrated in Figure 2.1, the rise of handgun production begun in the mid-1980s and its subsequent decline in the late 1990s closely parallels the murder rate—a relationship that public health researcher Garen J. Wintemute (2002) argues is causal. It is important to note that four of the top ten producers of semiautomatic pistols during the 1990s were "Ring of Fire" manufacturers (see Wintemute, 2002, 57); seven of the top ten guns used by juveniles (seventeen and under) in the commission of crime in 2000 were "Ring of Fire" semiautomatic pistols (with the Lorcin Engineering .380 at the top of the list), as were five of the top ten crime guns used by those between the ages of eighteen and twenty-four, and three of the top ten for those twenty-five and older. For all ages combined, "Ring of Fire" semiautomatics accounted for five of the top ten guns used in crime (and for which successful trace requests were made; see Bureau of Alcohol, Tobacco and Firearms, 2002, Table 5, 15–17).

Gun control proponents see two basic solutions to the cheap handgun problem: First, get their production outlawed; second, stop their trafficking into the hands of youths and criminals. The first strategy is being tried at the state level. Maryland has had a law banning the manufacture and sale of cheap handguns since 1989; at least one analysis reveals that the Maryland law has had an effect in reducing the number and use of these weapons (see Webster, Vernick, and Hepburn, 2002). Five other states currently have such laws (California, Hawaii, Illinois, Minnesota, and

FIGURE 2.1
Handgun Homicide and Seimautomatic Pistol Production by Year, 1976–2002

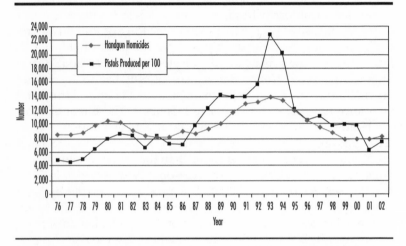

Sources: American Firearms Industry Magazine (2005); Bureau of Alcohol, Tobacco and Firearms (2005); Bureau of Justice Statistics (2005; for homicide data); 1996-1997 pistol production estimated from Wintemute (2002, 64).

Note: Pearson r = .83 (p. < .0001)

South Carolina).[4] Although the effectiveness of a combination of lawsuits and California's 1999 law has yet to be carefully studied, they have forced several "Ring of Fire" manufacturers out of business, while others have opted to leave the state (fleeing to nearby Arizona, Nevada, and Utah). It is important to note that compared with its peer nations (other economically developed democracies), the United States stands out regarding its lax restrictions on the owning of handguns, as well as with regard to the percentage of households that have a handgun. Virtually all of the U.S. peer nations put severe restrictions on handgun ownership (e.g., limiting them to the police; selected private security guards; and selected veterans of the military; see United Nations, 1999, Table 1.1). Indeed, as noted in Chapter 1, handguns are either outlawed or restricted so severely that ownership is extremely rare in most European countries, as well as in peer nations Japan, Australia, New Zealand, and Canada.

The second strategy focuses on reducing the trafficking of these guns from federally licensed firearms dealers into the wrong hands. This trafficking most commonly occurs via *straw* purchases. These are sometimes done on a small scale, such as when a noncriminal acquaintance of a criminal buys a gun for the criminal or when an older acquaintance buys a gun for a juvenile; but they also occur on a much larger scale involving straw-purchasing rings. In the latter case, one or more street-level unlicensed dealers buy multiple guns from a licensed dealer then sell them in the private market (person-to-person on the street, at yard sales or gun shows, or elsewhere). Because of their low cost, Saturday night specials are especially attractive to straw-purchasing rings. Most juveniles and criminals get their guns either through theft or from the trafficking of guns from federally licensed dealers to the street through unscrupulous middlemen or corrupt dealers (Wintemute, 2002; also see Pierce, Braga, Hyatt, and Koper, 2004).

Tracing Crime Guns

Pierce, Braga, Hyatt, and Koper (2004) are four of a small number of researchers that have been given access to the Bureau of Alcohol, Tobacco, Firearms and Explosives (ATF) gun tracing data. Their analyses reveal several facts about trafficking that could be used to reduce the supply of guns to the illegal market. The Gun Control Act of 1968 allows for the gathering of data that trace any given firearm from its manufacturing or importation through its first retail sale. Manufacturers, importers, distributors, and federal firearms licensees (FFLs—mainly gun retailers and pawnbrokers) must maintain records of all gun transactions, for example, sales and shipments. FFLs are also required to report multiple handgun sales and stolen weapons to the ATF. A particular trace begins when a law enforcement agency submits a request to the ATF's National Tracing Center to find all existing information on a firearm suspected of being used in the commission of a crime. Tracing is possible because every firearm is stamped with a unique serial number. Using 1999 data, Pierce, Braga, Hyatt, and Koper (2004) found that three-quarters of all trace requests involve handguns, especially semiautomatic pistols. Importantly, only one in ten traced guns is possessed by the purchaser—strong evidence of illegal gun trafficking. Of similar importance, and a similarly strong indicator of trafficking, they found that nearly a third of all traced crime guns are sold less than four years prior to their recovery after a crime. That there are corrupt dealers involved in the trafficking is evidenced by the fact that only about

1 percent of the nearly 81,000 active FFLs are associated with more than half (54.5 percent) of the successfully traced crime guns.

Controlling the Trafficking of Cheap Handguns and Other Firearms—Monitoring FFLs and One-Gun-per-Month Laws

Two gun control measures that have a reasonable probability of success have been developed out of the analysis of crime-gun trace data: First is the closer scrutiny of FFLs, and second is eliminating multiple gun purchases (and thus addressing the problem of large-scale straw purchases). The 1993 Federal Firearms Licensee Reform Act, the 1993 Brady Handgun Violence Prevent Act (the "Brady Law"), and the 1994 Violent Crime Control and Law Enforcement Act have combined to improve the background checking done on prospective FFLs to ensure that they are not criminals and are, instead, legitimate dealers in compliance with local and state gun laws. FFLs are now required to report multiple handgun sales and thefts to local and state law enforcement. The FFL fee was raised from $30 to $200 for the first three years, with $90 for renewals. In response, the number of FFLs fell from 287,000 in 1993 to 80,523 by the end of 1999. The ATF has increased its inspections of FFLs and now requires interviews for new applications and selected renewals—with future efforts focusing on the tiny percentage of FFLs whose guns have a relatively high probability of being traced to crimes. Nineteen states have their own dealer monitoring laws (Alabama, California, Connecticut, Delaware, Georgia, Hawaii, Indiana, Maryland, Massachusetts, New Hampshire, New Jersey, New York, North Carolina, Pennsylvania, Rhode Island, South Carolina, Tennessee, Virginia, and Washington), though no systematic study has yet been done to assess their effectiveness.

Eliminating multiple gun sales has been central to gun control efforts in a growing number of states. For example, Virginia enacted its famous "one-gun-per-month" law in June 1993, after realizing that many of the guns sold in its state ended up as crime guns in New York, New Jersey, and several states in New England. This law restricts individuals from buying more than a single gun in any thirty-day period. The number of crime guns recovered in New York, New Jersey, and southern New England (Connecticut, Massachusetts, and Rhode Island) that originated in Virginia dropped from one in three between September 1989 and June 1993, to one in six between July 1993 and March 1995 (see Weil and Knox, 1996). Gun control advocates would like similar action taken to shrink the trafficking of guns from Mississippi to the greater Chicago area (labeled by law enforcement as the "Iron Pipeline"). Chicago has strict laws controlling the sale of guns, requiring, for example, a firearm owner's identification card and a seventy-two-hour waiting period. On the other hand, anyone with a Mississippi driver's license can buy as many guns as they like without a waiting period. Chicago gang members recruit family members and acquaintances in Mississippi to buy guns (Join Together, 2004b). Mississippi authorities are well aware of this gun pipeline, but have addressed the problem only through a public education media campaign called "Don't Lie for the Other Guy." The campaign provides educational materials to Mississippi gun dealers on identifying straw purchasers; it also involves a public awareness campaign to warn potential straw purchasers of the tragic consequences that their behavior can invite (Join Together, 2004c).

The success of Virginia's one-gun-per-month law has prompted many states and municipalities to consider similar legislation to curb trafficking. California and Maryland have recently passed one-gun-per-month laws, as have many municipalities. For example, New York City passed the Gun Industry Responsibility Act in early 2005, creating a "Code of Responsible Conduct" for gun dealers and manufacturers and a one-gun-per-month law.

Gun rights advocates see no real problem with cheap handguns. They contend that restricting such weapons only serves to disarm the poor from defending themselves and thus, ultimately, increases crime (as thieves will be less fearful about robbing the poor). Gun rights advocates also repeatedly lobby Congress to further restrict the already tight access of researchers to ATF crime-gun trace data. A favorite tactic is to tack on amendments to spending bills, as has been common in recent years (see, for example, Hulse, 2004). Moreover, gun rights advocates see no purpose to one-gun-per-month laws and won a notable victory in South Carolina in the spring of 2004 when it repealed its one-gun-per-month law (Join Together, 2004d). The logic that some South Carolina lawmakers used in repealing the law demonstrates the importance and the need for national legislation. The law had originally been passed because gun traffickers were buying handguns in bulk and driving them to Washington, D.C., New York, and Chicago, where they were sold to gang members and street criminals. But as one lawmaker who voted for the repeal observed, "There's still a fairly high percentage of guns going to New York [City] from [other] southern states . . . [it is thus obvious that] there are ways to circumvent the South Carolina law that there [is] no way to prevent" (Join Together, 2004e, 1).

Assault Weapons Control

Although the most common crime weapon is a handgun (for example, of the 9,638 individuals murdered with a gun in 2003, 80 percent [7,710] were killed with a handgun), during the 1980s the U.S. public became particularly fearful of assault weapons. They were implicated in a number of gang killings, but when Patrick Purdy used an AKS assault rifle[5] to gun down thirty-four children (killing five of them) in a Stockton, California, school playground in January 1989, California and six other states banned their sale (Connecticut, Hawaii, Maryland, Massachusetts, New Jersey, and New York; note that Maryland and Hawaii banned assault pistols only). At the federal level, President George H. W. Bush responded with an executive order in March 1989 that put a temporary ban on the importation of AK-47 assault rifles and selected similar weapons. This sparked the introduction of several bills in Congress to outlaw or restrict assault pistols, rifles, and shotguns. President Bill Clinton eventually brokered one of the bills through Congress as part of the Violent Crime Control and Enforcement Act of 1994. The assault weapons provision banned 19 named guns and approximately 200 other guns that fit the generic definition of an "assault weapon" for a period of 10 years. This definition emphasized that selected pistols (e.g., the TEC-9 and the MAC-10), rifles (e.g., the AK-47), and shotguns (e.g., the SWD Street Sweeper, or Striker-12) were not appropriate for civilian use. Although the NRA and many other gun rights groups complained that it was impossible to give a generic, operational definition of an "assault weapon," congressional researchers agreed with gun control groups that there were certain characteristics that differentiated military-style from civilian-style (for use in hunting and target shooting, as well as self-defense) weapons. Among the characteristics that define an assault weapon are "a more compact design, a barrel less than twenty inches in length, extensive use of stampings and plastics in its construction, lighter in weight (six to ten pounds), a pistol grip or thumbhole stock, a folding or telescoping grip, a barrel shroud, a threaded barrel for adding a silencer or flash suppressor, and the ability to receive a

large clip that holds twenty to thirty bullets" (Spitzer, 2002a, 35)—
the last of which is their most functionally important feature
(Koper, 2004, 1). Several foreign manufacturers tried to make
minor alterations to their assault weapons to evade the law, but
President Clinton signed an executive order in April 1998 to ban
the importation of fifty-eight foreign-made substitutes. Nevertheless, a Violence Policy Center (2004) study found that U.S. manufacturers were generally successful in evading the ban using the
same strategy of foreign manufacturers, the most famous example of which was the Bushmaster XM15-M4-A3 assault rifle used
by John Allen Muhammad and John Lee Malvo in October 2002
to murder ten people and injure three others in the infamous
Washington, D.C. sniper case.

The federal assault weapons ban was enacted by a Democ-
rat-controlled Congress and a Democrat president. A decade after
its passage, in September 2004, a Republican Congress and president (George W. Bush) allowed it to quietly die amid accusations
that the ban was an ineffective crime-fighting tool and that it
needlessly curbed the rights of gun owners (see, for example, National Rifle Association, 2005a). For gun control advocates, the
death of the assault weapons ban was a setback. They were especially frustrated because there is empirical support for the ban's
effectiveness—despite the continued yearly manufacture and sale
of tens of thousands of assault weapon clones during the ten-year
ban (weapons that evaded the 1994 ban by making minor, cosmetic changes to banned guns). In particular, a U.S. Department
of Justice study reveals that the use of assault weapons in crime
dropped significantly in the first two years after the ban, and that
this drop could not be explained by other variables, including the
overall drop in gun crime during the late 1990s (Roth and Koper,
1999). Indeed, in the first year after passage, requests for ATF assault weapon traces declined 20 percent. Other studies revealed
that the reduction of assault weapons used in crime continued
throughout the 1990s (the Brady Center to Prevent Gun Violence,
2004; Koper, 2004). Assault weapons that were specifically named
in the 1994 federal assault weapons act declined from 5.23 percent
of all crime guns (according to the ATF National Tracing Center
data) to 1.1 percent between 1993 (the year before it took effect)
and 2001; and when "copycat" assault weapons (similar to those
specifically named in the 1994, but with minor, cosmetic modifications) are added in, the corresponding percentages are 6.15
(1993) and 2.57 (2001)—see Figure 2.2.[6]

FIGURE 2.2

Banned Assault Weapons and Copycats as a Percentage of all Crime Guns, 1993–2001

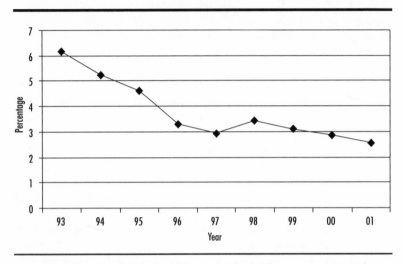

Sources: Adapted from data presented in Koper (2004, pp. 42-43) and Brady Center to Prevent Gun Violence (2004, p.11).

Since the early 1980s, assault weapons have been the "'weapons of choice' for drug traffickers, gangs, terrorists, and paramilitary extremists" (Brady Center to Prevent Gun Violence, 2004, 3). Indeed, Spitzer (2002a, 36) points out that while assault weapons accounted for only 2–3 percent of all firearms owned in the United States in the early 1990s, they accounted for 6–8 percent of gun crimes.

Beyond their greater use in crime, a central part of the rationale for the special regulation of assault weapons is that they facilitate "the rapid firing of high numbers of shots, which allows offenders to inflict more wounds on more persons in a short period of time, thereby increasing the expected number of injuries and deaths per criminal use" (Roth and Koper, 1999, 7; cf. Koper, 2004, 81). This argument is supported by a comprehensive study of gun attacks in Jersey City, New Jersey from 1992 through 1996. More particularly, Reedy and Koper (2003) found that attacks with semiautomatic pistols resulted in higher numbers of gunshot victims than attacks with revolvers (note: semiautomatics have magazine clips that hold a greater number of rounds than revolvers).

Ballistic Fingerprinting

A ballistic fingerprint is the unique set of markings left on a shell casing and bullet after firing. Law enforcement has used ballistic analysis in criminal investigations since the early 1930s, but advancements in computer image resolution technologies over the past decade have brought ballistic fingerprinting into the forefront of crime analysis. In 1997, the ATF and FBI set up the National Integrated Ballistics Identification Network (NIBIN) to keep a national-level database of digitalized ballistic fingerprints of guns involved in crime incidents. As Daniel W. Webster (2002b, 1), codirector of the Johns Hopkins Center for Gun Policy and Research, observes, "it is now common practice for law enforcement agencies to obtain ballistic fingerprints from firearms recovered from criminal suspects and crime scenes, and to attempt to match the ballistic fingerprints to those taken from other crime scenes."

The October 2002 Washington, D.C., sniper case brought into public discussion a key proposal of gun control advocates—that NIBIN should be expanded to hold ballistic fingerprints of *all* firearms, not just crime guns. Gun control advocates argue that had the NIBIN database existed for all firearms, the snipers could have been identified and consequently apprehended much more quickly. Sarah Brady of the Brady Campaign to Prevent Gun Violence told newspaper reporters, "if a nationwide ballistic fingerprinting system had existed (in the [D.C.] sniper case), police would have been able to trace the bullets to a specific gun" (as quoted in Franscell, 2002). NIBIN's success supports the claim of gun control advocates: For example, between March 2000 and July 2002, information in the database "resulted in 8.800 successful matches that linked 17,600 crimes" (Webster, 2002b, 1). Braga and Pierce report that the Boston Police Department realized a sixfold increase in the monthly number of ballistic matches after replacing traditional ballistics methods with NIBIN. Ballistic fingerprinting now plays a key role in connecting crime scenes "that occur within and across the different Boston Police districts," as well as "in the development of intelligence that better focuses Boston gun law enforcement operations" (2004, 2).

Opponents of expanding NIBIN maintain that criminals will respond by altering their guns after initial ballistic fingerprints are made. This is not inconceivable, as such alterations can be readily accomplished by using a small file to alter the firing pin or barrel. Moreover, opponents claim that an expanded NIBIN would only further encourage criminals to steal the guns they want to use in crime or to use false identification when buying them at a gun show or retail detailer. Finally, opponents contend that it would be "yet another infringement on constitutional rights, and creates a system that makes confiscation much easier," as phrased by Dudley Brown, executive director of Rocky Mountain Gun Owners (quoted in Franscell, 2002).

Gun rights proponents observe that the two states requiring universal ballistic fingerprinting, New York and Maryland, have seen little success. For example, a Maryland State Police (2004) study concluded that "there have been no crime investigations that have been enhanced or expedited through the use of [Maryland's Integrated Ballistics Identification System]."[7] Similarly, a study of New York's ballistic fingerprinting database revealed that it had "not solved a single crime in the more than three years since its debut" (as reported by the National Rifle Association, 2005b). However, Webster (2002b, 2) points out that Maryland and New York are limited by the lack of an equivalent national database. This is especially true for New York, as its highly restrictive state and local gun regulations force criminals to buy their guns from street dealers obtaining guns from states where there are few restrictions.

Bullet Serial Numbers

Recent advances in computer imagery have opened up the possibility of "micro-stamping" serial numbers on every newly manufactured bullet. This kind of coding system already exists in other industries, including everything from soda cans to Tic Tac breath mints. Firing tests reveal that a micro-stamp can even survive the mangling that can occur after a bullet hits a solid object. Crime-gun tracing expert Glenn Pierce of Northeastern University believes that this technology holds great promise for the control of violent gun crime, as does the California Police Chiefs Association. California is presently considering a bullet-coding law that would require all *handgun* ammunition packed in a particular box to carry the same code; the buyer's identity would be electronically recorded and linked with the ammunition by swiping his or her driver's license.[8]

Registration

The National Rifle Association (2005b) contends that ballistic fingerprinting and bullet coding are backdoors to a national system of gun registration, which is far and away the worst form of gun control that gun rights advocates can imagine (aside from the actual confiscation of guns from law-abiding citizens). Gun registration means keeping a permanent record of a firearm sale in a central location. It is a critical component of the gun violence control efforts of our peer nations—where it is believed to reduce the supply of guns to criminals. As noted earlier, many crime-gun traces reveal that the possessor purchased the gun from a licensed retailer; and gun control advocates believe that a well-publicized, national registration system would deter many would-be criminals from ever obtaining guns. Cross-nationally, the United States again stands out regarding the laxity of its gun regulations, because it is the only economically developed democracy that does not have an integrated system for registering firearms and keeping track of their owners (see United Nations, 1999, Table 2.5).[9] If a U.S. citizen buys a gun from a federally licensed firearm retail dealer, his or her name and address, as well as the gun make, model, and serial number, are submitted to the ATF's National Tracing Center. If the gun is used in a crime, law enforcement officials may request this information from the Tracing Center, but if the gun has been resold in the private market, there is no national law that requires the new owner to register it, and the ATF loses track of the weapon.

Currently eight states (California, Connecticut, Hawaii, Maryland, Massachusetts, Michigan, New Jersey, New York) and the District of Columbia have some form of mandated gun registration, but as noted earlier, the crime- and violence-prevention effect of these mandates are greatly mitigated because they are easily evaded by crossing a state line to purchase a gun where registration is not required. Gun rights advocates contend that even if the United States had a national registration system of all firearms—whether purchased from a federal licensed retailer or in the private resale market—there would be little impact on gun violence and crime because "criminals do not register their firearms. Tracing of crime guns through the use of registration leads law enforcement back to the last law-abiding person in the chain of possession" (Caplan, 2002, 256). Moreover, gun rights advocates contend that registration would violate the spirit of the Second Amendment: If the government has registration lists, they can use them to disarm the citizenry and thus prevent it from resisting a tyrannical government. Despite public opinion polls consistently revealing that the U.S. public supports the registration and licensing of all firearms (see references cited in Chapter 1, as well as Figure 1.3), the 1986 Firearm Ownership Protection Act was designed, in large part, with the goal of preventing the federal government from setting up national registries of firearms and their owners.

A 2001 study conducted at the Center for Gun Policy and Research at Johns Hopkins University touches on the potential effectiveness of mandatory registration. More particularly, Webster, Vernick, and Hepburn (2001) found that states with mandatory firearms registration and licensing have a third of their crime guns sold in-state compared with three-quarters of crime guns in states not requiring registration and licensing. The researchers conclude that "mandatory registration makes it easier to trace guns used in crime to their last known legal owner, and to investigate possible illegal transfers. In combination, these laws have the potential to significantly restrict gun acquisition by high risk individuals through stricter eligibility criteria, safeguards against falsified applications, and increased legal risk and costs associated with illegal gun transfers to proscribed individuals" (184).

Licensing

Closely related to the concept of gun registration is the licensing of gun owners. Obtaining a license (or permit) usually involves a thorough background check and a waiting period ranging from 3 to 180 days (as is the case in New York). Gun control advocates defend licensing on several grounds: "It prevents certain categories of individuals, including criminals, children, and those considered mentally incompetent, from gaining easy access to guns; it ensures that those having guns demonstrate some degree of competency . . . ; it facilitates criminal prosecutions, and it restricts the accessibility of an inherently dangerous commodity based, for example, on the needs of one's occupation" (Spitzer, 2002b, 360). The potential effectiveness of the licensing of individual gun buyers on gun violence and crime is indicated by the Johns Hopkins study noted earlier, where it was found that states requiring licenses had two and a half times fewer crime guns traceable back to an in-state dealer compared with states not requiring licenses (Webster, Vernick, and Hepburn, 2001). The potential effectiveness of requiring the strict licensing and monitoring of gun dealers is indicated by the finding that just 1 percent of gun dealers account for more than half of all traceable crime guns (see *Tracing Crime Guns* above).

Here again, the United States stands out when compared with its peer nations (United Nations, 1999, Table 2.7), which universally require a purchaser to obtain a license before buying a gun (often with a training requirement before a license is issued—see next section). Currently, thirteen U.S. states require a prospective gun buyer to obtain a license for buying a handgun (California, Connecticut, Hawaii, Illinois, Iowa, Massachusetts, Michigan, Minnesota, Missouri, Nebraska, New Jersey, New York, North Carolina) and four for the purchase of a "long gun" (rifle or shotgun; California, Hawaii, Massachusetts, New Jersey); in addition, nineteen states have licensing requirements for dealers that go beyond federal regulations (with the goal of deterring illegitimate dealers—those willing to sell to criminals and minors—by requiring either periodic inspection of dealer transactions, or on-demand inspection by law enforcement agents; these states are Alabama, California, Connecticut, Delaware, Georgia, Hawaii, Indiana, Maryland, Massachusetts, New Hampshire, New Jersey, New York, North Carolina, Pennsylvania, Rhode Island, South Carolina, Tennessee, Virginia, and Washington).

Gun rights advocates hold licensing in the same disdain as they do registration and for the same reasons: Criminals don't get licenses, and law-abiding citizens are having their Second Amendment rights violated—ultimately risking the confiscation of their firearms. Moreover, the NRA contends on its Web site that the "licensing of America's 60–65 million gun owners and their estimated 230 million firearms would require creation of a huge bureaucracy at tremendous taxpayer cost," with no "tangible" benefit (National Rifle Association, 2005c).

Training

Several of the states requiring an individual to obtain a license before obtaining a gun require that successful applicants complete a safety course (Connecticut, Hawaii, Massachusetts, and Michigan). No national training law exists. Somewhat surprisingly, this does not, unlike other serious gun control measures, put the United States in a category of its own when compared with its peer nations (United Nations, 1999, Table 2.3).[10] However, many states—including Colorado, Kansas, Minnesota, Missouri, New Mexico, Ohio, Virginia, and Wisconsin—require a gun safety course before issuing an individual a permit to carry a concealed firearm, and almost all states require a safety training course before minors may receive a hunting license.

At first wash, it would seem that gun safety training would be a key component of the legislative agenda of gun control advocates. Although training in the safe practice of handling and storing guns is indeed part of the agenda, and is related to the Child Access Prevention laws discussed earlier, empirical studies have been unable to show the effect gun control advocates would expect or like to see. For example, one national survey of gun owners found that those who had received formal training "were more likely to store their guns in the least safe way"—that is, "loaded and unlocked"—even after controlling for more than a dozen factors, including whether the gun was kept for protection (Hemenway, 2004, 84; the study referred to was authored by Hemenway, Solnick, and Azrael, 1995; several other studies have yielded similar findings—see Hemenway, 2004, 84–87). Many public health researchers are especially wary of gun safety programs aimed at children, such as the NRA's "Eddie Eagle" youth gun safety course (see, for example, Dolins and Christoffel, 1994; Hemenway, 2004). The problem, as they see it, is that such programs serve to increase children's curiosity and interest in guns, thus increasing their desire to handle them.

Gun rights advocates see safety courses as one of the twin pillars of effective gun control—the other is keeping criminals from obtaining guns. According to the NRA, "voluntary firearms safety training, not government intrusion, has decreased firearms accidents." The NRA's safety programs are conducted throughout the nation by 62,000 certified instructors. "Youngsters learn firearm safety in NRA programs offered through civic groups such as the Boy Scouts, Jaycees, the American Legion, and schools. NRA's Eddie Eagle GunSafe® program teaches children pre-K through sixth grade that if they see a firearm without supervision, they should 'STOP! Don't Touch. Leave the Area. Tell an Adult.' Since 1988, the program has been used by more than 22,000 schools, civic groups, and law enforcement agencies to reach 18 million children" (National Rifle Association, 2005d).

However, Hemenway (2004, 84) points out that even though "the NRA continuously touts Eddie Eagle, no evaluation study shows that it or any similar program reduces inappropriate gun use." Indeed, the evidence currently points the other way. Hardy (2002) found that thirty-four children ages four to seven who had done training on gun safety acted no more cautiously around guns than thirty-six children who had not received such training: In both sets of children, about half played with a semiautomatic pistol when given the opportunity. Hardy deemed the training a failure—guns are simply too tempting and too dangerous, and many children lack the mental maturity to appreciate the meaning of the gun safety training they receive, as well as the consequences of an accidental shooting (a fact lost on many parents, as Hardy's interviews with them revealed). Rather than relying on kids to handle guns safely, this aspect of the public health approach to gun control would place the burden on parents to keep their guns and ammunition locked up and out of the sight and minds of children (see the earlier section on *Controlling Guns in the Home: Child Access Protection Laws*).

Point-of-Sale Controls

Background Checks

The 1993 Brady Law is one of the few major gun control measures existing on the national level in the United States. It originally mandated a five-business-day waiting period before an individual could buy a handgun—allowing for a background check on the prospective buyer, as well as providing a "cooling off" period to deter the impulsive purchase of a gun to commit suicide or a violent crime. Since its enactment, an individual is barred from buying a handgun if he or she: (1) has been convicted of a crime carrying a minimum one-year sentence (in 1996, this was extended to any conviction for domestic violence); (2) is under a violence-related court restraining order; (3) is a fugitive; (4) is a minor (under twenty-one for handguns, under eighteen for "long guns," that is, rifles and shotguns); (5) is an illegal alien; (6) is the resident of a mental institution or has been certified mentally unstable; (7) has renounced his or her citizenship; or (8) has ever been arrested for using or selling drugs. This list originated with the 1968 Gun Control Act, which also barred the sale of handguns (and long guns) to these categories of people, but had no enforcement mechanisms (an individual signed a statement saying he or she was not in one of the categories barred from possessing or buying a firearm, but there was no investigative follow-up under the auspices of the federal government). In 1998, the background check provisions of the Brady Law were extended to long guns, and the five-day waiting period was eliminated and replaced by an instant, computerized background check system.[11] However, many states have imposed their own waiting periods—ranging from 2 days for Alabama, Nebraska, South Dakota, and Wisconsin; to 3 days for Florida, Illinois, and Iowa; to 5 days for Washington; to 7 days for Indiana, Maryland, Minnesota, Missouri, New Jersey, North Carolina, and Rhode Island; to 10 days for California; to 14 days for Hawaii; to 30 days for Massachusetts; and to a whopping 180 days for New York.

The public health approach to controlling gun violence places central importance on the screening of prospective gun buyers. It points to the success of the Brady Act in preventing convicted felons—and other individuals at high risk for committing violence—acquiring guns from federally licensed retail dealers. From the beginning of 1994 (the first full year after the Brady Act was implemented) through the end of 2002 (the most recent year for which data are available), 45,717,000 background checks produced 917,000 denials (a rejection rate of 2.1 percent). The most common reason for rejection was a felony indictment or conviction, followed by domestic violence (a conviction or restraining order), with most of the remaining rejections falling under one of the following categories: fugitive from justice, mental illness or disability, or drug addiction (Bureau of Justice Statistics, 2003b). Many gun rights enthusiasts scoff at such data and point out that criminals typically don't go to retail dealers to buy their guns. This contention has considerable empirical support: In its review of the relevant scientific studies, the National Research Council (2005, Chapter 4) reports that the majority of criminals obtain their guns through sources other than retail dealers—for example, by theft, sales in the private (or so-called secondary) market (e.g., at gun shows, flea markets, or between private individuals), or via straw purchases (e.g., a friend or a relative without a criminal record making the original retail purchase). Gun rights advocates also point to a 2001 U.S. General Accounting Office (GAO) finding that would-be criminals can easily thwart the Brady Law by using false IDs. GAO agents had no problem buying guns using fake identification cards that they constructed with simple computer software and an inexpensive laminator. They pulled off their scam at a variety of licensed gun retailers in every state in which they tried: Arizona, Montana, New Mexico, Virginia, and West Virginia. They ultimately concluded that "the instant background check does not positively identify purchasers of firearms," nor can it "ensure that the prospective purchaser is not a felon" (as quoted in Longley, 2001).

The Secondary Market

That a person prohibited from purchasing or possessing a firearm can easily do so by turning to the *secondary market* is the one of the hottest topics in the national debate over gun control—and one of the sorest points from the perspective of gun control advocates. The secondary market consists of the many forms of private sales transacted between individuals. Although many of these occur on the street or in the privacy of homes, a large number occur at gun shows, flea markets, and swap meets. The ATF estimates that more than 4,000 gun shows alone are held annually in the United States. Though many of the dealers at these gun shows are federally licensed, as many as 50 percent are not (see Bureau of Alcohol, Tobacco and Firearms, 1999). There are currently no federal enforcement mechanisms to govern the secondary market, although congressional legislation is regularly proposed to do so.[12] The end result is that "large numbers of firearms at these public markets are sold anonymously; the seller has no idea and is under no obligation to find out whether he or she is selling a firearm to a felon or other prohibited person. If any of these firearms are later recovered at a crime scene, there is virtually no way to trace them back to the purchaser" (Bureau of Alcohol, Tobacco and Firearms, 1999, 1). Note that eighteen states have their own laws that require purchases between private parties to involve a background check of the purchaser from either a federally licensed dealer or law enforcement agency (California, Connecticut, Hawaii, Illinois, Indiana, Iowa, Maryland, Massachusetts, Michigan, Minnesota, Missouri, Nebraska, New Jersey, New York, North Carolina, Pennsylvania, Rhode Island, and Tennessee). However, half of the top ten states in which gun shows are conducted are not on this list (in ranking order): Texas, Florida, Oregon, Ohio, and Nevada (the remaining top ten states are Pennsylvania, Illinois, California, Indiana, and North Carolina; see Bureau of Alcohol, Tobacco and Firearms, 1999, 4).

In the spring of 2005, the *Buffalo News* ran a lengthy story exposing the kind of horrific consequences that the lack of regulations at gun shows can have. Street criminal James Nigel Bostic crossed from the strict gun control state of New York into the less restrictive state of Ohio in 2000, where he purchased 250 handguns at various gun shows. He then returned to New York and sold them on the streets of Buffalo to drug dealers, thieves, and gang members. During the next four years, 100 of Bostic's guns were recovered and linked to an array of violent crimes, including murder, kidnapping, assault, and robbery (*Buffalo News*, 2005). The Bostic case is similar to many ATF investigations, which together "paint a disturbing picture of gun shows as venues for criminal activity and a source of firearms used in crimes" (Bureau of Alcohol, Tobacco and Firearms, 1999, 7).

However, many gun rights advocates place no blame for street crime on unregulated gun shows. As the NRA states on its Web page, if the gun show loopholes in federal law were closed, criminals would simply find another means to get their guns, for example, "from theft or burglary, the black market, or friends and family members" (National Rifle Association, 2005e).

"Shall Issue" (Right-to-Carry) Concealed Weapons Laws

During the 1990s, a revolution occurred in state-level concealed weapons laws, one bemoaned by the advocates of strong gun control. During the first third of the twentieth century, forty-two states banned most private citizens from carrying concealed firearms (with special exceptions being made for occupational purposes, e.g., private security).[13] These bans received little public resistance, even from gun enthusiasts. However, beginning with the state of Florida in 1987, and in the decade and a half that followed, twenty-eight states enacted "shall issue" laws, allowing for the average citizen to acquire, relatively easily, a concealed weapons permit to carry a handgun. By 2005, there were thirty-seven such states.[14] The usual requirements are not hard to meet: a background check revealing no felony convictions or domestic violence abuse incidents and a training course in gun safety and operation. Concealed weapons are prohibited in two states (Illinois and Nebraska) and difficult for the average citizen to obtain in eleven others (so-called may issue states: Alabama, California, Connecticut, Delaware, Hawaii, Iowa, Maryland, Massachusetts, New Jersey, New York, and Rhode Island). "May issue" implies that the final decision to issue a permit rests with local or state law enforcement agencies, who are generally reluctant to do so.

Gun control advocates feared that the enactment of such laws would bring with it a rise in handgun violence; they predicted, for example, a rise in (a) spur-of-the-moment shootings;

(b) the number of criminals carrying guns (knowing that some of the public might now be armed); and (c) gun theft and thus the putting of more guns into the hands of criminals, as gun possession in the law-abiding population will increase the number of firearms available for stealing. But what gun control advocates feared has not yet come to pass. On the contrary, most crime categories, including gun-related crimes, fell after 1995; and as pointed out in Chapter 1, so have the number of gun owners. Some gun control advocates, such as the Brady Campaign (2005a), credit the enactment of the 1993 Brady Law for the fall in the crime rate, while some gun rights advocates, such as the National Rifle Association, credit the sweeping liberalization of concealed weapons laws (claiming criminals become fearful when "potential victims are armed"; National Rifle Association, 2005f). Neither claim is valid. Empirical studies of the effects of "shall issue" laws have produced findings that are neither plain nor easy to interpret. As revealed in Table 2.2, the differences between the "shall issue" states and those with significant restrictions on concealed weapons permits are minimal and not statistically significant. More complex statistical analyses are no more revealing. For example, when controls for poverty, racial heterogeneity, region, and other significant correlates of crime are added, and when the dependent variable list is expanded to include other indicators of crime, as well as changes over time, researchers obtain the same relatively weak and insignificant differences between these two sets of states. In one of the most comprehensive studies to date, Donahue (2003, 290) concludes that "shall-issue laws may not increase crime as much as many feared." Moreover, and quite notably, "the typical gun permit holder is a middle-aged Republican white male, which is a group at relatively low risk of violent criminal victimization with or without gun ownership." So it is not clear why there should be any "substantial crime reduction benefits . . . by arming this group further." If there is any significant effect, according to Donahue, it will be reflected in the creation of a greater level of social unease, because citizens are likely to become apprehensive when they realize that "greater numbers of individuals walking through shopping malls, schools, and churches and sitting in movie theatres are carrying lethal weapons." Most public health researchers would agree with Donahue's assessment of current concealed weapons laws and find little benefit in their existence or growth, and, indeed, would prefer their repeal (see, for example, Hemenway, 2004, 244–251).

TABLE 2.2
Rate per 100,000 Inhabitants of Violent Crime and Murder by Existence of a "Shall-Issue" (Right-to-Carry) Law, 2003

	States without a Shall-Issue law (N=16)[a]	States with a Shall-Issue law (N=34)	Difference[b]
Average Violent Crime Rate[c]	480.2	467.2	13.0
Average Murder Rate	5.4	5.8	−0.4

Source: Rates calculated from Federal Bureau of Investigation (2004) raw data.

Notes: (a) In 2005, the NRA considered 12 states as infringing upon the 2nd Amendment rights of their citizens by not allowing them to readily obtain a concealed weapons permit—that is, by not having a "shall-issue" concealed weapons law: California, Delaware, Hawaii, Illinois, Iowa, Maryland, Massachusetts, Minnesota, Nebraska, New Jersey, New York, and Rhode Island. Four more states were on this list in 2003 (the latest year that FBI UCR crime data are available): Colorado, Connecticut, Missouri, and Ohio. This yields a total of 16 states for the first column.

(b) Neither difference between the two sets of states is statistically significant calculating a standard one-way analysis of variance: for the Violent Crime Rate, F=.924, sig.=.341; for the Murder Rate, F=.659, sign.=.411.

(c) "Violent crimes" are defined as murder, rape, robbery, and aggravated assault.

Gun Buyback Programs

The final gun control measure falling under the public health approach is the groundswell of gun buyback programs that dozens of cities have developed over the past two decades. A typical program is Jersey City's "Operation Lifesaver." In one three-week stretch in 2005, the city collected 897 guns by offering amnesty to the individuals turning in the guns, as well as cash: $25 for a BB gun, $150 for a revolver, and $250 for a semiautomatic weapon. The guns ranged from cheap Saturday night specials to fully functioning machine guns (see George, 2005). Hemenway's (2004, 217–220) review of the evidence on the effectiveness of gun buyback programs leads him to conclude that they "may have . . . some beneficial effects, including reducing accidents and suicides, but [they do] not help rid the streets of the weapons most commonly used in fatal criminal shootings." For example, a review of firearm fatality surveillance data for Milwaukee in the late 1990s revealed that five specific makes of handguns accounted for nearly half of the firearm deaths but only 6 percent of the guns collected in the city's buyback program.

An interesting variant of the buyback program is the *toy* gun version. In this case, a community agency will offer to give a child another kind of toy in exchange for a toy gun. For example, during the summer of 2004, the city of Central Falls, Rhode Island, hosted a toy gun turn-in event, in which children threw their toy guns into a "bashomatic" (a trash compactor that crushed them). The Rhode Island State Attorney General's Office funded this and similar events in several Rhode Island cities in 2004 and 2005. Community activist Angel Garcia observes that the point of the program is "to get children and adults thinking about society's use of guns . . . It's not just about gun removal, it's about educating our families, enlightening kids about safe play. As a person that works with kids, I tend to want to err on the side of caution. Guns shouldn't be part of everyday development." Garcia's views were echoed by Rhode Island Attorney General Patrick Lynch: "Any chance we get to stop and talk to kids and engage them and try to explain the danger associated with guns is good" (Garcia and Lynch quotes excerpted from Pina, 2004).

Gun rights advocates view buyback programs as exercises in futility. Even worse, the NRA contends that such programs "can result in the disarming of future crime victims who could have used the guns defensively to prevent death, injury, or property loss" (National Rifle Association, 2005g).

The Law Enforcement Approach

If you use a gun illegally, you will do hard time.

—President George W. Bush
Project Safe Neighborhoods (2005a)

*Do you favor or oppose mandatory prison sentences for felons
who commit crimes with guns?*

% Favor: 89

—The Gallup poll
Frank Newport (1999)

From our review of the key public health approaches to controlling gun violence, it is obvious that gun control and gun rights advocates have fundamental differences in values and worldviews. From the public health stance, too many guns with too few controls is a root cause of many contemporary social problems; from the gun rights stance, guns have become simply a scapegoat for many of our contemporary social problems. Nevertheless, both sides concur that the enforcement of current gun laws is critical to reducing gun violence and its costs to society. More specifically, both agree that violence-prone lawbreakers should be denied the right to buy and possess guns. When these individuals are caught, they should be taken off the streets with stiff prison sentences, especially if they are in possession of a firearm. Like the public health approach, the *law enforcement* approach is complex and multifaceted. Aspects of it that are particularly important to consider are the enforcement of current laws, gun-focused/place-oriented community policing, and gun courts.

Enforcement of Current Gun Control Laws

As gun-violence researcher Lawrence Southwick Jr. (2002b, 186) observes, often times the "issue of enforcement of gun laws is really a cover for opposing new gun laws. Those on one side of the issue argue that 'we need to make a law restricting guns,' while those on the other side say 'we don't need new laws—we need enforcement of existing gun laws'." That said, both sides of the gun debate want aggressive enforcement of current laws regarding illegal possession, sale, transfer, or use of a firearm.

The most common weapons offense category is the possession of a firearm by a prohibited person (usually a convicted felon); the second most common category is the use of a firearm during the commission of a violent crime (e.g., bank robbery) or drug trafficking (about half of the arrests in this second category). These two categories account for nearly 90 percent of the average 6,700 federal weapons arrests that occur each year, as well as of the majority of the 200,000 or so weapons arrests made by state and local police. There are many other categories of weapons-related arrests, the most significant of which include the receipt or possession of an unregistered firearm; the unlawful importation, manufacture, distribution, shipment or receipt of a firearm; and the possession of a stolen gun (see Scalia, 2000; Southwick, 2002b).

Gun-Focused/Place-Oriented Community Policing

In response to the rising gun violence of the 1980s, the U.S. Department of Justice, working in conjunction with state and local authorities, and coordinating its key law enforcement groups (the ATF, FBI, and Drug Enforcement Administration [DEA]), developed Project Triggerlock in 1991. Over the years, Triggerlock has been expanded and reformulated—to accommodate the unique circumstances of various metropolitan areas—under dozens of guises in hundreds of local and regional jurisdictions (program titles include Project Exile, Operation Ceasefire, Project Felon, Project Safe Neighborhoods, Triggerlock II, and many others). Funding for most of these has come through Project Safe Neighborhoods, the centerpiece of the federal government's efforts to control gun violence during President George W. Bush's two terms in office. Other funding has been channeled through the Community Oriented Policing Services (created as part of the Violent Crime Control and Law Enforcement Act of 1994), and the Safe Streets Violent Crime Initiative (see Center for Problem-Oriented Policing, 2005; Federal Bureau of Investigation, 2001; Gun Owners Foundation, 2005; National Center for State Courts, 2005; Project Safe Neighborhoods, 2005b; U.S. Department of Justice, 2000). These programs use federal firearm statutes—for example, those barring the possession of firearms by high-risk individuals, including convicted felons, drug dealers, and domestic abusers— to prosecute gun-toting offenders in *federal* ("U.S. District") courts, where convictions rates are typically much higher and penalties much stiffer than in state and local courts.[15] For example, approximately 86 percent of those arrested on a federal weapons charge are convicted, and 92 percent of them serve prison time, averaging 107 months. In contrast, only about 16 percent of those arrested on a state or local weapons charge are convicted, while 67 percent of them end up in prison, averaging only 45 months (see Southwick, 2002b, Table 1; cf. Scalia, 2000, and Bureau of Justice Statistics, 2004). The programs often contain media campaigns to increase public awareness of gun crime and its ramifications, including the death and maiming of innocent victims, the financial losses suffered by the community, and the stern penalties gun-carrying criminals will face when turned over to the federal judicial system. Sometimes the programs incorporate a "carrot" approach—for example, increasing funding for school and community development agencies, especially those that seek to take teens and young adults off the streets through recreational, educational, and job-placement programs.

Two highly publicized Triggerlock-type programs are Boston's Gun Project/Operation Ceasefire (GPOC) and Richmond's

(VA) Project Exile. Gun rights advocates have extolled both as shining successes of the law enforcement approach to controlling gun violence. Begun in May 1996, Boston's GPOC aims to reduce gun violence by disarming gang members. It created a task force composed of the office of the U.S. District Attorney, the Massachusetts State Probation Office, the ATF, the DEA, the FBI, the State Department of Youth Services, the county district attorney, area clergy, neighborhood street workers, and several community development organizations. GPOC strongly incorporated both "carrot" and "stick" approaches. For example, it sent gang-unit police, community-agency street workers, and clergy to schools and street corners gang members frequented to send a loud and clear message: Use a gun, and you will suffer the maximum consequences; carry a gun, and law enforcement will find you, and the judicial system will make sure that you suffer the maximum consequences. When, for example, a gang member was stopped for a traffic violation, if a search of the vehicle turned up a gun, or even a single bullet, the results were immediate arrest and speedy disposition in federal court. In the months following GPOC's inception, there were dozens of federal weapons indictments and arrests. Recovered guns were subjected to ATF traces, and many were linked to multiple crimes, which in turn subjected the possessors to even harsher punishment. More extensive traces often turned up illegitimate gun dealers, who were rounded up and quickly prosecuted. Many of the eighty federally licensed firearms dealers in the Boston area were known to sell guns to street criminals. However, fearing prosecution, sixty-five of them decided to surrender their licenses or not to seek renewal.

On the "carrot" side, the Boston Jobs Project was created to help street youths get job training and eventual job placement through the Boston Private Industry Council. Employers have been enticed into hiring these high-risk youth, because each youth comes with a "voucher" from the recommending individual (usually a police or probation officer, a Department of Youth Services caseworker, or a minister). The voucher guarantees the employer that the recommending individual will keep tabs on the new worker (e.g., checking in on the person to make sure he or she is going to work; making sure that the person has been assigned a case manager to assist in finding substance abuse services, transportation, housing, child care, and mental health counseling; see the Boston Strategy to Prevent Youth Violence, 2005).

In 2001, Harvard University and the City University of New York researchers concluded that GPOC was a huge success: The multifaceted program was credited with significant reductions in Boston area youth homicide (a 63 percent drop in the first two years following its inception), reports of "shots fired" called into the police (a 32 percent drop), and gun-assault incidents (a 25 percent drop; see Braga, Kennedy, Waring, and Piehl, 2001). Moreover, these reductions could not be accounted for by other factors, such as changes in the Boston job market or in the size and composition of the youth population.

A prototype of the "stick" emphasis of the law enforcement approach to controlling gun violence, Richmond's Project Exile seeks to deter illegal gun use by diverting weapons-related offenses from the state to the federal court system—with the expected benefits of higher convictions rates and stiffer prison sentences. Begun in February 1997, the project provides training to law enforcement agents on federal gun laws and proper procedures for search and seizure, and it funds an advertising campaign telling would-be criminals that any gun offense will be dealt with swiftly and sternly by the judicial system. Gun rights enthusiasts have extolled the program and credited it with reducing firearm-related murders by 40 percent during its first year alone. The State of Virginia was so impressed with the project that it developed its own statewide "Exile" program, passing a law mandating a minimum sentence of five years for those having a prior conviction for a violent felony and who are convicted of possessing a firearm (see Virginia Exile, 2005).

Some scholars are not particularly impressed with GPOC or Project Exile. They point out that gun-violence rates were dropping throughout the country in the late 1990s, and many cities, without these kinds of community policing programs, experienced just as dramatic reductions (see, most notably, Winship, 2002, and Raphael and Ludwig, 2003). However, when the National Research Council (2005, 234) reviewed the effects of similar programs in Kansas City, Indianapolis, Pittsburgh, and New York, it concluded that the evidence was "compelling"—that they work, and that they can reduce violent crime in a community and not merely displace it from one neighborhood to another.

Triggerlock-type programs suffered two setbacks during their first decade. First, in December 1995, the U.S. Supreme Court ruled in *Bailey v. United States* (516 U.S. 137, 116 S.Ct. 501) that persons in possession of a gun when arrested for a violent or drug-trafficking crime must have actually used it (e.g., firing or brandishing) if they were to be charged with a distinctive weapons offense apart from the actual crime. This immediately reduced the number of weapons charges made in federal district courts (see Scalia, 2000). Before *Bailey*, for example, if a drug dealer had a pistol under his or her car seat, federal prosecutors would charge the individual not only with drug dealing but also with using a weapon in the commission of a crime; the additional weapons charge added significant prison time if the individual was convicted on the drug charge. However, if the drug dealer is already a convicted felon, then an illegal firearm possession charge can of course still be made.

A second setback came at the end of 2004, when Congress cut $45 million that was directly earmarked to fund gun prosecutions from the proposed budget for Project Safe Neighborhoods. Another $106 million was cut from the budget that would have funded an ATF program meant to track and intercept illegal purchases of guns by youths. Many gun control advocates and law enforcement officials felt that these cutbacks sent "a troubling message about the federal commitment of fighting gun crime and trafficking" (Lichtblau, 2004, 32).

However, both setbacks were temporary. In the case of *Bailey v. United States*, federal prosecutors began channeling many of the weapons-possession cases for first-time drug and violent-crime offenders to state court systems (where many were prosecuted for violation of particular state-level firearms laws). Moreover, even though the two years immediately following the Bailey decision (1996–1997) saw consecutive decreases in the number of federal firearms cases brought to U.S. District Courts (bottoming out at 3,162), by 1998 the number climbed back to pre-*Bailey* levels and has risen every year to its current average of approximately 6,700 cases per year (Maguire and Pastore, 2004, Table 5.10, 405). The resurgence in cases was due largely to the increasing number of urban areas adopting Project Triggerlock-type programs. As of the end of 2005, it appears that improved cooperation among federal, state, and local officials is capable of overcoming losses of direct funding for gun prosecutions and gun trafficking control—as the general funding for Project Safe Neighborhoods (around $200 million per year) and for the ATF has remained intact.

Gun Courts

The establishment of the Gun Court sends a clear message that we are serious about making the streets of Philadelphia safer. The Gun Court, as demonstrated in other cities, is a useful tool to more closely monitor the sentences imposed in gun cases.

—Pennsylvania State Senator Dwight Evans
Kimberly Turner (2004)

A variant of Project Triggerlock-type programs are local area *gun courts*. The first to appear in the modern era was in Providence, Rhode Island, in September 1994.[16] The court put gun-related prosecutions on the fast track. Before its creation, the average time for the disposition of a gun case—through a plea bargain or the start of a trial—was 518 days, with a conviction rate of 67 percent. After the special court was created, the maximum time for the disposition of a gun case fell to 126 days, while the conviction rate rose to 87 percent (see U.S. Department of Justice, 2000, Profile No. 37). The speed of disposition and increased probability of conviction experienced in Providence encouraged many other jurisdictions to create gun courts, among the most notable are those in Birmingham, Detroit, Indianapolis, Minneapolis, New York City, Philadelphia, Seattle, and Washington, D.C. The motivating idea of courts specializing in gun cases is that "the judicial system can play an important role in reducing firearms offenses through speedier dispositions, mandatory sentences, and [in some cases] intensive service delivery" (Sheppard and Kelly, 2002). When gun cases get mixed into the mélange of cases that are part of everyday local-area courts, overworked and "impatient judges frequently give defendants mild or probationary sentences in exchange for a waiver of their right to a lengthy jury trial. Channeling the cases to a gun court [ensures] that gun crimes are not ignored or reclassified at the demand of a public defender who threatens the judge with a jury trial" (Weyrich, 2000). Gun courts are the offspring of the drug court movement of the early 1990s, which were based on the same underlying reasoning regarding combating the illegal drug problem.

A variant within the gun court movement is the *juvenile* gun court. Because so much gun violence is perpetrated by young offenders, and because societal norms hold that we should try to save such offenders from a lifetime of crime and its consequences (injury, death, prison), gun courts specializing in juveniles began to appear in the mid-1990s. In contrast to their adult counterparts, juvenile gun courts typically use a carrot-and-a-stick approach. The best known is Jefferson County's Juvenile Gun Court in Birmingham, Alabama. Established in the spring of 1995, its core features were swift action (either a guilty plea or the start of a trial within ten working days); a twenty-eight-day boot camp alternative for offenders considered at low risk for violence; a parent education program; a substance abuse program; community service; and a high level of supervision after release from boot camp or the state detention facility. According to the Alabama Department of Youth Services, the military-style boot camp aims "to develop and enhance positive behavior characteristics in delinquent youth through counseling, and includes self-concept development, academics, and physical fitness in a highly structured, intensive program" (as quoted in Sheppard and Kelly, 2002). The parent education program brings parents together with judicial officials, mental health counselors, and family specialists for fifteen hours of class work spread over a period of ten weeks. The emphases include the costs of gun violence to victims, offenders, and families, and instruction on improving parent-youth communication skills. The program is mandatory, and parents are threatened with jail time if they do not comply. Community service includes neighborhood cleanup and graffiti removal while under close supervision of the local police. Community service is part of an intensive post-release program that includes an 8:00 P.M. curfew (8:30 on weekends), home visits by the police and the juvenile's probation officer, intermittent drug testing; and the completion of a six-week substance abuse and anger management course.

Gun courts are clearly a success when measured by speed of disposition, conviction rates, and severity of sentences. On these measures, other gun courts have found success similar to Providence's. For example, within its first eight months New York City's Brooklyn Gun Court tripled its jail sentences from 14 to 44 percent, increased the average sentence from ninety days to one year, and eliminated probation-only sentences for felony offenders (Join Together, 2003b). However, regarding the real aim of virtually all gun control measures, little systematic research has been done to see if gun courts actually reduce rates of violence in the wider community. As of 2005, the best empirical study on this issue focused on Birmingham's Jefferson County Youth Gun

Court. University of Alabama researchers compared a group of Birmingham youth who had been processed through the Youth Gun Court with two other groups over a four year period (1995–1999): a group of Birmingham youths who served time at the state detention center and were not processed through the gun court and its programs, but who received limited post-release supervision; and a group of youths who were processed through the juvenile court system of the nearby community of Bessemer, which did not include post-release supervision. On the positive side, the group that had gone through gun court had the lowest recidivism rate (17 percent), compared with 37 percent for the other Birmingham youths and 40 percent for the Bessemer youths. On the other hand, even though violent crime in Birmingham dropped dramatically during the four-year period, by 57 percent, it had a comparable drop in Bessemer (54 percent). The National Research Council (2005, 221) has concluded that there is too little research on gun courts to assess their crime-prevention effectiveness. The U.S. Department of Justice is more optimistic, however, and recommends that gun courts should be part of more comprehensive crime-fighting plans, which is how they are viewed by law enforcement and other public officials in all communities where they currently exist (see Sheppard and Kelly, 2002).

The Lawsuit Approach

A recent court case found that gun manufacturers were liable
for shootings committed with weapons they had
manufactured and that they had been allowed to flow illegally
into certain states with strict anti-gun laws. What is your
opinion? Should gun manufacturers be held liable when their
weapons are used in this manner, or not?

% Yes, should: 41

—The Gallup Poll
Mark Gillespie (1999)

[Regarding Cincinnati's lawsuit against gun manufacturers,]
the Court finds as a matter of law that the risks associated
with the use of a firearm are open and obvious and matters of
common knowledge. [They] cannot be a basis for fraud or
negligent misrepresentation. [Gun makers and

> distributors] have no ability to control the misconduct of
> [the responsible] third parties.
>
> —Judge Robert Ruehlman
> *Cincinnati v. Beretta U.S.A. Corp* (Oct. 7, 1999)

> *John Allen Muhammad and John Lee Malvo were convicted in
> connection with a series of sniper shootings using a
> Bushmaster XM-15 E2S .223 caliber semi-automatic assault
> rifle in the fall of 2002. Muhammad and Malvo obtained the
> Bushmaster assault rifle through the gross negligence of gun
> dealer Bull's Eye Shooter Supply and gun manufacturer
> Bushmaster Firearms. Bull's Eye ran its gun store in such a
> grossly negligent manner that scores of its guns routinely
> "disappeared" from its store and it kept such shoddy records
> that it could not even account for the Bushmaster assault rifle
> used in the sniper shootings when asked by federal agents for
> records of sale for the weapon. At least 238 guns
> "disappeared" from Bull's Eye in the last three years alone.*

> *Bushmaster deliberately continued to utilize Bull's Eye as a
> Bushmaster gun dealer and supplied it with as many guns as
> Bull's Eye wanted, despite years of audits by the Bureau of
> Alcohol, Tobacco and Firearms showing that Bull's Eye had
> dozens of missing guns. If Bull's Eye and Bushmaster had
> acted responsibly in the sale of their guns, Muhammad and
> Malvo would not have been able to obtain the assault rifle
> they needed to carry out their shootings, as they were
> prohibited purchasers under federal law. This suit seeks
> damages for the injuries caused by the gun industry's
> negligence and the public nuisance their negligence created as
> well as the intentional acts of Muhammad and Malvo.*

> —The Legal Action Project (2005a)[17]

Frustration with the lack of progress of the public health and law enforcement approaches to controlling gun violence has led many gun control advocates to place their hope with the judicial system—using it to sue manufacturers, wholesalers, retailers, and gun owners in civil court. Five types of lawsuits have been filed over the past three decades: product liability suits against manufacturers for having produced and sold defective guns; suits against dealers for negligent sales to persons prohibited from possessing guns; suits against gun manufacturers for intentional shootings; suits against individuals when their guns have been used in either intentional or unintentional shootings; and litigation initiated by cities and states against manufacturers and distributors to recover costs associated with gun violence, including for healthcare and police services (see Denning, 2002; Firearms Litigation Clearing House, 2005; Legal Action Project, 2003, 2005b). The primary aim of all of these lawsuits is to reduce gun-related crime, suicide, and accidents by reducing the overall number of firearms afloat in society; the number of firearms that fall into the hands of high-risk individuals (criminals; juveniles; the mentally ill or incompetent); and the number of firearms that lack modern safety features (e.g., trigger locks; magazine disconnect safeties). A secondary aim is to recover monetary compensation for the victims of gun violence, both at the individual and community levels. A cascade of these lawsuits began in the mid-1990s, and has continued unabated into the 2000s. Many received strong support from various gun control groups, who provided both lawyers and funding. The two largest groups are the Legal Action Project of the Brady Center to Prevent Gun Violence (http://www.gunlawsuits.org/) and the Educational Fund to Stop Gun Violence (http://www.csgv.org/issues/litigation /index.cfm). Most of the lawsuits involve multiple appeals of lower-court decisions, and most take—or are still taking—years to unfold to their final conclusions. The overall effect of the suits has yet to be determined, but beginning in 2006 the filing of such suits will all but cease, as in the fall of 2005 Congress passed the Protection of Lawful Commerce in Arms Act. The Act prohibits new "civil liability actions" against manufacturers, distributors, dealers, and importers of firearms or ammunition products, and their trade associations, for any harm caused by the criminal or unlawful misuse of firearms or ammunition. (Note, however, that the Act does not exempt those in the gun industry breaking the law or selling defective weapons or ammunition.)

Gun rights advocates contend that the use of civil lawsuits to control firearms and the violence associated with them is illegitimate and lacking in legal merit. Rather, they see the problems of firearms violence as resting with the criminals who misuse guns and with the carelessness of particular individuals who become involved in accidental shootings. Moreover, they believe that individuals, organizations, and communities that have filed these lawsuits ignore the "positive consequences" of guns, that is, their defensive use, which can prevent "many violent, predatory criminals from committing future crimes" (Izumi, 1999). Finally, they believe the relatively few lawsuits against the gun industry that have been won, and the even fewer that have been successful in the appeals process, supports their viewpoint. In sum, the "courts should not use the judiciary to effectuate gun control reform. This function is better served by Congress or state legislatures" (Bonney, 2000, p. 202). This particular line of reasoning ignores, however, that the most notable lawsuit victories have occurred as out-of-court agreements. Examples include the $2.5 million settlement against gun retailer Bulls Eye and gun manufacturer Bushmaster in 2004 for their responsibility in the 2002 Washington D.C. sniper shootings; the $1 million settlement against a West Virginia pawnbroker for selling 12 handguns to an obvious straw purchaser (one of the guns was eventually used to shoot two New Jersey police officers); and the 2005 settlement against Smith & Wesson for its failure to childproof its Model 915 pistol (see Butterfield, 2004; Potter, 2005).

Product Liability and Other Legal Theories Used in Gun Lawsuits

Observing the success of product liability suits in the 1980s and early 1990s against the tobacco industry, many victims of gun violence began similar actions against the gun industry. The initial success against tobacco was not winning the suits. Until the landmark Master Settlement Agreement of 1998, plaintiffs had generally lost or had positive judgments set aside.[18] Instead, success was seen as the growing public awareness of the health problems associated with tobacco products. Similarly, the success of gun-related lawsuits has largely been in the area of increasing public awareness of the careless business practices of the gun industry that have allowed hundreds of thousands of firearms to find their way into the hands of felons and teenagers. Success has also been reflected in greater public awareness of the health-related and other costs of the gun violence to society. In a relatively small number of cases, the suits have actually motivated changes in the manufacture of guns to improve their safety, and the way in which gun dealers do business (e.g., training employees to recognize straw purchasers). They have also produced a handful of out-of-court financial settlements for the victims of gun violence.

The details of the more important lawsuits can be found in Chapter 6 of this *Handbook*.

As Kopel (2002, 482) observes, "Lawsuits involving manufacturing defects are uncontroversial." For example, a gun is considered defective if it fires when dropped or when the safety is on. In 1979, the Alaskan Supreme Court upheld damages to a plaintiff who had sued gun manufacturer Sturm, Ruger & Company for its defective .41 caliber revolver. Hundreds of accidental discharges of this gun had been reported since 1953, and the Court held that the "manufacturer knew that its product was defectively designed and that injuries and deaths had resulted from the design defect, but continued to market the product in reckless disregard of the public's safety" (*Sturm, Ruger & Co., Inc. v. Day*, as quoted in Violence Policy Center, 2005). Many other "manufacturing-defect lawsuits have resulted in many victories by plaintiffs, leading manufacturers of substandard guns (particularly cheap European imports) to improve their guns" or pull them off the market (Kopel, 2002, 482).[19]

The controversy between gun control and gun rights advocates arises when other legal theories are invoked. These include (a) *specific design-defects* suits going beyond shoddy safeties and firing pins, for example the lack of indicators that let the handler know whether a gun is loaded, trigger locks, and magazine safeties (making the gun incapable of firing a bullet left in the chamber after the ammunition clip is removed); (b) *general design-defect* suits holding that a particular gun (usually a handgun) "is by its very nature defective" because it is ultra hazardous—readily causing injury and death—and this hazard outweighs any sporting or other benefits the gun might have (Kopel, 2002, 483); (c) *negligent marketing*, for example, wholesalers selling their weapons to gun show vendors instead of strictly to dealers doing business in the normal way, that is, from retail stores; and (d) *public nuisance* suits, which have been the basis for many of the actions that various cities have brought to court to recover losses associated with gun violence—for example, those related to their burdens on local healthcare and law enforcement systems; the usual contention is that manufacturers have created a public nuisance by flooding the community with guns and that local and state gun control does not work because dealers can readily cross into and then return from nearby states where gun laws are lax.

Immunity Legislation

In response to the large number of litigations and the possibilities of losing billions of dollars in settlements, the tobacco industry sought, unsuccessfully, to have Congress grant tobacco companies immunity from liability lawsuits. Similarly, over the past decade, major legislation was proposed and debated each year in Congress intended to provide the gun industry similar immunity. The legislation was regularly defeated until the fall of 2005, when the U.S. Congress passed the Protection of Lawful Commerce in Arms Act barring any future lawsuits against firearm and ammunition manufacturers and dealers for any harm caused by the criminal misuse of a gun.

Before the Protection of Lawful Commerce in Arms Act was passed, many U.S. states had already passed legislation preventing counties and local communities from filing public nuisance and design-defect lawsuits against gun manufacturers and their distributors.[20] As with the spate of "shall issue" (right-to-carry) and preemption laws—preventing local communities from passing firearms laws stricter than those of the state—that were passed in the 1990s, the firearm-industry immunity laws represent major victories for gun rights advocates.

Notes

1. These 2001 data are provided only for exemplary purposes. They are taken from the NVISS, which presently includes Connecticut, Maine, Utah, Wisconsin, Allegheny County (PA), and San Francisco County (CA). Thanks to David Hemenway, Head of the Harvard Injury Control Research Center and the Harvard Youth Violence Prevention Center, for providing the data.

2. The developed nations used for the calculation of these percentages are Australia, Austria, Belgium, Canada, Denmark, Finland, Germany, Greece, Japan, Liechtenstein, Luxembourg, New Zealand, Norway, Spain, Sweden, Switzerland, and the United Kingdom. Only Finland, Liechtenstein, and Luxembourg do not require the locking up of guns, and only Luxembourg does not require the locking of ammunition.

3. Of the nations listed in note number 2, only Finland, Germany, and Norway do not have strict laws regulating the transportation of firearms.

4. Note that the District of Columbia has a ban on *all* handguns, not just Saturday night specials.

5. The AKS is a variant of the infamous AK-47 military assault rifle that is used by military groups around the world.

6. Note that the NRA rejects the validity of crime gun trace research; for a detailed account of its rejection, see National Rifle Association (2005a).

7. After the Maryland State Police report came out, the Maryland ballistics database did yield success in a murder conviction in which no weapon was found but shell casings found at the scene were eventually linked with a casing on file with Maryland's Integrated Ballistics Identification System. The casings all matched a weapon purchased by the murderer's girlfriend three weeks before the killing. The ballistics "evidence was the cornerstone of our case," said Glenn F. Ivey, the Prince George's [Maryland] state's attorney. "It was powerful evidence. I hope this verdict helps our efforts to have the [Maryland Integrated Ballistics Identification System] continued and expanded" (as quoted in Castaneda and Snyder, 2005).

8. Glenn Pierce's opinion was expressed in a personal communication on April 29, 2005. For more information on the California legislation, see Join Together (2005) and Sweeney (2005). The status of the California legislation can be monitored by checking the California State Legislature's Web site: http://www.leginfo.ca.gov/pub/bill/sen /sb_0351-0400/sb_357_bill_20050602_history.html (last accessed on June 2, 2005).

9. Records in our peer nations are generally maintained for both handguns and long guns (rifles and shotguns) and are not publicly available, except in Norway. Records are maintained and organized at different levels, depending on the nation; for example, they are organized at the local level in Finland, Germany, Norway, Sweden, and the United Kingdom; at the regional level in Australia and Switzerland; and at the national level in Belgium, Canada, Greece, Japan, Liechtenstein, New Zealand, and Spain.

10. Eight countries require mandatory safety training before an individual can purchase a firearm: Australia, Belgium, Canada, France, Japan, New Zealand, Norway, and Spain. Nine other nations are similar to the United States in not requiring training: Austria, Denmark, Finland, Germany, Greece, Liechtenstein, Luxembourg, Sweden, and the United Kingdom.

11. The Brady Law requires federal firearms licensees (FFLs) to request background checks on individuals attempting to receive a firearm. Its permanent provisions, which went into effect on November 30, 1998, required the U.S. attorney general to establish the National Instant Criminal Background Check System (NICS) so that any FFL can be supplied immediate feedback on whether the receipt of a

firearm by a prospective transferee would violate Section 922 (g) or (n) of Title 18 of the United States Code or state law. The NICS Section, located at the FBI's Criminal Justice Information Services Division in Clarksburg, West Virginia, provides full service to FFLs in twenty-seven states and four U.S. territories. Upon completion of the required Bureau of Alcohol, Tobacco, Firearms and Explosives (ATF) Form 4473, FFLs contact the FBI's NICS Section, via a toll-free telephone number or electronically through the NICS E-Check System via the Internet, to request a background check with the descriptive information provided. The NICS is customarily available seventeen hours a day, seven days a week, including holidays (except for Christmas).

Fourteen states have agencies acting on behalf of the NICS in a full Point-of-Contact (POC) capacity. These POC states, which have agreed to implement and maintain their own Brady-type NICS Program, conduct firearm background checks for FFLs' transactions in their respective states by electronically accessing the NICS. Upon completion of the required ATF Form 4473, the FFLs conducting business in the POC states contact a designated state agency to initiate a NICS background check in lieu of contacting the FBI NICS Section.

Additionally, ten states are currently sharing responsibility with the NICS Section by acting as partial POCs. Partial-POC states have agencies designated to conduct checks for handguns and/or handgun permits, while the NICS Section handles the processing of the state's transactions for long gun purchases. For more information on the NICS, see Federal Bureau of Investigation (2005).

12. For example, see the *Gun Show Loophole Closing Act of 2003* (S 1807, proposed by Senators McCain, Reed, DeWine, and Lieberman). Organizations advocating strict gun control closely monitor these proposals, e.g., see the Brady Campaign (http://www.bradycampaign .org/legislation/federal/) and the Coalition to Stop Gun Violence (http://www.csgv.org/issues/gunshow/).

13. The exceptions—Georgia, Indiana, Maine, New Hampshire, North Dakota, South Dakota, Vermont, and Washington—had either had no restrictions or had "shall issue" provisions allowing the average citizen to obtain a concealed weapons license to carry a handgun on his or her person.

14. Alaska and Vermont allow the average citizen to carry a concealed weapon with no special permit required. The National Rifle Association (2005f) claims there are thirty-eight states, as they include Connecticut as a "may issue"-with-few-restrictions state. In fact, it is a "may issue" state where it is difficult for the average citizen to obtain a permit to carry a concealed handgun. The twelve states that

the NRA considers infringing upon Second Amendment rights by not readily allowing concealed weapons are California, Delaware, Hawaii, Illinois, Iowa, Maryland, Massachusetts, Minnesota, Nebraska, New Jersey, New York, and Rhode Island.

15. Thus the gun-focused community-policing strategy incorporates the *sentence enhancement* approach to controlling gun violence, whereby those using guns in the commission of crimes are given stiffer prison sentences (a longer sentence, usually with a reduced possibility of parole). Sentence enhancement laws usually only work well in the context of gun-focused community-policing programs. Blumstein (1995, 417) insightfully observes that the threat of longer prison sentences "is undoubtedly very effective at deterring white collar crimes that tend to be committed by middle class individuals, [but it is] probably less effective in deterring the crimes committed by underclass individuals, who are the primary occupants of prisons, and for whom the increment of pain associated with prison time may be far less severe than it would be for those ensconced in a comfortable job." For reviews of the complex literature on the effects of sentence-enhancement laws, see National Research Council (2005, Chapter 9) and Raphael and Ludwig (2003).

16. Chicago created a Gun Court in the early 1930s to handle the huge volume of gun-related crimes it experienced in that era.

17. This case was settled out of court on September 8, 2004, resulting in a $2.5 million award for the plaintiffs. The plaintiffs were the families of some of the sniper victims (Conrad Johnson, James L. "Sonny" Buchanan Jr., Hong Im Ballenger, Premkumar Walekar, Sarah Ramos, and Linda Franklin), as well as two victims who survived the shooting, Rupinder "Benny" Oberoi and thirteen-year-old Iran Brown.

18. "On November 23, 1998, the attorneys general and other representatives of forty-six states, Puerto Rico, the U.S. Virgin Islands, American Samoa, the Northern Mariana Islands, Guam, and the District of Columbia signed an agreement with the five largest tobacco manufacturers (Brown & Williamson Tobacco Corporation, Lorillard Tobacco Company, Philip Morris Incorporated, R. J. Reynolds Tobacco Company, Commonwealth Tobacco, and Liggett & Myers), ending a four-year legal battle between the states and the industry that began in 1994 when Mississippi became the first state to file suit. Four states (Florida, Minnesota, Mississippi and Texas) had previously settled with tobacco manufacturers for $40 billion. . . . The agreement settle[d] all antitrust, consumer protection, common law negligence, statutory, common law and equitable claims for monetary, restitutionary, equitable and injunctive relief alleged by any of the settling states with respect to the year of payment or earlier years and cannot be modified in any way unless all the parties

agree to the modification. Over the next [two decades], states will [continue] to receive over $206 billion from the settlement," with funds first made available in June of 2000 (excerpted from Wilson, 1999).

19. Note that when Congress created the Consumer Product Safety Commission in 1972, it specifically exempted domestically manufactured guns from any consumer safety standards (see Brady Campaign, 2000, 4).

20. According to the National Rifle Association (2005h), thirty-three states have immunization laws. However, the Brady Campaign (2005b) notes that only eleven states prohibit both city/county *and* individual lawsuits (Alaska, Arkansas, Colorado, Indiana, Kentucky, Louisiana, Michigan, New Hampshire, North Dakota, Ohio, and South Dakota), while eighteen allow individual lawsuits, even though they prohibit city and county suits (Alabama, Arizona, Florida, Georgia, Idaho, Kansas, Maine, Mississippi, Missouri, Montana, Nevada, North Carolina, Oklahoma, Pennsylvania, Tennessee, Texas, Utah, and Virginia). In 2002, California repealed its state law that had granted special lawsuit immunization to the gun industry; the twenty-one other states that do not grant special immunity are Connecticut, Delaware, Hawaii, Illinois, Iowa, Maryland, Massachusetts, Minnesota, Mississippi, Missouri, Nebraska, New Jersey, New Mexico, New York, Oregon, Rhode Island, South Carolina, Vermont, Washington, Wisconsin, and Wyoming.

References

American Firearms Industry Magazine. 2005. "Production: 1973–1995." http://www.amfire.com/american_firearms_043.htm. Accessed April 2, 2005.

Ayres, Ian, and John D. Donohue III. 2003. "Shooting Down the More Guns, Less Crime Hypothesis." *Stanford Law Review* 55 (April): 1193–1312.

Azrael, Deborah, Catherine Barber, David Hemenway, and Matthew Miller. 2003. "Data on Violent Injury." In *Evaluating Gun Policy: Effects on Crime and Violence,* ed. Jens Ludwig and Philip J. Cook, 412–430. Washington, DC: Brookings Institution Press.

Blumstein, Alfred. 1995b. "Prisons." In *Crime,* ed. James Q. Wilson and Joan Petersilia, 387–419. San Francisco: Institute of Contemporary Studies Press.

Bonney, Shaun R. 2000. "Using the Courts to Target Firearm Manufacturers." *Idaho Law Review* 378: 167–202.

Boston Strategy to Prevent Youth Violence. 2005. *The Boston Strategy to Prevent Youth Violence: The Programs*. http://www.bostonstrategy.com /programs.html. Accessed June 4, 2005.

Brady Campaign to Prevent Gun Violence. 2000. *The Enforcement Fable: How the NRA Prevented Enforcement of the Nation's Gun Laws*. Washington, DC: Brady Campaign to Prevent Gun Violence (originally published by the Center to Prevent Handgun Violence). March 21. http://www.brady-campaign.org/pdf/facts/reports/enforcement_fable.pdf. Accessed June 17, 2005.

———. 2005a. "Crimes with Guns Down Faster Than Violent Crimes Overall." http://www.bradycampaign.org/facts/research/?page= bradyred&menu=gvr. Accessed May 27, 2005.

———. 2005b. "Special Protection for the Gun Industry: State Bills." http://www.bradycampaign.org/facts/issues/?page=immun_state. Accessed May 27, 2005.

Brady Center to Prevent Gun Violence. 2004. On *Target: The Impact of the 1994 Federal Assault Weapons Act*. Washington, DC: Brady Center to Prevent Gun Violence. http://www.bradycampaign.org/xshare/200403 /on_target.pdf. Accessed June 1, 2005.

Braga, Anthony A., David M. Kennedy, Elin J. Waring, and Anne Morrison Piehl. 2001. "Problem-Oriented Policing, Deterrence, and Youth Violence: An Evaluation of Boston's Operation Ceasefire." *Journal of Research in Crime and Delinquency* 38 (3): 195–225.

Braga, Anthony A., and Glenn L. Pierce. 2004. "Linking Crime Guns: The Impact of Ballistics Imaging Technology on the Productivity of the Boston Police Department's Ballistics Unit." *Journal of Forensic Sciences* 49 (4): 1–6.

Buffalo News. 2005. *Gun by Gun*. June 12. http://buffalonews.com/ editorial/20050612/1018407.asp. Accessed June 13, 2005.

Bureau of Alcohol, Tobacco and Firearms. 1999. *Gun Shows: Brady Checks and Crime Traces*. http://www.atf.treas.gov/pub/treas_pub/gun_show .pdf. Accessed May 24, 2005.

———. 2000. *Federal Firearms Regulations Reference Guide*. http://www .atf.gov/pub/fire-explo_pub/2000_ref.pdf. Accessed March 22, 2005.

———. 2002. *Crime Gun Trace Reports (2000) National Report*. http:// www.atf.gov/firearms/ycgii/2000/index.htm. Accessed March 29, 2005.

———. 2005. *Annual Firearms Manufacturing and Export Report[s]*. 1998–2003 http://www.atf.gov/firearms/stats/index.htm. Accessed March 30, 2005.

Bureau of Justice Statistics. 2003b. *Background Checks for Firearms Transfers, 2002*. Washington, DC: U.S. Department of Justice. http:// www.ojp.usdoj.gov/bjs/pub/pdf/bcft02.pdf. Accessed May 23, 2005.

———. 2004. *State Court Sentencing of Convicted Felons, 2002: Statistical Tables.* Washington, DC: Office of Justice Programs, U.S. Department of Justice.

———. 2005. *Homicide Trends in the U.S.: Weapons Used, 1976–2002.* http://www.ojp.usdoj.gov/bjs/homicide/weapons.htm. Accessed March 31, 2005.

Butterfield, Fox. 2004. "Gun Dealer Settles Case over Sale to Straw Buyer." *New York Times,* June 23: A-14.

Caplan, David I. 2002. "Gun Registration." In *Guns in American Society: An Encyclopedia of History, Politics, Culture, and the Law,* Vol.1, ed. Gregg Lee Carter, 255–258. Santa Barbara, CA: ABC-CLIO.

Castaneda, Ruben, and David Snyder. 2005. "Ballistics Database Yields 1st Conviction." *Washington Post,* April 2: B01.

Center for Problem-Oriented Policing. 2005. *Responses to the Problem of Gun Violence among Serious Young Offenders.* http://www.popcenter.org /Problems/problem-gun_violence.htm.. Accessed June 2, 2005.

Cook, Philip J., and Jens Ludwig. 2003. "Pragmatic Gun Policy." In *Evaluating Gun Policy: Effects on Crime and Violence,* ed. Jens Ludwig and Philip J. Cook, 1–40. Washington, DC: Brookings Institution Press.

Cummings, Peter, David C. Grossman, Frederick P. Rivara, and Thomas K. Koepsell. 1997. "State Gun Safe Storage Laws and Child Mortality Due to Firearms." *Journal of the American Medical Association* 278: 1084–1086.

Denning, Brandon. 2002. "Firearms Litigation Clearing House." In *Guns in American Society: An Encyclopedia of History, Politics, Culture, and the Law,* Vol. 1, ed. Gregg Lee Carter, 209. Santa Barbara, CA: ABC-CLIO.

Dolins, Judith C., and Katherine K. Christoffel. 1994. "Reducing Violent Injuries: Priorities for Pediatrician Advocacy." *Pediatrics* 94: 638–651.

Donohue, John J. 2003. In *Evaluating Gun Policy: Effects on Crime and Violence,* ed. Jens Ludwig and Philip J. Cook, 287–324. Washington, DC: Brookings Institution Press.

Federal Bureau of Investigation. 2001. *Safe Street Violent Crime Initiative Report, Fiscal Year 2000.* Washington, DC: Federal Bureau of Investigation, U.S. Department of Justice.

———. 2004. *Uniform Crime Reports: Crime in the United States, 2003.* http://www.fbi.gov/ucr/03cius.htm. Accessed January 25, 2005.

———. 2005. *NICS Program Summary.* http://www.fbi.gov/hq/cjisd /nics.htm. Accessed May 22, 2005.

Firearms Litigation Clearing House. 2005. "Frequently Asked Questions about Firearms Litigation." http://www.csgv.org/issues/litigation /faq_litigation.cfm. Accessed June 14, 2005.

Franscell, Ron. 2002. "Gun 'Fingerprinting' Plan Raises Privacy Fears." *Denver Post*, October 29. Available online at: http://www.law-forensic .com/cfr_bullid_04.htm. Accessed May 2, 2005.

George, Jason. 2005. "Buyback Nets 897 Firearms in Jersey City." *New York Times*, February 10: B-5.

Gillespie, Mark. 1999. "New Gun Control Efforts Draw Mixed Support from Americans." July 13. Available online for Gallup poll subscribers at http://www.gallup.com/poll/. Accessed January 31, 2005.

Grossman, David C., et al. 2005. "Gun Storage Practices and Risk of Youth Suicide and Unintentional Firearm Injuries." *Journal of the American Medical Association* 293: 707–714.

Gun Owners Foundation. 2005. *Summary of District Gun Violence Reduction Strategies*. http://www.gunowners.com/AppendixA.htm. Accessed June 1, 2005.

Hardy, Marjorie S. 2002. "Teaching Firearm Safety to Children: Failure of a Program." *Journal of Developmental and Behavioral Pediatrics* 23: 71–76.

Hemenway, David. 2002. "Accidents, Gun." In *Guns in American Society: An Encyclopedia of History, Politics, Culture, and the Law*, Vol. 1, ed. Gregg Lee Carter, 2–3. Santa Barbara, CA: ABC-CLIO.

———. 2004. *Private Guns, Public Health*. Ann Arbor: University of Michigan Press.

Hemenway, David, S. J. Solnick, and Deborah Azrael. 1995. "Firearm Training and Storage." *Journal of the American Medical Association* 272: 46–50.

Hulse, Carl. 2004. "After Disputes, Congress Passes Spending Plan." *New York Times*, January 23: A1.

Izumi, Lance. 1999. "Gun Lawsuits: Misfired Public Policy." *Capital Ideas* 4 (18): 1–2. Available on line at: http://pacificresearch.org/pub/cap /1999/99-04-12.html. Accessed June 17, 2005.

Join Together. 2003a. "Brady Campaign: Good News from the States." Boston: Boston University School of Public Health: http://www .jointogether.org/gv/news/alerts/print/0,2060,566646,00.html. Accessed March 22, 2005.

———. 2003b. "NYC to Expand Gun Courts." Boston: Boston University School of Public Health. http://www.jointogether.org/z /0,2522,568257,00.html. Accessed April 20, 2005.

———. 2004a. "National Police Group Sets Guidelines for Home Gun Storage." Boston: Boston University School of Public Health: http://www.jointogether.org/z/0,2522,569767,00.html. Accessed March 21, 2005.

———. 2004b. "Gun Pipeline Extends from Mississippi Delta to Chicago." Boston: Boston University School of Public Health: http://www.jointogether.org/z/0,2522,568998,00.html. Accessed March 22, 2005.

———. 2004c. "Miss. Authorities, Gun Dealers Fight Illegal Gun Sales." Boston: Boston University School of Public Health: http://www.jointo gether.org/z/0,2522,574052,00.html. Accessed March 21, 2005.

———. 2004d. "S.C. Limit on Gun Purchases Lifted." Boston: Boston University School of Public Health: http://www.jointogether .org/z/0,2522,571094,00.html. Accessed March 21, 2005.

———. 2004e. "S.C. Lawmakers Vote to Repeal One-Gun-a-Month Law." Boston: Boston University School of Public Health: http://www .jointogether.org/z/0,2522,571044,00.html. Accessed March 21, 2005.

———. 2005. "Bullet-Coding Measure Gaining Support in California." Boston: Boston University School of Public Health: http://www .jointogether.org/z/0,2522,576844,00.html. Accessed May 2, 2005.

Kopel, David. 2002. "Product Liability Lawsuits." In *Guns in American Society: An Encyclopedia of History, Politics, Culture, and the Law,* Vol. 2, ed. Gregg Lee Carter, 482–485. Santa Barbara, CA: ABC-CLIO.

Koper, Christopher S. 2004. *Updated Assessment of the Federal Assault Weapons Ban: Impacts on Gun Markets and Gun Violence, 1994–2003.* Philadelphia: Jerry Lee Center of Criminology, University of Pennsylvania.

Legal Action Project. 2003. *Smoking Guns: Exposing the Gun Industry's Complicity in the Illegal Gun Market.* Washington, DC: Brady Center to Prevent Gun Violence. http://www.bradycenter.org/xshare/pdf/reports/smokingguns.pdf. Accessed June 19, 2005.

———. 2005a. "Conrad Johnson, et al. v. Bull's Eye Shooter Supply, et al., No. 03-2-03932-8, Superior Court of the State of Washington, Pierce County." http://www.gunlawsuits.org/docket/casestatus.php ?RecordNo=79. Accessed June 15, 2005.

———. 2005b. "The Legal Action Project: Representing Gun Violence Victims and the Public Interest in the Courts." http://www.gunlawsuits .org/. Accessed June 15, 2005.

Lichtblau, Eric. 2004. "Key Antigun Program Loses Direct Financing." *New York Times,* December 2: 32.

Longley, Robert. 2001. "Fake IDs Foil Brady Check—GAO." http:// usgovinfo.about.com/library/weekly/aa032801a.htm. Accessed May 28, 2005.

Lott, John R., Jr., and John E. Whitley. 2002. "Safe Storage Gun Laws: Accidental Deaths, Suicides, and Crime." *Journal of Law and Economics* 44: 659–689.

Maguire, Kathleen, and Ann L. Pastore, eds. 2004. *Sourcebook of Criminal Justice Statistics 2002.* Washington, DC: U.S. Department of Justice.

Maryland State Police. 2004. *MD-IBIS Progress Report #2: Integrated Ballistics Identification System.* Pikesville, MD: Forensic Sciences Division, Maryland State Police.

Merrill, Vincent. C. 2002. *Gun-in-Home as a Risk Factor in Firearm-Related Mortality: A Historical Prospective Cohort Study of United States Deaths, 1993.* Ph.D. dissertation, Department of Environmental Health Science and Policy, University of California, Irvine.

Milkovits, Amanda. 2005. "Two Arrested in Teen's Killing." *Providence Journal,* June 30: A1–A2.

National Center for State Courts. 2005. *Gun Violence: State Links.* http:// www.ncsconline.org/WC/Publications/KIS_SpeProGunStatesPub.pdf. Accessed June 2, 2005.

National Research Council. 2005. *Firearms and Violence: A Critical Review.* Committee to Improve Research Information and Data on Firearms. Charles F. Wellford, John V. Pepper, and Carol V. Petrie, editors. Committee on Law and Justice, Division of Behavioral and Social Sciences and Education. Washington, DC: The National Academies Press.

National Rifle Association. 2005a. *Good Riddance to the Clinton Gun Ban.* Fairfax, VA: NRA Institute for Legislative Action. http://www .nraila.org/Issues/FactSheets/Read.aspx?ID=158. Accessed May 1, 2005.

———. 2005b. *Ballistic Fingerprinting Not Effective.* Fairfax, VA: NRA Institute for Legislative Action. http://www.nraila.org/CurrentLegislation /Read.aspx?ID=1128. Accessed May 2, 2005.

———. 2005c. *Licensing and Registration.* Fairfax, VA: NRA Institute for Legislative Action. http://www.nraila.org/Issues/FactSheets/Read .aspx?ID=28. Accessed May 12, 2005.

———. 2005d. *Firearm Safety in America 2005.* Fairfax, VA: NRA Institute for Legislative Action. http://www.nraila.org/Issues/FactSheets/Read .aspx?ID=120. Accessed May 15, 2005.

———. 2005e. *Gun Shows: An American Tradition 2005.* Fairfax, VA: NRA Institute for Legislative Action. http://www.nraila.org/Issues/ FactSheets/Read.aspx?ID=157. Accessed May 25, 2005.

———. 2005f. *Right-to-Carry 2005.* Fairfax, VA: NRA Institute for Legislative Action. http://www.nraila.org/Issues/FactSheets/Read .aspx? ID=18. Accessed May 26, 2005.

———. 2005g. *The False Hope of Gun Turn-In Programs.* Fairfax, VA: NRA Institute for Legislative Action. http://www.nraila.org/Issues/ FactSheets/Read.aspx?ID=29. Accessed May 26, 2005.

————. 2005h. Courts Reject Lawsuits against Gun Makers. Fairfax, VA: NRA Institute for Legislative Action. http://www.nraila.org /Issues/FactSheets/Read.aspx?ID=37. Accessed June 16, 2005.

New York Times. 2004. "'Smart Gun' Research Advances." January 11: 14NJ (Late Edition, East Coast).

Newport, Frank. 1999. "Americans Support Wide Variety of Gun Control Measures." June 16. Available online for Gallup poll subscribers at http://www.gallup.com/poll/. Accessed January 28, 2005.

Pierce, Glenn L., Anthony A. Braga, Raymond Hyatt Jr. and Christopher S. Koper. 2004. "Characteristics and Dynamics of Illegal Firearms Markets: Implications for a Supply-Side Enforcement Strategy." *Justice Quarterly* 21 (2): 391–422.

Pina, Tatina. 2004. "Toy Guns Target of 'Bashing' Event's Anti-Violence Message." *Providence Journal* (Blackstone Valley Edition), August 20: C-1.

Potter, Tim. 2005. "Gunmaker Settles Suit with Former Wichita Family." *Wichita Eagle,* April 28: A-1.

Project Safe Neighborhoods. 2005a. "If you use a gun illegally, you will do hard time (George W. Bush)." http://www.projectsafeneighborhoods .gov/ Accessed June 1, 2005.

————. 2005b. *About Project Safe Neighborhoods: A National Network to Reduce Gun Crime.* http://www.projectsafeneighborhoods.gov/about.asp. Accessed June 1, 2005.

Raphael, Steven, and Jens Ludwig. 2003. "Prison Enhancements: The Case of Project Exile." In *Evaluating Gun Policy: Effects on Crime and Violence,* ed. Jens Ludwig and Philip J. Cook, 251–286. Washington, DC: Brookings Institution Press.

Reedy, Darin C., and Christopher S. Koper. 2003. "Impact of Handgun Types on Gun Assault Outcomes: A Comparison of Gun Assaults Involving Semiautomatic Pistols and Revolvers." *Injury Prevention* 9: 151–155.

Roth, Jeffrey A., and Christopher S. Koper. 1999. *Impacts of the 1994 Assault Weapons Ban: 1994–96.* Washington, DC: National Institute of Justice, U.S. Department of Justice. NCJ 173405 (March). http://www .ncjrs.org/pdffiles1/173405.pdf. Accessed June 1, 2005.

Scalia, John. 2000. *Federal Firearm Offenders, 1992–1998.* Washington, DC: U.S. Department of Justice. NCJ 180795 (June).

Sheppard, David, and Patricia Kelly. 2002. *Juvenile Gun Courts: Promoting Accountability and Providing Treatment.* Washington, DC: Office of Juvenile Justice and Delinquency Prevention, Office of Justice Programs, U.S. Department of Justice. http://www.ncjrs.org/html/ojjdp /jaibg_2002_5_1/contents.html. Accessed June 4, 2005.

Smothers, Ronald. 2004. "New Jersey Tells of Progress in Developing a 'Smart Gun'." *New York Times*, January 7: B5.

Southwick, Lawrence, Jr. 2002a. "Saturday Night Specials." In *Guns in American Society: An Encyclopedia of History, Politics, Culture, and the Law*, Vol. 2, ed. Gregg Lee Carter, 516–519. Santa Barbara, CA: ABC-CLIO.

———. 2002b. "Enforcement of Gun Control Laws." In *Guns in American Society: An Encyclopedia of History, Politics, Culture, and the Law*, Vol. 1, ed. Gregg Lee Carter, 186–190. Santa Barbara, CA: ABC-CLIO.

Spitzer, Robert J. 2002a. "Assault Weapons." In *Guns in American Society: An Encyclopedia of History, Politics, Culture, and the Law*, Vol. 1, ed. Gregg Lee Carter, 34–35. Santa Barbara, CA: ABC-CLIO.

———. 2002b. "Licensing." In *Guns in American Society: An Encyclopedia of History, Politics, Culture, and the Law*, Vol. 1, ed. Gregg Lee Carter, 360–361. Santa Barbara, CA: ABC-CLIO.

Stolberg, Sheryl Gay. 2004. "Senate Vote to Require Safety Locks on Guns." *New York Times*, February 27: A18.

Sweeney, James P. 2005. "Senate OK likely for bullet coding, tracking system." April 27. San Diego *Union-Tribune*. http://www.signonsandiego.com/news/state/20050427-9999-1n27bullet.html. Accessed May 2, 2005.

Turner, Kimberly. 2004. "Evans among Officials Announcing Philadelphia Gun Court." Harrisburg, PA: House of Representatives (News Release). http://www.pahouse.com/pr/Evans/203010504.htm. Last Accessed June 17, 2005.

United Nations. 1999. *United Nations International Study on Firearm Regulation*. Vienna, Austria: Crime Prevention and Criminal Justice Division, United Nations Office.

U.S. Department of Justice. 2000. *Promising Strategies to Reduce Gun Violence*. Washington, DC: U.S. Department of Justice, NCJ 173950. Also available at: http://ojjdp.ncjrs.org/pubs/gun_violence/contents.html. Accessed June 11, 2005.

U.S. General Accounting Office. 1991. *Accidental Shootings: Many Deaths and Injuries Caused by Firearms Could Be Prevented*. Washington, DC: U.S. General Accounting Office.

Vernick, Jon S., Z. F. Meisel, and Stephen P. Teret, et al. 1999. "'I didn't know the gun was loaded': An Examination of Two Safety Devices That Can Reduce the Risk of Unintentional Firearm Injuries." *Journal of Public Health Policy* 20 (4): 427–440.

Violence Policy Center. 2004. *United States of Assault Weapons: Gunmakers Evading the Federal Assault Weapons Ban*. Washington, DC: Violence Policy Center. http://www.vpc.org/studies/USofAW.htm. Accessed June 2, 2005.

————. 2005. *The Endgame: Any Settlement of Firearms Litigation Must Address Three Specific Areas of Gun Industry Conduct and Include a Strict Enforcement Mechanism.* Washington, DC: Violence Policy Center. http://www.vpc.org/studies/endprod.htm. Accessed June 16. 2005.

Virginia Exile. 2005. "Law Enforcement Services, Virginia Exile. Department of Criminal Justice Services, Commonwealth of Virginia. http://www.dcjs.virginia.gov/exile/index.cfm. Accessed June 3, 2005.

Webster, Daniel W. 2002a. "Child Access Prevention (CAP) Laws." In *Guns in American Society: An Encyclopedia of History, Politics, Culture, and the Law,* Vol. 1, Gregg Lee Carter, 110–111. Santa Barbara, CA: ABC-CLIO.

————. 2002b. *Comprehensive Ballistic Fingerprinting of New Guns: A Tool for Solving and Preventing Violent Crime.* Baltimore, MD: Center for Gun Policy and Research, Bloomberg School of Public Health, Johns Hopkins University.

Webster, Daniel W., Jon S. Vernick, and L. M. Hepburn. 2001. "Relationship between Licensing, Registration, and Other Gun Sales Laws and the Source State of Crime Guns." *Injury Prevention* 7: 184–189.

————. 2002. "Effects of Maryland's Law Banning Saturday Night Special Handguns on Homicides." *American Journal of Epidemiology* 155 (5): 406–412.

Webster, Daniel W., Jon S. Vernick, April M. Zeoli, and Jennifer A. Manganello. 2004. "Association between Youth-Focused Firearm Laws and Youth Suicides." *Journal of the American Medical Association* 292 (5): 594–601.

Weil, Douglas S., and Rebecca C. Knox. 1996. "Effects of Limiting Handgun Purchase on Interstate Transfer of Firearms." *Journal of the American Medical Association* 275 (22): 1759–1761.

Weyrich, Noel. 2000. "The Orphaned Gun Fix." Philadelphia: *Philadelphia City Paper.* July 13, http://citypaper.net/articles/071300/cb.citybeat .gun.shtml. Accessed June 1, 2005.

Wilson, Joy Johnson. 1999. *Summary of the Attorneys General Master Tobacco Settlement Agreement.* http://academic.udayton.edu/health/ syllabi/tobacco/summary.htm. Accessed June 15, 2005.

Winship, Christopher. 2002. *End of a Miracle? Crime, Faith, and Partnership in Boston in the 1990's.* (March). Cambridge, MA: Department of Sociology, Harvard University. http://www.wjh.harvard.edu/soc/faculty /winship/End_of_a_Miracle.pdf. Accessed June 15, 2005.

Wintemute, Garen J. 1994. *Ring of Fire: The Handgun Makers of Southern California.* Sacramento, CA: The Violence Prevention Research Program.

————. 2002. "Where the Guns Come From: The Gun Industry and Gun Commerce." *Children, Youth, and Gun Violence* 12 (2): 55–71.

Wintemute, Garen J., Stephen P. Teret, and J. F. Kraus. 1987. "When Children Shoot Children: Eighty-Eight Unintended Deaths in California." *Journal of the American Medical Association* 257 (22): 3107–3109.

Zimring, Franklin E. 2003. "Continuity and Change in the American Gun Debate."In *Evaluating Gun Policy: Effects on Crime and Violence,* eds. Jens Ludwig and Philip J. Cook, 441–454. Washington, DC: Brookings Institution Press.

3

Chronology

Each side in the contemporary debate over gun control uses history selectively, emphasizing events supporting its views and ignoring or discounting those that do not. In contrast, this chapter presents the broad range of watershed events that have shaped the debate, some of which support the "gun rights" side, and others of which support the "gun control" side.

600–700   The Anglo-Saxon tradition of requiring all free men (non-serfs) to keep and bear arms begins and continues unabated for 500 years. All landowners are required to keep armor and weapons; and there is a yearly review of arms.

1181   England's King Henry II authors the *Assize of Arms*, requiring all free men (most of whom are landowners) to own weapons. While continental European society is split between an armed nobility and a disarmed peasantry, in England free men are required to possess arms and to bear them in the defense of the community.

1215   England's King John is forced to sign the *Magna Carta* (the "Great Charter of Liberties") guaranteeing the right of free men to revolt against a government that does not follow the laws of the land. As part of this right, free men can petition the government to redress

1215 (cont.)   their grievances and to bear arms against it if their petitions are ignored. To ensure that government will respect this right, free men are expected to possess their own weapons (the number and quality commensurate with their rank and wealth). The framers of the U.S. Constitution are greatly influenced by the *Magna Carta,* as partly reflected in the First (the right " . . . to petition the Government for a redress of grievances") and Second (". . . the right of the people to keep and bear Arms, shall not be infringed") Amendments.

1285   England's King Edward I issues the Statue of Winchester, acknowledging that the English military is equivalent to its self-armed citizenry. The military is to repeal foreign invaders, assist local officials in apprehending lawbreakers, and resist internal tyranny.

1639–1689   To maintain his status as absolute monarch beholding to no one, least of all the members of the English Parliament, King Charles I carries out a succession of arms seizures from his parliamentary enemies. To ensure that firearms do not fall into the hands of his foes, Charles orders his gunsmiths to produce records of all weapons they manufacture, along with a list of their purchasers. They are also ordered to report weekly to the ordinance office the number of guns made and sold that week. Individuals wanting to travel with a gun must obtain a license, and the importation of firearms is banned.

In retaliation, Parliament enacts a series of statutes that allows the legislative body to confiscate arms from the citizenry and to deny the right of weapons possession to those thought loyal to Charles, including "Papists, and other persons who are voted to be Delinquents by both or either of the Houses of Parliament . . . or that have been present with or aiding His Majesty . . . or such Clergymen and others that have publicly preached or declared themselves to oppose, disgrace or revile the proceedings of both or either Houses of Parliament." Parliament orders that the "Arms, Ammunition, and Horses fit for Service in the War" be seized from such individuals (Ordinance of 9 January 1642).

Parliament eventually prohibits all but the landed elite from owning firearms. In the Hunting Act of 1671, all persons not owning lands that produced at least 100 pounds in annual rental (which relatively few estates did) are barred from possessing firearms; moreover, those qualifying to own arms are given the power to search the premises of their tenants and to seize any firearms that might be found.

During his brief reign, King James II, the successor of Charles I, continues the practice of disarming citizens thought disloyal to the monarchy. The war between the Crown and Parliament ends with the Glorious Revolution in 1688 and the ascension of William and Mary to the throne. James II is not dead, but living in exile in France, which means that William and Mary must seek legitimacy from Parliament. After much debate, Parliament eventually rules that James's living in exile is tantamount to his voluntarily giving up the throne; thus, the monarchy of William and Mary is deemed rightful. The cost for receiving legitimacy is high, however, and William and Mary are forced to abide by Parliament's "Declaration of Rights." The forerunner of the U.S. Constitution's Bill of Rights, this declaration outlines the basic rights of Englishmen, among which is a clear restoration of the individual's right to keep and bear arms.

1690–1776 The restored Anglo-Saxon tradition of all free men having the right, and even the duty, to keep and bear arms is transferred to Colonial America, where all the colonies individually pass militia laws requiring universal gun ownership. Hunting is essential to many families, and in light of immediate threats from the French, Dutch, Spanish, and Native Americans, it is not surprising that colonial militia statutes require that all able-bodied males be armed and trained. Intellectually, the colonial elite imbibe the writings of Whig political philosophers, who emphasize decentralized government, fear of a standing army, and the right of the common people to keep and bear arms in defense of themselves—against criminals, foreign powers, and especially the state itself.

1776–1783 Critical in setting the stage for the Revolutionary War is the British attempt to take away the firearms of Massachusetts colonialists. The first battle at Lexington in April 1776 is touched off when British soldiers set out to disarm a group of local militiamen.

Colonialists bent on independence fear that the British will soon try to disarm not only the residents of Massachusetts, but also residents of the other twelve colonies. Indeed, their fears receive confirmation when Britain's Colonial Undersecretary William Knox circulates to Crown officials the tract "What Is Fit to be Done with America?," which, among other things, advises that "The Militia Laws should be repealed and none suffered to be re-enacted, & the Arms of all the People should be taken away, . . . nor should any Foundery or manufactuary of Arms, Gunpowder, or Warlike Stores, be ever suffered in America, nor should any Gunpowder, Lead, Arms or Ordnance be imported into it without License" (as quoted in Peckman, 1978, 176).

As the Revolutionary War gets under way, the individual states adopt constitutions and declarations of rights that are partly shaped by perceived and actual British attempts to disarm Americans. Four states (Pennsylvania, North Carolina, Vermont, and Massachusetts) include the right to bear arms in their formal declarations of rights.

1787–1791 The right to bear arms is a core issue during the U.S. Constitutional Convention's deliberations in 1787. States' rights advocates emphasize that citizens in new republics should fear standing armies at all costs. These advocates are quick to invoke the historical record of 1767–1776 in Massachusetts, where the British army's presence inflamed and abused the local population—and where that standing army tried to weaken the people by disarming them. States' rights advocates are also quick to point to the dismal records of Charles I, Oliver Cromwell, and James II, who used their militaries to disarm and tyrannize much of the English populace between 1639 and 1688. States' rights advocates—also known as "Antifederalists"—

make up the majority of delegates, but their zeal is tempered by the ineffective governance existing under the Articles of Confederation (1778–1789), which have kept the federal government weak and the governments of the states strong.

Federalists are also fearful of standing armies, but see the survival of the United States depending on a strong national government—a government that, among many other things, has its own army and navy. The great compromise between proponents and opponents of federalism is reflected in Article I, Section 8 of the Constitution and the Second Amendment of the Bill of Rights. In Article I, Section 8, Congress is granted the power to raise and support an army (8.12); provide and maintain a navy (8.13); call forth the militia to execute the laws of the Union, suppress insurrections, and repel invasions (8.15); provide for organizing, arming, and disciplining the militia, and for governing such part of them as may be employed in the Service of the United States (8.16).

Concessions to satisfy the Antifederalists include the right of the states to appoint officers to the militia and to train militiamen (according to standards set by Congress). State militias are seen as counteracting forces to the potential might of a standing federal army. Fears of a standing army are further assuaged by giving the civilian Congress control over the military's purse strings and by requiring that the secretary of war (defense) be a civilian.

Nagging doubts over the power of the states to maintain and control militias are addressed in the First Congress and eventually alleviated with the passage of the Second Amendment. States' rights advocates want certainty that federal power will not be used to annul state sovereignty.

1792   The First Congress passes the Militia Act of 1792. The act demands all able-bodied (free) men between the ages eighteen and forty-five to own a firearm and ammunition and to be willing to put their weapons to use when called upon by the federal government. Each man is required to: "provide himself with a

1792
(cont.)

good musket or firelock, a sufficient bayonet and belt, two spare flints, and a knapsack, a pouch with a box therein to contain not less than twenty-four cartridges, suited to the bore of his musket or firelock, each cartridge to contain a proper quantity of powder and ball: or with a good rifle, knapsack, shot-pouch and powder-horn, twenty balls suited to the bore of his rifle, and a quarter of a pound of powder, and shall appear, so armed, accoutred and provided, when called out to exercise, or into service, except, that when called out on company days to exercise only, he may appear without a knapsack" (Militia Act, Ch. 33, 1 Stat. 271–274, 1792).

The deliberations of the First Congress on the Militia Act reveal no instance of any representative questioning whether individual citizens had the right to possess a firearm. On the contrary, the representatives agonize over how well citizens should be armed—fearing that the average citizen cannot bear too much cost. One congressman asserts that "as far as the whole body of the people are necessary to the general defence, they ought to be armed; but the law ought not to require more than is necessary; for that would be a just cause of complaint" (as quoted in Shalhope, 1982). In response, other legislators argue that those Americans who do not possess arms should have them supplied by the states. Such discussions clearly indicate that the problem perceived by the representatives is how to get arms into the hands of the people, not how to restrict their possession.

1800–1900 Even though stories of frontier violence are popular, the level of violence—especially gun violence—in non-frontier America is but a fraction of that actually occurring on the frontier, which itself is considerably less than that depicted in the Wild West shows and dime novels of the era. As soon as a frontier area is secured and towns established, violence quickly recedes—especially personal violence—and so do gun ownership and gun carrying. In established metropolitan areas violence tends to be at the *group* level, coming in periodic waves in the form of riots and pogroms. Such frays pit older immigrant groups against more recent arrivals: Protestants against Catholics, Yankees against Irishmen, blacks and their white abolitionist friends against Irishmen and other whites, Chinese against whites, Mexicans against "Anglos." The issues are usually economic and involve disputes over jobs, turf, and the public largess. Even though some killing occurs, most egregiously during the New York City draft riots, where Irish immigrants ran amuck and murdered dozens of African-Americans, the fighting in New York and elsewhere rarely involves guns and is often limited to fisticuffs. When fists are not the order of the day, bats, rocks, swords, and fire are the most common weapons, because few industrial workers can afford to buy a gun. In response to the group violence, cities start organizing police forces in the 1840s. By the middle of the 1870s, all major cities have professional police forces, and by the century's end so do most smaller communities. In the last quarter of the nineteenth century, urban police forces are buttressed by state National Guard units, which are formed to help combat the labor violence that is becoming common in Northern and Midwestern cities.

Frontier peoples' readiness to cooperate for their mutual protection belies the myth of frontier individualism and of the lone pioneer—as extolled in dime novels—conquering the West with rifle and six-shooter. The gun violence associated with famous range wars (as in Johnson County, Wyoming, in 1891), gunfighters (like Billy the Kid, Bat Masterson, Wild Bill Hickok), cattle towns (such as Dodge City and Abilene, Kansas), mining towns (à la Deadwood, South Dakota; Tombstone, Arizona; Virginia City, Nevada), and stagecoach robberies (as of the Butterfield line and of Wells Fargo) are, for the most part, the vivid creations of pulp fiction writers.

As frontier settlements become "civilized," local officials are quick to put controls on guns. Thousand of local, county, and state gun-control laws are passed to protect the public and maintain law and order. A typical gun law is the Indiana statute that "every person,

1800–1900   not being a traveller, who shall wear or carry any dirk,
(cont.)   pistol, sword in a sword-cane, or other dangerous
            weapon concealed, shall upon conviction thereof, be
            fined in any sum not exceeding one hundred dollars"
            (*Laws of Indiana, 1831*, as quoted in Cramer, 1994, 72).
            Prohibitions against concealed weapons are increas-
            ingly common by the mid-1800s, as are laws against
            the discharging of a weapon within city limits. By the
            late 1800s, most communities have laws dictating that
            firearms cannot be carried publicly unless a person is
            hunting, taking the weapon for repair, or going to or
            from a military muster.
                With few exceptions, challenges of such laws in the
            courts fail. Many of the legal arguments are based on
            Second Amendment rights, either as detailed in the
            Bill of Rights or as reformulated in various state con-
            stitutions. However, the courts routinely rule along
            the lines of an 1840 judgment by the Alabama
            Supreme Court: "A Statute, which, under pretence of
            regulating the manner of bearing arms, amounts to a
            destruction of the right, or which requires arms to be
            so borne as to render them wholly useless for the pur-
            pose of defence, would be clearly unconstitutional.
            But a law which is intended merely to promote per-
            sonal security, and to put down lawless aggression
            and violence, and to that end inhibits the wearing of
            certain weapons in such a manner as is calculated to
            exert an unhappy influence upon the moral feelings of
            the wearer, by making him less regardfull of the per-
            sonal security of others, does not come in collision
            with the constitution" (as quoted in Kennett and An-
            derson, 1975, 161).

1865–1866   In the post–Civil War South, *Black Codes* are enacted in
            Alabama, Arkansas, Florida, Georgia, Louisiana, Mis-
            sissippi, North Carolina, South Carolina, Tennessee,
            and Texas. These statutes deprive African-Americans
            of many basic rights, including the right to own
            firearms. For example, a Mississippi law dictates that
            "no freedman, free Negro, or mulatto not in the mili-
            tary service of the United States government, and not
            licensed so to do by the board of police of his or her

county, shall keep or carry firearms of any kind, or ammunition, dirk, or Bowie knife" (as quoted in Cramer, 1994, 72). Such laws contribute to keeping African-Americans servile and degrade their ability to defend themselves.

1871–1977 The National Rifle Association (NRA) is founded in 1871. In its early years, it is a small shooting association sponsoring rifle matches and sharpshooter classes. It is a favorite child of the Department of the Army, many of whose leaders view the NRA as helping to keep the general population "militia ready." As part of this task, the NRA is commissioned to train members of the New York National Guard to shoot well. However, its state funding is cut off in 1879, and the organization falls into disarray.

The NRA is revived in 1903, when Congress creates the National Board for the Promotion of Rifle Practice (NBPRP) to promote civilian rifle practice (another attempt by the military to ensure that civilians are militia ready). An appendage of the War Department, the civilian-run NBPRP has several trustees of the NRA on its executive board. This is a critical turning point for the organization, because these trustees work with Congress to achieve passage of Public Law 149, authorizing the sale of surplus military weapons, at cost, to rifle clubs meeting NBPRP standards. One of these standards is that the club must be sponsored by the NRA.

In 1910, Congress authorizes the giving away of surplus weaponry to NRA-sponsored clubs, and in 1912, Congress begins funding NRA shooting matches. The association benefits greatly, and membership climbs from several hundred to several thousand by 1917. The end of World War I greatly increases the number of surplus weapons made available to the NRA, and membership rises steadily as prospective members are motivated by the allure of a free new rifle and a place to shoot it. By the mid-1930s, the first period in which the NRA actively involves itself in anti-gun control activity, the organization has grown to 35,000 members.

1871–1977   Compared with the organization it will become in the
(cont.)   1980s, the NRA of the 1930s is moderate and re-
strained in its attempts to influence public policy. In
response to the proposed National Firearms Act of
1934, the NRA develops its first clear philosophy on
gun control. Although recognizing the bill's virtuous
aim of fighting gangsterism, the NRA deems it a potential threat to firearms owners and decides to fight
those portions of it that are not directly aimed at gangsters—namely, the sections dealing with a system of
national gun registration. This philosophy is refined
over the years until the late 1970s, when it is solidified
to its present status, which is that virtually all gun
control regulations should be resisted.

The decision to oppose the gun-registration portion
of the 1934 bill is accompanied by the development of
a set of tactics that remains with the NRA to the present day. It circulates editorials, press releases, and
open letters throughout the sporting and gun-owning
communities. It urges its members and potential sym-
pathizers to telegram or write congressional representatives. The NRA is rewarded with a huge influx of
anti-registration mail, resulting in the eventual dele-
tion of the reference to "all weaponry" and the substi-
tution of "machine guns and sawed-off shotguns" in
the final version of the National Firearms Act of 1934.
The NRA's growing involvement in public policy results in an invitation to work with the Justice Department and Congress in developing the Federal
Firearms Act of 1938. As with the earlier legislation,
the NRA accepts minimal regulation but makes sure
strong restrictions, such as a system of national licensing, are kept out of the law.

Although the NRA is not especially large or well
funded in the 1930s, it finds its interests more or less
readily accepted because there is no gun control
movement and no organization dedicated to gun control (like the modern-day Brady Campaign to Prevent
Gun Violence).

After World War II, nine million demobilized veterans re-enter civilian life with a new interest in
firearms. Tens of thousands of ex-GIs join the NRA,

giving it a much greater potential to wield power over public policy. However, the vast majority of these new members have little interest in gun control issues per se and great interest in recreational shooting. The NRA's programs and publications begin to reflect this transformation in membership. The NRA changes from an organization motivated by the nation's need for military preparedness to one reflecting the interests of hunters, target shooters, and other recreational gun enthusiasts. Today, the NRA's headquarters has affixed above its front doors "The Right of the People to Keep and Bear Arms, Shall Not Be Infringed" (the last half of the Second Amendment). But in 1958, the NRA's main entrance was emblazoned with the words "Firearms Safety Education, Marksmanship Training, Shooting for Recreation."

Well into the 1970s, the NRA continues on a moderate course. For example, the NRA of the late 1960s and early 1970s endorses the banning of Saturday night specials (cheaply made handguns). In 1968, the NRA editorializes: "Shoddily manufactured by a few foreign makers, hundreds of thousands of these have been peddled in recent years by a handful of U.S. dealers. Prices as low as $8 or $10 have placed concealable handguns within reach of multitudes who never before could afford them. Most figure in 'crimes of passion' or amateurish holdups, which form the bulk of the increase in violence. The Administration . . . possesses sufficient authority to bar by Executive direction these miserably-made, potentially defective arms that contribute so much to rising violence" (National Rifle Association, 1968a, 16).

The NRA reaffirms its stance against Saturday night specials by observing that it does "not necessarily approve of everything that goes 'Bang!'" (National Rifle Association, 1968b, 16). In what sounds astounding by the position of the NRA today ("there is no such thing as a good gun control law"), Executive Vice President Franklin L. Orth testifies before Congress that "the National Rifle Association concurs in principle with the desirability of removing from the market crudely made and unsafe handguns . . . [because] they have no

1871–1977   sporting purpose, [and] they are frequently poorly
(cont.)   made. . . . On the Saturday night special, we are for
            [banning] it 100 percent. We would like to get rid of
            these guns" (as quoted in Sugarmann, 1992, 42). As for
            the place of the Second Amendment in debate over
            gun control, the official *NRA Fact Book on Firearms
            Control* in the 1970s notes that the amendment is of
            "limited practical utility" in arguing against gun con-
            trol (as quoted in Sugarmann, 1992, 48).
               The voices of moderation within the NRA are si-
            lenced in 1977, when a palace coup by Second
            Amendment hardliners ousts those leaders seeing the
            NRA as primarily a hunting and sport-shooting asso-
            ciation (see "Revolt at Cincinnati" below).

1876   In *U.S. v. Cruikshank,* the U.S. Supreme Court renders
            its first major decision on the Second Amendment.
            The Court rules that the amendment offers no ab-
            solute right to the individual. Louisiana state officials,
            many of whom belonged to the Ku Klux Klan, are
            challenged for conspiring to disarm a meeting of
            African-Americans. Attorneys for the African-Ameri-
            cans argue that the Second Amendment is meant to
            protect the right of all citizens to keep and bear arms.
            However, the Supreme Court maintains that the offi-
            cials have the legal prerogative to disarm the African-
            Americans in protection of the common weal. More
            particularly, the Court holds that "bearing arms for a
            lawful purpose . . . is not a right granted by the Con-
            stitution." The Court rules that the Second Amend-
            ment is not "incorporated," meaning that it only ap-
            plies to the federal government, not to state
            governments. The states do not have to honor it, al-
            though they cannot prevent citizens belonging to the
            militia from possessing their own firearms—as long as
            the firearms are appropriate for use in the militia.
               Despite this decision supporting their contention
            that the Second Amendment should pose no barrier to
            the enactment of strict gun-control laws, at least at the
            state level, many advocates of the gun control move-
            ment are not particularly eager to tout *U.S. v. Cruik-
            shank.* The racist ruling justified keeping former slaves

unarmed and in a position of vassalage in the South, thereby partly counteracting the effect of the Emancipation Proclamation. This fact is not lost on many African-American and Jewish jurists, or on interest groups opposing gun regulation such as the National Rifle Association. Even though African-Americans and Jews generally tend to support strict gun control, some contend that regulations on gun possession are a means for suppressing a society's minorities and for allowing unjust rulers to hold sway because they control most weaponry.

1886   The U.S. Supreme Court addresses the Second Amendment for a second time in *Presser v. Illinois.* Herman Presser, the leader of a German-American labor group called the *Lehr und Wehr Verein* (the "Learning and Defense Club"), is arrested for parading the group through downtown Chicago while carrying a sword. He is accused of conducting an "armed military drill," which can legally be done only with a license, under Illinois statutes in force at the time. Presser appeals, invoking the Second Amendment in his defense. The Supreme Court rules against him, citing the *U.S. v. Cruikshank* decision discussed earlier. Again, the Court contends that the Second Amendment has not been "incorporated" and thus cannot be foisted upon the individual states. And as was the case with *Cruikshank,* the Supreme Court's decision smacks of bigotry—in this instance, through the repression of exploited immigrant laborers trying to improve their collective lot via unionization.

1903–1990 Congress passes the Militia Act of 1903, also known as the Dick Act (named after the Ohio Congressman who sponsors the legislation, Rep. Charles Dick, himself a National Guard officer). The act separates the organized militia, to be known as the "National Guard" of the state, from the "Reserve Militia" (which, in actuality, has not existed for decades). It mandates that the U.S. government arm, train, and drill the guards.

In 1916, Congress passes the National Defense Act, increasing federal support for the guards, and also

1903–1990 further subsumes them under national military rules,
(cont.) organization, and authority. They operate under a dual enlistment system, whereby a guard member is simultaneously part of the relevant *state* guard and the *National* Guard.

Federal authority over the state guards is recognized by the Supreme Court in 1990 in *Perpich v. Department of Defense,* where it rules that state governors have control over their state guards for state purposes, but that the governors cannot prevent the U.S. government from using the state guards as it sees fit. As the Supreme Court observes in its 1965 *Maryland v. U.S.* decision, "The National Guard is the modern Militia reserved to the States by Art. I . . . of the Constitution."

1911 New York State passes the Sullivan Law, requiring a license for both the purchase and carry of handguns. Such licenses are rarely issued. The law eventually serves to redefine the meaning of "gun control," making it much stricter than it has previously been conceived. However, gun rights advocates point out that it has little effect on violent crime and is motivated, at heart, by xenophobic fears within the mainstream white Anglo-Saxon leadership of New York, who want to keep firearms out of the hands of Italian immigrants. It is estimated that seven of ten of those arrested during the first three years of the law are of Italian descent. While the Sullivan Law applies to the entire state, it is actually aimed at New York City, where the large foreign population is thought overly turbulent and overly prone to criminal activity. Due to the xenophobic nature of the Sullivan Law, some critics point to it as an example of using "gun control" to quash minority interests.

1927 Congress passes the Mailing of Firearms Act of 1927, also known as the Miller Act, prohibiting sending concealable firearms through the U.S. Post Office. As originally proposed, the act would ban the interstate shipping of all handguns except service revolvers. However, strong opposition from legislators in gun manufacturing states combined with similarly strong opposition from legislators in the southern and western states, many of whom believe it violates the Second Amendments right to keep and bear arms, almost completely neutralize the act by restricting its provisions to the U.S. Post Office. The law is easy to skirt until passage of the Gun Control Act of 1968, because mailers can legally send guns via private mail delivery companies such as UPS (United Parcel Service).

1929   The Saint Valentine's Day Massacre in Chicago shocks the nation. Four members of Al Capone's gang, two dressed as police officers, ruthlessly mow down seven members of a rival Chicago gang using Thompson submachine guns. The murders prompt several gun control proposals in Congress, two of which eventually pass (the National Firearms Act of 1934 and the Federal Firearms Act of 1938).

1934   The first major federal gun control legislation is passed as the National Firearms Act of 1934. It mandates all persons engaged in the business of selling "gangster-type" weapons—such as machine-guns, sawed-off shotguns, and silencers—and all owners of these to register with the Collector of Internal Revenue and pay applicable taxes for the firearm transfer. Because criminals are unlikely to register their weapons, the effect is to give law enforcement authorities a new reason to arrest gangsters (possession of an unregistered weapon). Trade in these weapons is also dramatically reduced.

1938   The second major federal gun control legislation is passed as the Federal Firearms Act of 1938. It imposes the first federal limitations on the sale of ordinary firearms. It requires manufacturers, dealers, and importers of guns and handgun ammunition to obtain a Federal Firearms License. Dealers must maintain records of the names and addresses of persons to whom firearms are sold. Gun sales to persons convicted of violent felonies are prohibited.

1939–1942 In *United States v. Miller* (1939), the U.S. Supreme Court makes its third major ruling bearing on the Second Amendment. As with *U.S. v. Cruikshank* and *Presser v. Illinois*, the Court's decision supports the concept that both federal and state governments can restrict who may and may not own a gun and can also regulate the sale, transfer, receipt, possession, and use of selected categories of firearms. More specifically, the Court rules that the federal government has the right, which it exercised in the National Firearms Act of 1934, to control the transfer of (and in effect, to require the registration of) certain firearms. In this particular case, the sawed-off shotgun, a favorite weapon of gangsters, is deemed unprotected by the Second Amendment. The ruling reads, in part: "In the absence of any evidence tending to show that possession or use of 'shotgun having a barrel of less than eighteen inches in length' at this time has some reasonable relationship to the preservation or efficiency of a well regulated militia, we cannot say that the second amendment guarantees the right to keep and bear such an instrument." Lower court decisions involving the National Firearms Act and the kindred Federal Firearms Act use even more direct language. In upholding the National Firearms Act, the district court declares in *United States v. Adams* (1935) that the Second Amendment "refers to the Militia, a protective force of government; to the collective body and not individual rights." A later district court decision, *United States v. Tot* (1942), cites this ruling in upholding the Federal Firearms Act. These court decisions make clear that no personal right to own arms exists under the federal Constitution.

On the other hand, gun rights advocates point out that in its *Miller* ruling, the Supreme Court noted that the writers of the Constitution clearly intended that the states had both the right and the duty to maintain militias and that a "militia comprised all males physically capable of acting in concert for the common defense . . . . And, further, that ordinarily when called for service, these men were expected to appear bearing arms supplied by themselves and of the kind in common use at the time. . . . This implied the general obligation of all adult male inhabitants to possess arms, and with certain exceptions, to cooperate in the work of defense. The possession of arms also implied the possession of ammunition, and authorities paid quite as much attention to the latter as to the former." Thus, the full text of the Supreme Court decision mitigates the impact of its decision on sawed-off shotguns. Such weapons have no place in a militia and thus are not protected, but the general principle of ordinary citizens owning arms and ammunition is clearly preserved.

1958–1961 The Federal Aviation Act of 1958—and its amendments contained in Public Law 87-197 of 1961—bar individuals from bringing on board a passenger aircraft any firearm, ammunition, or firearm part (except in the form of check-in luggage).

1963 Using a false name, Lee Harvey Oswald buys an imported Italian military rifle for less than $20 from a mail-order dealer in Chicago. He uses it to assassinate President John F. Kennedy. The ease with which he has obtained the weapon stuns many Americans, and soon there are numerous bills brought before Congress to regulate the gun market. These bills are combined and reformulated many times until they result in the Omnibus Crime Control and Safe Streets Act of 1968 and its sister legislation, the Gun Control Act of 1968.

1965 The Texas Tower Shooting shocks the nation. On August 1, ex-Marine sharpshooter Charles Whitman climbs the clock tower on the University of Texas campus in Austin with seven firearms. He methodically kills fifteen people and wounds thirty-one others. Whitman's victims include the unborn child of an eighteen-year-old pregnant student, whom he shot through the abdomen. The shooting spree ends when two Austin police officers and a civilian subdue and kill the sniper. An autopsy reveals a golf-ball sized tumor in Whitman's brain.

1965
(cont.)

The Texas Tower massacre and its immediate aftermath are played out many times over the next four decades: A mass-murder shooting shocks the nation and sparks local, state, and national legislative proposals to control guns; within a few months, however, emotions die down and almost all of the proposals fail enactment.

1968

The assassinations of Reverend Martin Luther King Jr. and Senator Robert F. Kennedy, as do the urban riots exploding in hundreds of urban areas, increase national attention on gun violence and, according to many observers, the need for stronger gun control. Congress is finally motivated to pass twin bills containing serious gun control measures—the Omnibus Crime Control and Safe Streets Act of 1968 and the Gun Control Act of 1968 (GCA). More recent federal guns laws, including the 1993 Brady Law and the 1994 federal assault weapons ban, are generally enacted as amendments to the GCA statutes.

The GCA places severe restrictions on the importation of firearms and on the sale of guns and ammunition across state lines. Interstate pistol sales are banned. Interstate long gun sales are also banned, except when contiguous states enact laws to authorize such sales. Mail-order and package delivery service (e.g., UPS) gun sales are prohibited. Interstate ammunition sales are prohibited. The GCA also creates a "prohibited persons" list of those barred from possessing guns. The list is originally composed of convicted felons, alcoholics, drug users, "mental defectives," fugitives, persons dishonorably discharged from the military, and persons who renounced their citizenship. In 1996, the list is expanded to include those convicted of domestic violence or subject to a domestic violence restraining order.

The GCA leads to the creation of the Bureau of Alcohol, Tobacco and Firearms (ATF)—upgraded from its previous status as a division—within the Department of the Treasury. The ATF is the key federal agency assigned to effectuate gun control, but is hampered by lack of funding and restrictions placed on it by the gun rights leaning Congresses of the mid-1980s and of the post-1994 era.

1973–1978 From October 1973 through April 1974, the Zebra Killings in the San Francisco area captivate the public's attention and eventually strengthen the gun control movement both locally and nationally. The label given the killings is attributed to the fact that the killers are black and the victims mostly white. Fourteen people are murdered and seven wounded during the five-month killing spree.

Eight members of a Black Muslim cult called the "Death Angels" are eventually arrested; their motive is to incite a race war. Four are released for a lack of evidence, but the other four are convicted in 1976 and sentenced to life in prison.

The Zebra Killings, as well as the 1978 handgun murders of Mayor George Moscone and Supervisor Harvey Milk, are instrumental in strengthening political and public support for stricter gun control measures within the San Francisco Bay Area. The City and County of San Francisco approve a handgun ban in 1982, though it is subsequently overturned in state court. However, San Francisco and other Bay Area cities adopt a number of other local zoning and sales restrictions on guns that withstand legal challenges.

The Zebra killing of college student Nick Shields leads his father, Pete Shields, to become a gun control activist. Shields leaves an executive position with DuPont to become executive director of a fledging advocacy group, Handgun Control Inc. He plays a critical role in developing it into the premier organizational advocate for strengthening gun controls in the United States (it is renamed the Brady Campaign to Prevent Gun Violence in 2001).

1974–2005 The modern gun control movement begins in 1974 when Mark Borinsky founds the National Council to Control Handguns in Washington, D.C. In the late 1970s, it is renamed Handgun Control Inc., and in 2001, the Brady Campaign to Prevent Gun Violence.

1974–2005   Borinsky had been robbed at gunpoint as a graduate
(cont.)   student. The traumatic experience stays with him, and
upon graduation he decides to join a national group
promoting gun control. Alas, none exists. He fills the
void by starting his own.

The new organization finds sympathy for its cause
abounding within the federal government. Many
members of Congress are eager to work with an organization devoted to gun control. Indeed, many of
them were part of the Seventy-eighth Congress that
had passed the Omnibus Crime Control and Safe
Streets Act of 1968 and the kindred Gun Control Act of
1968. Though the acts ban the sale and possession of
guns to felons, drug addicts, illegal aliens, and the
mentally incompetent, they include no serious enforcement mechanisms. Many members of Congress
feel that rectifying this shortcoming is critical to realizing effective gun control.

The Treasury Department's Bureau of Alcohol,
Tobacco, and Firearms (ATF) welcomes an organization that will help in its fight to regulate and monitor
firearms. ATF's efforts to fulfill the promise of the federal gun control legislation of 1968 are stymied every
step of the way by gun rights legislators (prodded, in
part, by the NRA), and it is looking for allies. Most
egregiously, the ATF's proposal to begin a computerized system to record the serial numbers of all new
weapons and every firearms transaction of the nation's 160,000 federally licensed firearms dealers is
slashed from its budget in committee.

Other divisions of the Department of Justice also
welcome an organization devoted to gun control. For
example, the department's recently formed Bureau of
Justice Statistics has many staffers who are shocked by
the gun violence statistics they are amassing and are
subsequently eager to provide these statistics in edito-
rialized format ("guns are bad, just look at these
data!") to an organization like Borinsky's.

In the 1990s, the organization finds an ally in the federal government's Centers for Disease Control, whose
staffers are emotionally affected by the gun violence

data they are analyzing in much the same way as the emotions of their counterparts in the Bureau of Justice Statistics.

1977   The "Revolt at Cincinnati" occurs at the annual meeting of the National Rifle Association. It is a watershed event that will change the organization from one largely dedicated to promoting the sporting uses of firearms to one largely dedicated to fighting any and all forms of gun control.

Although some of the NRA's membership and leadership in the 1960s and early 1970s are radically opposed to any form of gun regulation, they are in the minority. In 1972, however, this minority begins an all-out—and eventually successful—effort to redefine the meaning and the primary mission of the NRA.

Executive committee member Harlon B. Carter leads this redefinition effort. In a July 1972 address to the NRA executive committee, Carter argues that the NRA philosophy on gun control—that some was necessary and good for society—is wrongheaded and needs to be replaced by a new philosophy, one of absolute resistance to any and all forms of gun regulation: "Any position we took [on gun control] back at that time is no good, it is not valid, and it is simply not relevant to the problem that we face today. The latest news release from NRA embraces a disastrous concept . . . that evil is imputed to the sale and delivery, the possession of a certain kind of firearm, entirely apart from the good or evil intent of the man who uses it and/or . . . that the legitimate use of a handgun is limited to sporting use" (as quoted in Sugarmann, 1992, Chapter 2).

Carter further argues that every gun has a legitimate purpose and that every law-abiding person, no matter what his or her age, should have the right to choose his or her own weapon according to what he or she thinks best. The argument is even carried to the point that children, because of their small hands, should have access to derringers (tiny handguns).

Largely through Carter's efforts, the minority view begins appearing more and more in the NRA's public

1977
(cont.)

statements. The moderate editorials that had occasionally appeared in the NRA's leading publication,
The American Rifleman, vanish as its editor is replaced,
partly through pressure applied by Carter, by a new
editor who promotes the idea that there can be nothing good about any kind of gun control.

During the mid-1970s, only 25 percent of the organization—according to the NRA's own estimate—consists of "nonshooting constitutionalists" (people dedicated to preserving full-scale private ownership of
firearms). But this does not prevent the complete
takeover of NRA leadership positions by the hardest
of the hard-liners against gun control at the NRA's
1977 annual meeting. The coup is led by Neal Knox (at
the time, editor of the gun magazines *Rifle* and *Handloader*), Robert Kukla (the new head of the NRA's lobbying wing, the Institute for Legislative Action), and
Joseph Tartaro (then the editor of *Gun Week*).

Knox, Kukla, and Tartaro lay the foundation for
their revolt by using their access to gun publications
to condemn the moderate direction the NRA is taking
(on being a hunting and conservation organization).
At the convention itself, they use their knowledge of
parliamentary procedure to methodically replace top
leaders with hardcore gun rights advocates such as
themselves. The "New NRA," as Carter calls it, will
become *the* gun lobby.

1980

On the evening of December 8, Mark David Chapman
uses a Charter Arms .38 caliber revolver—a classic
"Saturday night special"—to gun down John Lennon
in New York City. Lennon's murder stokes national interest in gun control and the still fledgling Handgun
Control Inc. (renamed the Brady Campaign to Prevent
Gun Violence in 2001) rockets from 5,000 to 80,000
dues-paying members in a matter of weeks.

In *Lewis v. United States,* the Supreme Court upholds
the Gun Control Act of 1968; it also reaffirms its 1939
decision on the Second Amendment as previously set
forth in *United States v. Miller.* The Court concludes
that "restrictions on the use of firearms are neither

based upon constitutionally suspect criteria, nor do they trench upon any constitutionally protected liberties." The Court further expresses its view that the Second Amendment guarantees no right to keep and bear a firearm that does not have "some reasonable relationship to the preservation or efficiency of a well-regulated militia."

In *Lewis*, the Court addresses the case of an individual convicted of a burglary in Florida in 1961, whose conviction for the offense is never overturned, even though it is ruled unconstitutional under the Sixth and Fourteenth Amendments (the individual had not been provided with counsel to assist in his defense). The Court holds, however, that the constitutionality of the petitioner's conviction has no bearing on his liability under the Gun Control Act of 1968. The Court maintains that any felony conviction, even an invalid one, is sufficient to prohibit possession of a firearm.

1982   In *Quilici v. Village of Morton Grove,* the Seventh Circuit of the U.S. Court of Appeals upholds a ban on the possession of handguns by ordinary persons in Morton Grove, Illinois. The court declares that the Second Amendment preserves the *collective* right of a state's citizens to form a militia and not the absolute right of an *individual* to keep and bear firearms.

The 1981 Morton Grove law exempts those needing a handgun for occupational purposes—such as police officers, prison officials, members of the armed forces, and security guards. It also exempts licensed gun collectors. A resident owning a handgun can keep it, as long as the gun is stored at a local gun club (although nonworking, antique firearms may be kept at home).

Soon after enactment, gun rights advocates file a lawsuit claiming that the Morton Grove law is in violation of both the U.S. and Illinois State Constitutions. A lower federal court rules in favor of Morton Grove, as does the appeals court. The appeals court declares that "construing the [Second Amendment] according to its plain meaning, it seems clear that the right to bear arms is inextricably connected to the preservation

1982	of a militia." The decision is appealed to the U.S.
(cont.)	Supreme Court, but it declines to hear the case.

The ruling in *Quilici* is consistent with other federal court decisions confirming the militia-based meaning of the Second Amendment—though in 2001, a federal appeals court rules in *U.S. v. Emerson* that the amendment guarantees an individual right to possess and bear firearms (see below).

Quilici v. Village of Morton Grove receives enormous publicity and fuels the increasingly hot fires of the national debate over gun control. The village's law banning handguns, as well as the lower and appeals court decisions in favor of it, are huge symbolic victories for those favoring stricter gun control. In reaction, gun rights advocates work with public officials in the small town of Kennesaw, Georgia, to pass a local ordinance *requiring* that all heads of households own a firearm and ammunition. The law was entirely symbolic, as there is no provision for enforcement; moreover, the law itself includes several clauses "excusing" those not wanting to own a gun for moral or religious reasons, or because they are a convicted felon or mentally or physically disabled.

Although gun rights advocates are delighted when Kennesaw's crime rates fall in the succeeding year, and point to it as evidence of the validity of the "more-guns-produce-less-crime" thesis, gun control advocates note that crime rates have fallen in the Village of Morton Grove as well. Criminologists David McDowall, Allan Lizotte, and Brian Wiersema publish a more systematic analysis of the crime rates in small towns promoting or discouraging gun ownership in the journal *Criminology* in 1991. They find that the crime reductions observed in Kennesaw are more likely part of a normal crime fluctuation than a real response to the mandatory gun ownership ordinance.

1984   On July 18, James Huberty leaves his home announcing to his wife that he is "going to hunt humans." He enters a MacDonald's restaurant in San Ysidro, California, and uses three high-powered weapons to methodically slaughter twenty patrons and employees, wounding another nineteen. The carnage stops when he is mortally wounded by a police sniper. Because one of his weapons is an Uzi semiautomatic rifle, gun control advocates press state legislators for restrictions on assault weapons, but it will take another California massacre, four and a half years later in Stockton, before action is finally taken. See below.

1986   The Firearms Owners' Protection Act (FOPA)—known also as the McClure-Volkmer Act—is passed against the protests of gun control advocates. FOPA curtails many of the more stringent provisions of the Gun Control Act of 1968. Most notably, it (a) allows federally licensed firearms dealers to sell guns away from their principal place of business as long as the sales comply with all relevant laws (thus allowing these dealers to sell their wares at gun shows, flea markets, and on the street); (b) limits the Bureau of Alcohol, Tobacco, and Firearms' (ATF) inspections of a gun dealer to once per year; (c) prohibits the ATF from creating a national gun registry; (d) removes federal restrictions on interstate ammunition sales; and (e) re-legalizes interstate long gun sales (if the seller is a federally licensed firearms dealer, and the sale is legal in the buyer's home state).

The Armed Career Criminal Act increases the penalties for firearm possession by "prohibited persons" as specified in the Gun Control Act of 1968.

The Law Enforcement Officers Protection Act bans so-called cop killer handgun bullets—or more accurately, bullets with very dense cores—that are capable of piercing bullet-resistant vests and other body armor.

1989   On January 17, Patrick Purdy enters a Stockton, California, schoolyard and fires 105 rounds from a semiautomatic assault rifle, killing five children and wounding twenty-nine others. The slaughter mobilizes public and political support for gun control throughout the nation. California responds quickly and enacts the Roberti-Roos Assault Weapons Control

1989 *(cont.)*	Act of 1989. Six other states soon follow with legislation restricting the sale of assault weapons (Connecticut, Hawaii, Maryland, Massachusetts, New Jersey, and New York). At the federal level, President George H. W. Bush, even though a member of the NRA and a gun rights proponent during his election campaign, responds with an executive order in March that places a temporary ban on the importation of AK-47 assault rifles and selected similar weapons. Several bills are introduced in Congress to outlaw or restrict assault pistols, rifles, and shotguns. President Bill Clinton eventually brokers one of these through Congress as part of the Violent Crime Control and Enforcement Act of 1994.
1990	Enacted as Public Law 101-647, the Crime Control Act of 1990 bans the importing of—and manufacturing from—foreign parts of certain semiautomatic firearms designated as "assault weapons." The Act also creates Gun-Free School Zones, making it a federal crime to carry a firearm within 1,000 feet of a school; however, this provision is overturned in a circuit court ruling in 1993, which is subsequently upheld by the Supreme Court in *United States v. Lopez* (1995).
1991	The Killeen, Texas, massacre unfolds on the afternoon of October 16, when George Hennard Jr., plows his truck into Luby's Cafeteria. Repeatedly firing and then reloading two handguns, he kills twenty-three people, wounds twenty-one others, and then kills himself. It is the worst single-day murder total by a single gunman in U.S. history. Two of Hennard's victims are the parents of Suzanna Gratia. Gratia normally travels with a handgun for self-protection, but keeps it in her car to be in compliance with Texas law, which in 1991 does not allow ordinary citizens to carry concealed weapons. She testifies ruefully at a public hearing that she might have been able to save her parents if she had had her gun in her purse: "I had a perfect shot at him. It would have been clear. I had a place to prop my hand. The guy was not even aware of what we were doing. I'm

not saying that I could have saved anybody in there, but I would have had a chance" (as quoted in Kopel, 2002, 335). Gratia's testimony becomes instrumental in changing the political climate in Texas and many other states regarding right-to-carry laws. And in the mid-1990s eleven states, including Texas, adopt a right-to-carry law. (Note that thirty-eight states now allow ordinary citizens to carry concealed handguns—that is, they have the "right to carry"; see Chapter 2.)

1993–2001 On July 1, 1993, Gian Luigi Ferri, a disgruntled former client, enters the law office of Pettit and Martin at 101 California Street in San Francisco. Armed with three handguns, two of them TEC-DC9 assault pistols, he kills eight people and wounds another six in the law office and in neighboring offices. The police quickly arrive and corner him in a stairwell, where he commits suicide. Although California had banned the sale of assault weapons after the Stockton schoolyard massacre of 1989, Ferri easily obtains his at a gun show and pawn shop in Nevada.

The 101 California Street massacre sparks outcries for strong gun controls and contributes to the passage of the 1994 federal assault weapons ban. The massacre also spawns the historic lawsuit *Merrill v. Navegar*, resulting in the first appeals court decision to rule that under certain circumstances a gun manufacturer can be held negligent when its weapons are used in the commission of crime.

Navegar, under the business name Intratec Firearms Inc., manufactures high-capacity assault pistols under the names KG-9 and TEC-9 during the 1980s. The weapons are popular with criminals and street gang members. When the District of Columbia and other jurisdictions enact laws restricting the TEC-9 (and other assault weapons by model name), Navegar responds by making a minor alteration to the pistol and renaming it the "TEC-DC9" to evade the laws (according to some former employees, the "DC" is inserted to mock the Washington, "D.C." Assault Weapons Control Act of 1990; see DeBell, 2002). The

1993–2001   features appealing most to criminals remain un-
(cont.)   changed—a high-capacity magazine and a threaded
barrel to screw on a silencer. The company touts the
TEC-DC9's "firepower" and "excellent resistance to
fingerprints" (see Henigan, 2002).

The *Merrill v. Navegar* lawsuit is filed in May 1994.
California (101) street victims and their families argue
that Navegar's negligent actions contributed to the
massacre. The company's advertising is said to appeal
to criminals. Indeed, Navegar executives testify that
they are well aware of their product's stature as the
preeminent assault weapon used in crimes and that
they welcome the publicity stemming from its use in
notorious acts of violence because of the resulting
spike in sales.

A California Superior Court judge dismisses the
suit before trial, ruling that Navegar's guns are legally
manufactured and sold and that the company cannot
be held liable for what others do with their guns. In a
landmark ruling in September 1999, the California
Court of Appeals disagrees. The court holds that
Navegar owes the plaintiffs and the general public a
duty to exercise reasonable care and not to create risks
above and beyond those inherent in the presence of
firearms in society.

On August 6, 2001, the California Supreme Court
votes 5–1 to reverse the court of appeals ruling on
other grounds, finding that a California statute, passed
in 1983, bars imposing any liability on Navegar.

On November 30, 1993, President Clinton signs the
Brady Handgun Violence Prevention Act requiring a
five-government-business-day waiting period for the
purchase of a handgun. The waiting period allows
time for a thorough background check of the prospective buyer; it also allows for a "cooling off" period to
minimize impulse purchases that might lead to suicide
or criminal violence. Five years after enactment, the
five-day waiting period is eliminated and replaced by
the National Instant Criminal Background Check System (NICS). The check must be completed within three
days, but almost all are completed within a few hours.

Gun rights advocates challenge the Brady Act as a violation of states' rights under the Tenth Amendment. In 1997, the U.S. Supreme Court strikes down the provision requiring local police to conduct background checks in *Printz v. United States.* Despite the ruling, handgun background checks continue on a voluntary basis in most areas until the NICS is operational in late 1998.

Gun control advocates bemoan that background checks only apply to licensed retail dealers. At gun shows and flea markets, guns can be bought and sold by unlicensed individuals in many states.

On December 7, 1993, Colin Ferguson shoots twenty-five people, killing six of them, on a Long Island commuter train in Garden City, New York. Carolyn McCarthy's husband is killed, and her son seriously injured in the attack. She successfully runs for Congress in 1996 after her representative, Dan Frisa, votes against an assault weapons ban. McCarthy's campaign focuses on one issue, gun control.

1994   The Gun Free Schools Act of 1994 requires that any state receiving federal education funds "shall have in effect a State law requiring local educational agencies to expel from school for a period of not less than one year a student who is determined to have brought a weapon to a school."

Enacted under Title XI as part of the Violent Crime Control and Law Enforcement Act of 1994, the federal "assault weapons ban" prohibits for ten years the future manufacture and transfer of nineteen named assault weapons and approximately 200 firearms covered by the law's generic definition of an "assault weapon." It also bans large capacity ammunition feeding devices—those that could hold more than ten rounds. The ban does not apply to assault weapons already in circulation.

Although gun rights advocates complain that it is impossible to give a generic, operational definition of an "assault weapon," Congress agrees with gun control groups that there are certain characteristics

1994
(cont.)
differentiating military-style from civilian-style (for use in hunting and target shooting, as well as self-defense) weapons. Among these characteristics of military-style weapons are a compact design, a barrel less than twenty inches, a pistol grip or thumbhole stock, a folding or telescoping grip, a threaded barrel for adding a silencer or flash suppressor, and the ability to receive a large-capacity ammunition clip (holding more than ten rounds).

1996 The Lautenberg Amendment to the Gun Control Act of 1968, also called the Domestic Violence Offender Gun Ban, expands prohibition of gun purchase, ownership, or possession to include persons convicted of domestic violence misdemeanor offenses.

1997 On June 4, Massachusetts Attorney General Scott Harshbarger sets forth the state's new *Consumer Protection Regulations on Handgun Safety.* Harshbarger bases the sweeping new gun controls on a state statute against "unfair or deceptive trade practice." He claims it is unfair or deceptive to sell handguns that: (1) do not have tamper-resistant serial numbers; (2) do not meet high standards for accidentally discharging when dropped on a hard surface; (3) do not have trigger locks; (4) do not have strong trigger pulls (which can prevent the average five-year-old child from firing it); and (5) have a barrel less than three inches long.

In protest, gun industry representatives file a lawsuit claiming that Harshbarger has overstepped his authority. Harshbarger loses, but the Massachusetts Supreme Court overturns the decision in June 1999. To prevent further suits, the Massachusetts legislature enacts a law giving the attorney general the necessary authority to create the new handgun regulations. The Brady Campaign to Prevent Gun Violence and other gun control organizations extol Harshbarger's efforts as a model for emulation by other states.

1998–2005 A wave of schoolyard shootings stun the nation and spark dozens of state and federal legislative proposals to tighten up gun laws, almost none of which are enacted. The most shocking shootings occur in 1998, in Littleton, Colorado, and in 2005, in Red Lake, Minnesota. In Littleton, two Columbine High School students kill twelve fellow students, one teacher, and then themselves, and in Red Lake, a sixteen-year-old shoots to death his grandfather and his companion in their home, and then seven others on his high school campus—the murdering halted when he shoots himself to death. Sandwiched between these two massacres are many other shooting sprees by teenage boys that gain national attention, including those in Santee, California; Springfield, Oregon; Pearl, Mississippi; West Paducah, Kentucky; Jonesboro, Arkansas; Edinboro, Pennsylvania; Raleigh, Virginia; and Conyers, Georgia. Typical of the reaction following each of these shootings is the introduction of a bill in the U.S. Congress following the Columbine tragedy that would have required background checks on *all* gun purchasers, not just those buying their weapons from federally licensed dealers. Much of the general public and many members of Congress are stunned into supporting this particular legislation when it is learned that three of the weapons used at Columbine were acquired through a straw purchase at a gun show (a friend of one of the killers made the straw purchase at the gun show—that is, she bought the guns *not* for herself, but to give to the boys). New Jersey Senator Frank Lautenberg leads the legislative efforts, but his bill (aimed at closing the "gun show loophole," whereby gun transactions between private individuals, many of which occur at gun shows, are not subject to purchaser background checks) is defeated on 51–47 vote. Gun rights lobbyists, spearheaded by the NRA, take credit for the defeat.

2000–2003 President Clinton announces the *Smith & Wesson Settlement Agreement* on March 17, 2000. The agreement involves the gun manufacturer and industry giant Smith & Wesson, the federal government, the states of New York and Connecticut, and several cities and counties. In return for the dismissal of lawsuits that the governmental bodies had filed (seeking compensation for the gun-related violence they had incurred),

2000–2003 Smith & Wesson agrees to implement major changes
(cont.)   in the design and distribution of its guns. More specifically, the company promises to begin incorporating
the following safety features: internal locking systems;
"authorized user technology" (making the gun func-
tional only for an authorized user, normally the
owner); "chamber loaded" indicators; child safeties;
and hidden serial numbers to prevent obliteration.
Moreover, Smith & Wesson agrees to distribute their
guns only to dealers willing to: make no sales at gun
shows unless there are background checks on all purchasers at the show; make sales only to individuals
passing a certified firearms safety course or exam;
pass a comprehensive exam on recognizing suspect
buyers (e.g., "straw purchasers"); and implement security procedures to prevent gun thefts.

The landmark agreement represents the first time
that any gun manufacturer has been willing to alter its
sales and distribution practices to prevent criminals,
juveniles, and other high-risk individuals from obtaining guns. However, fierce opposition to the agreement
quickly arises from other gun manufacturers, gun retailers, gun rights organizations, and many gun owners. The opposition is successful and impedes implementation of the provisions. Smith & Wesson's sales
plummet. It is sold to Saf-T-Hammer, which renames
the manufacturer the Smith & Wesson Holding Corporation. Even though Saf-T-Hammer produces safety
devices that prevent unauthorized gun use and unintentional firearm accidents, it wants to reverse Smith &
Wesson's plummeting sales and introduces a .50 caliber revolver in 2003. The revolver is so powerful that
it can blast through police protective vests, and its introduction receives huge criticism from gun control
advocates. However, gun rights organizations applaud
Smith & Wesson's return to the fold. For example, in
the NRA publication *The American Rifleman,* there is the
acclamation that "Smith & Wesson has re-established
itself as an American handgun icon—a status it lost in
the backlash of its now infamous agreement with the
Clinton administration" (Mayer, 2003, 55).

2001   In *United States v. Emerson*, the New Orleans-based
        Fifth Circuit Court of Appeals becomes the first fed-
        eral court to declare that the Second Amendment
        guarantees individuals—as opposed to members of
        groups such as the National Guard—the right to own
        guns. The court concludes "that the history of the sec-
        ond amendment reinforces the plain meaning of its
        text, namely that it protects individual Americans in
        their right to keep and bear arms whether or not they
        are a member of a select militia."
            The *Emerson* ruling is a striking departure from pre-
        vious state and federal court decisions, which empha-
        size that the Second Amendment is meant to grant a
        collective right to the citizens of a state to maintain a
        militia. Gun control advocates criticize the court's in-
        terpretation but take heart that the court also makes
        clear that the federal government has the right to reg-
        ulate arms. More specifically, the court notes that the
        individual-rights interpretation of the Second Amend-
        ment "does not mean that those rights may never be
        made subject to any . . . restrictions." In this particular
        instance, the court upheld the indictment of Dr. Timo-
        thy Joe Emerson, who had challenged the confiscation
        of his firearm after being served with a domestic-
        violence related restraining order (Dr. Emerson was
        challenging the 1994 federal Violence against Women
        Act that allowed for the confiscation).

2002   John Allen Muhammad and John Lee Malvo use a
        Bushmaster assault rifle in October to murder ten
        people and injure three others in the Washington,
        D.C., area. The shooting spree prompts gun control
        advocates to call for the creation of a national ballistic
        fingerprinting database, in which all firearms would
        have on file digital images of their shell casing and (in
        the case of rifles and handguns) bullet markings. They
        contend that such a database would have led law en-
        forcement authorities to identify the snipers much
        sooner. These advocates also contend that the shoot-
        ing spree is strong evidence for strengthening and ex-
        tending the federal ban on assault weapons.

2002 *(cont.)*	The United States Customs Service and the Bureau of Alcohol, Tobacco, and Firearms (ATF) announce that they will begin enforcement of the Nonimmigrant Aliens Firearms and Ammunition Amendments to the Gun Control Act of 1968 (as enacted by Congress in 1998 as Public Law 105-277). These amendments require nonimmigrant aliens wanting to bring firearms or ammunition into the United States for hunting or sporting purposes to obtain an import permit from ATF prior to entering the country.
2004	Tucked away in an omnibus spending package approved by both houses of Congress in January are provisions reducing the length of time the Department of Justice can maintain background-check records on firearm sales: from ninety days to twenty-four hours. Records are kept on file to ensure that if an individual prohibited from buying guns (e.g., a convicted felon) is inadvertently allowed to make such a purchase, the mistake can be corrected. Gun control advocates complain that requiring these records to be destroyed within twenty-four hours makes it nearly impossible for the Justice Department to correct errors, and the end result will be the arming of more criminals. This contention has empirical support: In a 2002 study, the federal government's General Accounting Office asserts that if background records are destroyed within twenty-four hours "the FBI would lose certain abilities to initiate firearm-retrieval actions when new information reveals that individuals who were approved to purchase firearms should not have been. Specifically, during the first 6 months of the current 90-day retention policy, the FBI used retained records to initiate 235 firearm-retrieval actions, of which 228 (97 percent) could not have been initiated under the proposed next-day destruction policy" (General Accounting Office, 2002, 4).

Despite the protests of gun control advocates, the 1994 federal assault weapons ban, originally enacted to last for ten years, is allowed to expire in September. U.S. gun manufacturers were generally successful in evading the ban by making cosmetic changes to their assault weapons. The most infamous example is the Bushmaster assault rifle that John Allen Muhammad and John Lee Malvo use in their October 2002 Washington, D.C., killing spree.

A Department of Justice study reveals that the use of assault weapons in crime dropped significantly in the years following the ban and that this drop was not explainable by the overall drop in gun crime during the late 1990s. Assault weapons specifically named in the 1994 ban declined from about 5 percent of all crime guns, according to the ATF National Tracing Center data, to about 1 percent between 1993 (the year before it took effect) and 2001.

In December, the U.S. Attorney General's Office publishes a lengthy memorandum concluding that "the Second Amendment secures a personal right of individuals, not a collective right that may only be invoked by a State[,] or a quasi-collective right restricted to those persons who serve in organized militia units" (U.S. Department of Justice, 2004). Gun rights activists applaud the opinion, even though its interpretation of the Second Amendment is disputed by some constitutional historians and many gun control advocates.

2005   In June, landmark gun control bills are introduced in the California state legislature. The first requires the laser "micro-stamping" of a serial number on every newly manufactured bullet. This kind of coding system works well in many other consumer product industries (e.g., soda cans are so stamped). Firing tests reveal that a micro-stamp can even survive the mangling that can occur after a bullet hits a solid object. The California bullet-coding law would require all *handgun* ammunition packed in the same box to carry identical codes. The name of the purchaser would be linked to the ammunition through electronic recording of driver's license information.

The second landmark bill requires that semiautomatic pistols be equipped with technology that can imprint microscopic identifying information of any

2005
(cont.)

shell casing fired from a particular gun. The recently patented technology uses the firing pin to imprint the identification mark onto the shell casing.

Congress passes the Protection of Lawful Commerce in Arms Act (S.397; H.R.800) into law. The act prohibits "civil liability actions" against manufacturers, distributors, dealers, and importers of firearms or ammunition products and their trade associations, for any harm caused by the criminal or unlawful misuse of firearms or ammunition. The act does not exempt those in the gun industry that break the law or sell defective weapons or ammunition. However, gun control advocates see this legislation as a major setback. Although civil lawsuits are not won in the courtroom, many yield major out-of-court settlements that promote reform in the gun industry. For example, a $2.5 million settlement against gun retailer Bulls Eye and gun manufacturer Bushmaster is reached in 2004 for their responsibility in the 2002 Washington D.C. sniper shootings. Both the retailer and the manufacturer revise their inventory-control procedures to reduce the probability of the theft of their guns and to let law enforcement know immediately if a theft actually occurs.

References

Cramer, Clayton E. 1994. *For the Defense of Themselves and the State: The Original Intent and Judicial Interpretation of the Right to Keep and Bear Arms.* Westport, CT: Praeger.

DeBell, Matthew. 2002. "TEC-DC9 Pistol." In *Guns in American Society: An Encyclopedia of History, Politics, Culture, and the Law,* Vol. 2, ed. Gregg Lee Carter, 575–576. Santa Barbara, CA: ABC-CLIO.

General Accounting Office. 2002. *Potential Effects of Next-Day Destruction of NICS Background Check Records.* (Report No.: GAO-02-653). July.

Henigan, Dennis A. 2002. "California Street (101) Massacre." In *Guns in American Society: An Encyclopedia of History, Politics, Culture, and the Law,* Vol. 1, ed. Gregg Lee Carter, 95–96. Santa Barbara, CA: ABC-CLIO.

Kennett, Lee, and James LaVerne Anderson. 1975. *The Gun in America: The Origins of a National Dilemma.* Westport, CT: Greenwood Press.

Kopel, David. 2002. "Killeen Texas, Massacre." In *Guns in American Society: An Encyclopedia of History, Politics, Culture, and the Law*, Vol. 1, ed. Gregg Lee Carter, 333–336. Santa Barbara, CA: ABC-CLIO.

Mayer, Scott. 2003. "'Do You Feel Lucky . . .' .500 S&W Magnum." *American Rifleman*, 151 (May): 54–57, 93.

McDowall, David, Allan J. Lizotte, and Brian Wiersema. 1991. "General Deterrence through Civilian Gun Ownership: An Evaluation of the Quasi-Experimental Evidence." *Criminology* 29: 541–559.

National Rifle Association. 1968a. "Are We Really So Violent?" *American Rifleman*, February: 16.

———. 1968b. "Restraint on . . . Cheap Handguns Wins Favor." *American Rifleman*, March: 16.

Peckman, Howard H., ed. 1978. *Sources of American Independence: Selected Manuscripts from the Collection of the William Clements Library, Vol. 1*. Chicago: University of Chicago Press.

Shalhope, Robert E. 1982. "The Ideological Origins of the Second Amendment." *Journal of American History* 69: 599–614.

Sugarmann, Josh. 1992. *National Rifle Association: Money, Firepower, Fear*. Washington, DC: National Press Books.

U.S. Department of Justice. 2004. "Whether the Second Amendment Secures an Individual Right: Memorandum Opinion for the Attorney General." August 24. http://www.usdoj.gov/olc/secondamendment2.htm. Accessed June 17, 2005.

4

Federal Gun Laws

This chapter reviews the major federal gun laws as of 2005. Many of the provisions of these laws are extremely difficult for the average person to decipher. The descriptions given here are written in plain English, which, unfortunately, slightly increases the chance that some aspects of the laws have been lost in translation. Thus, this chapter should not be used for legal purposes.

Descriptions rely heavily on their respective entries in Gregg Lee Carter, ed., *Guns in American Society: An Encyclopedia of History, Politics, Culture, and the Law, Vols. I and II* (Santa Barbara, CA: ABC-CLIO, 2002). Much more comprehensive accounts can be found in Stephen Halbrook's *Firearms Law Deskbook: Federal and State Criminal Practice* (Eagan, MN: Thomson/West Group, 2004) and Alan Korwin and Michael P. Anthony's *Gun Laws of America* (Phoenix, AZ: Bloomfield Press, 2005).

The following three organizations provide Web presentations of federal firearms regulations: (1) the National Rifle Association (http://www.nraila.org/GunLaws/FederalGunLaws .aspx?ID=60); (2) the Firearms Law Center (http://www.firearms lawcenter.org/content/Federallawsummary.asp); and (3) the Bureau of Alcohol, Tobacco, Firearms and Explosives (http:// www.atf.gov/pub/fire-explo_pub/2000_ref.htm).

The most important change in federal legislation in the past five years was the expiration of the 1994 federal assault weapons ban (as set forth in the Title XI as part of the Violent Crime Control and Law Enforcement Act of 1994). The politics of the creation and demise of this ban are discussed in detail in Chapter 2.

155

1927

Mailing of Firearms Act (Miller Act)

Officially entitled "An Act Declaring Pistols, Revolvers, and Other Firearms Capable of Being Concealed on the Person Nonmailable and Providing Penalties," this act was the first federal legislation aimed at controlling guns. Also known as the Miller Act, it sought to prohibit interstate shipment of all concealable handguns (except service revolvers). Still in effect today, the act prohibits sending through the United States Post Office pistols and other firearms that could be concealable weapons.

In actuality, the law was easy to skirt, because mailers could legally send guns via private delivery companies such as UPS.

1934

National Firearms Act

The National Firearms Act (NFA) of 1934 mandated all persons who were engaged in the business of selling "gangster-type" weapons—such as machine guns, sawed-off shotguns, and silencers—and all owners of these to register with the Collector of Internal Revenue and pay applicable taxes for the firearm transfer.

The NFA was enacted under the taxing power granted to Congress in Article I, Section 8 of the U.S. Constitution. It is administered by the secretary of the Treasury, who has delegated all responsibilities to the Bureau of Alcohol, Tobacco, and Firearms (BATF), which was upgraded from a division to a bureau in 1972. Among its central provisions, the NFA instituted a unique system of registration whereby NFA-related firearms are registered to their owners in a central registry maintained by BATF. In addition, the NFA prohibits the transfer or manufacture of NFA-related firearms without the prior approval of the BATF. The written application forms require, among other things, that the person submit a photograph and fingerprint card to the BATF.

It should be noted that approximately one-half century later (in 1986), Congress banned the sale of new machine guns altogether—except for the government. Section 922(o) of the Firearms Owners' Protection Act (FOPA) of 1986 now prohibits a private citizen from possessing or transferring a machine gun that was not made and registered before May 19, 1986, unless such transfer or possession is authorized by federal or state governments or their departments or agencies. Since the enactment of FOPA, BATF will not approve any NFA application to make, transfer, and pay the $200 tax on any machine gun made after May 19, 1986.

1938

Federal Firearms Act

The Federal Firearms Act imposed the first federal limitations on the sale of ordinary firearms. It was aimed at those involved in selling and shipping firearms through interstate or foreign commerce. The law required the manufacturers, dealers, and importers of guns and handgun ammunition to obtain a Federal Firearms License (at an annual cost of one dollar) from the Internal Revenue Service. Dealers had to maintain records of the names and addresses of persons to whom firearms are sold. Gun sales to persons convicted of violent felonies were prohibited.

However, the legislation was substantially weakened when Congress struck from it any provision that would empower the Justice Department to prosecute gun shippers and manufacturers who unintentionally put guns into the hands of criminals. They could only be prosecuted if they "knowingly" sold guns to criminals, but they were not required to do any background checking of buyers.

1958

Federal Aviation Act

As part of the Federal Aviation Act, individuals flying on passenger aircraft are barred from bringing on board any firearm, ammunition, or firearm part, except as part of their check-in luggage. The Transportation Security Administration summarizes the law and its related amendments in its 2005 circular *Transporting Firearms and Ammunition* (http://www.tsa.gov/public/display ?content=09000519800ac232). Firearms declared to the air carrier during the ticket counter check-in process must meet the following regulations:

- The firearm must be unloaded.
- The firearm must be carried in a hard-sided container.
- The container must be locked.
- The passenger must provide the key or combination to the screener if it is necessary to open the container, and then remain present during screening to take back possession of the key after the container is cleared.
- Any ammunition transported must be securely packed in fiber (such as cardboard), wood or metal boxes or other packaging specifically designed to carry small amounts of ammunition.
- Firearm magazines/clips do not satisfy the packaging requirement unless they provide a complete and secure enclosure of the ammunition (e.g., by securely covering the exposed portions of the magazine or by securely placing the magazine in a pouch, holder, holster or lanyard).
- The ammunition may also be located in the same hard-sided case as the firearm, as long as it is properly packed as described above.
- Black powder and percussion caps used with black-powder type firearms are not permitted in carry-on or checked baggage.

The regulations are strictly enforced. Violations can result in criminal prosecution and the imposition of civil penalties of up to $10,000 per violation.

1968

Gun Control Act

Those statutes that are now called the Gun Control Act (GCA) were actually combined from two different bills: the Gun Control Act, and the Omnibus Safe Streets and Crime Control Act. Most of the statutes are found at 18 U.S. Code secs. 921–929. New federal gun laws (e.g., the Brady Act, the 1994 "assault weapon" ban) are usually codified as amendments to the GCA statutes.

The GCA's most important provisions include restrictions on sales of guns and ammunition across state lines, restrictions on the import of firearms, creating the "prohibited persons" list of classes of persons who are barred from possessing guns, and creating a point-of-sale system of gun owner registration.

"Prohibited persons" consist of anyone with any type of felony conviction no matter how distant or nonviolent, alcoholics, drug users, "mental defectives," fugitives, persons dishonorably discharged from the military, and persons who renounced their citizenship. In the 1990s, the list was expanded to include people with any domestic violence misdemeanor conviction and persons subject to domestic violence restraining orders. The ban on sales, but not possession, was also applied to persons under indictment by the Firearms Owners' Protection Act of 1986.

Interstate pistol sales were banned. Interstate long gun sales were banned, except when contiguous states enacted laws to authorize such sales. Mail-order and package delivery service (e.g., UPS) gun sales were shut down. Interstate ammunition sales were prohibited. All of these bans applied only to purchases by consumers. Federal Firearms License (FFL) holders—including gun manufacturers and wholesalers—were still allowed to sell across state lines to each other, and to use the mails. A new class of FFL was created for gun collectors, allowing them to engage in interstate and mail-order transactions for "curios and relics," but requiring them to submit to various registration and paperwork rules.

FFL sales of handguns were banned to persons under the age of twenty-one. Long gun (rifle or shotgun) sales to persons under eighteen were also banned. In addition, the secretary of the treasury was given authority to ban the import of any gun not "particularly suitable for or readily adaptable to" sporting purposes. Imports of foreign military surplus firearms were prohibited.

The GCA also amended a separate federal law, the National Firearms Act (NFA) of 1934. As noted previously, the NFA (26 U.S. Code sec. 5801 et seq.) had imposed a taxation and registration system on machine guns, short shotguns, short rifles, and silencers. The GCA amended the NFA by creating a new category of prohibited weapons: "destructive devices" (e.g., mortars, grenades).

Finally, the GCA led to the creation of the Bureau of Alcohol, Tobacco, and Firearms (BATF)—upgraded from its previous status as a division—within the Department of the Treasury.

Concerns about abusive enforcement of the GCA eventually led Congress to pass the Firearm Owners' Protection Act of 1986, which curtailed some provisions of the GCA, while leaving the basic structure intact.

1986

Firearms Owners' Protection Act (McClure-Volkmer)

Enacted as Public Law 99-308, 100 Stat. 449 in 1986, the Firearms Owners' Protection Act (FOPA)—known also as the McClure-Volkmer Act—made technical changes to the Gun Control Act of 1968 (GCA). FOPA prohibited forfeitures of personal firearms on charges for which a defendant had been acquitted; prohibited punishment of unintentional violations by the GCA (by requiring that the government prove that the violation was willful or knowing); clarified what was meant by the GCA requirement that a Federal Firearms Licence (FFL) was necessary for persons "engaged in the business"; allowed a FFL holder to sell guns away from their principal place of business as long as the sales complied with all relevant laws (thus allowing FFL holders to sell guns at gun shows); reclassiffied certain paperwork violations as misdemeanors; limited Bureau of Alcohol, Tobacco, and Firearms (BATF) inspections of gun dealers to one per dealer per year (while still allowing unlimited inspections in case of a criminal investigation); required BATF to process FFL applications in a timely manner and not to deny the application without good cause; imposed controls on BATF license revocations; provided for the award of attorney's fees against BATF if the court found that that case was abusive; prohibited BATF from creating a national gun registry; removed federal restrictions on interstate ammunition sales; relegalized interstate long gun sales (if the seller is an FFL, and the sale is legal in the buyer's home state); and broadened the scope of firearms allowed to be imported. FOPA left in tact the GCA banning of consumers being able to purchse handguns across state lines.

The GCA had created a mandatory sentence for use of a gun in a federal crime of violence. FOPA extended this to drug trafficking crimes, and added a thirty-year sentence for a machine gun or silencer.

FOPA did not end the debate about proper federal implementation of the GCA. BATF regulation-writing under GCA/FOPA, as well as enforcement of GCA/FOPA, remain objects of great controversy, with allegations that BATF is implementing the statute too stringently or too loosely.

Armed Career Criminal Act

Enacted as Public Law 99-570, the Armed Career Criminal Act increased the penalties for possession of firearms by "prohibited persons" as specified in the Gun Control Act of 1968.

Law Enforcement Officers Protection Act

Enacted as Public Law 99-308, the Law Enforcement Officers Protection Act bans so-called cop killer handgun bullets—or more accurately, bullets with very dense cores—that are capable of piercing bullet-resistant vests and other body armor.

1988

Undetectable Firearms Act (Terrorist Firearms Detection)

Codified at 18 U.S. Code section 922(p), the Undetectable Firearms Act, also known as the Terrorist Firearms Detection Act, arose in response to the development of plastic guns that combined the use of plastic polymers with metallic firearm components. The act banned the manufacture, importation, possession, receipt, and transfer of guns with less than 3.7 ounces of metal.

Although the bill was prospective only and had no effect on any existing gun, it helped set the stage for the 1994 congressional ban on "assault weapons."

1990

Crime Control Act

Enacted as Public Law 101-647, the Crime Control Act of 1990 bans the importing and manufacturing from foreign parts of certain semiautomatic firearms designated as "assault weapons"; other types of semiautomatic rifles, shotguns, and pistols were still allowed to be imported. The act also created Gun-Free School Zones, making it a federal crime to carry a firearm within 1,000 feet of a school; however, this portion of the act was overturned in a circuit court ruling in 1993—that was subsequently upheld by the ruling of the Supreme Court in *United States v. Lopez* (1995).

1993

Brady Handgun Violence Prevention Act

Enacted by Congress as Public Law 103-159; 107 Statute 1536, the Brady Act required a five-government-business-day waiting period for the purchase of a handgun, for the purpose of conducting a background check on the prospective buyer, and to provide a cooling off period in order to minimize impulse purchases that might lead to violence. Five years after enactment of the law, the five-day waiting period was eliminated and replaced by an instant background check system.

Handgun purchases are to be rejected if the applicant has been convicted of a crime that carries a sentence of at least a year (not including misdemeanors); if there is a violence-based restraining order against the applicant; if the person has been convicted of domestic abuse, arrested for using or selling drugs, is a fugitive from justice, is certified as mentally unstable or is in a mental institution, or is an illegal alien or has renounced U.S. citizenship. (Note that this list of prohibited persons was created earlier by the Gun Control Act of 1968 and its subsequent amendments.) The Brady law also authorized $200 million per year to help states improve and upgrade their computerization of criminal records, increased federal firearms license fees from $30 to $200 for the first three years and $90 for renewals, made it a federal crime to steal firearms from licensed dealers, barred package labeling for guns being shipped (to deter theft), required state and local police to be told of multiple handgun sales (such sales were already required to be reported to the Bureau of Alcohol, Tobacco, and Firearms), and said that police must make a "reasonable effort" to check the backgrounds of gun buyers. In addition, it provided for ending the five-day wait after five years, to be replaced with an instant background check, which began in December 1998. Such checks are conducted through information provided by the FBI's National Instant Criminal Background Check System (NICS). The check must be completed within three days, but 95 percent of the background checks are completed within two hours, according to a U.S. Justice Department report. Even though waiting periods are no longer required by the national government, nineteen states have their own, ranging from a few days to several months. They include Alabama, California, Connecticut, Florida, Illinois, Indiana, Kansas, Maryland, Massachusetts, Minnesota, Missouri, New Jersey, New York, North Carolina, Ohio, Rhode Island, South Dakota, Washington, and Wisconsin.

Opponents of the law, including the NRA, challenged its constitutionality—not as a violation of the Second Amendment's right to bear arms, but as a violation of states' rights under the Tenth Amendment. In 1997, a sharply divided Supreme Court struck down the law's provision requiring local police to conduct background checks in the case of *Printz v. United States* (521 U.S. 898). The majority ruling did not challenge or address the propriety of restricting handgun sales. Despite the ruling, handgun background checks generally continued on a voluntary basis. From the time of the law's enactment through 2000, nearly 600,000 handgun sales were blocked as the result of the law (about 2.5 percent of all handgun purchases). In addition, the increase in federal firearms license fees—coupled with vigorous BATF efforts that had already been under way—helped reduce the number of license holders from nearly 300,000 to about 74,000 by 2000, as most license holders were not storefront dealers, but private individuals who were willing to pay the low fee in order to save money on their own gun purchases.

Brady law supporters complain that the background check provision only applied to licensed dealers. At gun shows and flea markets in most states, guns can be bought and sold by unlicensed individuals. An estimated 40 percent of gun sales occur at gun shows, flea markets, among friends, and other unregulated "secondary market" venues (over 4,000 gun shows are held every year). National legislative efforts to close this so-called gun-show loophole failed in 1999 and 2000.

1994

Gun Free Schools Act

The Gun Free Schools Act of 1994 (20 U.S.C. Chapter 70, Sec. 8921) requires that any state receiving federal education funds "shall have in effect a State law requiring local educational agencies to expel from school for a period of not less than one year a student who is determined to have brought a weapon to a school."

Violence Against Women Act

Under statute 18 U.S.C. 922 (g)(8) of the Violence Against Women Act of 1994, it is unlawful for anyone subject to a domestic violence protection order to ship, transport, or possess any firearm or ammunition. Under statute 18 U.S.C. 922 (g) (9), it is likewise unlawful for anyone who has been convicted in any court of a misdemeanor crime of domestic violence to ship, transport, or possess any firearm or ammunition. Finally, under statute 18 U.S.C. 922 (g) (1), it is a federal crime for anyone convicted in any court of a crime punishable by imprisonment for a term exceeding one year to ship, transport, or possess any firearm or ammunition.

1996

Lautenberg Amendment (Domestic Violence Offender Gun Ban)

The Lautenberg Amendment to the Gun Control Act of 1968 [18 U.S.C. §922(d)(9)], also called the Domestic Violence Offender Gun Ban, closed what gun control advocates considered a loophole in federal regulations. The amendment expanded prohibition of gun purchase, ownership, or possession to include persons convicted of domestic violence misdemeanor offenses. Previously such bans covered only convicted felons.

Following its passage, the amendment came under fire from some law enforcement organizations. Leaders of those groups were responding to complaints from members prohibited from carrying firearms because of previous misdemeanor domestic violence convictions.

2002

Nonimmigrant Aliens Firearms and Ammunition Amendments

In 2002, the United States Customs Service and the Bureau of Alcohol, Tobacco, and Firearms (ATF) announced that they would begin enforcement of the Nonimmigrant Aliens Firearms and Ammunition Amendments to the Gun Control Act of 1968 (as enacted by Congress in 1998 as Public Law 105-277). These amendments require nonimmigrant aliens wanting to bring firearms or ammunition into the United States for hunting or sporting purposes to obtain an import permit from ATF prior to entering the country.

2004

Background Check Restriction

In January 2004, as part of the Fiscal Year 2004 Consolidated Appropriations Bill (Public Law 108-199), Congress approved provisions reducing the length of time the Department of Justice can maintain background-check records on firearm sales: from ninety days to twenty-four hours. Records are kept on file to ensure that if an individual prohibited from buying guns (e.g., a convicted felon or individual under a domestic violence restraining order) is inadvertently allowed to make such a purchase, the mistake can be corrected. Gun control advocates have complained that requiring these records to be destroyed within twenty-four hours has resulted in the Justice Department being unable to correct most errors, and their expectation is that more guns will end up in the hands of those prohibited from possessing them. However, gun rights proponents note that if a background check produces a rejection, then all information related to that potential sale is kept indefinitely.

Guidelines for Studies Using Tracing Data

Also as part of the Fiscal Year 2004 Consolidated Appropriations Bill (Public Law 108-199), Congress set new requirements on crime-gun tracing data gathered and released by the Bureau of Alcohol, Tobacco, Firearms and Explosives. More particularly, the bureau must include a "disclaimer" when it releases studies based on tracing data. The disclaimer must "make clear that trace data cannot be used to draw broad conclusions about firearms-related crime." The disclaimer should specifically note that traced firearms "do not constitute a random sample and should not be considered representative of the larger universe of all firearms used by criminals."

2005

Protection of Lawful Commerce in Arms Act

The Protection of Lawful Commerce in Arms Act (S.397; H.R.800) was passed into law in the fall of 2005. The act prohibits "civil liability actions" against manufacturers, distributors, dealers, and importers of firearms or ammunition products and their trade associations, for any harm caused by the criminal or unlawful misuse of firearms or ammunition. It does not, however, exempt those in the gun industry who break the law or sell defective weapons or ammunition.

5

State Gun Laws

Many news and gun-related organizational Web sites provide comprehensive presentations of state gun regulations, including: (1) the Bureau of Alcohol, Tobacco, Firearms and Explosives (http://www.atf.treas.gov/firearms/statelaws/22edition.htm); (2) the National Rifle Association (http://www.nraila.org/GunLaws/Default.aspx); (3) the Brady Campaign to Prevent Gun Violence (http://www.bradycampaign.org/legislation/state/); (4) Bloomfield Press (http://www.gunlaws.com/links/); (5) MSNBC (http://www.msnbc.com/modules/cnp/cnp_Front.asp); (6) CNN (http://www.cnn.com/SPECIALS/1998/schools/gun.control/); and (7) Common Sense about Kids and Guns (http://www.kidsandguns.org/study/stateinfo.asp). The best scholarly presentation and analysis of recent state gun laws is Jon S. Vernick and Lisa M. Hepburn's "State and Federal Gun Laws" (pp. 345–411 in Jens Ludwig and Philip J. Cook, eds., *Evaluating Gun Policy: Effects on Crime and Violence*, Brookings Institution Press, 2003).

Table 5.1 presents the major state gun laws as of 2005. It does not contain information on every possible gun-related law, but focuses on those that are at the center of the national debate over gun control. As presented in Chapter 2, gun control advocates believe that all of the following should be regulated at the national level, as state-level laws are often easily evaded by simply crossing the border between a strict and lax gun-control state: waiting periods registration, licensing (permits to purchase), juvenile possession and sales, records of sale, secondary sales regulations, restrictions on assault weapons, ballistic fingerprinting, and limiting gun purchases to once per month. The last two columns in Table 5.1 (Part II) list the "grade" each state receives for the strictness of its gun control laws according to two of the strongest organizations advocating gun control—the Brady Campaign to Prevent Gun Violence and the Open Society Institute. Of course, whether one views a Brady Campaign "A" or an Open Society "S" ("strong gun control laws") as good or bad depends whether one is a "gun control" versus a "gun rights" advocate.

Federal gun control laws do not preempt those at the state level. Rather, federal laws set the minimum standard for all states. For example, federal law does not allow the sale of handguns to individuals under the age of eighteen, but Connecticut, Hawaii, Illinois, Iowa, Maryland, Missouri, Ohio, Rhode Island, South Carolina, and Washington have set a higher age minimum (twenty-one), which trumps the federal requirement. On the other hand, as noted in Chapters 1 and 2, most states now have "preemption" laws that discourage localities from enacting their own gun control measures. More particularly, no local law in these states can be stricter than the state-level equivalent. The only states without a preemption law are Alaska, Hawaii, Illinois, Kansas, Nebraska, New Hampshire, and Ohio. Connecticut, Massachusetts, New Jersey, and New York have preemption through judicial ruling (as opposed to state statutes), and Massachusetts allows local ordinances if they receive state legislature approval.

TABLE 5.1
Key State Gun Laws—Part I
Purchase

STATE	(A) NICS Background Check[A]	(B) State Waiting Period[B]	(C) Registration Laws[C]	(D) Permit to Purchase Required[D]	(E) Juvenile Possession Laws[E]	(F) Juvenile Sales Laws[F]	(G) Record of Sale[G]	(H) Secondary Sales Law[H]	(I) Restrictions on Assault Weapons[I]	(J) Ballistic Fingerprinting[J]	(K) One-Gun-Per-Month Law
Alabama	YA1	YB1	N	N	N	YF1	YG1	Y	N	N	N
Alaska	YA1	N	N	N	YE1	N	YG2	N	N	N	N
Arizona	YA2	N	N	N	YE2	YF1	N	N	N	N	N
Arkansas	YA1	N	N	N	YE2	YF1	N	N	N	N	N
California	YA2	YB2	N	N	YE2	YF2	YG1	Y	Y	N	N
Colorado	YA2	N	N	N	YE2	YF1	Y	N	N	N	N
Connecticut	YA2	YB3	Y	YD1,D2,D3	N	YF3	YG1	Y	Y	N	N
Delaware	YA1	N	N	N	YE2	YF1	Y	N	N	N	N
Florida	YA2	YB4	N	N	YE2	YF1	N	N	N	N	N
Georgia	YA2	N	N	N	YE3	YF3	N	N	N	N	N
Hawaii	YA2	YB5	Y	YD1,D2,D4	YE1	YF1	YG3	Y	YI1	N	N
Idaho	YA1	N	N	N	YE2	YF4	Y	N	N	N	N

(continues)

TABLE 5.1
Key State Gun Laws—Part I
Purchase (continued)

STATE	(A) NICS Background Check[A]	(B) State Waiting Period[B]	(C) Registration Laws[C]	(D) Permit to Purchase Required[D]	(E) Juvenile Possession Laws[E]	(F) Juvenile Sales Laws[F]	(G) Record of Sale[G]	(H) Secondary Sales Law[H]	(I) Restrictions on Assault Weapons[I]	(J) Ballistic Fingerprinting[J]	(K) One-Gun-Per-Month Law
Illinois	YA2	YB6	N	YD2,D3,D4	YE2	YF1	Y	Y	N	N	N
Indiana	YA3	N	N	N	YE2	YF1	YG1	Y	N	N	N
Iowa	YA3	YB7	N	YD2,D5	YE4	YF3	N	Y	N	N	N
Kansas	YA1	N	N	N	YE2	YF1	N	N	N	N	N
Kentucky	YA1	N	Y	N	YE2	N	N	N	N	N	N
Louisiana	YA1	N	N	N	N	YF1	YG3	N	N	N	N
Maine	YA1	N	N	N	N	YF4	Y	N	N	N	N
Maryland	YA3	YB8	N	N	YE3	YF3	YG1	Y	YI1	Y	Y
Massachusetts	YA1	YB8,B11	N	YD1,D2,D4,D5	YE3	YF3	YG1	Y	Y	N	N
Michigan	YA3	N	N	YD1,D2	YE2	YF1	Y	Y	N	N	N
Minnesota	YA1	YB9	N	YD2,D5	YE2	YF1	YG1	Y	N	N	N
Mississippi	YA1	N	N	N	YE1	YF1	N	N	N	N	N
Missouri	YA1	YB9	N	YD2,D5	N	YF1	N	Y	N	N	N

TABLE 5.1
Key State Gun Laws—Part I
Purchase (continued)

STATE	(A) NICS Background Check[A]	(B) State Waiting Period[B]	(C) Registration Laws[C]	(D) Permit to Purchase Required[D]	(E) Juvenile Possession Laws[E]	(F) Juvenile Sales Laws[F]	(G) Record of Sale[G]	(H) Secondary Sales Law[H]	(I) Restrictions on Assault Weapons[I]	(J) Ballistic Fingerprinting[J]	(K) One-Gun-Per-Month Law
Montana	YA1	N	N	N	YE5	N	N	N	N	N	N
Nebraska	YA3	YB10	N	YD2,D5	YE2	YF1	N	Y	N	N	N
Nevada	YA2	N	N	N	YE5	YF1	N	N	N	N	N
New Hampshire	YA3	N	N	N	YE1	YF1	YG1	N	N	N	N
New Jersey	YA2	YB11	N	YD2,D4,D5	YE2	YF1	YG1	Y	Y	N	N
New Mexico	YA1	N	N	N	YE6	N	N	N	N	N	N
New York	YA3	YB12	N	YD2,D5	YE3	YF3	YG1	Y	Y	Y	Y
North Carolina	YA3	YB13	N	YD2,D5	YE2	YF1	Y	Y	N	N	N
North Dakota	YA1	N	N	N	YE2	YF1	N	N	N	N	N
Ohio	YA1	N	N	N	N	YF2	N	N	N	N	N
Oklahoma	YA1	N	N	N	YE2	YF1	N	N	N	N	N
Oregon	YA3	N	N	N	YE2	YF1	N	N	N	N	N

(continues)

TABLE 5.1
Key State Gun Laws—Part I
Purchase (continued)

STATE	(A) NICS Background Check^A	(B) State Waiting Period^B	(C) Registration Laws^C	(D) Permit to Purchase Required^D	(E) Juvenile Possession Laws^E	(F) Juvenile Sales Laws^F	(G) Record of Sale^G	(H) Secondary Sales Law^H	(I) Restrictions on Assault Weapons^I	(J) Ballistic Fingerprinting^J	(K) One-Gun-Per-Month Law
Pennsylvania	YA2	N	N	N	YE2	YF1	YG1	Y	N	N	N
Rhode Island	YA1	YB8	N	N	YE2	YF1	Y	Y	N	N	N
South Carolina	YA1	N	N	N	YE3	YF3	N	Y	N	N	N
South Dakota	YA1	N	N	N	YE2	YF1	N	N	N	N	N
Tennessee	YA2	N	N	N	YE2	YF1	N	N	N	N	N
Texas	YA1	N	N	N	N	YF1	N	N	N	N	N
Utah	YA2	N	N	N	YE2	YF1	N	N	N	N	N
Vermont	YA2	N	N	N	YE1	YF4	Y	N	N	N	N
Virginia	YA2	N	N	N	YE2	YF1	YG1	N	N	N	N
Washington	YA3	YB14	N	N	YE2	YF3	N	N	N	N	N
West Virginia	YA1	N	N	N	YE2	YF1	N	N	N	N	N
Wisconsin	YA3	YB1	N	N	YE2	YF1	N	N	N	N	N
Wyoming	YA1	N	N	N	N	N	Y	N	N	N	N

TABLE 5.1
Key State Gun Laws—Part II

		OTHER		STRENGTH OF GUN LAWS	
	(L)	(M)	(N)	(O)	(P)
STATE	CAP Law[L]	Average Citizen Has Right to Carry a Concealed Handgun	Preemption Law	Brady Grade[O]	Open Society Grade[P]
Alabama	N	NM1	Y	F	WP3
Alaska	N	YM2	YN1	D-	WP3
Arizona	N	Y	Y	D	WP3
Arkansas	N	Y	Y	D	WP3
California	Y	NM1	YN1	A-	MP2
Colorado	N	Y	N	D	WP3
Connecticut	Y	NM1	YN2	A-	MP2
Delaware	Y	NM1	Y	C	WP3
Florida	Y	Y	YN1	D+	WP3
Georgia	N	Y	Y	D	WP3
Hawaii	Y	NM1	N	A-	SP1
Idaho	N	Y	Y	F+	WP3
Illinois	Y	NM3	N	B+	MP2
Indiana	N	Y	Y	D	WP3
Iowa	Y	NM1	Y	C+	WP3
Kansas	N	NM3	N	C+	WP3
Kentucky	N	Y	Y	F	WP3
Louisiana	N	Y	Y	F	WP3
Maine	N	Y	Y	D-	WP3
Maryland	Y	NM1	YN1	A-	MP2
Massachusetts	Y	NM1	YN2	A-	SP1
Michigan	N	Y	Y	D+	WP3
Minnesota	Y	Y	Y	C-	WP3
Mississippi	N	Y	Y	F	WP3

(continues)

TABLE 5.1
Key State Gun Laws—Part II (continued)

STATE	(L) CAP Law[L]	OTHER			STRENGTH OF GUN LAWS	
		(M) Average Citizen Has Right to Carry a Concealed Handgun	(N) Preemption Law		(O) Brady Grade[O]	(P) Open Society Grade[P]
Missouri	N	Y	Y		D+	WP3
Montana	N	Y	YN1		F	WP3
Nebraska	N	NM3	N		B-	WP3
Nevada	Y	Y	Y		D	WP3
New Hampshire	N	Y	N		D-	WP3
New Jersey	Y	NM1	YN2		A-	MP2
New Mexico	N	Y	Y		F	WP3
New York	N	NM1	YN2		B+	MP2
North Carolina	Y	Y	Y		C	WP3
North Dakota	N	Y	Y		D	WP3
Ohio	N	Y	N		D-	WP3
Oklahoma	N	Y	Y		D-	WP3
Oregon	N	Y	Y		C-	WP3
Pennsylvania	N	Y	Y		D+	WP3
Rhode Island	Y	NM1	Y		B-	WP3
South Carolina	N	Y	Y		D+	WP3
South Dakota	N	Y	Y		D	WP3
Tennessee	N	T	Y		D+	WP3
Texas	Y	Y	Y		D-	WP3
Utah	N	Y	Y		D-	WP3
Vermont	N	YM2	Y		D-	WP3
Virginia	Y	Y	Y		C-	WP3
Washington	N	Y	Y		D+	WP3

(continues)

TABLE 5.1
Key State Gun Laws—Part II (continued)

		OTHER		STRENGTH OF GUN LAWS	
	(L)	(M)	(N)	(O)	(P)
STATE	CAP Law[L]	Average Citizen Has Right to Carry a Concealed Handgun	Preemption Law	Brady Grade[O]	Open Society Grade[P]
West Virginia	N	Y	Y	D	WP3
Wisconsin	Y	NM3	Y	C+	WP3
Wyoming	N	Y	Y	F	WP3

A National Instant Check System (NICS) is a mandatory, computerized system that provides instant information for criminal background checks on all firearm purchases.

A1 FBI performs NICS checks on both handguns and long guns.

A2 The state conducts NICS checks for all firearms purchases and for permits for handguns and long guns.

A3 The state performs NICS checks for handgun purchases, but the FBI performs NICS checks for long gun purchases.

B Some states have their own waiting periods to obtain a permit to purchase and/or for actual purchase.

B1 Two-day waiting period for handguns.

B2 Ten-day waiting period for any firearm.

B3 Up to fourteen-day wait to acquire permit to purchase a handgun.

B4 Three-day waiting period for handguns.

B5 Up to fifteen-day wait to acquire permit to purchase any firearm.

B6 Three-day waiting period to purchase a handgun, one-day waiting period for a long gun.

B7 Up to three-day wait to acquire permit to purchase a handgun.

B8 Seven-day waiting period for handguns.

B9 Up to seven-day wait to acquire permit to purchase a handgun.

B10 Up to two-day wait to acquire permit to purchase a handgun.

B11 Up to thirty-day wait to acquire permit to purchase any firearm.

B12 Up to six-month wait to acquire permit to purchase a handgun, though in practice, waits of more than half a year are common, especially in New York City.

B13 Up to thirty-day wait to acquire permit to purchase a handgun.

B14 Five-day waiting period for handguns.

(continues)

TABLE 5.1
Key State Gun Laws—Part II (continued)

C Registration Law requires a record of the transfer or ownership of a specific handgun.

D1 Safety training required.

D2 Permit for handgun purchase is required.

D3 Buyer must be at least twenty-one years of age.

D4 Permit for long gun purchase is required.

D5 Background check is required, before issuing a permit to purchase.

E Federal Law prohibits possession of handguns for those under eighteen (except under certain circumstances, namely, hunting, ranching, and target shooting); otherwise state law dictates possession of long guns for juveniles, and of handguns for those who are eighteen to twenty years old.

E1 Must be sixteen years old.

E2 Must be eighteen years old.

E3 Must be twenty-one years old.

E4 Must be twenty-one for handguns, and eighteen for rifles or shotguns.

E5 Must be fourteen years old.

E6 Must be twenty years old.

F1 Must be eighteen years old.

F2 Must be eighteen for firearms, and twenty-one for handguns.

F3 Must be twenty-one years old.

F4 Must be sixteen years old.

G Some states require dealers to retain a record of sale, for a short period of time, while others want it sent to a state agency.

G1 Record of sale must be sent to state agency.

G2 Required for pawnshops only.

G3 Registration of all firearms is required.

H Some states prohibit secondary sales or require that such sales be registered or routed through a licensed firearms dealer.

I1 Assault pistols only.

L Also known as safe gun storage laws, CAP laws require gun owners to store their firearms in a manner that would prevent children and teens from gaining unauthorized access.

L1 Sale of safety lock is required.

L2 Partial; only dealer warning signs are required.

M1 "May Issue (implies difficulty in the average citizen obtaining a concealed firearm permit)"

M2 Citizens generally have the right to carry a concealed weapon and do not need a special permit.

M3 "All concealed firearms are prohibited."

(continues)

TABLE 5.1
Key State Gun Laws—Part II (continued)

N Preemption laws are state laws that generally prohibit localities from enacting any gun control regulations that are in conflict with state-level regulations, especially any that would be stricter than those of the state.

N1 Partial.

N2 Preemption through judicial ruling.

O The Brady Campaign to Prevent Gun Violence 2004 Report Card—Detailed Grade Information (http://www.bradycampaign.org/facts/reportcards/2004/details.pdf). The higher the letter grade, the tougher the state's gun laws.

P Open Society Institute, Gun Control in the United States: A Comparative Survey of State Firearm Laws (http://www.soros.org/initiatives/justice/articles_publications/publications/gun_report_20000401/GunReport.pdf). States are individually scored on their gun laws out of a maximum possible score of 100%. The higher the score, the tougher the state's gun laws.

P1 "S" Strong (>71).

P2 "M" Moderate (20–70).

P3 "W" Weak (<20).

6

Major Court Cases

As pointed out in Chapter 2, disappointment over lack of progress with legislative approaches to controlling gun violence has led many gun control advocates to use the judicial system to pursue their cause. Suing manufacturers, wholesalers, retailers, and gun owners in civil court became a common tactic of the gun control movement during the 1990s. Five types of lawsuits were filed:

- product liability suits against manufacturers for producing and selling defective guns;
- suits against dealers for negligent sales practices that result in prohibited persons (e.g., convicted felons) acquiring guns;
- suits against gun manufacturers for intentional shootings;
- suits against individuals for not keeping their guns secure, resulting in the guns being used in crimes, suicides, or accidents;
- litigation initiated by communities against manufacturers and dealers to recover the health-care and criminal justice costs related to gun violence.

Gun control advocates pursue these suits for a variety of reasons, including compensation for victims, but the ultimate goal is to reduce gun-related crime, suicides, and accidents by reducing the likelihood of guns falling into the hands of high-risk individuals (e.g., criminals; juveniles; the mentally ill or incompetent).

These lawsuits have received strong support from various gun control groups, including the Legal Action Project of the Brady Center to Prevent Gun Violence (http://www.gunlawsuits.org/) and the Educational Fund to Stop Gun Violence (http://www.csgv.org/issues/litigation/index.cfm).

Gun rights advocates contend that lawsuits are misused when filed to control gun violence. Criminals and individuals who abuse firearms are responsible for gun violence, not the makers or sellers of the weapons involved. Gun rights advocates also believe that those filing lawsuits are either unaware of—or refuse to acknowledge—the benefits of guns, more particularly their defensive use. According to these advocates, law-abiding citizens using their firearms to fend off criminal attack not only save themselves from harm but also give relief to the health care and criminal justice systems.

On the other hand, gun rights advocates are not afraid to use the courts to overturn legislation they believe infringes on their constitutional right "to keep and bear arms." Over the years, many such individuals—often with the backing of powerful gun rights groups such as the NRA—have filed suit against the government. With few exceptions, the plaintiffs have lost these cases. That is, the courts have ruled that there is no inherent problem between the general Second Amendment right for individuals to own and use guns and specific laws to regulate such ownership and use (see http://www.lcav.org/content/secondamendment.asp and http://www.lcav.org/content/secondamendment_state.asp for a comprehensive listing of these decisions at the federal and state levels).

In recent years, gun rights advocates have been successful in their pursuit of "immunity" legislation that prevents gun manufacturers and dealers from being sued for the consequences of the misuse of their firearms. Nineteen U.S. states have passed legislation preventing counties and local communities from filing public nuisance and design-defect lawsuits against gun manufacturers and their distributors. At the federal level, immunity legislation was passed into law in the fall of 2005 (The Protection of Lawful Commerce in Arms Act; S.397; H.R.800). The federal legislation will have the ultimate effect of all but ceasing the filing of civil suits by gun control advocates against the manufacturers, distributors, retailers, and importers of the gun industry.

Anderson v. Bryco Arms Corp. (pending) (No. 00-L-007476 [Circuit Court, Cook County, Illinois])

Benjamin Nathaniel Smith, a member of the white supremacist World Church of the Creator, was denied the right to purchase guns from a federally licensed firearms dealer in Peoria Heights, Illinois, in June 1999. He was under a domestic violence restraining order and thus was a prohibited purchaser. To bypass the law, Smith sought out Donald Fiessinger, who was selling guns from his home. Smith bought two handguns from Fiessinger, including a Bryco .380 caliber semiautomatic handgun. Over a two-year period, Fiessinger had bought seventy-two firearms, usually cheaply made handguns (Saturday night specials), from Old Prairie Trading Post in Pekin, Illinois. He would then resell them. Old Prairie never questioned him about the transactions, despite the high volume and the penchant for such guns to end up in criminal hands.

Smith used the Bryco .380 in a shooting spree against African-Americans, Asian-Americans, and Jews during the weekend of July 4, 1999. Smith killed two individuals and seriously wounded nine others.

The Legal Action Project for the Brady Center to Prevent Gun Violence brought a civil lawsuit against the gun manufacturer Bryco Arms, as well as against the gun shop and trafficker. The suit was brought on behalf of three of the wounded victims (including Reverend Stephen Anderson), the widow and children of one of the fatally wounded victims, and the family of another fatally wounded victim. The suit claimed negligence and public nuisance against the parties that armed Smith.

Bryco Arms Corporation was accused of irresponsible sales and distribution methods, since the manufacturer had not taken reasonable actions to prevent prohibited purchasers from acquiring their guns and failed to prevent large-volume sales of their guns to traffickers. Despite attempts by Bryco Arms and Old Prairie Trading Post to have the case dismissed, the court ruled that the suit should move forward. Robert Hayes, a gun dealer of Old Prairie Trading Post, was indicted on thirteen counts of violating federal firearms sales laws, including illegally selling the Bryco .380 to Fiessinger. In addition, Fiessinger was accused of illegally selling the gun to Benjamin Smith. Both pled guilty and were sentenced to prison. Since then, Hayes has filed for bankruptcy. As of the summer of 2005, the case against Bryco is ongoing.

Armijo v. Ex Cam, Inc. (1987)
(656 F. Supp. 771, 1987)

In 1983, Dolores Armijo's brother shot and killed her husband while she and her daughter looked on in fear and horror. When the brother turned to shoot Dolores and her daughter, the gun jammed and their lives were saved. Filing suit in the U.S. District Court for New Mexico, Ms. Armijo sought damages from the importer and manufacturer of the cheaply made handgun (Saturday night special) used in the murder. The suit alleged that the selling of the gun was an "ultra hazardous activity" that put the community at risk. The court rejected this argument and determined there was no precedent established in New Mexico to collect damages from the importer and distributor, Ex Cam, Inc., as well as no basis in product liability legal theory. When examining the liability aspect, the court considered such rules as strict product liability; hazardous production principle; negligence liability; and a strict liability specifically related to Saturday night specials. The court found that none of these requisites were met and also claimed that for Ms. Armijo to win the case, she needed to prove the weapon was defective. Ironically, this was found impossible to do, as the firearm had been successfully used to slay Mr. Armijo. The district court's decision was upheld when it was appealed to the U.S. Court of Appeals for the Tenth Circuit (843 F.2d 406). In a similar case in Maryland, the state Supreme Court did accept the "ultra hazardous activity" argument in ruling for the plaintiff in *Kelley v. R. G. Industries, Inc.* (q.v.).

Aymette v. State (1840)
(2 Humphrey [21 Tenn.] 154 [1840])

In a case that would take nearly one hundred years to realize its full consequences, the Tennessee Supreme Court ruled that the state's legislature had the power to prohibit the carrying of a concealed weapon. The decision supported an 1837 state law that prohibited the concealed carrying of such weapons. The court ruled that the law was not in conflict with the state constitution that allowed any free white man the right to keep and bear arms for personal defense. The *Aymette* decision did not follow the precedence of a similar case in Kentucky, where in *Bliss v. Commonwealth* (q.v.), an appeals court ruled that a similar law was in conflict with the state's constitutional protection of the right to keep and bear arms.

William Aymette had appealed his conviction of carrying a concealed bowie knife on the grounds that the decision infringed upon his state constitutional right to keep and bear arms. However, the Tennessee judges ruled that Aymette had no such right in this instance because the bowie knife was not traditionally used for military purposes and thus would not help him fulfill his duty of serving in the state militia if he were ever called to do so. They declared this kind of knife was common in brawls and robberies and therefore presented a danger to the peace and safety of others. The court also stated the constitution did not prevent the legislature from regulating weapons to protect the welfare of others. This rationale would be used almost a hundred years later by the U.S. Supreme court in its *United States v. Miller* (q.v.) ruling, one of the few times that the Supreme Court has dealt directly with how the Second Amendment should be interpreted.

Bailey v. United States (1996)
(516 U.S. 137, 1996)

In May 1989, Roland Bailey was found in possession of thirty grams of cocaine in his car after being pulled over by the local police. A loaded pistol was also found in the trunk. As the firearm was useful for drug trafficking, he was charged with violating the Gun Control Act of 1968. A jury found Bailey guilty on both the drug and weapons charges. The Court of Appeals for the District of Columbia Circuit upheld the guilty verdicts.

In a separate case, Candisha Robinson was arrested for selling crack cocaine. Upon a search of her apartment, police found an unloaded firearm in a locked trunk in her bedroom closet. Similar to Bailey, Robinson was found guilty of both drug and weapons charges, despite the fact that there was no evidence in either case that the firearms had been directly used as part of any drug dealings. However, in the Robinson case the appeals court reversed the weapons verdict, ruling that a firearm in close proximity to drugs does *not* establish a violation of the statute, which claims the gun must be in "use."

Since this contradicted the Bailey decision, the cases were consolidated for a consistent ruling in the District of Columbia Circuit Court of Appeals. The Court upheld the Bailey conviction and ruled against Robinson. The defendants appealed to the U.S. Supreme Court, claiming "use" should only be interpreted as actual employment of the gun. The Court agreed and overturned their weapons-related convictions. It ruled that "proximity and accessibility" are not enough to classify the guns as having been in "use." Thus, it sided with a narrow interpretation of the law, claiming the Gun Control Act of 1968 statute that was allegedly violated required that the firearms be in actual, not intended, use.

The *Bailey* decision had an immediate impact in significantly reducing the number of weapons charges processed in federal district courts. Before *Bailey*, if a drug dealer had a pistol anywhere in his or her car or dwelling, federal prosecutors would charge the individual not only with drug dealing but also with using a weapon in the commission of a crime; the additional weapons charge added significant prison time if the individual was convicted on the drug charge.

Barrett v. United States (1976)
(423 U.S. 212, 1976)

In April 1972, convicted felon Pearl Barrett purchased a revolver from a federally licensed firearms dealer. The gun had been manufactured in Massachusetts and sold in Kentucky. Barrett was charged and found guilty of violating a provision of the Gun Control Act of 1968 prohibiting convicted felons from receiving a gun or ammunition that had been transported through interstate or foreign commerce. Because he had made an *intrastate* purchase of the firearm that was not associated with the previous *interstate* transfer, Barrett argued for an acquittal. However, he was found guilty and the court of appeals upheld the decision.

Upon appeal, the U.S. Supreme Court upheld the conviction. The Court did not agree with Barrett's contention that the legislation was only meant to apply to interstate trafficking in which a purchaser was receiving a firearm directly from an out-of-state dealer. On the contrary, the Court found that the law was meant to keep firearms out of the hands of convicted felons and could be applied broadly, including to any intrastate transactions where it was found that the firearm had ever traveled in interstate commerce. In its decision, the Supreme Court referred to *United States v. Tot* (q.v.), in which it had ruled that the Federal Firearms Act of 1938 could be used to keep convicted felons from possessing firearms.

Barron v. Baltimore (1833)
(32 U.S. 243, 1833)

In *Barron v. Baltimore,* the U.S. Supreme Court ruled that the Bill of Rights pertains only to the national government, not to state or local governments. John Barron was a co-owner of a profitable wharf in the harbor of Baltimore, but as the city expanded, large amounts of sand accumulated. Without deep waters, ships were unable to approach the wharf, and Barron began to lose money. He brought suit against the city for reimbursement of his losses, claiming the Fifth Amendment prohibited divesting property without just compensation. Barron won his case, but the verdict was reversed in the court of appeals.

When Barron appealed to the U.S. Supreme Court, Chief Justice John Marshall handed down the unanimous judgment that the Bill of Rights applied only to the national government, and that the Court had no jurisdiction over the case. Over the years, the decision was mitigated, however, as several of the first ten amendments were "incorporated" through congressional and court action to make them applicable to state and local governments. A key exception, however, has been the Second Amendment, which has never been incorporated. Gun control advocates see this as leaving state and local governments free to develop gun control regulations, while gun rights advocates argue that *Barron v. Baltimore* has been overturned by the incorporation doctrine.

Beecham v. United States (1994)
(511 U.S. 368, 1994)

In *Beecham v. United States,* the U.S. Supreme Court examined the issue of whether a convicted felon's right to possess firearms could be restored. The case involved two defendants, Lenard Ray Beecham and Kirby Lee Jones, both of whom had been found guilty of violating the Gun Control Act of 1968, which bans gun possession by convicted felons. However, the individuals had their civil rights restored by their respective states.

In federal district court, cases were filed asking whether the state can restore an individual's right to possess guns. The courts decided that the state can restore the right and negate federal restrictions (as dictated, in this case, by the Gun Control Act of 1968). However, the Fourth Circuit Court of Appeals reversed the decisions. The U.S. Supreme Court agreed, claiming that state restoration did not eliminate the gun prohibitions that had come from federal law. In its ruling, the Court found that in order for persons convicted of a felony to receive reprieve from the Gun Control Act of 1968, their civil rights must be restored by the federal government itself. Such restoration is unlikely to happen, because it must be done by presidential pardon or by special application to the Bureau of Alcohol, Tobacco, Firearms and Explosives; however, Congress has prohibited the bureau from acting on such application in its annual appropriations bills since 1992.

Bernethy v. Walt Failor's, Inc. (1982) (97 Wn.2d 929, 653 P.2d 280)

Leaving his estranged wife, Phoebe, at a bar, an inebriated Robert Fleming went to a nearby gun store to buy a shotgun and ammunition. Before the store owner, Walt Failor, could complete the purchase, however, Fleming grabbed the gun and a box of shells and fled. Fleming returned to the bar and shot Phoebe to death. On behalf of the three Fleming children, Carolee Bernethy sued Failor and his store for wrongful death. The case was quickly dismissed, the court ruling that the Bernethy had no legal cause for action. However, after appeal, the Supreme Court of Washington ruled that the case was prematurely dismissed—that the plaintiff's case should be heard.

The case was thus returned to the original court. Backed up by a witness, Failor claimed he was unaware that Fleming was drunk, despite smelling alcohol. He also claimed that he had not sold the gun, but that it had been stolen. On the other hand, Fleming claimed he had urinated in his pants before entering the store and could not even hold himself up. Other witnesses testified that Fleming was heavily intoxicated. Washington state law did not have a specific law banning the sale of firearms to intoxicated individuals, but did have a statute prohibiting sale to those who were incompetent. The judge ruled that Bernethy had grounds for a civil suit, and her case was given over to a jury trial.

This decision was potentially significant for the advocates of gun control, because it establishes that gun retailers can be held liable for the unlawful use of firearms if it can be shown the seller could have reasonably foreseen that such a harmful action would be taken. However, other courts have rejected the logic of this decision and have not held the manufacturer or gun dealer supplying a firearm used in a crime liable for the misuse of the gun they have sold. Moreover, the U.S. Congress passed the Protection of Lawful Commerce in Arms Act (S.397; H.R.800) in the fall of 2005. The act prohibits future civil liability suits against manufacturers and dealers of firearms and ammunition products for any harm caused by their criminal misuse.

Bliss v. Commonwealth (1822)
(12 Ky. [2 Litt.] 90, 1822)

Bliss v. Commonwealth confirmed the individual's right to keep and bear arms as put forth in the Kentucky state constitution. After being arrested for carrying a concealed weapon, a sword in a cane, Bliss was found guilty in a local court. However, he appealed, asserting that the statute under which he was convicted conflicted with the state constitution's guarantee of citizens having the right to keep and bear arms for self-defense. The state Supreme Court agreed and overturned Bliss's conviction.

Bryan v. United States (1998)
(524 U.S. 184, 1998)

Sillasse Bryan was charged with selling firearms without a federal license, violating a section of the Firearms Owners' Protection (McClure-Volkmer) Act of 1986 (FOPA). In the trial, evidence was presented that Bryan was selling firearms without a federal

license. Despite showing that Bryan knew he was acting unlawfully, there was no evidence brought forth that Bryan was aware
of the specific federal law that bans dealing in firearms without a
license. The trial judge did not inform the jury that in order for
Bryan to be found guilty he must be aware of the specific law he
was breaking. Instead the judge instructed the jury that a person
is guilty if he or she acts "willfully" in a way that disregards or
disobeys the law. The jury found Bryan guilty, but he appealed,
claiming the judge had not given proper instructions to the jury.
The court of appeals affirmed the decision, claiming the trial
judge had acted properly.

Upon appeal to the U.S. Supreme Court, the original decision
was again upheld. The Court interpreted "willfully" as only requiring proof that the individual knew his behavior was against
the law, not that the defendant knew the exact federal licensing
law he was violating. Thus, this was an example of the general
legal principle that ignorance of the law is no excuse for breaking
it. The case is important to gun control activists because they see
FOPA as a weakening of the Gun Control Act of 1968, which originally established the requirement that firearms dealers must be
federally licensed. However, in this instance, the strength of the
1968 legislation was maintained.

Burton v. Sills (1968)
(248 A. 2d 521, 1968)

The plaintiffs in this case included individuals affiliated with a
sportsmen's club, gun dealers, and corporation that promoted
firearm shooting. These members of the gun industry filed a complaint that the New Jersey Gun Control Law was unconstitutional. The law required the licensing of manufacturers and dealers and identification cards for purchasers. The case was rejected
by the New Jersey Supreme Court, because it held that the Second
Amendment grants a collective, not an individual, right. In short,
the court viewed the law as not impairing the state's organized,
active militia, and was therefore not in violation of the Second
Amendment. Moreover, the court found that "New Jersey's Gun
Control Law is highly purposed and conscientiously designed toward preventing criminal and other unfit elements from acquiring firearms while enabling the fit elements of society to obtain
them with minimal burdens and inconveniences."

Caron v. United States (1998)
(524 U.S. 308, 1998)

The Gun Control Act of 1968 prohibits convicted felons from possessing firearms. The Armed Career Criminal Act of 1986 allows for "enhanced" (stiffer) sentences when a three-time violent felon violates the 1968 prohibition. Gerald Caron had been convicted of several serious offenses, but was still allowed under the state laws of Massachusetts to possess rifles and shotguns (although not handguns) because the required amount of time had passed since his convictions. However, he was arrested for threatening a man and his family with a firearm. Six rifles and thousands of rounds of ammunition were seized from Caron's home, and he was eventually convicted of violating the Gun Control Act of 1968 (he was a "prohibited" person yet still possessed firearms). Moreover, he was given an enhanced sentence because he was a three-time convicted felon.

Caron appealed his conviction and enhanced sentencing. He contended that federal law should not apply to him because the state had restored his civil rights with respect to possessing rifles and shotguns. The U.S. Court of Appeals for the First Circuit upheld his conviction and enhanced sentence, as did the U.S. Supreme Court. The Supreme Court ruled that even though his civil rights had been restored and the *state* had allowed him to possess certain firearms, Caron was still accountable for his violation of the *federal* Gun Control Act of 1968 and still subject to the enhanced sentencing provided for in the Armed Career Criminal Act of 1986.

Cases v. United States (1942)
(131 F. 2d 916, 1942)

Jose Cases Velazquez was convicted of violating sections of the Federal Firearms Act of 1938 prohibiting anyone with a violent-crime conviction from receiving a gun or ammunition through interstate or foreign commerce. The conviction, handed down in the District Court of the United States for Puerto Rico, was upheld by the U.S. Court of Appeals for the First Circuit.

A friend of the defendant had bought ten .38 caliber rounds from a hardware store. Three days later Velazquez used some of this ammunition to shoot a patron at a beach club in Carolina,

Puerto Rico. Since Velazquez had a previous conviction for a violent crime, he was charged with violating the Federal Firearms Act of 1938.

Among the several arguments the defendant presented was that the act infringed on his Second Amendment right to keep and bear arms. The court again ruled against him, citing *United States v. Miller* (q.v.). More specifically, it held that the government can prevent the keeping and bearing of arms by individuals as long as it does not violate the people's ability to form a well-regulated militia. Since Valazquez had no evidence that his firearm served any such purpose, the court held there had been no constitutional violation.

Ceriale v. Smith & Wesson Corp. et al. (pending)
(No. 99 L 5628 [Circuit Court, Cook County, Illinois])

Ceriale v. Smith & Wesson Corp. et al. is a landmark case in the battle of gun control advocates for stronger controls over firearms. It represents the first time a court has decided that individual victims of gun violence can bring charges of "public nuisance" against the gun industry. Families of murdered Chicago police officer Michael Ceriale and four other victims of unrelated criminal shootings filed the suit against two dozen gun manufacturers and distributors. The plaintiffs allege that Smith & Wesson, along with many other of the largest handgun manufacturers in the nation, created a public nuisance by cultivating an illicit market for handguns that has allowed them to easily end up in the hands of prohibited individuals—namely, juveniles and street gang members. More specifically, the manufacturers were charged with (a) producing negligently designed handguns that have been specifically geared to serve the needs of juveniles and gang members who use weapons for violent criminal purposes (e.g., having large-capacity ammunition clips); (b) negligently marketing these handguns to emphasize characteristics of the weapons that appeal to juveniles and gang members who intend to use the guns for criminal purposes; and (c) negligently distributing these handguns in a "no-holds barred way"—that is, without any supervision or training of handgun dealers. The effect of these actions have "combined to create an epidemic of violence by arming thousands of juvenile gang members in Chicago and throughout Cook County and to create a situation where many Chicago children feel pressured to obtain handguns to protect themselves from other children with handguns. The actions and omissions of all of the Handgun Manufacturers in the design, marketing and distribution of their handguns have created and are perpetuating a public nuisance in the City of Chicago."

After a motion to dismiss by the defendants was denied, the gun industry appealed the decision to the Illinois Appellate Court, which ruled that the suit could continue. However, the case may fall victim to the federal Protection of Lawful Commerce in Arms Act (S.397; H.R.800), which passed in the fall of 2005. The act prohibits "civil liability actions" against manufacturers and dealers for any harm caused by the criminal or unlawful misuse of the firearms and ammunition they make or sell. Whether the new federal legislation can be applied to this particular case is yet to be decided by the courts.

City of Las Vegas v. Moberg (1971) (82 N.M. 626, 1971)

In the *City of Las Vegas v. Moberg*, the Court of Appeals of New Mexico voided a city ordinance for violating the state constitution. When Leland Moberg, armed with a holstered pistol, went to the police department of Las Vegas, New Mexico, to report a robbery, he was arrested for violating a city ordinance that prohibited the carrying of a deadly weapon, open or concealed, within the city limits. Moberg was convicted of carrying a deadly, concealed weapon. However, he appealed and was granted a second trial. He was again found guilty, though this time for carrying a nonconcealed weapon. Moberg again appealed, and his conviction was eventually overturned by the Court of Appeals of New Mexico. Citing previous decisions in *State v. Rosenthal* (q.v.), *In re Brickey* (q.v.), and *State v. Kerner* (q.v.), the court ruled that the local ordinance was in violation of the state constitutional right of citizens to keep and bear arms. In the court's opinion, it was acceptable to have an ordinance prohibiting the carrying of *concealed* weapons, but not banning their open carry.

City of Salina v. Blaksley (1905)
(83 P. 619, 72 Kan. 230, 1905)

James Blaksley was convicted in a city police court of carrying a revolver while intoxicated within the city limits of Salina, Kansas. Upon appeal, both the district court and the Kansas Supreme Court upheld the conviction. Blaksley argued that the General Statutes of 1901, which allowed the city council to prohibit and punish the carrying of deadly weapons, including firearms, violated the state constitution. The bill of rights within the constitution gave people the right to keep and bear arms for security. However, the Kansas Supreme Court ruled that this right was intended for the people collectively, not individually. Since Blaksley could not show that he was part of an organized militia, the weapons-carrying charge for which he was convicted was not protected by the state constitution. The court's decision joined a long line of judicial decisions—at both the state and federal level, which continued for the next century—favoring a restrictive interpretation of the Second Amendment (that it guarantees a collective, *not* an individual, right).

Commonwealth v. Davis (1976)
(369 Mass. 886, 1976)

While conducting a search of Hubert Davis's apartment for narcotics, police found a shotgun with a barrel less than eighteen inches long. Davis was charged with and found guilty of violating a Massachusetts law prohibiting the ownership of such a firearm. Davis appealed for a new trial on the basis that his right to bear arms under both the Massachusetts and the U.S. Constitutions had been violated. However, the Supreme Judicial Council of Massachusetts ruled that such a law violated neither the state nor the federal constitution. The court held that the right to keep and bear arms was a collective right given to the citizens of a state, not to individuals per se. Moreover, the National Guard represented the state's militia, and since Davis was not a member, he had no constitutional right to keep and bear arms. In justifying its decision, the court cited *United States v. Miller* (q.v.).

Conrad Johnson, et al. v. Bull's Eye Shooter Supply, et al. (2003)
(No. 03-2-03932-8 [Superior Court of the State of Washington, Pierce County])

Representing the families of victims and survivors of the Washington, D.C.-area sniper shootings that occurred in the fall of 2002, the Legal Action Project for the Brady Center to Prevent Gun Violence and a Washington state law firm filed a civil lawsuit against the snipers as well as the dealer and manufacturer of the gun used in the crimes. The snipers, John Allen Muhammad and John Lee Malvo, used a Bushmaster XM-15 E2S .223 caliber semiautomatic assault rifle obtained from Bull's Eye Shooter Supply of Tacoma, Washington. The dealer was notorious for not keeping accurate records of transactions that occurred; for example, in a three-year period, 238 guns "disappeared" from the shop. In addition, the dealer failed to produce documentation of the transaction in which Muhammad and Malvo, both of whom were prohibited from purchasing firearms under federal law, obtained the gun. Even though the Bureau of Alcohol, Tobacco, Firearms and Explosives had previously audited the dealer and found shoddy recordkeeping, Bushmaster Firearms Inc. of Windham, Maine, the manufacturer of the gun, continued to supply the dealer with as many guns as desired.

The suit consisted of three claims. First, negligence on the part of Bull's Eye Shooter Supply for its irresponsible business practices, as well as on the part of Bushmaster Firearms, Inc., for failing to discontinue transactions with the dealer despite knowledge of its negligent activities. Second, Bull's Eye Shooter Supply and Bushmaster Firearms, Inc., were charged with being a public nuisance for acting in such a negligent manner that the public was endangered. Finally, Muhammad and Malvo were accused of intentional, harmful actions. The suit sought monetary compensation, along with the complete end of irresponsible practices by the manufacturer and distributor—which had allegedly continued even after it was made apparent the snipers obtained their gun from Bull's Eye.

The case ended with an out-of-court settlement, in which Bull's Eye Shooting Supply agreed to pay the plaintiffs $2 million and Bushmaster Firearms, Inc., agreed to pay another $500,000.

Bushmaster Firearms also agreed to educate dealers about safer business practices. The settlement is seen as a major victory for gun control advocates, because it was the first time a manufacturer had ever paid damages for negligence related to a crime of violence, and it was the largest settlement ever paid by a dealer.

Dickerson v. New Banner Institute, Inc. (1983)
(460 U.S. 103, 1983)

The chairman of the board of the New Banner Institute, Inc., David Kennison, was charged in Iowa for violating a state law prohibiting the carrying of concealed weapons. The case involved the kidnapping of his estranged wife, and in a bargain with the district attorney, Kennison pled guilty to the weapons offense. The judge gave him probation, instead of the possible five-year prison term that could have been meted out. Kennison's record was cleared upon the completion of his probation.

Subsequently, on behalf of New Banner, Kennison applied to the Bureau of Alcohol, Tobacco, and Firearms (ATF) for a license to deal in firearms. On his application, he did not reveal his Iowa offense, and the license was granted. However, when ATF discovered Kennison's previous guilty plea, it revoked the license. The Gun Control Act of 1968 prohibited a person convicted of a crime carrying a sentence with more than one year from becoming a firearms dealer. Kennison protested because his criminal record had been cleared prior to the license application, and the case ended up in the federal district court of South Carolina (where the company was located). The district upheld the license revocation. However, upon appeal, the U.S. Court of Appeals for the Fourth Circuit reversed the district court decision. The ATF, for which G. R. Dickerson was the chief, appealed to the U.S. Supreme Court. In a 5–4 vote, the Supreme Court reversed the court of appeals decision and upheld the original ruling that the company should not be granted a firearms license. The Court observed that Kennison had admitted guilt to a charge that carried with it a stiff prison term that prevented individuals from later dealing in firearm transactions. It emphasized that Kennison was exactly the kind of unsavory person that Congress had in mind when it enacted this portion of the Gun Control Act of 1968, barring convicted felons from dealing in firearms.

Farmer v. Higgins (1990)
(907 F. 2d 1041, 1990)

One provision of the Firearm Owners' Protection (McClure-Volk-mer) Act of 1986 was prohibiting a private citizen from possess-ing a machine gun unless the individual had acquired the weapon before May 19, 1986. In October 1986, the Bureau of Al-cohol, Tobacco, and Firearms (ATF) refused to issue J. D. Farmer Jr. a permit to make a machine gun for his private collection. Farmer protested and brought his case to the federal district court in northern Georgia, which ruled in his favor. However, ATF ap-pealed, and the United States Court of Appeals reversed the deci-sion. The appeals court ruled that the denial to grant a license was not unconstitutional, since the ability to make and register ma-chine guns was only allowed "under the authority" of the federal, state, or local government. Subsequently, the U.S. Supreme Court refused to hear the case.

Fresno Rifle and Pistol Club, Inc. v. Van de Kamp (1992)
(965 F. 2d 723, 1992)

In *Fresno Rifle and Pistol Club, Inc. v. Van de Kamp,* several gun or-ganizations, including the Fresno Rifle and Pistol Club, argued that the federal Civil Marksmanship Program (CMP) took prior-ity over California's Robert-Roos Assault Weapons Act (AWCA). The AWCA prohibited the manufacture, sale, transfer, possession, distribution, and importation of firearms categorized as "assault weapons." The firearm groups based their argument on the prem-ise that the law banned the use of weapons that the CMP sanc-tioned for instructional and competitive purposes. A federal dis-trict court decided against the groups, claiming that the CMP was not intended to take precedence over gun control measures in the AWCA.

The Ninth Circuit Court of Appeals refused to overturn the district court's decision. It observed that no punishment had been imposed on firearms manufacturers or gun organizations—as was claimed in the original suit—and that the law was designed only for the protection of the citizens of California. The original suit also claimed that AWCA violated the Second Amendment right to keep and bear arms. However, citing numerous previous judicial decisions, the appeals court ruled that the amendment only applied to the federal government, not the states.

Harris v. State (1967)
(432 P. 2d 929, 1967)

Edward Mark Harris was arrested for shoplifting cigarettes in a Reno, Nevada, supermarket. Upon searching Harris, police found a tear gas pen, which was banned by state law. Harris was convicted, but he appealed on the grounds that the law was an infringement upon his right to keep and bear arms as guaranteed by the Second Amendment to the U.S. Constitution. The appeals court refused to overturn his conviction. The court observed that the amendment applies only to the federal government, not the states, and that this right is a collective right of the citizens to arm its state militia, *not* an individual right of private citizens to keep and bear weapons.

Huddleston v. United States (1974)
(415 U.S. 814, 1974)

The Gun Control Act of 1968 makes it unlawful for a person to make a false statement when acquiring a gun from a federally licensed firearms dealer. In *Huddleston v. United States*, the U.S. Supreme Court decided that this law applies to an individual redeeming a firearm from a pawnshop.

During the 1960s, William C. Huddleston Jr. had been convicted of writing bad checks, a felony that could have gotten him fourteen years in prison, even though he only served a thirty-day jail term. In October 1971, Huddleston pawned three rifles to a pawnshop that held a federal firearms license. Upon redemption of the rifles, Huddleston filled out a U.S. Department of Treasury form, where he answered "no" to a question asking if he had previously been convicted of a crime carrying a punishment of more than one year. If he had answered "yes," he would have been unable to collect the firearms.

For his false statement, Huddleston was convicted in federal district court for violating the Gun Control Act of 1968. On appeal, he argued that the act did not apply to redeeming firearms from a pawnshop. However, the U.S. Court of Appeals for the Ninth Circuit rejected his appeal, as did the U.S. Supreme Court. The Supreme Court rejected Huddleston's claims that his property had been taken without proper compensation; that the Treasury form had been filled out through coercion, and that he was unaware of the sentence that came with conviction of writing bad checks. In sum, the Court concluded that redemption of a firearm from a licensed pawnshop did fall under the purview of the Gun Control Act of 1968 and that the intent of the act was to prevent persons like Huddleston—with histories of serious criminal offenses—from possessing firearms.

Ileto v. Glock, Inc. (pending) (349 F.3d 1191, 2003); (370 F.3d 860, 2004)

On August 10, 1999, convicted felon and white supremacist Buford O. Furrow used a 9mm Glock handgun to murder postal worker Joseph Ileto and injure four children at a Jewish Community Center in Granada Hills, California. Family members of the victims filed a suit of negligence and public nuisance against Glock, Inc. and several other gun manufacturers. The plaintiffs, represented in part by The Educational Fund to Stop Gun Violence, claimed that the practices employed by the defendants allowed easy access to deadly weapons by dangerous persons such as Furrow. In particular, the claim stated that the defendants did not take precautions to prevent a criminal market in firearms and that it was foreseeable that such harm would occur because of this irresponsibility. Thus, it was alleged there was a link between the negligence of the firearms manufacturers and Furrow's resulting shooting spree.

However, the U.S. District Court for the Central District of California dismissed the case, observing that product liability lawsuits against the gun industry were prohibited in California. Such a prohibition had also led to the dismissal of *Merrill v. Navegar* (q.v.). In what would be the first federal appellate-level decision claiming that negligence and public nuisance can be filed against the firearms industry, the Ninth Circuit Court of Appeals reversed the district court's decision in *Ileto v. Glock, Inc.* and sent the case back to the district court for further proceedings. The court of appeals specifically separated the case from that of product liability and made clear that the lawsuit revolved around negligence and public nuisance. The case is ongoing as of the summer of 2005, but may become a casualty of the Protection of Lawful Commerce in Arms Act (S.397; H.R.800), which was passed into law in the fall of 2005. This act prohibits lawsuits against the gun industry for the criminal misuse of firearms and ammunition. The courts have yet to decide if the new federal legislation can be applied to this particular case.

In re Brickey (1902)
(8 Idaho 597, 70 P. 609 [1902])

The Supreme Court of Idaho ruled that a state statute prohibiting private persons from carrying deadly weapons within the limits of a town or village in Idaho contravened the Second Amendment. The petitioner, L. D. Brickey, was convicted of violating the statute, but appealed on the grounds that his right to keep and bear arms had been violated. In making its decision, the court examined both the Second Amendment and the state's constitutional provision granting the right to bear arms for self-defense. The court held that the legislature may regulate the manner in which such weapons are carried and the exercise of police power in such regulation, but cannot enact a complete prohibition. The statute was thus determined void.

Kalodimos v. Village of Morton Grove (1984)
(103 Ill. 2d 483, 1984)

In *Kalodimos v. Village of Morton Grove*, the appellant challenged the ordinance in the village of Morton Grove banning handguns as a violation of both the Second Amendment of the U.S. Constitution and the Illinois Constitution. The state constitution grants the right to keep and bears arms, subject to police power. In its decision, the Illinois Supreme Court ruled that the Second Amendment does not grant an individual right, but a collective one, and that the ban on handguns did not violate the state constitution. However, the court was quick to point out that a complete ban on firearms would be a violation of both federal and state constitutional guarantees. The decision followed the ruling of *Quilici v. Village of Morton Grove* (q.v.), in which the court ruled that the ban on handguns was not in violation of either the U.S. or the Illinois Constitution, and that the ban was put in place to prevent injuries and accidents related to firearms.

Kelley v. R. G. Industries, Inc. (1983) (497 A. 2d 1143, 1983)

An assailant shot and wounded grocery store clerk Olen J. Kelley during an armed robbery. The assailant used a Rohm Revolver, manufactured by R. G. Industries, Inc. Kelley brought suit against R. G. Industries for liability. The company responded that the firearm was not defective and performed as designed. Moreover, the company held that it should not be held accountable for the actions of someone it had no control over, in this instance the armed robber. The case ended up at the Maryland Supreme Court, which decided against Kelley's claims that marketing handguns is an "abnormally dangerous activity" and that such weapons are "abnormally dangerous products." The gun had performed as intended and under Maryland law, the court ruled it could not hold the manufacturer liable for the injuries suffered. However, the court decided that cheaply made handguns (Saturday night specials) have no legitimate use for law, sport, or personal protection and are a weapon of choice for criminals. The court used material from the U.S. Congress and the Maryland General Assembly in deeming that Saturday night specials should be distinguished from other firearms because of their high probability of being used in crime. In addition, the court found that the Gun Control Act of 1968 banned the importation of firearms that are not used for law enforcement, the military, or sport. In conclusion, the court found that the manufacturers and sellers of a Saturday night special should be aware that the weapon being sold is often used for criminal activity. In a revision of common law, the court decided a new area of strict liability could be applied to the producers of Saturday night specials for the injuries suffered from the firearms. If the firearm used could be established as a Saturday night special, the manufacturer and seller could be held liable. In this case, the Rohm revolver used in the crime met the requirements of being a Saturday night special (a short-barreled gun made of low-grade metal).

Lewis v. United States (1980)
(445 U.S. 55, 1980)

In 1961, George Calvin Lewis Jr. was convicted of breaking and entering, even though he had no attorney to represent him. After this incident, in *Gideon v. Wainwright,* the U.S. Supreme Court ruled that states were required to provide counsel for all defendants who could not afford it. In 1977, Lewis was again arrested; this time for knowingly receiving and possessing a firearm, thus violating the Gun Control Act of 1968—which prohibits convicted felons from possessing a gun.

At his trial, Lewis argued that since he had not had a counsel in his previous case, that the conviction had violated his constitutional rights and was thus retroactively invalid. The court ruled against him, claiming that the constitutionality of that ruling did not bear any relation to his current trial. The U.S. Court of Appeals for the Fourth Circuit affirmed the decision. On further appeal, the U.S. Supreme Court upheld the decisions of the lower courts, determining that any felony conviction, even if allegedly invalid, is adequate grounds on which to ban possession of a firearm. Furthermore, the Court saw no language in the act that would allow for a defendant to challenge a previous conviction.

Maryland v. United States (1965)
(381 U.S. 41, 1965)

After a Maryland Air National Guard trainee accidentally flew his jet into a commercial airliner, the estates of the commercial pilots and the airline company filed a suit against the United States government under the Federal Tort Claims Act. It was acknowledged that the trainee was at fault, but in order for the national government to be held liable, it had to be determined if the National Guard pilot was acting in a military or civilian capacity at the time. A federal district court ruled that the pilot was acting as a civilian under the federal government and therefore the government should be held liable.

However, the case was appealed and eventually heard by the U.S. Supreme Court. The Court ruled that the pilot was an employee of Maryland, not of the United States. The Court held that the National Guard was the modern successor of the militia reserved to the states in the U.S. Constitution, and that the state has direct authority over such individuals. Therefore, the Tort Claims Act did not apply because military and civilian personnel of the National Guard are employees of the state. Gun control advocates applauded the Supreme Court's ruling, because it maintains that the National Guard constitutes the state militia and therefore, other privately organized militias, as well as private citizens in general, are not part of a militia. The upshot is that private citizens need not keep arms, because they will not be called to serve the militia; if they do serve in the National Guard, they will be provided with weapons.

Maxfield v. Bryco Arms, et al. (2003) (Alameda Co., Calif., Super. Ct., No. C–841636–4)

On April 6, 1994, seven-year-old Brandon Maxfield was left a quadriplegic when he was accidentally shot by a family friend trying to unload a .380-caliber Bryco handgun. The cheaply made handgun—a so-called Saturday night special—could only be unloaded when the safety was off. Brandon's parents filed suit against Bryco, claiming that its gun was unsafe for several reasons, including the fact that the trigger lock had to be released before it could be unloaded. The suit claimed that if the firearm had been designed and manufactured with proper safety features the accident would have never happened.

On May 7, 2003, the Superior Court of the State of California for Alameda County awarded $50.9 million in compensatory damages to the plaintiff. The jury found the manufacturer, Bryco Arms, and its owner, Bruce Jennings, 35 percent liable. They found two distributors that had shipped the gun as well as the pawnshop where the gun had been purchased 13 percent liable. The parents and the shooter were also judged liable. The jury found it was reasonable to assume an ordinary consumer could be harmed by the defective gun, owing to its lack of safety features. They awarded Brandon $50.9 million in damages, though it is unlikely he will ever see the money. Bryco immediately filed for bankruptcy, and an appeal was filed and is still pending.

Merrill v. Navegar, Inc. (2001)
(26 Cal. 4th 465. 2001)

On July 1, 1993, Gian Luigi Ferri walked into the law firm of Petit and Martin in a high-rise building in San Francisco. Using a semi-automatic .45 caliber pistol, a TEC-9, and a TEC-DC9, he murdered eight people in the building, injured six others, and then committed suicide in what became known as the 101 California Street Massacre. Marilyn Merrill, who was left a widow from the event, and other members of the victims' families brought a suit against the producers of the TEC semiautomatic pistol models, Navegar, Inc., which operated under the name Intratec. The suit alleged that the company carried out negligent marketing and distribution of the firearms. The TEC models were known to be a weapon of choice for criminals and were marketed as very deadly firearms. In fact, company executives viewed the notoriety their weapons received as crime guns positively—since it boosted sales. The weapons were also very easy to modify, including adding silencers, and were hard to gather fingerprints from. Ferri had outfitted his TECs with Hell-Fire triggers, so the weapons would fire at a faster rate. Though the TECs had been legally manufactured in Florida, they were prohibited from being sold in California. Using a fake ID, Ferri had purchased his TECs in Nevada.

Despite the advantages the TEC models might afford criminals, the district court in San Francisco ruled that the gun manufacturer could not be held responsible. However, the court of appeals reversed the decision and ruled that Navegar, Inc. could be held liable for the negligence claim. The decision was the first appellate ruling in the United States to hold a gun manufacturer liable for selling a firearm. The court held that manufacturers had a duty to use reasonable care to prevent risks beyond those already inherent of guns.

The case was appealed to the Supreme Court of California, which reversed the appellate court decision. The Supreme Court ruled that the manufacturer could not be held liable, because California law granted gun manufacturers "immunity" from civil liability lawsuits involving the criminal or other misuse of their firearms. The decision looked narrowly at the issue involved, only deciding on the particular claim that was brought against the manufacturer. It did not address the broader subject of whether a gun manufacturer can ever be held liable for the criminal use of the firearms they produce.

Miller v. Texas (1894)
(153 U.S. 535, 1894)

After Franklin P. Miller was convicted of murdering a police officer, he lost his appeal to the Court of Criminal Appeals of Texas. He then brought his case to the U.S. Supreme Court, claiming several infringements on his rights. Miller claimed the state statute under which he had been originally arrested for carrying a pistol in public, called An Act to Regulate the Keeping and Bearing of Deadly Weapons, violated his Second Amendment right to keep and bear arms. Moreover, the state allowed his arrest for violating the statute without first obtaining a warrant, which Miller contended violated the Fourth Amendment of the U.S. Constitution, protecting citizens from unreasonable searches and seizures. Lastly, Miller argued that the state statute violated the Fifth Amendment, which protects citizens from deprivation of life, liberty, or property without due process of law, and the Fourteenth Amendment, which says no state can violate the rights of U.S. citizens.

The Supreme Court found that the state statute did not violate the Second or the Fourth Amendments, and even if they were breached, the amendments only apply to the federal government, not to the states. In addition, the Court would not consider the violation of the Fourteenth Amendment, because the complaint was not issued in the original case trial. The *Miller* decision is one of many that gun control advocates use to support their contention that the Second Amendment does not prevent state or local governments from imposing strict regulations on firearms.

Muscarello v. United States (1998)
(524 U.S. 125, 1998)

Federal law mandates a five-year prison term for an individual who "uses or carries a firearm" during a drug-trafficking crime.

Upon a search of Frank J. Muscarello's truck, which he was using to transport marijuana, police officers found a handgun locked in the glove compartment. Muscarello argued that keeping a gun in a locked glove compartment does not fall within the reach of the statutory phrase "carries a firearm." In a separate case, federal agents found guns in the locked trunk of a car used by drug dealers Donald Cleveland and Enrique Gray-Santana. The defendants in both cases were found guilty of breaking the federal law regarding "carrying" a firearm during drug-trafficking. The cases were combined when they were appealed to the U.S. Supreme Court.

In *Muscarello v. United States*, the Supreme Court upheld both appeals court decisions by a 5 to 4 vote. The defendants had claimed that "carrying" a firearm meant that it had to be on the person. However, the Court decided that "carries a firearm" also applies to an individual who knowingly possesses and conveys a gun in his or her vehicle during drug-trafficking. The Court emphasized that Congress had created the law to prevent dangerous situations involving both drugs and guns, not strictly confining "carrying" to being on a person involved in the illegal activity.

Nunn v. State (1846)
(1 Ga. 243, 1846)

Hawkins H. Nunn was found guilty in a lower court of carrying a pistol, an activity that Georgia law prohibited ordinary citizens from doing. Nunn appealed his conviction on the basis that he had been denied his right to keep and bear arms. The Georgia Constitution did not grant this right, so the Supreme Court of Georgia cited the Second Amendment to the U.S. Constitution in overturning Nunn's conviction. However, the court did not deem the right as absolute: It declared that state's ban on carrying *concealed* weapons was constitutional, because it did not interfere with the general right of citizens to keep and bear arms. In 1877, Georgia amended its state constitution to read: "The right of the people to keep and bear arms shall not be infringed, but the General Assembly shall have power to prescribe the manner [in] which arms may be borne."

People v. Zerillo (1922)
(219 Mich. 635, 189 N.W. 927, 1922)

James Zerillo, an unnaturalized foreign-born resident of Michigan, was charged with possessing a revolver without a permit—a violation of state game law. At his trial, he argued that his state constitutional guarantee that the right of "every person . . . to keep and bear arms for the defense of himself and the state" had been violated. Earlier judicial rulings had held that the state constitution only protected individuals from using arms for self-defense, not for hunting or sport. Even though Zerillo had not been charged with hunting a wild animal, a lower court found him guilty.

However, upon Zerillo's appeal to the Supreme Court of Michigan, the guilty verdict was overturned. The court ruled that the right to keep and bear arms for self-defense extended to unnaturalized foreign-born residents, and that it would be a violation of the state constitution if Michigan game law disallowed noncitizens this right. In short, because Zerillo had not been using his pistol for hunting or sport, but only for self-defense, his state constitutional rights had been violated.

Presser v. Illinois (1886)
(116 U.S. 252, 1886)

Presser v. Illinois was set in motion when Herman Presser, the leader of a German-American labor group called the *Lehr und Wehr Verein* (the "Learning and Defense Club"), was arrested for parading the group through downtown Chicago while carrying a sword. More specifically, he was arrested for conducting an "armed military drill," which could legally be done only with a license, under Illinois statutes in force at the time. Presser appealed, invoking the Second Amendment in his defense. The Supreme Court judged against him, citing its *U.S. v. Cruikshank* (q.v.) ruling. As in the *Cruikshank* case, the Court contended that the Second Amendment had not been "incorporated"—meaning that it only applied to the federal government, not to state governments. As in the *Cruikshank* ruling, the Court also took the opportunity to reaffirm that the "States cannot . . . prohibit the people from keeping and bearing arms, so as to deprive the United States of their rightful resource for maintaining the public security, and disable the people from performing their duty to the General Government." In other words, the individual states did not have to honor the Second Amendment, except that they could not prevent citizens belonging to the militia from possessing their own firearms—as long as the firearms were appropriate for use in the militia. And, as was the case with *Cruikshank*, the Supreme Court's decision in *Presser* smacked of bigotry—in this instance, in the repression of exploited immigrant laborers trying to improve their collective lot via unionization. Nevertheless, gun control advocates often put *Presser v. Illinois* on center stage as evidence that there are no constitutional reasons why the government—local, state, or federal—cannot strictly regulate deadly weapons, including firearms.

Printz v. United States (1997)
(521 U.S. 898, 1997)

The 1993 Brady Handgun Violence Prevention Act required that local law enforcement officers perform background checks on prospective handgun purchasers. This was intended as an interim duty (approximately five years) until the attorney general created a national computerized system to conduct "instant" background investigations. In separate cases, county sheriffs Jay Printz and Richard Mack challenged the constitutionality of this provision in their respective states of Montana and Arizona. The sheriffs argued that this aspect of the Brady Act violated the Tenth and Thirteenth Amendments of the Constitution—more specifically, they contended that local officials should not have to assume the work of a federal agency (the Department of Justice), especially without pay. The federal district court in each case agreed with the sheriffs. However, when the *Mack* case moved forward to the Ninth Circuit Court of Appeals, the lower court decision was reversed and the requirement that local officials do the background checks required by a federal law was deemed constitutional.

The *Printz* and *Mack* cases were consolidated and argued before the U.S. Supreme Court as *Printz v. United States*. In a 5 to 4 decision, the Court ruled that the Brady Act's demand on local law enforcement officials was indeed a violation of the Tenth

Amendment. The Court emphasized that state legislatures are not subject to federal authority and that the national government could not require that the states fulfill a federal duty, even if it was only on an interim basis. Thus, the Brady background-check demand on local officers was, at best, a polite request—one that they could accept or decline, but there was no requirement. Although regarded as a victory for gun rights advocates, the decision had little real impact, because the interim check period was almost over and the national instant background check system would soon be operational. Moreover, most local officials continued to perform background checks, as the Supreme Court stated they were allowed, but not required, to do.

Quilici v. Village of Morton Grove (1981) (532 F. Supp. 1169 N.D. Ill., 1981; 695 F.2d 261; 7th Cir. 1982; cert. denied, 464 U.S. 863, 1983)

Handgun owner Victor Quilici moved to Morton Grove, Illinois, after the village had enacted a local law banning ownership of working handguns. There were a number of people who could be exempted, including members of the National Guard and licensed collectors. Quilici challenged the law, claiming it infringed upon the right to keep and bear arms granted by the Illinois Constitution and the Second Amendment; he also contended that the law did not adhere to the Ninth and Fourteenth Amendments. However, he lost his case, and the decision was upheld by the U.S. Court of Appeals for the Seventh Circuit in *Quilici v. Village of Morton Grove*.

The court cited *Presser v. Illinois* (q.v.) and *United States v. Miller* (q.v.) in deciding that the *individual* is not granted the right to possess a firearm, except as he or she may serve in the state militia; and furthermore, the Second Amendment does not apply to the states, only to the federal government. The court also held that the state constitution granted the right to keep and bear *certain* firearms, not all, and the government had the power to regulate this right to protect the safety and health of the people. This decision was consistent with more than thirty other federal court decisions regarding the Second Amendment—that it was about the collective right of the citizens of a state to form and arm a militia and not about guaranteeing the individual the right to keep and bear arms. The court also found that the Fourteenth Amendment does not grant all provisions of the Bill of Rights to the states. Finally, the court ruled against the argument that the Ninth Amendment grants certain other rights than those cited in the Constitution, specifically the right to own or possess firearms.

Robertson v. Baldwin (1897)
(165 U.S. 275, 1897)

Robert Robertson and other fellow seamen balked at finishing their service on the sailing vessel *Arago*. Even though they had signed contracts to complete a tour of duty with the ship, they were unhappy with their working conditions and refused to return to it after a port stop in Astoria, Oregon. They were arrested and convicted of violating U.S. maritime law. Robertson and the other defendants argued that their commitments were unconstitutional—violating the protection against involuntary servitude specified in the Thirteenth Amendment. The convictions were appealed all the way to the U.S. Supreme Court. The Supreme Court upheld the convictions. Of special interest to modern day advocates of gun control, the Court contended constitutional amendments were not immune to change, and it supported its contention with a Second Amendment example. More specifically, Justice Henry Brown wrote in the decision, the Second Amendment ". . . . is not infringed by laws prohibiting the carrying of concealed weapons."

Schubert v. DeBard (1980)
(398 N.E. 2d. 1339, 1980)

In *Schubert v. DeBard*, an Indiana appeals court found that a police administrator could not deny a law-abiding citizen a license to own a handgun for personal protection. After Joseph L. Schubert received a threatening letter, he applied for a permit to carry a handgun for protection. Under law, the chief of police, or an equivalent, was to do a background investigation and then forward a recommendation to the superintendent of the Indiana State Police. In Schubert's case, the permit was denied because the superintendent saw no reasonable need for the weapon. Schubert appealed the denial to a trial court judge, who upheld the superintendent's decision. However, when the case was heard before the intermediate Indiana Court of Appeals, the superintendent was found to have overstepped his authority, and Schubert was granted his license. The decision was applauded by gun rights activists and helped to set the stage for the flurry of right-to-carry laws passed in Florida and two dozen other states after 1987. Currently, thirty-seven states have "shall issue" laws allowing for the average citizen to acquire, relatively easily, a concealed-weapons permit to carry a handgun.

Shettle v. Shearer (1981)
(425 N.E. 2d 739, 1981)

In a trial court, the superintendent of the Indiana State Police, John T. Shettle, was ordered to issue a license to James F. Shearer to carry a handgun. Shettle appealed, arguing that Shearer did not provide a sufficient self-defense reason for the requested license. Shearer had claimed he had a "medical condition" and any assault could be life-threatening; thus, he needed an extraordinary capacity to defend himself. Shearer had obtained a physician's letter supporting his claim of the debilitating nature of his medical condition. In appellate court, Shearer won his case and Shettle was forced to grant a handgun license. As with *Schubert v. DeBard* (q.v.), gun rights advocates praised the decision—a decision that set the stage for the spate of right-to-carry laws that passed in Florida and dozens of other states after 1987. Currently, thirty-seven states allow the average law-abiding citizen to obtain a permit to carry a concealed handgun, the usual requirements only being a background check and passing a gun safety course.

Sklar v. Byrne (1984)
(556 F. Supp. 136, 1983; 727 F.2d 633, 1984)

The Chicago City Council banned the possession of all handguns within city limits that had not been registered by April 10, 1982. On April 15, 1982, Jerome Sklar moved from the Chicago suburb of Skokie—where he had his handgun legally registered—to Chicago proper and immediately tried to register his handgun. His application was duly rejected.

Sklar appealed his rejection to federal district court, where he lost; and then to the seventh circuit court of appeals, where he lost again. The courts reaffirmed the judicial decision made in *Quilici v. Village of Morton Grove* (q.v.), which held that a community had the right to ban handguns to secure the safety of the public. The courts also rejected Sklar's argument that he had been denied equal protection under the law, as laid out in the Fourteenth Amendment of the U.S. Constitution. More particularly, Sklar claimed that the Chicago ordinance violated his right to travel freely, since he could not move to Chicago without surrendering his firearm. However, the appellate court observed that Sklar had not been singled out—that all residents and newcomers to Chicago were equally affected by the ordinance.

Smith & Wesson Settlement Agreement (March 17, 2000)

The nation's largest gun manufacturer, Smith & Wesson, agreed to a landmark settlement with the federal government, two states, and several cities and counties on March 17, 2000. The deal would dismiss lawsuits brought against the company by state and local governments, as well as grant the assurance that the federal government would not file suit, in exchange for modifications in Smith & Wesson's marketing, manufacturing, and design practices. President Bill Clinton announced the settlement, which the Legal Action Project for the Brady Center to Prevent Gun Violence participated in, and stated that the agreement "says that gun makers can and will share in the responsibility to keep their products out of the wrong hands. And it says that gun makers can and will make their guns much safer without infringing on anyone's rights." At first wash, the settlement appeared to be one of the major events in the history of gun control in the United States.

Per terms of the agreement, Smith & Wesson would make their weapons safer and their marketing more responsible. For example, their guns would be equipped with new safety features, including internal locking systems, authorized-user technology, chamber-loaded indicators, child-safety devices, and hidden serial numbers (to prevent their destruction by criminals). Smith & Wesson would sell its firearms only through authorized dealers who would abide by new, more stringent requirements—including training on recognizing "straw purchasers" (legal buyers purchasing guns for prohibited buyers; for example, a convicted felon using his girlfriend with no criminal record to buy a gun). The gun industry as a whole was outraged. In retaliation, thousands of retailers and tens of thousands of gun rights consumers boycotted Smith & Wesson. It worked and the agreement was completely scuttled when the British conglomerate that owned Smith & Wesson sold the company to a former executive, Robert Scott. Soon after taking over, Scott announced that he would not abide by the agreement, and Smith & Wesson was welcomed back by the gun industry and gun rights advocates.

Smith v. United States (1993)
(508 U.S. 223, 1993)

John Angus Smith was charged with multiple firearm and drug-trafficking violations upon offering to trade his MAC-10 to an undercover officer for cocaine. Federal law requires a minimum five-year prison term for an individual who "uses" a firearm in relation to drug trafficking. Moreover, a "sentence enhancement" of a minimum thirty-year term is required if the firearm is a machine gun or equipped with a silencer. Since Smith had modified the MAC-10 so that it was automatic, he was subject to the lengthier sentence. A jury found Smith guilty on all accounts, and he was given the thirty-year minimum. The Court of Appeals for the Eleventh Circuit rejected Smith's argument that "use" of a firearm only pertains to situations in which the gun is acting as a weapon—for example, being fired or brandished. However in *United States v. Harris*, a different appeals court rendered a decision that did not concur with the Eleventh Circuit's in the *Smith* case. For this reason, the U.S. Supreme Court agreed to hear the case.

The Supreme Court rejected Smith's appeal, taking the broadest possible interpretation of the word *use*; it decreed that a firearm employed as a medium of transaction was indeed in "use." In its ruling, the Court cited *Astor v. Merritt* (1884), which contained the passage "to derive service from," as part of the definition of "use." Writing for the majority in the 6–3 decision, Sandra Day O'Connor maintained that "the introduction of guns into drug transactions dramatically increases the danger to society, whether the guns are used as a medium of exchange or as protection for the transaction or dealers. . . . The fact that a gun is treated momentarily as an item of commerce does not render it inert or deprive it of its destructive capacity. Rather, as experience demonstrates, it can be converted instantaneously from currency to cannon" (*Smith v. United States*, 1993, 237–240).

Sonzinsky v. United States (1937)
(300 U.S. 506, 1937)

The 1934 National Firearms Act (NFA) imposed tax and registration requirements for firearms transactions involving machine guns, sawed-off shotguns, and silencers. It required all dealers and owners of these weapons to register with the Internal Revenue Service and pay any applicable taxes. The real meaning of the legislation was not to collect taxes but to prohibit the ownership and sale of such "gangster-type" weapons. Harold Sonzinsky was convicted in an Illinois district court of violating the NFA. He appealed to the court of appeals, where his conviction for dealing in firearms without paying the special tax was upheld. The U.S. Supreme Court eventually agreed to hear the case because of the constitutional issues it raised—could the federal government use its power to collect taxes in such a creative manner that it was actually effecting gun control? Sonzinsky claimed that the tax imposed on him was not genuine, but was a punishment for dealing in certain types of weapons. Indeed, in the 1930s the $200 transfer tax was greater than the cost of a new machine gun. Sonzinsky further claimed that the authority to regulate firearms belonged solely to the states. However, the Supreme Court ruled that it could not interpret—nor did it care about—the motives of Congress in establishing the NFA tax, and it let Sonzinsky's conviction stand.

Springfield, Inc. v. Buckles (2000)
(116 F. Supp. 2d 85 [U.S. District Court for the District of Columbia, 2000], on appeal, No. 00-5409 [U.S. Court of Appeals for the D.C. Circuit, 2000])

The Gun Control Act of 1968 generally prohibits the importation of firearms into the United States. However, there are a few exceptions, one of which gives the Department of the Treasury the authority to approve the importation of firearms intended for *sporting purposes*. The definition of this term is open to interpretation. In 1989, the Treasury Department prohibited the importation of semiautomatic rifles that incorporated certain military features—such as a folding stock and a short barrel—because they were not identified as having such sporting purposes. In 1998, the department extended the list of banned features to include detachable large-capacity military magazines. One major importer, Springfield, Inc., filed a lawsuit in protest, arguing that the Treasury Department's use of the sporting purposes test was in violation of the true intent of the Gun Control Act of 1968.

In *Springfield, Inc. v. Buckles* (Bradley Buckles was the director of the Treasury Department's gun-law enforcement agency, the Bureau of Alcohol, Tobacco, and Firearms), the federal district court rejected Springfield, Inc.'s claims. The court agreed that firearms that can hold large-capacity magazines are not intended for sporting purposes and can thus be banned from importation. The decision was unsuccessfully appealed to the U.S. Court of Appeals for the District of Columbia.

Staples v. United States (1994)
(511 U.S. 600, 1994)

A provision of the National Firearms Act of 1934 (NFA) prohibits the possession of certain unregistered firearms, including fully automatic ("machine") guns. Upon a legal search of the home of Harold E. Staples III, local police and Bureau of Alcohol, Tobacco, and Firearms agents seized a semiautomatic rifle that had been modified to fire automatically (one pull of the trigger fires more than one shot). At his trial in federal district court, Staples argued that he should not be held criminally responsible, because he did not know his gun was an automatic—he claimed he had never fired it that way. However, the government argued that criminal intent (mens rea) did not have to be established under this provision of the NFA. Moreover, the government claimed mens rea was not required, because the defendant was dealing with a dangerous device, and the defendant did not need to be aware of the exact criminal statutes in place regarding such a weapon (common law asserts that ignorance of the law is no excuse for breaking it). The district court judge rejected Staples's defense, and he was convicted.

The U.S. Supreme Court agreed to hear Staples's appeal. The Court concurred with Staples that mens rea—also a critical part of common law—was critical for the prosecutor to establish because normal use of a semiautomatic weapon can degrade its trigger mechanism turning it into an automatic weapon without the owner's knowledge. Moreover, the punishment for an NFA violation is so harsh—up to a ten-year prison sentence—that it would be unfair to impose it on an individual who had been unaware that he or she was breaking the law. As such, the Court overturned Staples's conviction.

State v. Boyce (1983)
(61 Ore. App. 662, 658 P. 2d 577, 1983)

Michael Boyce was found guilty of violating a Portland, Oregon, ordinance prohibiting anyone from carrying a loaded weapon in public, including in his or her vehicle. Boyce had been pulled over for speeding, after which the police found a loaded .32 caliber semiautomatic handgun on the front seat. Taking his case to the state court of appeals, Boyce argued that the city ordinance violated the state constitution guaranteeing individuals the right to keep and bear arms for defense "of themselves, and the State." In coming to its decision, the appeals court reviewed a previous Oregon Supreme Court ruling in *State v. Kessler* (q.v.), which had found that ordinary citizens have the right to possess weaponry for self-defense. The appeals court also reviewed the judicial ruling in *Christian et al. v. La Forge*, in which it was held that a "guaranteed right" can be restricted to protect the safety and welfare of the public. In the end, the appeals court found that the prohibition on the carrying—on one's person or in one's vehicle—of a *loaded* firearm was justified to protect the public.

State v. Kerner (1921)
(181 N.C. 574, 1921)

O. W. Kerner was carrying boxes through the streets of Kernersville, North Carolina, when another man challenged him to a fight. Kerner went to his office and returned to the scene with his pistol in plain sight. He was subsequently arrested for violating the Public-Local Laws of 1919, which prohibited the carrying of a weapon off personal property without a permit. The local court found Kerner not guilty. The state of North Carolina appealed, but the state Supreme Court upheld the not-guilty verdict.

Kerner based his defense on the right to keep and bear arms granted by the Second Amendment to the U.S. Constitution, as well as by the state constitution of North Carolina. The Supreme Court ruled that the Second Amendment did not apply, citing *United States v. Cruikshank* (q.v.), since the amendment only pertains to the federal government and not the states. However, the Court agreed with Kerner that his right to carry a nonconcealed firearm was protected by the state constitution. The Court observed that the right to keep and bear arms for protection had played an important part in the history of the United States, in general, and of North Carolina, in particular.

State v. Kessler (1980)
(Or. 614 P. 2d 94, 1980)

After Randy Kessler engaged in a verbal and physical confrontation with his apartment manager, police arrested Kessler at his residence. During his arrest, the police found two billy clubs in his apartment, and they charged him not only with disorderly conduct but also with possessing a "slugging weapon"—contrary to state and local law. At his trial, Kessler argued that the Oregon Constitution protected his right to keep and bear arms for self-defense. His argument failed, and he was found guilty on both charges. Kessler appealed his case all the way to the Supreme Court of Oregon. Because Kessler kept the clubs in his home and did not carry them on the street, the Oregon Supreme Court agreed with him that his state constitutional right to "bear arms" for defense of both himself and of the state had been violated, and his weapons conviction was thus overturned.

State v. Rosenthal (1903)
(75 Vt. 295, 55 A 610, 1903)

In *State v. Rosenthal*, the Supreme Court of Vermont ruled in that the local ordinance of Rutland, Vermont, prohibiting the carry of a concealed weapon without written approval from the mayor or chief of police, infringed upon the state constitutional guarantee that "the people have a right to bear arms for defence [*sic*] of themselves and the State." Andrew Rosenthal had been charged with violating the Rutland ordinance, but he successfully argued his case in a lower court. The State of Vermont appealed the decision on behalf of Rutland, claiming that the city council had been granted the power by its charter to enact a broad range of laws to protect its citizens, including restricting the carrying of concealed weapons. The Supreme Court's decision has remained in effect to the present day. Vermont and Alaska are the only two states allowing the average citizen to carry a concealed weapon with no special permit required. (In thirty-six other states, citizens passing a background check and a gun safety course can readily obtain a permit to carry a concealed handgun.)

Stevens v. United States (1971)
(440 F. 2d 144, 149, 1971)

In *Stevens v. United States*, the United States Court of Appeals for the Sixth Circuit ruled that the Second Amendment grants a collective right of the individuals of a state to form and arm a militia, but guarantees no absolute right of the individual "to keep and bear Arms." As such, the court upheld a provision of the Gun Control Act of 1968 prohibiting convicted felons from receiving, possessing, or transporting a firearm. In particular, the court denied the appeal of convicted felon Frank James Stevens to overturn his guilty verdict for possessing a 9mm Astra semiautomatic pistol.

Strickland v. State (1911)
(72 S.E. 260, 1911)

J. L. Strickland had been convicted of carrying a pistol without a license. He appealed on the basis that the Georgia statute prohibiting the carrying of a revolver without a license violated the Second Amendment to the U.S. Constitution and the state constitution. The state constitution affirms that "the right of the people to keep and bear arms shall not be infringed, but the General Assembly shall have power to prescribe the manner in which arms may be borne." After Strickland pled his case before the Supreme Court of Georgia, the court ruled that the state statute was not unreasonable and did not violate either the Second Amendment or the Georgia constitution. In support of its decision, the court cited *United States v. Cruikshank* (q.v.) and *Presser v. Illinois* (q.v.), both of which held that the Second Amendment only limited the power of the federal government to enact overly restrictive gun control legislation, not that of the states.

United States v. Adams (1935)
(11 F. Supp. 216, S.D. Fla, 1935)

The defendant in this case was convicted of violating the National Firearms Act of 1934 (NFA) in failing to pay a tax that was placed on importers, manufacturers, and dealers of machine guns, sawed-off shotguns, and silencers. The defendant argued that the tax was unconstitutional because it was not intended to raise revenue but to control guns; moreover, it was a violation of the Second Amendment to the U.S. Constitution.

In *United States v. Adams*, the southern district court of Florida ruled against the defendant. It was found that the Second Amendment argument was not applicable, because the right to keep and bear arms only referred to the "militia" and not to individuals. The court acknowledged that collecting revenue was not the prime motive of the NFA, but cited the Harrison Narcotic Control Act of 1914 as an example of how the federal government had used taxation to effect another goal—in that case, the reduction of drug-trafficking. The U.S. Supreme Court had upheld the Harrison Act as constitutional in *United States v. Doremus*.

United States v. Cruikshank (1876)
(92 U.S. 542, 1876)

In *U.S. v. Cruikshank*, the U.S. Supreme Court made the first of its eventual five rulings on how the Second Amendment to the United States Constitution should be interpreted ("*A well regulated Militia, being necessary to the security of a free State, the right of the people to keep and bear Arms, shall not be infringed . . .*").

The case began when Louisiana state officials—who happened to be members of the Ku Klux Klan—were challenged for conspiring to disarm a meeting of African-Americans. Attorneys for the African-Americans argued that the Second Amendment protected the right of all citizens to keep and bear arms. However,

the Supreme Court held that the officials had the legal prerogative to disarm them in protection of the common weal. In short,
the court held that "bearing arms for a lawful purpose . . . is not
a right granted by the Constitution." More specifically, the Court
ruled that the Second Amendment was not "incorporated,"
meaning that it only applied to the federal government, not to
state governments. The states did not have to honor it, except that
they could not prevent citizens belonging to the militia from possessing their own firearms—as long as the firearms were appropriate for use in the militia.

Although this ruling supports their contention that the Second Amendment should pose no barrier to the enactment of strict
gun control laws, at least at the state level, many modern-day gun
control advocates are not particularly eager to tout *U.S. v. Cruikshank*. The ruling was racist—providing a justification for keeping
former slaves unarmed and in a position of vassalage in the South,
thereby partly counteracting the effect of the Emancipation Proclamation. This fact is not lost on many African-American and Jewish jurists, or on interest groups opposed to gun regulation such as
the National Rifle Association. Even though African-Americans
and Jews generally tend to support strict gun control, some such
jurists have contended that regulations on gun possession are a
means for suppressing a society's minorities and for allowing unjust rulers to hold sway because they control all weaponry.

United States v. Emerson (2001)
(270 F.3d 203 [5th Cir. 2001])

Dr. Timothy Joe Emerson was indicted for violating a federal statute
prohibiting an individual under a domestic violence restraining
order from possessing a firearm. He successfully argued at his trial
that the statute violated his Second Amendment rights to keep and
bear arms, and his case was dismissed. The federal prosecutor appealed the dismissal to the U.S. Court of Appeals for the Fifth Circuit, and the original indictment was reinstated. The appeals court
held that the statute in question was both reasonable and constitutional. However, to the great dismay of gun control advocates and
the great satisfaction of gun rights advocates, the court broke with
the traditional interpretation of the Second Amendment that had
been rendered in previous federal courts. More specifically, the
court held that the amendment not only confers upon the citizens of

a state the right to form and arm a militia (the traditional interpretation), but also confers upon the individual the right to keep and bear arms "whether or not they are a member of a select militia." Legal scholars point out that this breaking with tradition was only dictum—that is, unnecessary to the result of the case and thus not binding to other courts. The decision has yet to be appealed to the U.S. Supreme Court. Both gun control and gun rights advocates are wary of trying to get the Supreme Court to rule on the Second Amendment, because both sides are unsure if the ruling would be in its favor. Thus, they are content to let judicial interpretations of the amendment continue to be contested only in lower courts.

United States v. Freed (1971)
(401 U.S. 601, 1971)

In the Gun Control Act of 1968, Congress expanded the number of firearms that had to be registered by amending the National Firearms Act of 1934 (NFA); in particular, individuals were now required to register any hand grenades they possessed. The amendment specified that a registrant's information could not be used against him or her in prosecution for possession of the weapon before registration. In a California federal district court, Donald Freed was charged with possessing unregistered hand grenades in violation of the amended NFA. Freed claimed the amendment violated his Fifth Amendment right to not incriminate himself; the trial judge agreed, and he was found not guilty. Had Freed revealed his possession of the grenades, he would have been in violation of a California state law prohibiting their ownership. The court also declared that the prosecutor did not prove that Freed had *scienter*— that is, knowledge that the crime was being committed.

Upon direct appeal to the U.S. Supreme Court, the district court's decision was overturned. In a unanimous vote, the Supreme Court held that the amendment in question did not violate the Fifth Amendment, because Section 5848 of the NFA specifically prohibited a registrant from being prosecuted for possession of a banned weapon prior to registration. The Court also ruled that *scienter* did not have to be proven, because the NFA "requires no specific intent or knowledge that the hand grenades were unregistered." The prosecution only had to show that Freed knew the objects in his possession were hand grenades—which it had done. The Court cited previous cases in which criminal intent, or mens rea, did not have to be established when the crime involved a serious threat to society. (Note, however, that twenty-three years later, in *Staples v. United States* [q.v.], the Supreme Court ruled quite differently—holding that mens rea must be established when prosecuting an NFA weapons violation.)

United States v. Hutzell (2000)
(217 F. 3d 966, 969 8th Cir., 2000)

Cody Hutzell was arrested and charged with violating the federal law prohibiting anyone convicted of a domestic violence misdemeanor from possessing a firearm. Hutzell pleaded guilty but reserved his right to contend that he was unaware of the law at the time, as many others would have been. The court dismissed this argument and found him guilty as charged.

Upon appeal to the U.S. Court of Appeals for the Eighth Circuit, the decision was upheld. However, the court referred to *United States v. Miller* (q.v.) in making its decision, and its ruling included an interpretation of the Second Amendment that gun rights advocates applauded: "an individual's right to bear arms is constitutionally protected." However, gun control advocates were quick to point out that the court also held that "the possession of a gun, especially by anyone who has been convicted of a violent crime, is nevertheless a highly regulated activity, and everyone knows it." Thus, even though the court supported the *individual's* right to keep and bear arms, it acknowledged that the right was not absolute—that reasonable gun regulations were in full accordance with the Constitution.

United States v. Lopez (1995)
(514 U.S. 549, 1995)

In 1992, twelfth-grader Alphonso Lopez Jr. brought a concealed .38 caliber handgun to his high school in San Antonio, Texas. He was arrested for violating the 1990 Gun-Free School Zones (GFSZ) Act, which prohibited the possession of a firearm within 1,000 feet of a school. At his trial, Lopez's attorney argued that the GFSZ Act violated the U.S. Constitution because it had nothing to do with the regulation of interstate commerce, the guise under which it had been passed. However, Lopez was found guilty.

Upon appeal, the Court of the Appeals for the Fifth Circuit reversed the lower-court decision. The U.S. Supreme Court concurred with the argument that Lopez's attorney had laid forth in the original trial and thus affirmed the court of appeals's decision. Congress subsequently amended the GFSZ Act to read that the firearm involved in any GFSZ violation must have traveled through interstate commerce. As most firearms meet this condition, the power of the act was left intact.

United States v. Miller (1939)
(307 U.S. 174, 1939)

In the past 130 years, five U.S. Supreme Court rulings have dealt directly with the Second Amendment. In each instance, the ruling has supported the notion that various levels of governments can restrict who may and may not own a gun and can also regulate the sale, transfer, receipt, possession, and use of specific categories of firearms. *United States v. Miller* is one of the most important of these five rulings. Significantly, unlike two of the other most important rulings—*U.S. v. Cruikshank* (q.v.) and *Presser v. Illinois* (q.v.)—*United States v. Miller* does not leave gun control advocates feeling morally uncomfortable.

In *U.S. v. Cruikshank*, Louisiana state officials (members of the Ku Klux Klan) were challenged for conspiring to disarm a meeting of African-Americans. The Supreme Court held that "bearing arms for a lawful purpose . . . is not a right granted by the Constitution." Although this ruling supports the contention that the Second Amendment should not prevent the passage of strict gun control laws, it was racist—keeping former slaves unarmed and thus unable to resist violent white racism in the South. Similarly, in *Presser v. Illinois*, the Court's decision, though supporting the position of gun control advocates, was bigoted. In effect, it contributed to the repression of exploited immigrant laborers trying to improve their working conditions through public demonstration and unionization.

A more morally palatable starting point for gun control advocates contending that there is no constitutional basis preventing strict gun control is *United States v. Miller*. The case involved Jack Miller and Frank Layton of Arkansas, who had been charged with unlawfully transporting an unregistered weapon, a double-barreled, sawed-off shotgun, across state lines—a violation of the

1934 National Firearms Act (NFA). The federal district court ruled for Miller and Layton on the grounds the NFA violated the Second Amendment. However, when the case reached the Supreme Court, it ruled that the federal government had the right, which it exercised in the NFA, to control the transfer and registration of certain firearms. More particularly, the sawed-off shotgun, a favorite weapon of gangsters and which had been specifically named in the NFA, was deemed unprotected by the Second Amendment. The ruling reads, in part: "In the absence of any evidence tending to show that possession or use of 'shotgun having a barrel of less than eighteen inches in length' at this time has some reasonable relationship to the preservation or efficiency of a well regulated militia, we cannot say that the second amendment guarantees the right to keep and bear such an instrument." Lower court decisions involving the NFA and the kindred 1938 Federal Firearms Act used even more direct language. In upholding the NFA, the district court held in *United States v. Adams* (q.v.) that the Second Amendment "refers to the Militia, a protective force of government; to the collective body and not individual rights." Another district court decision in *United States v. Tot* (q.v.) referred to this ruling in upholding the Federal Firearms Act. Both court decisions made clear that the Second Amendment does not protect the right of the *individual* to own a firearm, except as he or she might need it to participate in the state militia.

However, the *Miller* ruling also lends support to the contention of gun rights advocates that the Second Amendment does confer an individual right. More specifically, the Court observed that the writers of the Constitution clearly intended that the states had both the right and the duty to maintain militias and that a "militia comprised all males physically capable of acting in concert for the common defense. . . . And, further, that ordinarily when called for service, these men were expected to appear bearing arms supplied by themselves and of the kind in common use at the time. . . . This implied the general obligation of all adult male inhabitants to possess arms, and with certain exceptions, to cooperate in the work of defense. The possession of arms also implied the possession of ammunition, and authorities paid quite as much attention to the latter as to the former." Thus, the full text of the Supreme Court decision mitigates the impact of its ruling on sawed-off shotguns. Such weapons had no place in a militia and were thus not protected, but the general principle of ordinary citizens owning arms and ammunition was clearly preserved.

United States v. Oakes (1977)
(564 F. 2d 384, [10th Cir. 1977])

Ted E. Oakes was convicted of possessing an unregistered machine gun, and upon appeal to the Tenth Circuit Court of Appeals, the decision was upheld. Oakes used two arguments in his defense. First, the Second Amendment granted every citizen the absolute right to keep and bear arms. Second, even if some would deny this interpretation, he was a member of a militia in the state of Kansas, the "Posse Comitatus"—and even those rejecting the individual-rights interpretation of the Second Amendment did not reject the collective-rights interpretation (that the amendment was meant to allow ordinary citizens to be armed so that they could participate in the state militia). However, the appeals court rejected both arguments: The Second Amendment did not protect the individual right to bear arms; and Oakes's unregistered firearm bore no relationship to the state militia, which was most certainly *not* the Posse Comitatus.

United States v. One Assortment of 89 Firearms (1984)
(465 U.S. 354, 1984)

In 1977, the Bureau of Alcohol, Tobacco, and Firearms (ATF) seized a store of firearms from the home of Patrick Mulcahey, charging him with knowingly dealing in firearms without a federal license. Mulcahey admitted that he was a collector and dealer, but claimed that the federal agents had entrapped him into illegal transactions. Mulcahey was eventually acquitted. Despite his acquittal, the ATF seized his firearms, arguing that they should be forfeited according to the Gun Control Act of 1968. In a close decision, the United States Court of Appeals for the Fourth District reversed the lower court ruling and declared that the civil forfeiture could not go forward. The court held that the forfeiture was punitive and violated the constitutional guarantee against double jeopardy. It was also decided that the ruling to confiscate the arms was prohibited by the principle of *collateral estoppel*—the facts established in one case cannot be reargued in another case.

The federal government appealed to the U.S. Supreme Court, which, in a unanimous ruling, overturned the appellate court decision. The Court deemed that the forfeiture of the collection could continue even though Mulcahey had been acquitted of the criminal charges because the forfeiture proceedings did not constitute a criminal proceeding. As is well known, the burden of proof in civil proceedings is weaker than in criminal proceedings: A criminal case must be proved beyond a reasonable doubt, while a civil case can be proved only by a preponderance of the evidence. In addition, the Court deemed the forfeiture remedial, not punitive, and decided that it did not violate the rule of double jeopardy. The Court's decision provided part of the motivation for Congress to pass the Gun Owners' Protection (McClure-Volkmer) Act of 1986. This act prohibits firearm forfeitures if the government's criminal case against a gun owner fails.

United States v. Tot (1942)
(131 F. 2d 261, 1942)

While arresting Frank Tot at his residence for stealing cigarettes from an interstate shipment, federal officers found a .32 caliber Colt semiautomatic pistol. Tot was a convicted felon and thus in violation of the Federal Firearms Act of 1938 (FFA), which banned felons from receiving a firearm involved in interstate commerce. Although Tot was merely in possession of the pistol, federal agents assumed that it had traveled through interstate commerce. At his trial, Tot argued that the pistol had been obtained through an illegal search—in violation of the Fourth Amendment; further, he contended there was no proof he had received it through interstate commerce and that the Second Amendment afforded him the right to keep a firearm. The district court rejected all of these arguments, and he was found guilty of violating the FFA.

The U.S. Court of Appeals for the Third Circuit affirmed the conviction, citing *United States v. Miller* (q.v.) and *Aymette v. State* (q.v.) as precedence for the legality of the FFA and the inapplicability of the Second Amendment. The appellate court observed that Tot had offered up the gun to federal agents without prompting. It also opined that the rights guaranteed in the Second Amendment did not apply to individuals, but to the states to protect themselves from any tyrannies that might arise from the national government.

Undeterred, Tot appealed to the U.S. Supreme Court, which agreed to hear the case on grounds that Tot's Fifth Amendment rights might have been violated. The Court found that the government only presumed Tot had received the pistol through interstate commerce without providing any evidence. As such, the Court held that procedural due process guaranteed in the Fifth Amendment had not been fulfilled, and it overturned Tot's conviction. Gun control advocates point out that the Supreme Court felt no need to review the appellate court's interpretation of the Second Amendment—that this amendment provides no guarantee for the right of the *individual* to keep and bear arms.

United States v. Warin (1976)
(530 F. 2d 103, 1976)

In *United States v. Warin*, the U.S. Court of Appeals for the Sixth Circuit affirmed the federal district court's conviction of Francis J. Warin for possessing a firearm that was not properly registered. The weapon, a 9mm prototype submachine gun, had to be registered with the Department of Justice according to the National Firearms Act of 1934 (as amended by the Gun Control Act of 1968).

Warin was a firearms designer and had built the submachine gun himself. At his trial and during his appeal, he stated he had built the weapon to be sold to the federal government. He argued that he had broken no law because the Second Amendment protected his right to keep and bear a weapon capable of being used by the military or a militia. Warin further claimed that he was part of a "sedentary militia"—in other words, he was a citizen who had the right to be in—and could potentially serve in—the state militia.

The appellate court rejected his arguments. It observed that the Second Amendment guaranteed a collective state right to support a militia, not an individual right to bear arms. Since Warin was not part of an organized militia, under the Second Amendment, he did not have the right to keep a submachine gun. The Court cited *United States v. Miller* (q.v.) and *United States v. Tot* (q.v.) as evidence that the Second Amendment does not protect the right of an individual to keep and bear arms.

7

Biographical Sketches

This chapter presents brief biographies of many of the key politicians, researchers, and activists involved in the gun control debate as it has evolved in the United States over the past four decades. A few have retired, and a few are deceased, but most are still very much involved in their gun-related activities.

The key criterion for selection is the degree to which their work has come to public attention—or more precisely, to my attention in the mainline journals, popular magazines, and newspapers that I read. About one-quarter are researchers, another quarter are politicians, and one-half are activists with high profiles in their advocacy organizations. Although no attempt was made to present any kind of balance based on which side of the gun debate they fall—those favoring the rights of gun owners versus those favoring greater gun control—there is, indeed, near perfect balance: Forty-eight percent are on the gun rights side, and 52 percent are on the gun control side. Thus, even though many of those on the gun rights side often complain that the media and the faculty of major universities are biased against guns, in fact the likes of George W. Bush, Charlton Heston, John Ashcroft, Senator Larry Craig (q.v.)* (R-Idaho), and other strong gun rights proponents get (or have gotten) strong media coverage, as do the National Rifle Association and many of the academicians and intellectuals who question the effectiveness and constitutionality of gun control legislation. On the other hand, there

---

Note that quod vide (q.v.) references a complete entry in this section.

is a noticeable gender imbalance: Four out of five are men, which reflects their dominance in academia, national politics, and the high-level positions of voluntary organizations deeply involved in the national debate over gun control.

Aborn, Richard (1952–)

Richard Aborn's belief that the United States needs strong gun control laws began when he worked in the Manhattan District Attorney's office from 1979 to 1984. On a daily basis, he witnessed the ravages of gun violence in the inner city. In 1992, he took over as president of Handgun Control, Inc. (HCI) and the Center to Prevent Handgun Violence (CPHV), positions he held through 1996. (In 2001, these organizations were respectively renamed the Brady Campaign to Prevent Gun Violence and the Brady Center to Prevent Gun Violence.)

In his quest for more stringent gun control, Aborn supported the 1993 Brady Handgun Violence Prevention Act and the Assault Weapons Ban of 1994. He has fought for mandatory registration laws for handguns as well as for stringent background checks and safety training for prospective purchasers. His priorities include limiting gun purchases to one per month and banning cheaply made handguns (Saturday night specials). Aborn also supports a waiting period on firearm purchases, handgun transfer registration, and the complete prohibition of guns for those convicted of misdemeanors. He believes that to pay for firearms-related injuries, there should be a heavy tax on ammunition and gun sales, as well as for dealer licenses.

Aborn helped begin the STAR (Straight Talk about Risks) program to educate school children on the dangers of gun violence and was critical in getting it under way in New York City. He has worked as a consultant on violence and youth for the Ford Foundation and has assisted a New York task force aimed at preventing violent crime. Currently, he sits on the board of the advocacy group New Yorkers against Gun Violence.

Ashcroft, John (1942–)

John David Ashcroft was the seventy-ninth attorney general of the United States during the first term of President George W. Bush (q.v.). A man of deep religious upbringing, Ashcroft has been labeled a conservative Christian Republican. After graduating from Yale University in 1964, he obtained a J.D. degree from the University of Chicago in 1967. He served two terms as the attorney general of Missouri and was governor of the state from 1984 through 1992. In 1994, Ashcroft was elected to the Senate. He sat on the Senate Judiciary Committee and was Chairman of the Constitution Subcommittee. After Ashcroft lost in his reelection bid in the fall of 2000, president-elect Bush appointed him attorney general.

Ashcroft served as U.S. attorney general until November 2004, during which time he was a strong proponent of the rights of gun owners. He believed that much of what passes as "gun control" simply punishes those who responsibly use firearms while doing nothing to reduce gun-related violence. Ashcroft supported, for example, the shortening of the time that the federal government can keep records of instant background checks on gun buyers (from ninety days to twenty-four hours). As governor, he supported (unsuccessfully) the right of Missourians to carry concealed firearms. As is typical of strong supporters of gun rights, he believes the best way to fight gun crime is through strong criminal penalties for those violating firearms-related laws, which he strived to do while he was attorney general.

Ayoob, Massad (1948–)

Massad Ayoob founded the Lethal Force Institute (LFI) in 1981, an organization dedicated to educating civilians and law enforcement officers in self-defense and deadly force. He is currently the director of the LFI as well as a part-time police captain in New Hampshire. Ayoob is the author of many books, articles, and videos about combat and weaponry. His books include *In the Gravest Extreme: The Role of the Firearm in Civilian Self Defense* and *The Truth about Self Protection.* Ayoob is recognized as one of the best gun instructors in the United States, and his firearm skills have won him numerous titles. His proficiency in self-defense and firearms has placed him as an expert witness in court cases involving violent confrontations. In 1987, he became the chair of the firearms committee for the American Society of Law Enforcement (ASLET) and was voted the Outstanding American Handgunner of the Year in 1988.

Ayoob believes that the Second Amendment grants the individual the right "to keep and bear Arms." He believes that the amendment grants the ordinary citizen the right to carry a gun, which can be a great asset in fending off a criminal attack. He contends that guns provide an especially effective means of self-defense for women, because they overcome women's generally smaller stature relative to that of many criminal attackers. In his view, licensing and taxes for firearms create a civil rights violation, because they deter the poor and minorities from having ready access to guns.

Barnes, Michael D. (1943–)

Michael D. Barnes is the president of the Brady Campaign to Prevent Gun Violence and the Brady Center to Prevent Gun Violence. These organizations were formerly known as Handgun Control, Inc. (HCI) and the Center to Prevent Handgun Violence (CPHV), respectively. Barnes served in the Marine Corps before graduating from the University of North Carolina and earned his J.D. from the George Washington University Law School. He served in the U.S. House of Representatives for the Eighth Congressional district of Maryland from 1979 to 1987. During this time, he chaired the House Subcommittee on Western Hemisphere Affairs and worked with Mothers Against Drunk Driving. Before assuming his present position in March 2000, he was a partner in the law firm of Hagan & Hartson. Barnes has recently helped form an alliance between the Million Mom March and the Brady Campaign and the Brady Center.

Barr, Bob (1948–)

Bob Barr represented the Seventh District of Georgia as a Republican congressman in the U.S. House of Representatives from 1995 to 2003. During his time in office, he was an outspoken proponent for the rights of gun owners. He introduced legislation banning civil suits against gun manufacturers and proposed limiting the responsibility for gun manufacturers when their products were used to commit crimes. Barr fought to eliminate the Bureau of Alcohol, Tobacco, and Firearms, and he worked toward reducing the power of federal law enforcement agencies regarding gun control. He vehemently opposed the 1993 Brady Handgun Violence Prevention Act as well as the Assault Weapons Ban of 1994. As is typical for those on the gun rights side of the gun debate, Barr believes that strong penalties for breaking gun laws is the best means for controlling gun violence; he thus worked to increase prison sentences for convicted felons using guns to commit crimes.

After receiving his B.A. from the University of Southern California in 1970, Barr worked as an official for the Central Intelligence Agency (CIA), while earning an M.A. from George Washington University (1972) and a law degree from Georgetown University (1977). During his political career, Barr served as a senior member of the House Judiciary Committee, the vice chairman of the Government Reform Committee, and a member of the Financial Services Committee. He was awarded the Gun Rights Legislator of the Year by the Citizens Committee for the Right to Keep and Bear Arms, the Congressional Leader of the Year by American Shooting Sports Council, the Freshman Legislator of the Year by the Conservative Political Action Committee, and the Freedom Award from the Law Enforcement Alliance of America. As of 2005, he sits on the board of directors for the National Rifle Association and has received numerous honors for his efforts on behalf of the rights of gun owners.

Bates, Madeleine "Lyn" (1946–)

Madeleine "Lyn" Bates is a founder and the vice president of AWARE (Arming Women Against Rape and Endangerment), a nonprofit organization dedicated to educating women on self-defense. AWARE focuses on helping women to protect themselves from a variety of crimes, including stalking. Bates received her B.S. from Carnegie Mellon University and her Ph.D. from Harvard University. She is a skilled shooter and has become a leading educator in self-defense and firearms for women, winning the Tactical Advocate Award for teaching and writing from the American Tactical Shooting Association in 1997. Bates has lectured for the American Society of Law Enforcement Training, Women in Federal Law Enforcement, the International Women Police Association, the American Society of Criminology, and the American Women's Self-Defense Association. She also writes for *Women & Guns* and is the author of *Safety for Stalking Victims: How to Save Your Privacy, Your Sanity, and Your Life.*

Beard, Michael K. (1941–)

Michael K. Beard is the president and founder of the Coalition to Stop Gun Violence (CSGV). The organization, originally named the National Coalition to Ban Handguns, is composed of many groups with interests in social justice, public health, religion, civic, and child welfare—all of which strive for the reduction of firearms-related death and injury. An important branch of CSGV is the Educational Fund to Stop Gun Violence (EFSGV). CSGV and EFSGV have focused their efforts on trying to close illegal gun markets, creating a greater grassroots gun control movement, strengthening laws regulating firearms, and filing litigation against the gun industry. Beard graduated from the School of Government and Public Administration and the School of International Service at American University. He is a frequent guest on television and radio talk shows, where he promotes stronger gun control, and his writing on this topic regularly appears in newspapers across the country. In addition, Beard has testified before the U.S. House of Representatives and the U.S. Senate, during which he spoke against the McClure-Volkmer (Firearm Owners' Protection) Act of 1986.

Bell, Carl C. (1947–)

Dr. Carl C. Bell is the director of Public and Community Psychiatry at the University of Illinois at Chicago. He is a graduate of the University of Illinois and received his M.D. from Meharry Medical School. He is the president and CEO of the Community Mental Health Council and Foundation, Inc.; former chairman of the National Medical Association's Section on Psychiatry; and a founding member and past board chairman of the National Commission on Correctional Health Care. His research focuses on public health, especially as it relates to African-Americans. He is a coauthor of *Suicide and Homicide among Adolescents,* a clinical and epidemiologic study into youth suicide and homicide. In acknowledging the importance of his research, he was presented with the E. Y. Williams Distinguished Senior Scholar Award of the Section on Psychiatry of the National Medical Association as well as with the American Psychiatric Association President's Commendation, Violence.

Bell believes that easy access to firearms can lead to more suicides and homicides. Noting that most physical confrontations are the result of flawed interpersonal relations, he claims guns can add a deadly dynamic to a fight between individuals who are familiar with one another. He especially advocates limiting the access to firearms by children and career criminals.

Biden, Joseph, Jr. (1942–)

Since 1972, Democrat Joseph Biden Jr. has represented Delaware as a U.S. Senator. He is a graduate of the University of Delaware and the Syracuse University College of Law. He is currently the ranking Democrat on the Senate Foreign Relations Committee and the cochairman of the International Narcotics Control Caucus, in addition to being an adjunct professor at the Widener University School of Law. He strongly supported the 1993 Brady Handgun Violence Prevention Act, and he played a critical role in the passage of the Violent Crime Control and Law Enforcement Act of 1994, also known as the Biden Crime Law, which included a ten-year ban on assault weapons.

Biden is one of a core group of senators committed to the idea that the high rate of gun violence in the United States is a function of its lack of strong gun control laws. Other members of this group include Barbara Boxer (q.v.) (Dem-Cal.), Dianne Feinstein (q.v.) (Dem-Cal.), Edward Kennedy (q.v.) (Dem-Mass.), Frank Lautenberg (q.v.) (Dem-N.J.), Jack Reed (Dem-R.I.), and Charles Schumer (q.v.) (Dem-N.Y.).

Blanchard, Kenneth V. F. (1962–)

As a gun rights activist, Kenneth V. F. Blanchard has used several different positions to advance his cause. Blanchard is a former U.S. marine and has worked in federal law enforcement. He is a specialist in security, terrorism, and firearm training and founded African American Arms & Instruction, Inc., to promote gun training and safety education. The organization would later merge with Royal Marksmanship Instruction and become Best Shot Professional Training and Consulting Group. Blanchard also established the Tenth Cavalry Gun Club, an organization designed to bring more minorities into the gun world and provide firearms education for those with guns in urban areas.

Blanchard holds the title of sergeant-at-arms and sits on the board of directors of the Law Enforcement Alliance of America (LEAA). A nonprofit group composed of law enforcement professionals, crime victims, and other individuals, LEAA seeks ways to reduce violent crime while preserving the right of citizens to defend themselves through the keeping and bearing of arms. In his activist role, Blanchard has appeared in all types of media outlets and spoken before various government bodies, helping to pass concealed carry weapons laws in several states that permit the ordinary citizen to carry a handgun. As of 2005, he is trying to promote the Armed Pilots Program. He is the author of *Black Man with a Gun: A Responsible Gun Ownership Manual for African Americans*, which extols the individual right to keep and bear arms.

Borinsky, Mark (1945–)

In 1974, Dr. Mark Borinksy founded the National Council to Control Handguns (NCCH) in Washington, D.C. While attending the University of Chicago as a graduate student in 1973, Borinsky was robbed at gunpoint, which motivated him to start NCCH. In 1980, the organization was renamed Handgun Control, Inc. (HCI). The original NCCH sought to ban all handguns, but HCI abandoned this position after realizing the U.S. public would not support it. HCI's new goal became the strict control of handguns, as well as other firearms associated with crime, including military-style assault rifles, shotguns, and pistols. The Center to Prevent Handgun Violence (CPHV) was founded in 1983 as an affiliate of HCI, with the aim of reducing gun violence through education, legal advocacy, research, and outreach. In 2001, HCI changed its name to the Brady Campaign to Prevent Gun Violence, and CPHV was renamed the Brady Center to Prevent Gun Violence. Despite being the founder of the best known and most powerful advocacy group for stronger gun control laws in the United States, Borinsky no longer remains active in the organization.

Boxer, Barbara (1940–)

Barbara Boxer, a Democratic senator from California known for her liberal stances, has been a strong advocate for strict gun control throughout her political career. After serving on the Marin County, California, Board of Supervisors from 1977 to 1983, she was elected to the House of Representatives in 1983. In 1992, she was elected to the Senate and currently sits on the Commerce, Foreign Relations, and Environment and Public Works Senate Committees. She is the Democratic Chief Deputy Whip and is a member of the Democratic Policy Committee's Committee on Oversight and Investigation. Boxer has shown a special interest in increasing funding for after-school programs and reducing violence among children and adolescents.

After supporting the 1993 Brady Handgun Violence Prevention Act and the Assault Weapons Ban of 1994, Boxer introduced several pieces of legislation herself. In 1996, she drew up the American Handguns Standards Act with three other senators to increase the safety standards on the production of handguns in order to take cheaply made models (Saturday night specials) off the street. Although this legislation did not pass, she was undeterred and has vigorously pursued other forms of gun control. For example, she introduced the Firearms Rights, Responsibilities, and Remedies Act that would have allowed for cities and groups to sue firearms dealers for civil damages; as has been the case for almost all forms of gun control legislation since 1994, this act did not pass. Her other (failed) attempts for stricter gun control have included the Child Safety Lock Act (that would have required all handguns sold in the United States to have child-safety locks) and legislation to require background checks for sales at gun shows.

Brady, James S. (1940–)

On March 30, 1981, John W. Hinckley Jr. used a cheap handgun to wound President Ronald Reagan in front of the Washington Hilton Hotel. He fired five other shots, one of them seriously injuring White House Press Secretary James S. Brady. Brady was shot in the forehead; prompt medical attention saved his life, but he was left with partial paralysis. He heroically remained the White House press secretary until the end of the Reagan Administration. He and his wife, Sarah Kemp Brady (q.v.), then focused all of their energies on strengthening gun control laws. They worked with Handgun Control, Inc. (HCI), for which Sarah became chair in 1989, to develop the strongest federal gun legislation that had been enacted since the Gun Control Act of 1968, the 1993 Brady Handgun Violence Prevention Act. Taking effect in February 1994, it required a five-day waiting period and background checks on all handguns bought from federally licensed firearms dealers. The Bradys soon went on to another victory with the passage of the landmark federal Assault Weapons Ban of 1994.

In honor of James and Sarah Brady, in 2001 Handgun Control, Inc. was renamed the Brady Campaign to Prevent Gun Violence, and the Center to Prevent Handgun Violence was renamed the Brady Center to Prevent Gun Violence. He is a member of the board of trustees of the Brady Center to Prevent Gun Violence, vice chairman of the National Head Injury Foundation, and vice chairman of the National Organization on Disability. Brady continues to advocate for strong gun control laws as well as for the rights of the disabled.

Brady, Sarah Kemp (1942–)

After her husband, James S. Brady (q.v.), was shot and partially paralyzed during the assassination attempt on President Ronald Reagan in 1981, Sarah Kemp Brady became a leading activist for strong national gun control legislation. Brady earned her B.A. from the College of William and Mary in 1964 and then became a teacher and an active politician for the Republican Party. Following the injury to her husband and an incident involving her young son finding a handgun on vacation, Brady joined Handgun Control, Inc. (HCI), becoming its chair in 1989. She later became chair of its sister organization, the Center to Prevent Handgun Violence (CPHV).

Along with her husband, she was a major force behind passage of the 1993 Brady Handgun Violence Prevention Act, which required a five-day waiting period and background checks on all handgun purchases made from federally licensed firearms dealers. In 2001, Sarah and James were honored when Handgun Control, Inc. was renamed the Brady Campaign to Prevent Gun Violence and the Center to Prevent Handgun Violence was renamed the Brady Center to Prevent Gun Violence. As of 2005, Sarah Brady remains the chair of both organizations.

Bush, George H. W. (1924–)

George Herbert Walker Bush was elected the forty-first president of the United States in 1988. The Republican platform included a strong gun rights plank, and the National Rifle Association (NRA) endorsed his candidacy. Although traditionally opposed to gun control, Bush changed his stance after the 1989 Stockton, California, schoolyard massacre in which Patrick Purdy used a semiautomatic assault rifle to kill five school children, wounding twenty-nine others. The massacre shocked Bush, and by executive order he put a temporary ban on the importation of the AK-47 and selected other military-style assault rifles. Although he did not support the Brady Handgun Violence Protection Act, which failed passage during his time in office, Bush endorsed stronger sentencing for the criminal use of semiautomatic firearms, as well as the prohibition of the production and sale of high-capacity ammunition magazines. Because of these modest efforts toward the stronger regulation of guns, the National Rifle Association did not support his reelection campaign in 1992.

Bush attended Yale University and served two terms as a representative to Congress from the seventh district of Texas. Before becoming vice president in 1980, he was ambassador to the United Nations, chairman of the Republican National Committee, and director of the Central Intelligence Agency (CIA). In 1995, he publicly resigned his lifelong membership in the NRA after the organization's executive vice president, Wayne R. LaPierre Jr. (q.v.), criticized agents of the Bureau of Alcohol, Tobacco, and Firearms, calling them "jack-booted thugs," in a fund-raising letter.

Bush, George W. (1946–)

Republican George Walker Bush is the forty-third president of the United States and the son of former president George H. W. Bush (q.v.). Like his father, the younger Bush is a strong advocate for the rights of gun owners and generally opposed to additional gun control legislation. Bush graduated from Yale University and received an M.B.A. from Harvard University. Before running for president in 2000, he was involved in the oil and gas business and at one point was part owner of the Texas Rangers. He was also the governor of Texas between 1994 and 2000.

Bush believes that the Second Amendment guarantees the *individual* the right to keep and bear arms. He thus supports the right of ordinary persons to carry concealed weapons. As is common for gun rights enthusiasts, he believes that gun control is best effected by strongly punishing those violating firearms laws. Not surprisingly, he is against civil lawsuits against gun manufacturers for the health-care and other economic costs incurred by gun violence. However, he does favor some aspects of the agenda of those wanting stronger gun control, including raising the legal age for owning guns from eighteen to twenty-one, banning "high-capacity" ammunition clips (those that hold more than ten rounds), and requiring background checks for purchases made at gun shows.

Calhoun, Deane (1944–)

Deane Calhoun is the executive director of Youth ALIVE!, an organization designed to prevent violence and create youth leadership in California communities. For her efforts, Calhoun was one of the 1995 honorees of the California Peace Prize, awarded to those helping to stop violence and to promote peace in local communities. She is a graduate of the College of Wooster and earned her M.A. from the University of Wisconsin. Calhoun is critical of the efforts of gun manufacturers to market their weapons to women. One of her reactions was to help start the gun control advocacy group Women against Gun Violence Campaign in California. She also worked in developing the multicity East Bay Corridor Partnership to reduce violence along California's Route 80, as well as helping in the passage of many gun control ordinances in the East Bay area. These include bans on cheaply made handguns (Saturday night specials), mandatory trigger lock requirements, prohibition of gun dealers doing business out of their homes or vehicles, and firearm tax increases for retailers.

Youth ALIVE!'s antiviolence programs include "Teens on Target" and "Caught in the Crossfire." Teens on Target uses peer educators to prevent violence in local communities; President William Jefferson "Bill" Clinton (q.v.) recognized it as one of the top violence prevention programs nationwide. It also won the National Crime Victim Service Award in 1994 from Attorney General Janet Reno and was named the "Most Innovative Violence Prevention Project in Los Angeles" by the Los Angeles City Council. Caught in the Crossfire provides counseling and rehabilitation services for young people that have participated in—or have been the victim of—gun violence.

Carter, Harlon (1913–1991)

For most of his life, Harlon Carter was a gun rights activist and a member of the National Rifle Association (NRA). He served many years on the NRA's national board of directors and was the organization's vice president from 1963 to 1965, before serving as its president from 1965 to 1967. He then served on the NRA's executive council and became head of the organization's political action wing, the Institute for Legislative Action (ILA) in 1975. Carter became head of the ILA with the clear goal of making the NRA *the* political voice for the rights of gun owners. His goal came to full fruition after the "Revolt at Cincinnati," in which several hardcore gun rights advocates took control of the NRA's leadership positions at the organization's annual convention meeting in 1977. Carter was elected executive vice president, and he and his cohorts—Neal Knox (q.v.), Robert Kukla, and Joseph Tartaro (q.v.)—set the NRA on the path it has taken ever since, opposing almost all gun control efforts.

Chisholm, Matthew C. C. "Sandy," III (1954–)

Matthew C. C. "Sandy" Chisholm III is the president and owner of North American Arms (NAA), a gun company that manufactures small pistols and revolvers. Although these guns could be classified as cheaply made handguns (Saturday night specials), the company does not fall under the ban of the Gun Control Act of 1968, because it is a U.S. manufacturer. The act only prohibits the importation of such firearms. Chisholm earned his B.S. from the University of Florida and his M.B.A from the University of Western Ontario. He previously worked for Teleflex, a large company that acquired Tally Manufacturing, a firm that made aerospace defense products and was also the parent company of the small gun manufacturing company, North American Arms. Teleflex had no interest in NAA, but there were no buyers, so Chisholm purchased it himself. With "Convenient, Reliable, Effective!" as its slogan, NAA markets its guns for personal protection—with women, law enforcement officers, outdoorsmen, and collectors providing the bulk of its buyers. Although NAA was one of the first gun manufacturers to voluntarily provide trigger locks for its firearms, Chisholm—like most strong gun rights advocates—is against gun control and instead emphasizes education, common sense, and personal responsibility.

Christoffel, Katherine Kaufer (1948–)

With a scientific and public health policy perspective, Katherine Kaufer Christoffel is one of the country's leading authorities on gun violence. Christoffel graduated from Radcliffe College and earned her M.D. from Tufts University and her M.P.H. from Northwestern University Medical School. She is an attending pediatrician at the Children's Memorial Hospital in Chicago, Illinois, and the director of Statistical Sciences and Epidemiology

Program. She is also a professor of pediatrics and preventive medicine at Northwestern University School of Medicine.

Christoffel has been a member of many panels, committees, and programs dedicated to reducing gun violence among children. She helped to refine the American Academy of Pediatrics's policy on firearms, calling for a ban on handguns. In 1993, Christoffel founded—and is currently board president of—the Handgun Epidemic Lowering Plan (HELP), an international network made up of various organizations dedicated to reducing gun injuries and deaths. She is strongly opposed to keeping handguns in homes with children and believes that a firearm can turn an everyday conflict into a deadly one. She has worked for laws mandating safety locks for gun owners and fought, unsuccessfully, to have the Assault Weapons Ban of 1994 renewed (it expired in September 2004 after Congress failed to renew it).

Clinton, William J. "Bill" (1946–)

As the forty-second president of the United States, Democrat William J. "Bill" Clinton was a strong advocate of gun control and instrumental in the passage of the strongest federal gun control legislation since the Gun Control Act of 1968. During his campaign for the presidency, Clinton was explicit about his support for gun control. After his election, he appointed gun control advocate Janet Reno as the U.S. attorney general. In his first term, he worked hard to push through Congress the 1993 Brady Handgun Violence Prevention Act, as well as the Assault Weapons Ban of 1994. Clinton endorsed strong penalties for gun law violators—a gun control policy appealing to both sides of the gun control debate (those favoring strong gun control versus those wanting to protect the rights of gun owners). Like all those on the gun control side of the debate, he believes that more restrictions on the sale and possession of handguns will lead to a reduction in violence. After the instant background check replaced the five-day waiting period on the purchase of firearms, Clinton pushed to renew the waiting period. He also proposed raising the legal age limit for owning guns from eighteen to twenty-one and enacting a background check period for *all* purchases at gun shows and other parts of the gun market involving transactions between private individuals (as opposed to between a private individual and a federally licensed gun dealer; such a transaction has required a background check of the purchaser since 1994).

Conyers, John, Jr. (1929–)

Democrat John Conyers Jr. entered the U.S. House of Representatives in 1964, where he has served the Michigan's Fourteenth Congressional District ever since. A staunch liberal, Conyers is the second most senior member of the House and the ranking member on the Democratic side of the House Judiciary Committee. He is also considered the dean of the Congressional Black Caucus, a group he helped found. Conyers received his B.A. and law degree from Wayne State University and was awarded the Southern Christian Leadership Conference Award for his civil rights efforts. Since being in the House, he has introduced the Hate Crimes Act, the Violence against Women Act, and the Public Safety Officers Benefits Act and was a major force behind the Help America Vote Act.

Conyers is a strong advocate for strict gun control. He has supported banning armor-piercing ammunition and opposed passage of the Firearms Owners' Protection Act of 1986, which dismantled some of the strong gun control features of the Gun Control Act of 1968. Conyers has also fought for prohibiting the production and importation of firearms that can go undetected through metal detectors, and he supported the 1993 Brady Handgun Violence Prevention Act and the Assault Weapons Ban of 1994. Conyers is the author of the Gun Safety Act, which would ban cheap domestic handguns and require trigger locks and other safety features on the production of new handguns. The act has met strong resistance by gun rights advocates in Congress and has yet to be passed into law.

Cook, Philip J. (1946–)

Philip J. Cook is currently the ITT/Sanford Distinguished Professor of Public Policy at the Terry Sanford Institute of Public Policy at Duke University. He is a much published and well-respected researcher on gun violence. His studies have led him to become a strong advocate for strict gun control. He has researched a broad range of gun-related issues, including the relationship between gun availability and violence, the defensive uses of guns against criminal attacks, and the economic costs of gun violence to contemporary society.

Cook and coresearcher Jens Ludwig (q.v.) authored the National Survey of Private Ownership of Firearms (http://www

.ncjrs.org/txtfiles/165476.txt), which produced an extensive inventory of gun ownership and use in the United States. Some of their findings were at odds with those of Gary Kleck (q.v.) and Marc Gertz regarding how often guns are used defensively (e.g., to thwart a robbery attempt). Cook and Ludwig found a considerably smaller number of defensive gun uses, and even that estimate is questionable. They concluded that the best estimate is given by the annual National Crime Victimization Survey, which puts defensive gun use at about 100,000 incidents per year (which contrasts sharply with Kleck and Gertz's estimate of 2.5 million). Cook's best known work is *Gun Violence: The Real Costs* (coauthored with Jens Ludwig), in which the annual cost of gun violence to the United States—adding together the burdens on the health care system, lost wages, lessened productivity, and lost tax revenues—is estimated to be $100 billion.

Cornell, Saul (1960–)

Saul Cornell is a professor of history at Ohio State University, where he serves as the director of the Second Amendment Research Center at the John Glenn Institute. He is an expert on early U.S. history and has extensively researched the history of the Second Amendment—his most important works include an edited collection of historical scholarship on the Second Amendment (*Whose Right to Bear Arms Did the Second Amendment Protect?*) and *A Well Regulated Militia: The Founding Fathers and the Origins of Gun Control in America.* His research is of critical importance to the contemporary debate on gun control and focuses on the contested nature of the right to bear arms throughout U.S. history. The advocates of the rights of gun owners—as articulated, for example, by the National Rifle Association—contend that the Second Amendment guarantees the *individual* the right to own and use arms for protection—personal protection, as well as against a tyrannical government. On the other hand, the proponents of gun control—as articulated, for example, by the Brady Campaign to Prevent Gun Violence—contend that the Second Amendment is a *collective* right that guaranteed states, not individuals, the right to form armed militias for protection in case the democracy of the fledgling nation failed.

Cornell argues that both sides of the contemporary debate lack a basic understanding of eighteenth-century American thought and language. The original understanding of the right to bear arms was as a *civic* right—the right of citizens to keep and bear those arms needed to meet their legal obligation to partici- pate in the militia. In Cornell's view, the collective-rights theory and individual-rights theory only crystallized in the decades after the Second Amendment was ratified. The notion of a civic right reflected the fears of the founding generation over standing armies and the abuses they might impose on the general popula- tion in the hands of a despotic government. The founders as- sumed that the average white property-owning man would pos- sess arms and ammunition, and that the community might ask such a man to defend it as part of the local militia. But there was no *individual* right as we think of the term today; for example, few in the late eighteenth century would have included women, people of color, or resident aliens as individuals possessing the right to "keep and bear Arms." The state expected that these guns would be closely regulated. Guns owned for self-defense that had little value for public defense—such as pistols—enjoyed no spe- cial constitutional protection. In sum, Cornell argues that rather than presenting a barrier to robust gun regulation, the Second Amendment *requires* it.

Cottrol, Robert J. (1949–)

Robert J. Cottrol is the Harold Paul Green Research Professor of Law at George Washington University. He earned his B.A. and Ph.D. from Yale University, and his J.D. from Georgetown Law School. Cottrol's research focuses on race relations in the contexts of U.S. legal history and criminal law. He is the editor of the much-cited volume *Gun Control and the Constitution: Sources and Explorations on the Second Amendment*. Cottrol's studies have led him to endorse background checks for firearms purchases to screen out those who shouldn't own a gun—most importantly, convicted felons. However, he argues that guns are an important tool for self-defense and that the ordinary citizen should have ready access to them. In particular, Cottrol contends that African- Americans and other minorities need to possess guns as a coun- tervailing power to a racist society—a society that has produced the likes of the Ku Klux Klan and police forces that have been known to treat minorities with extreme and undue harshness.

Currently gun rights and gun control advocacy groups do not work together on any aspect of the pressing social problem of gun violence in the United States. Cottrol believes this situation needs rectification and that there are several areas in which the two advocacy groups could profitably work together, especially in developing more creative measures of preventing guns from ending up in the hands of dangerous individuals.

Covey, Preston King (1942–)

Preston King Covey is the director of the Center for the Advancement of Applied Ethics at Carnegie Mellon University in Pittsburgh, Pennsylvania. He also serves as the Pennsylvania regional director for the National Institute of Law Enforcement Ethics. A significant part of his writings involve the role of firearms in contemporary society, including their connection to violence.

Covey's positive childhood experiences with firearms combined with his professional work on the ethics of gun ownership have led him to become a strong proponent of gun rights. Covey believes that guns are a legitimate means for self-defense in dire circumstances; guns should especially be made available to the weaker members of society, because they are the favorite prey of criminals. He also contends that there are far too many negative connotations given to guns in the media. Thus, for example, in 1994 he testified against a proposed ban on assault weapons before the Pennsylvania General Assembly; he argued that the term *assault* should be changed to *combat*, because the former term has a negative, aggressive connotation. He believes that the features of assault weapons that make them attractive to thugs and street gang members also make them attractive to law-abiding citizens wanting to defend themselves against criminal attack.

Covey is a certified firearms instructor, having taught for Defensive Training International, Inc., and for the Lethal Force Institute. He is currently a member of the International Association of Law Enforcement Firearms Instructors, the American Society of Law Enforcement Trainers, and the Allegheny County Sheriff's Reserve.

Craig, Larry E. (1945–)

A Republican Senator from Idaho, Larry E. Craig has been on the board of directors of the National Rifle Association since 1983. He is a strong proponent of the rights of gun owners. He represented Idaho in the U.S. House of Representatives in the 1980s and in

1990 was elected to the U.S. Senate and reelected in 1996 and 2002. He currently chairs the Republican Policy Committee and serves on the Congressional Sportsman's Caucus.

Craig believes in a limited government. He views most gun control legislation as infringing on the Second Amendment right of citizens "to keep and bear Arms." Not surprisingly, he did not back the 1993 Brady Handgun Violence Prevention Act, or the federal Assault Weapons Ban of 1994. He has voted against all legislative attempts to enact mandatory background checks for purchases made at gun shows. Like many gun rights advocates, Craig believes that the media focus too much attention on the number of crimes committed with guns, while ignoring the significant number of crimes that are prevented by firearms (e.g., when a law-abiding citizen brandishes a firearm to scare off a would-be mugger). In recent years, Craig has been at the forefront in introducing and advocating for the passage of legislation to exempt gun manufacturers from civil lawsuits for deaths and or injuries related to firearms.

Diaz, Tom (1940–)

Tom Diaz is a senior policy analyst at the Violence Policy Center (VPC) and has authored many studies on gun violence that are popular with gun control advocates. A former competitive shooter and past member of the National Rifle Association, Diaz's views on firearms have changed from that of a strong "gun rights" to a strong "gun control" stance. He is the author of *Making a Killing: The Business of Guns in America*, which details how firearm manufacturers have increased the lethality of guns to increase sales. In general, he argues that firearms are a major public health problem in the contemporary United States and that its gun control laws need strengthening to at least the level of the average western European nation.

Dingell, John D. (1926–)

Longtime United States House of Representatives Democrat John D. Dingell has fought gun control and worked for the rights of gun owners throughout his political career. He has represented the Fifteenth Congressional District of Michigan since 1955. He attended Georgetown University and received his law degree from there in 1952. While in office, he has been chair of House

Committee on Energy and Commerce and is a senior member on the Migratory Bird Conservation Committee.

Dingell has made attempts to shut down the Bureau of Alcohol, Tobacco, Firearms and Explosives (ATF), accusing it of being an embarrassment to the nation. Despite being such a strong critic of ATF, he resigned his National Rifle Association membership after its executive vice president, Wayne LaPierre (q.v.), labeled ATF agents as "jack-booted thugs" in a fund-raising letter.

Examples of Dingell's strong gun rights stance include his voting against the 1993 Brady Handgun Violence Prevention Act and his swamping efforts to require mandatory background checks on *all* purchases made at gun shows. With regard to the latter, his amendments to the House's Mandatory Gun Show Background Check Act ensured its defeat. The amendments included reducing the maximum amount of time during which law enforcement officials could have conducted criminal background checks on handgun purchases from three business days to twenty-four hours.

Faria, Miguel A., Jr. (1952–)

Miguel A. Faria Jr. came to the United States from Cuba when he was thirteen years old. He received his undergraduate degree and his M.D. from the University of South Carolina before becoming a clinical professor of surgery at Mercer University School of Medicine in Macon, Georgia (from which he is now retired). He is one of a small number of physicians professing a strong gun rights stance. During his professional career, he has sought equality of reporting for the gun rights side of the gun debate in the medical literature—a literature dominated by those seeking stronger gun control measures. His quest for equal reporting is likely rooted in his childhood, when he witnessed new leader Fidel Castro order all privately owned firearms confiscated. This confiscation, of course, reduced the possibilities for armed resistance against the Castro regime.

Faria was able to realize some balance in reporting when he became the editor of the *Journal of Medical Association of Georgia* in 1993, a position he held for two years. He used his editorship to ensure that there were writings reflecting the benefits of firearms, including their use as weapons of defense by law-abiding citizens protecting themselves from criminal attack. He argues that the health-care system's savings from deterred crimes far outweigh the present costs of gun violence to the system. Faria also sought balance of reporting when he became the editor of the *Medical Sentinel*, a position he held until 2003. The journal has since been renamed the *Journal of American Physicians and Surgeons*, and Faria maintains the title of editor emeritus.

Feinstein, Dianne (1933–)

Dianne Feinstein is the senior U.S. senator from California, having been first elected in 1992. Feinstein was president of the San Francisco Board of Supervisors when she discovered the bullet-riddled bodies of Mayor George Moscone and City Board member Harvey Milk on November 27, 1978. This horrific event solidified her strong gun control views. She replaced Moscone as mayor and immediately began working on a municipal ordinance prohibiting handgun ownership in the city. The Board of Supervisors eventually passed the ordinance in June 1982, but it was soon overturned by the California Court of Appeals.

Feinstein was instrumental in authoring and enacting the Assault Weapons Ban of 1994 and the Gun-Free Schools Act of 1994. The Assault Weapons Ban prohibited the manufacture and transfer of nineteen named assault weapons and approximately 200 rifles, shotguns, and pistols covered by the law's generic definition of an "assault weapon." It also banned large-capacity ammunition feeding devices (those holding more than ten rounds). The Gun-Free Schools Act requires that any state receiving federal education funds must have a law requiring local school districts to expel—for at least a year—any student who has brought a weapon to a school. Thwarted by a Republican-dominated Congress, Feinstein and many of her Democratic colleagues have been unsuccessful in recent years in trying to strengthen federal gun control laws. One of her greatest setbacks was the nonrenewal of the assault weapons ban, which had a "sunset" clause, limiting it to ten years; it expired on September 13, 2004, and all attempts to bring it to a renewal vote failed.

Gottlieb, Alan Merril (1947–)

In his quest to promote the *individual-rights* interpretation of the Second Amendment in public policy, Alan Merril Gottlieb founded the lobbying organization the Citizens Committee for the Right to Keep and Bear Arms (CCRKBA), along with its research affiliate, the Second Amendment Foundation (SAF) in 1974. He is currently the chairman of CCRKBA and vice president of SAF, working with Joseph P. Tartaro (q.v.) in producing the *Got-tlieb-Tartaro Report*, SAF's monthly newsletter.

Although a member of the National Rifle Association (NRA), Gottlieb believes that other gun rights organizations, such as the CCRKBA, often play a crucial role in mobilizing gun rights activists. He appears often on television and radio talk shows, and his writings are cited by many on the gun rights side of the national debate over gun control. His books include *The Gun Owner's Political Action Manual, The Rights of Gun Owners, The Gun Grabbers, Gun Rights Fact Book,* and *Guns for Women* (coauthored with George Fly). With David B. Kopel (q.v.), he also cowrote *Things You Can Do to Defend Your Gun Rights* and *More Things You Can Do to Defend Your Gun Rights,* which both offer practical advice on how ordinary citizens can become politically involved in protecting their Second Amendment right "to keep and bear Arms."

Gross, Daniel (1967–)

On February 23, 1997, Ali Abu Kamal used a .38 caliber Beretta handgun to murder two people and critically injure a third at the Empire State Building in New York City. Christoffer Burmeister, a member of the music band the Bushpilots, was killed. Fellow band member Matt Gross was critically injured with a gunshot to his head, although he exceeded all expectations and eventually recovered. The shooting motivated his brother, Daniel Gross, a partner in a New York advertising agency, to quit his job and devote his professional life to strengthening the nation's awareness of the public health epidemic of gun violence. Gross believes that stronger public awareness and practical education, especially applied to young people, can prevent the kind of tragedy that befell his brother. To this end, he cofounded, with Talmage Cooley, the gun control advocacy group PAX in 1998. PAX promotes the notion that self-defensive gun use is the exception, not the rule, and that household firearms are dangerous.

PAX concentrates its efforts on two national campaigns. The ASK Campaign pushes for parents to ask about guns before sending their children to someone else's home, and the SPEAK UP Campaign urges students to report weapons-related threats in their schools and neighborhoods. Through its mass media framework, PAX has become the nation's largest nonpolitical gun violence prevention organization. It uses marketing and grassroots professionals to spread its message and enjoys the strong support of many public health, law enforcement, and educational organizations.

Halbrook, Stephen P. (1947–)

Attorney Stephen P. Halbrook has taken his advocacy for gun rights to the United States Supreme Court three times and won. In his most famous case, *Printz v. United States,* Halbrook successfully argued that the federal background checks on retail gun purchases spelled out in the 1993 Brady Handgun Violence Prevention Act violated the Tenth Amendment and did not follow the principle of separation of powers between the federal government and the states. He was also successful in *United States v. Thompson/Center Arms Co.* in protecting a gun manufacturer from a special tax and regulatory system. Halbrook won as part of a team in the case of *Castillo v. United States,* which reevaluated the sentencing given to Branch Davidians after its 1993 shootout with the Bureau of Alcohol, Tobacco, and Firearms.

Halbrook earned his B.S. and Ph.D. from Florida State University before receiving his J.D. from Georgetown University Law Center. One of his major career goals has been to introduce the Second Amendment to critical, scholarly examination. To this end, he wrote *That Every Man Be Armed: The Evolution of a Constitutional Right,* which provides a broad historical assessment of the Second Amendment, and *Freedmen, the Fourteenth Amendment, and the Right to Bear Arms, 1866–1876,* which argues that the intent of the Fourteenth Amendment was to extend all constitutional guarantees to the newly freed slaves, including the right to "keep and bear Arms"; gun control laws in the post–Civil War South were little more than (quite successful) attempts to disarm African-Americans. Halbrook's *Firearms Law Deskbook: Federal and State Criminal Practice* is a leading reference for lawyers and judges involved in firearms cases. More recently he has studied how gun ownership and policies have historically affected European nations, as reflected in his book *Target Switzerland: Swiss Armed Neutrality in World War II*—wherein he argues that the Nazis bypassed Switzerland, in part, because every able-bodied Swiss man was armed.

Hammer, Marion P. (1939–)

Marion P. Hammer is a certified firearms instructor and the executive director of Unified Sportsmen of Florida. She was the first woman to become president of the National Rifle Association (NRA). A lifetime gun user, Hammer was a major figure in the passing of Florida's right-to-carry law in 1987, allowing for the ready licensing of ordinary citizens to carry concealed handguns. In 1992, she became second vice president of the NRA and in 1994 became first vice president. After the death of the president of the NRA in 1995, Hammer assumed the position and held it through 1998. She played a key role in the construction of the NRA National Firearms Museum, which opened in 1998. In addition to being a lifetime member of the NRA Executive Council, she is currently on the board of directors and the executive committee. Owing to her lifelong commitment to the organization, the NRA named its female philanthropy award the Marion P. Hammer Award.

Hammer was central in developing the NRA's Eddie Eagle program, which provides gun safety education to children. For her efforts, she was honored with National Citation of Outstanding Community Service by the National Safety Council and the American Legion's National Education Award. In 2004, Hammer was inducted into the Florida Women's Hall of Fame.

Hardy, David T. (1951–)

A strong advocate for the rights of gun owners, David T. Hardy has a private law practice in Arizona, which includes an emphasis on First and Second Amendment litigation. As a Second Amendment legal scholar and historian, Hardy has testified before Congress—criticizing the Gun Control Act of 1968 as allowing the prosecution for inadvertent and minor transgressions, and thus impinging upon the civil liberties of law-abiding citizens.

Hardy's law review articles have been referenced by the U.S. Supreme Court and eleven U.S. Circuit Courts of Appeals. He is the author of *Origins and Development of the Second Amendment*. He is also the coauthor, with Rex Kimball, of *This Is Not an Assault*, which examines the disastrous 1993 federal siege of the Branch Davidians complex outside of Waco, Texas. His most recent work, *Michael Moore Is a Big Fat Stupid White Man*, coauthored with Jason Clarke, is especially critical of Moore's (q.v.) depiction of the gun control issue in the film *Bowling for Columbine*.

Hatch, Orrin (1934–)

Utah's senior U.S. Senator, Orrin Hatch, is a strong proponent of the *individual-rights* interpretation of the Second Amendment, claiming that any limitation on the right to keep and bear arms is a violation of the founding fathers' intentions. Hatch graduated from Brigham Young University and the University of Pittsburg Law School before entering the Senate in 1976. He is one of the most powerful lawmakers on Capitol Hill, serving as the senior Republican member of the Senate Judiciary Committee and the second ranking Republican on the Senate Committee on Finance. He is also a member of the Senate Health, Education, Labor, and Pensions Committee, the Senate Select Committee on Intelligence, and the Joint Committee on Taxation.

In support of his Second Amendment beliefs, Hatch has voted against more stringent background checks on firearm purchases made at guns shows and for immunity legislation that would protect firearms manufacturers from civil lawsuits. Like most in the gun rights camp, he believes that controlling gun violence is best effected by strongly enforcing current gun laws. To this end, he strongly favors prosecuting gun-law violators in federal courts, where convictions rates are higher and sentences more severe than in the average state court. Unlike some staunch gun rights advocates, however, he supports trigger locks and locked storage boxes for firearms. (Many gun rights advocates feel that locked firearms mitigate their use for self-defense.)

Haymaker, Richard (1940–) and Holley Galland Haymaker (1944–)

In 1982, Louisiana State University professors Richard Haymaker and Holley Galland Haymaker were the host family for a Japanese exchange student, Yoshihiro "Yoshi" Hattori. On October 17 of that year, Yoshi and the Haymakers' teenage son, Webb, entered the carport of a Baton Rouge home they thought was hosting a Halloween party. Their costumes frightened homeowner Bonnie Peairs, who called for her husband, Rodney, to get his gun. With a .44 Magnum, Rodney stood at his doorway while the boys were in his carport. Yoshi, holding a camera in his hand—an object that may not have been identifiable in the dark—approached the man even after being told to "Freeze!" For whatever reason, perhaps not understanding that the term meant to stop,

Yoshi continued to approach. Tragically, Peairs shot and killed Yoshi.

Japan was shocked by the event, because handguns are all but prohibited in that country. Yoshi's parents traveled to the United States and worked with the Haymakers to create a petition calling for greater gun control in the United States. The petition was eventually signed by 1.7 million Japanese and 150,000 Americans and personally delivered to President William Clinton (q.v.) days before the Senate passed the 1993 Brady Handgun Violence Prevention Act.

Rodney Peairs was acquitted in his manslaughter trial. His attorney successfully argued that Louisiana law allows a homeowner the right of self-defense, even if it results in the death of an intruder. However, the Hattoris filed a civil lawsuit against Peairs and won a settlement of $653,000 on September 15, 1994. Peairs's homeowner's insurance company paid $100,000, of which the Hattoris received about $45,000 after the lawyer's fees and expenses had been paid. The Hattoris used the money to create the Yoshi's Gift foundation. Yoshi's Gift uses its funds to support gun control groups lobbying for stronger federal gun laws. The Haymakers went on to work for gun control with the Coalition to Stop Gun Violence and later helped to found Louisiana Ceasefire, a high-profile gun control advocacy group.

Hemenway, David (1945–)

David Hemenway is a professor at the Harvard School of Public Health and the director of both the Harvard Injury Control Research Center and the Harvard Youth Violence Prevention Center. He is a leading researcher on gun violence and its prevention from the public health perspective. His most important findings and recommendations are found in his 2004 book *Private Guns, Public Health*.

The public health approach to gun violence avoids dividing the world as it is most often done in the debate over gun control. Instead of concentrating on *individuals* and looking at the world as divided into criminals and noncriminals, those who commit suicide and those who do not, those who mishandle firearms and those who do not, the public health approach looks at the *social and physical environments* and how these encourage or discourage gun-related harm. The ultimate goal is to change these environments in such ways as to reduce this harm.

Hemenway contends that the improvement in motor vehicle safety in the United States over the past fifty years provides an excellent model for reducing gun violence. Between 1952 and 1999, the death rate per motor vehicle mile dropped 80 percent—not because drivers got any better, rather because comprehensive data collection and analysis revealed the many flaws in the design of cars (e.g., inflexible steering columns, unyielding dashboards, weak passenger compartments) and roadways (lack of shoulders, lack of guardrails), which were eventually corrected. He believes that in the area of firearms-related violence, the United States is currently where it was with motor vehicle safety in the early 1950s.

From the public health perspective, serious gun control has yet to be realized in the United States, in part, because we lack the comprehensive data to evaluate gun control measures. Hemenway argues that the nation needs a data collection system for gun violence similar to the National Highway Traffic Safety Administration's Fatality Analysis Reporting System (FARS). He is part of a multiorganizational team leading such an effort. In 1999, the Harvard Injury Control Research Center set up a violence reporting system in collaboration with the Medical College of Wisconsin and ten other medical organizations (university medical centers and health departments) around the country. Labeled the National Violent Injury Statistics System (NVISS), it has developed uniform standards for the collection and organization of data related to violent deaths. These standards are based on FARS, and they have the ultimate goal of doing what FARS has done for highway fatalities—that is, to reduce deaths by using multivariable analysis to ascertain the complex mix of causes that underlies incidents of firearms violence (though originally intended for firearms-related deaths, the system has been expanded to include all types of violent deaths). Hemenway and his colleagues have the ultimate goal of having NVISS adopted at the national level under the auspices of the Centers for Disease Control, which already has a similar pilot program under way (its National Violence Death Reporting System).

Henigan, Dennis A. (1951–)

As director of the Legal Action Project for the Brady Center to Prevent Gun Violence, Dennis A. Henigan has represented many individuals and communities in lawsuits in federal and state courts seeking to reform the gun industry and bring about safer practices on the part of gun manufacturers, dealers, and owners. Like most on the gun control side of the contemporary gun debate, Henigan does not believe that the Second Amendment guarantees citizens an individual right to keep and bear arms for private purposes. Thus, he sees no conflict between the Second Amendment and strict gun regulations. He has devoted much of his professional work in trying to make the gun industry more accountable for manufacturing unsafe firearms and more responsible for the needless deaths and injuries that occur from poor industry practices—including designing guns without feasible safety devices and maintaining a distribution system that supplies the underground market through corrupt and irresponsible retail dealers.

Henigan also believes that gun owners need to take utmost care in securing their weapons, and he assisted in bringing suit against gun owners who left a firearm accessible to a teen who accidentally killed a friend (as part of the groundbreaking *Dix v. Beretta*, which also included a product liability claim against the gun manufacturer, Beretta, for failing to have installed a chamber-loaded indicator and a locking device on its 92 Com-S 9mm handguns). Recently, he has been highly vocal in protesting "immunity legislation" that Congress passed in the fall of 2005 (the Protection of Lawful Commerce in Arms, sponsored by National Rifle Association Board Member and Idaho Republican Senator Larry Craig). This act protects gun manufacturers from civil lawsuits from individuals, communities, and states seeking to recover compensation for the costs they incur from gun violence. Since its passage, Henigan's top priority has become preserving the lawsuits he filed on the part of gun violence victims in spite of the new law, both by arguing that the cases come within the exceptions of the Act and by arguing that the Act is unconstitutional. He is also working with the Brady Center to inaugurate a new program during 2006 called Gun Industry Watch, which is designed to systematically expose the practices of the industry that contribute to gun violence.

Heston, Charlton (1924–)

As the president of the National Rifle Association (NRA) from 1998 to 2003, Charlton Heston used his celebrity status to bring national attention to the gun rights cause. Membership increased during his term, and his widespread popularity motivated the NRA to change its bylaws to allow him to remain the organization's president past normal term limits.

Heston was a successful Hollywood actor, starring in such films as *The Ten Commandments* and *Ben Hur*, for which he won an Academy Award for Best Actor in 1959. During President Lyndon B. Johnson's push for gun control legislation in 1968, Heston emerged as a celebrity supporter of gun control. However, he would later go on to say that this support was a mistake.

Despite being a very articulate speaker during his tours and media appearances, his critics accused him of not being knowledgeable enough about the issues and speaking about gun rights at inopportune times. In 2002, Heston publicly acknowledged he had been diagnosed with Alzheimer's disease, and in 2003 he resigned as president. That same year, he was awarded the Presidential Medal of Freedom from President George W. Bush (q.v.).

Homsher, Deborah (1952–)

Deborah Homsher of Cornell University's Southeast Asia Program is the author of *Women and Guns: Politics and the Culture of Firearms in America*. In her much-cited book, she studies pro-gun and anti-gun political agendas promulgated through the 1990s, investigating how individual women responded to aspects of these fierce debates and how the divisive techniques employed by partisans affected U.S. political life generally. She examines the roles guns play in the lives of women who hunt, attend pro- and anti-gun rallies, use firearms for protection, and are members of militias. She also details her interviews with women whose family members have been killed or wounded by guns, including African-American women living in an urban neighborhood blighted by drug trafficking and gun deaths. Rare in both the scholarly and popular commentary on firearms, Homsher does not come down firmly on either the gun rights or gun control side of the contemporary debate, but instead seeks to analyze the repetitive, passionate "talking points" used as ammunition by both sides and to understand how this discourse has developed out of U.S. history and promises to shape its future. The paperback version of her book includes an addendum of primary source documents: speeches and congressional testimony from notable pro-gun and anti-gun advocates.

Horwitz, Joshua M. (1963–)

Joshua M. Horwitz is the executive director of the Coalition to Stop Gun Violence (CSGV) and its sister organization, the Educational Fund to Stop Gun Violence (EFSGV). CSGV is made up of many religious and social justice groups, as well as child welfare advocates and public health professionals. The primary mission of CSGV and EFSGV is to reduce firearm death and injury. To this end, CSGV and EFSGV work toward building a strong grassroots gun control movement promoting stricter gun control laws, reform within the gun industry, and wider community awareness of the cost of gun violence and what can be done to reduce it. As do most of those believing that the United States needs stronger controls over its firearms, Horwitz contends that needless harm results from the bad practices common in the gun industry, including shoddy recordkeeping, inadequate training of sales personnel, and the manufacturing of guns lacking state-of-the-art safety devices; for example, chamber-loaded indicators and magazine disconnects. He also contends that lawsuits against the gun industry are an appropriate means for achieving CSGV and EFSGV's primary mission.

Horwitz has been central in developing EFSGV's most important efforts to reduce gun violence. These include the Right-to-Know Campaign to inform gun violence victims of their legal rights in the civil justice system; the Hands Without Guns program to change youth views on guns and violence through focusing on empowerment, education, and development; and a key offshoot of Hands Without Guns, the Positive Youth Development's Ymedia Program, which shows local organizers how to develop a youth group that can prepare an antiviolence media campaign appropriate for distribution via television, radio, movies, magazines, or the Internet. Most recently, Horwitz and his organizations have developed an intense lobbying effort, Protect Justice for Gun Victims, to combat the strong gun rights legislation currently under consideration in the U.S. Congress that would "immunize" the gun industry from civil lawsuits.

Hupp, Suzanna Gratia (1959–)

On October 16, 1991, at Luby's Cafeteria in Killeen, Texas, George Hennard Jr. murdered twenty-three people and wounded twenty-one others with two high-capacity magazine semiautomatic handguns, before killing himself. Suzanna Gratia Hupp escaped the massacre through a broken window, but both of her parents were killed. She usually carried a handgun for protection, but had left it in the car because she was afraid of being arrested for carrying a concealed weapon and losing her chiropractic license. Since the day of her parents' murders, she has become an advocate for the right of ordinary citizens to carry a concealed weapon. She believes there was a reasonable chance that she could have stopped Hennard from killing and wounding so many had her handgun been in her purse instead of her car.

Dr. Hupp was instrumental in getting Texas's right-to-carry law passed in 1996 and was elected to the Texas House of Representatives that same year. She has testified at legislative hearings across the country on behalf of ordinary citizens having the right to carry a concealed weapon if they can pass a simple background check to ensure that they are legal possessors under federal law (e.g., are not convicted felons or under a domestic-violence-related restraining order). The National Rifle Association awarded her the Sybil Ludington Women's Freedom Award, and she was the first Texan granted lifetime membership to the organization.

Hyde, Henry J. (1924–)

As a Republican member of the U.S. House of Representatives for the Sixth District of Illinois since 1975, Henry J. Hyde has become a strong advocate for strong federal legislation to regulate guns. He has been a member of the International Relations Committee since 1982, and currently serves as chairman. In addition, he has also been a ranking Republican on the House Select Committee on Intelligence and is on the House Judiciary Committee, for which he was chairman during President Bill Clinton's (q.v.) impeachment hearings. He is most famous for sponsoring the Hyde Amendment, which banned the use of federal funds to pay for abortions through Medicaid.

During his first years in Congress, Hyde was known as an opponent of gun control. However, over time he slowly changed his thinking until, by 1993, he became a major supporter of the Brady Handgun Violence Prevention Act. He also helped in the passage of the Assault Weapons Ban in 1994. Hyde supports a key component of the contemporary agenda of gun control advocates, background checks on *all* purchases made at gun shows.

And he has introduced legislation, as of yet with no success, to enact a gun-show background-check law. In 2005, Hyde announced that he would not seek another term in office because of health issues.

Kates, Don B., Jr. (1941–)

Attorney Don B. Kates Jr. has been one of the best-known proponents of the rights of gun owners for the past three decades. Like others on the gun rights side of the contemporary debate over gun control, he believes that the Second Amendment guarantees the *individual* the right "to keep and bear Arms," and thus views many forms of gun control as violating the Constitution. His strong advocacy for gun rights has a very personal dimension: Kates worked on civil rights cases in the South during the 1960s. His efforts were not popular with many in the white establishment, and he thus carried a gun for protection.

Kates's legal work has involved many gun-control cases. One of the most famous was *Doe v. San Francisco*, which he won when the California Court of Appeals found that the 1982 handgun ban in San Francisco did not comply with a state law restricting local firearm ordinances. As an author and an editor, Kates's writings have appeared in law journals and as chapters of several books well known to scholars studying the gun control issue, including a major coauthored chapter in David B. Kopel's (q.v.) *Guns: Who Should Have Them?* He is also the coeditor, with Gary Kleck (q.v.), of *The Great American Gun Debate: Essays on Firearms and Violence*. In addition to Second Amendment issues, Kates's writings have questioned much of the research growing out of the public health approach to the topic. For example, he argues that if handguns were eliminated (a gun control recommendation made by many public health researchers), more people would end up being killed because shotguns and rifles would be substituted—and they are generally deadlier than handguns. Kates has pointed out that when public health researchers extol the low violence of many western European nations (viewing it as a product of their strict gun control laws), they ignore the high rates of suicide in these nations—typically much higher than that of the United States. Using FBI Uniform Crime Reports and other data, he has also argued that firearms are abused by only a tiny proportion of the population—most of whom lack self-control and have had a long history of violence before ever using a gun to kill, injure, or rob another person. He claims it is a myth to think that the ordinary, law-abiding citizen who buys a gun with the intention of using it legally will be suddenly transformed into a criminal.

Kellermann, Arthur L. (1954–)

Dr. Arthur L. Kellermann, director of the Center for Injury Control at the Rollins School of Public Health and chair of the Department of Emergency Medicine at the Emory University School of Medicine, has published several influential—but controversial—studies on the relationship between having a firearm in the home and the increased risks of accidental death, homicide, and suicide. In one study, Kellermann and coresearcher Donald Reay examined firearm deaths in Seattle and found that guns kept in the home were forty-three times more likely to be involved in a suicide, homicide, or accidental death than to be used to kill in self-defense. In another study, conducted with John Henry Sloan and colleagues, Kellermann compared the rate of firearm-related homicides in Seattle, Washington to that of Vancouver, British Columbia (right across the Canadian border); these are two cities in the Pacific Northwest that are remarkably similar in many respects but operate under different national approaches to handgun control (Seattle under the lax gun control laws of the United States; Vancouver under the strict gun control laws of Canada). During the seven-year study period (1980–1986) these cities experienced virtually identical rates of burglary and robbery and had very similar rates of assault, but the overall rate of homicide in Seattle was 63 percent higher than that of Vancouver. Virtually all of this difference was attributable to a 4.8-fold higher rate of handgun-related homicide in Seattle. Rates of homicide by other means were not significantly different in the two cities.

Kellermann and his colleagues concluded the Seattle–Vancouver study with the observation that their results suggested that a more restrictive approach to handgun control may decrease national homicide rates. This recommendation inflamed gun rights activists and scholars, who have sharply criticized his research. They complained that there was no attempt to assess the positive influence of household guns for home defense. The Centers for Disease Control and Prevention (CDC) funded some of Kellermann's research (and that of similar studies conducted by other researchers), and the criticisms of this work eventually ended up in congressional debates over the CDC's budget. In the end, the CDC was barred from supporting any research in which the investigators might advocate for stronger gun control.

In a later study of gun carrying by juvenile offenders, Kellermann concluded that effective enforcement of existing gun control laws is sorely needed in the U.S. Many of the teenagers in his study reported that it was easy for adolescents to acquire firearms. In Kellermann's view, such reports imply that efforts to reduce the demand for illegal guns should be matched by efforts to reduce the supply. For example, safe storage of guns in the home could decrease diversion through burglary or theft. This cause would further be helped if adults illegally supplying guns to juveniles were identified and prosecuted.

Kennedy, Edward M. "Ted" (1932–)

Democrat Edward M. "Ted" Kennedy has been a Senator for Massachusetts since 1962. Known as one of the most liberal politicians in the country, he has been a major proponent of strengthening federal gun control laws. His ardor has been fueled, in part, by the murders of his brothers John and Robert Jr. by assassins using weapons that gun control advocates would have banned (a mail-order military rifle, in the case of John; and a cheap handgun in the case of Robert Jr.).

Kennedy supported the Gun Control Act of 1968, and since then, every other legislative effort to strengthen federal gun control laws—including the 1993 Brady Handgun Violence Prevention Act and the federal Assault Weapons Ban of 1994. He has fought all efforts to take steps backward—unsuccessfully so in the instances of the Firearm Owners' Protection Act of 1986 (which weakened the Gun Control Act of 1968) and the Assault Weapons Ban of 1994 (which expired in September 2004, after Congress failed to renew it). Kennedy supports the full agenda of the gun control movement and has backed proposed legislation to limit gun purchases to one per month, to require background checks on *all* purchasers at gun shows, and to mandate gun manufacturers to install state-of-the-art safety devices on their firearms. Kennedy represents the desires of his constituents quite well on the issue of gun control, because Massachusetts has the strongest gun regulations in the nation and rates the Brady Campaign letter grade of "A–." (The Brady Campaign gives each state a letter grade for the strength and quality of its gun control laws; the highest grade it gave in 2005 was an "A–," which only three other states merited—Connecticut, Maryland, and New Jersey).

Kleck, Gary (1951–)

Gary Kleck is a professor of criminology and criminal justice at Florida State University. His book *Point Blank: Guns and Violence in America* and its revised and updated sequel *Targeting Guns: Firearms and Their Control* are two of the most respected and often cited treatises on gun violence and the variable effects of gun control measures. The crux of the debate over gun control is whether guns contribute to violence. To gun control advocates, the answer is simple and obvious—guns and violence go hand in hand, and there is a host of epidemiological evidence to "prove" it (e.g., "a gun in the house is X times more likely to be used to kill a spouse or other family member than an intruder"; "the ecological correlation between the percentage of homes having a gun and the murder rate is consistently positive and strong"). Not so, argues Kleck. The ecological correlations are weak and inconsistent at the city, county, and cross-national levels of analysis; at the U.S.-state level of analysis, the correlation is significant and positive for homicide, but a good portion of it can be accounted for by the increased possession of firearms by concerned citizens for defensive purposes, not the other way around (that high prevalence of firearms encourages a high murder rate). The individual-level correlations are often negative: The person most likely to own a gun—an older, married, middle-class ruralite—is much less likely to be a victim or perpetrator of violence than the person least likely to own a gun—a younger, single, low-income urbanite. Kleck is especially critical of the research published in medical journals and many government reports, which tend to lack methodological sophistication—relying, for example, on bivariable associations that do not test for alternative explanations. In *Targeting Guns,* he shows that when proper control variables are introduced, these associations weaken greatly, disappear, or even reverse themselves. For instance, the positive correlation of living in a household with a gun and having a greater likelihood of being a victim of homicide disappears when one controls for criminal lifestyle (e.g., being a drug dealer or the member of a street gang). Similarly, Kleck argues that—although difficult to quantify—culture and heterogeneity, rather than strictness of gun laws, can account for most cross-national differences in violence, including the very high homicide rate of the United States when compared with that of the typical European nation or Japan.

Kleck's research has led him to have little confidence in many of the measures that gun control advocates hold dear. For example, relying on several respected social science studies, he argues that gun control laws regarding background checks and other purchasing requirements cannot keep guns out of the wrong hands, because most hardcore criminals acquire their guns by means other than buying from a federally licensed gun retailer (most often from a relative, friend, or acquaintance, or sometimes from a black market dealer or by theft). Indeed, stolen guns alone could supply criminals wanting to acquire a gun in any given year. Kleck also believes that banning assault weapons and cheaply made handguns from private ownership doesn't work because the former are implicated in only a tiny fraction of all gun crimes, and the latter are used as often by noncriminals, defensively, as by criminals.

Kleck's most controversial claim involves the positive uses of guns as weapons of defense. In 1995, he and Marc Gertz published "Armed Resistance to Crime: The Prevalence and Nature of Self-Defense with a Gun" in the *Journal of Criminal Law and Criminology*. His and Gertz's national survey revealed that there are somewhere in the neighborhood of 2.5 million defensive uses of guns occurring each year in the United States. This number has been criticized as unrealistically far too high by a number of scholars, including Philip J. Cook (q.v.), Jens Otto Ludwig (q.v.), David Hemenway (q.v.), and Robert J. Spitzer (q.v.). Like many skeptics of prohibitory gun controls, Kleck believes that the most effective means to control gun violence is to take firearms away from high-risk individuals (e.g., violent criminals) and to use more of the nation's resources to enforce current laws that prohibit these individuals from possessing guns.

Knox, Neal (1935–2005)

During his entire professional career, Neal Knox was one of the strongest and best known advocates for the rights of gun owners. He was central to launching or strengthening several gun publications, including *Gun Week, Handloader,* and *Rifle.* Over the years, he had a tumultuous relationship with the leading advocacy organization for gun rights, the National Rifle Association (NRA).

But in 1977, along with Harlon Carter (q.v.), Robert Kukla, and Joseph Tartaro (q.v.), Knox helped revolutionize and radicalize the NRA from a mostly apolitical organization seeing itself as a representative of the interests of hunters and recreational shooters to an uncompromisingly political organization that would be *the* voice for the rights of gun owners and *the* combatant against any and all forms of gun control. During this period, Knox became the head of the NRA's newly created lobbying branch, the Institute for Legislative Action, which has developed a strong presence on Capitol Hill and a strong grassroots movement to involve ordinary gun owners in local and state politics in resisting all legislative efforts at gun control. Later he would become the NRA's second and first vice presidents and a member of the board of directors. His views on how best to manage the organization brought him into clashes with executive vice president Wayne R. LaPierre Jr. (q.v.) and president Charlton Heston (q.v.), and he was eventually ousted as a board member in 1997.

In his role as a gun rights advocate, Knox was a major supporter of the Firearms Owners' Protection Act of 1986, which gun control advocates view as a major weakening of the Gun Control Act of 1968. He was also a vocal opponent of the Bureau of Alcohol, Tobacco, Firearms and Explosives—the federal organization charged with enforcing most of the nation's gun laws. To fund and promote the perspective that the Second Amendment protects the rights of the *individual* to "keep and bear Arms," Knox founded the Firearms Coalition (http://www.nealknox.com/). The coalition's Web site keeps gun rights enthusiasts informed on many of the key political battles over gun control and lets them know how they might become involved. On January 17, 2005, he passed away after losing his battle with colon cancer.

Kopel, David B. (1960–)

David B. Kopel is research director of the Independence Institute and an associate policy analyst at the Cato Institute. He has written extensively on the Second Amendment and on the failures of gun control. His writings are a favorite of those on the gun rights side of the contemporary national and international debates over gun control. He argues strongly that the Second Amendment grants *individuals* the right to bear firearms, including all types of semiautomatic firearms, to protect themselves from criminals and any despotic excesses on the part of the government.

Kopel's writings are highly critical of gun control measures, which he contends are often ineffective and sometimes in violation of the Second Amendment or state constitutional arms rights. His writings appear in a broad range of outlets, including law journals, books, and editorials in the popular press. He is the editor in chief of the *Journal on Firearms and Public Policy* and a member of the editorial board and a major contributor to the highly praised *Guns in American Society: An Encyclopedia of History, Politics, Culture, and the Law*. With Alan Merril Gottlieb (q.v.), he cowrote *Things You Can Do to Defend Your Gun Rights* and *More Things You Can Do to Defend Your Gun Rights*. He is the author of *Trust the People: The Case against Gun Control* and of a much cited examination of guns through the lens of history and culture, *The Samurai, the Mountie, and the Cowboy: Should America Adopt the Gun Controls of the Other Democracies?* (which won the 1992 Book of the Year award from the American Society of Criminology). With Paul H. Blackman, he coauthored *No More Wacos: What's Wrong with Federal Law Enforcement, and How to Fix It*. This book won the Thomas S. Szasz Award for Outstanding Contributions to the Cause of Civil Liberties from the Center for Independent Thought in 1997. With Andrew McClurg and Brannon Denning, he also coauthored the university-level textbook *Gun Control and Gun Rights*.

LaPierre, Wayne R., Jr. (1950–)

After joining the National Rifle Association's (NRA) Institute for Legislative Action (ILA) in 1978 as a lobbyist, Wayne R. LaPierre Jr. soon became its director of state and local affairs, and then the director of federal affairs. In 1986, he was promoted to executive director of ILA, taking control of its lobbying efforts. In 1991, LaPierre became the NRA's executive vice president and chief executive officer, positions he has held ever since. He is the organization's chief national spokesperson.

As one of the NRA's all-time most influential leaders, LaPierre has helped increase membership by the millions. Save for the passage of the 1993 Brady Handgun Violence Prevention Act and the Assault Weapons Ban of 1994, LaPierre's efforts have been largely successful. He led the NRA in a triumphant campaign to change state laws to include "preemption" provisions, whereby local communities cannot pass any law that is in conflict with statewide laws (thus, for example, the California Court of

Appeals ruled that San Francisco's ban on handguns was illegal because it was in violation of state law permitting private owner-ship of such weapons); currently forty-three states have either statutory or judicial preemption of local gun ordinances. LaPierre has also led the NRA to great success in getting many state legis-latures to pass "shall issue" right-to-carry laws, allowing for or-dinary citizens to readily obtain a permit to carry a concealed handgun (in thirty-eight states ordinary citizens can now carry concealed weapons). Currently, he is leading what appears will be a successful campaign to have the U.S. Congress pass "immu-nity" legislation for the gun industry—protecting gun manufac-turers from civil lawsuits seeking damages for the costs related to gun violence (either by individuals or by communities or states).

His very popular book, *Guns, Crime, and Freedom*, highlights the *individual-rights* interpretation of the Second Amendment. As is typical of those advocating strongly for the rights of gun own-ers, he argues that the only effective solution to gun violence is keeping guns out of the hands of criminals (as is dictated by the Gun Control Act of 1968); all other forms of gun control violate the Second Amendment rights of U.S. citizens, not to mention being largely ineffective. LaPierre also emphasizes the positive impacts of guns as weapons ordinary citizens can use to defend themselves against criminals. He believes the lack of an armed population has helped despotic governments take over in much of Africa and Asia, and he holds up Afghanistan in the 1980s as a nation whose citizens were able to overthrow a tyrannical, non-democratic government (a puppet of the then Soviet Union) be-cause they were armed—even though most of their weapons were small arms (rifles, shotguns, and handguns).

LaPierre has been involved in some highly publicized con-troversies. For example, he received severe criticism in the media when he accused President Bill Clinton (q.v.) of supporting radi-cal gun control legislation mainly for selfish political interests. LaPierre also made controversial statements about Bureau of Al-cohol, Tobacco and Firearms agents in a fund-raising letter shortly before the 1995 Oklahoma City bombing—calling them "jack-booted thugs"; in protest, former U.S. President George H. W. Bush (q.v.) resigned his membership from the NRA. De-spite such controversy, LaPiere's overall success in leading the NRA in its political endeavors has been great, as is partly indi-cated by *Fortune* magazine naming the organization the most in-fluential lobbying group in Washington, D.C.

Lautenberg, Frank R. (1924–)

New Jersey U.S. Senator Frank R. Lautenberg has supported strong gun control legislation throughout his political career. He voted for the 1993 Brady Handgun Violence Prevention Act and the federal Assault Weapons Ban of 1994. He is best known for his sponsorship of the 1996 Lautenberg Amendment, also known as the Domestic Violence Offender Gun Ban. The amendment closed what gun control advocates considered a loophole to the Gun Control Act of 1968 by expanding the prohibition of gun possession to include persons convicted of domestic violence misdemeanor offenses. Previously such bans covered only convicted felons. In recent years, he has worked, unsuccessfully, for the passage of federal gun laws that would require background checks on *all* purchasers at gun shows and for an extension to the Assault Weapons Ban, which expired in September 2004. He has led the fight against legislation that would "immunize" gun manufacturers from civil lawsuits, including the Protection of Lawful Commerce in Arms Act of 2005, sponsored by his Senate colleague, Idaho Republican Larry Craig (q.v.).

Lautenberg served in the U.S. Army during World War II and graduated from Columbia University with a degree in economics on the GI Bill. He was cofounder, chairman and chief executive officer of Automatic Data Processing (ADP) and served in the U.S. Senate from 1983 to 2001, before returning in 2003.

Lott, John R., Jr. (1958–)

In his groundbreaking and controversial book *More Guns, Less Crime: Understanding Crime and Gun-Control Laws,* John R. Lott Jr. came to the conclusion that U.S. states allowing ordinary citizens to carry concealed handguns have lower crime rates than those that do not. His interpretation is straightforward: Criminals are rational, and they are less likely to rape, rob, or assault when they are fearful that a potential victim may be armed. Lott points out that in countries that have strong gun-control laws and low gun-ownership rates, such as Canada or Great Britain, burglaries are often "hot"—that is, the homeowner or apartment dweller is on the premises when the criminal strikes. In contrast, in the United States, where a third of householders own a gun, hot burglaries are relatively unusual. In the United States, burglars are more fearful of being shot at by a potential victim, thus they spend a lot more time than their counterparts in Canada or Great Britain casing a house to make sure no one is home.

Lott's thesis has fueled rancorous debate on the effectiveness of gun control. Several respected scholars—who are nonetheless sympathetic to the gun control movement—have carefully reanalyzed Lott's data and have found his conclusions unwarranted. The most publicized of these reanalyses appeared in a 2003 *Stanford Law Review* article by Ian Ayres and John D. Donohue III ("Shooting Down the More Guns, Less Crime Hypothesis").

Lott's research has led him to be very critical of many of the measures that have been popularized by the gun control movement over the past two decades. In his most recent book, *The Bias against Guns: Why Almost Everything You've Heard about Gun Control Is Wrong*, he finds little empirical support for the gun-violence-reducing effects of waiting periods, buyback programs, gun show background checks, and bans on assault weapons. Like most in the gun rights camp, he sees gun control laws as hurting law-abiding citizens in their efforts to use their guns for self-defense or recreation, while providing none of the intended effects of reducing violence.

Lott received a Ph.D. in economics from the University of California at Los Angeles and has had research positions with the law schools of the University of Chicago and Yale University. In recent years, he has been a resident scholar at the American Enterprise Institute for Public Policy Research, a conservative "think tank" in Washington, D.C.

Ludwig, Jens Otto (1968–)

A professor at the Public Policy Institute of Georgetown University, Jens Otto Ludwig has studied crime and gun violence extensively throughout his entire professional career. He is affiliated with the Center for Gun Policy and Research at Johns Hopkins University, as well as with the National Consortium on Violence Research at Carnegie-Mellon University. Ludwig earned his Ph.D. in economics from Duke University, where he was a student of Philip J. Cook (q.v.).

With Cook, Ludwig analyzed the 1994 National Survey of Private Ownership of Firearms (NSPOF), which offered a comprehensive examination of gun ownership in the United States. Based on dramatically different estimates found in the NSPOF, as well as in the National Criminal Victimization Survey (NCVS), he has sharply criticized the research of Gary Kleck (q.v.) and Marc Gertz on their estimation of the number of defensive gun uses occurring each year (where ordinary citizens fend off a criminal attack with their guns, including by brandishing or firing it). Kleck and Gertz put the number at 2.5 million, while the NCVS puts it at about 100,000. In addition, Ludwig has challenged John R. Lott's (q.v.) "more guns, less crime" thesis that U.S. states with laws allowing ordinary citizens to carry concealed handguns realize significant drops in violent crime.

Ludwig was an expert witness for the Committee on Public Safety on the California Assembly and has supported the Canadian Firearms Act to place more restrictions on handguns. He and Cook wrote *Gun Violence: The Real Costs*, which is often cited by other scholars doing research on gun violence. Ludwig and Cook estimate the annual cost of gun violence—taking into consideration the burdens on the health care system, lost wages, lessened productivity, and lost tax revenues—at $100 billion. They coedited another volume that has also become very popular in scholarly circles, *Evaluating Gun Policy: Effects on Crime and Violence*. The overall thesis of *Evaluating Gun Policy* is that strict gun control can be effective in reducing violent crime, suicide, and accidental shootings.

MacNutt, Karen L. (1948–)

An active firearms competitor, attorney Karen L. MacNutt has gained a national reputation as a staunch supporter of the rights of gun owners. She believes that firearm ownership by law-abiding citizens is a right guaranteed by the Second Amendment and that gun control laws often infringe upon this right. Placing restrictions on guns only hurts the ordinary citizen and gives greater power to criminals. In her Boston law practice, she has defended individuals charged with violating the Bartley-Fox Act, a Massachusetts law that mandates a jail term for anyone caught carrying a handgun without a license.

MacNutt is a consulting attorney for several gun-rights advocacy organizations, including the Second Amendment Foundation (SAF), the National Rifle Association, and the Gun Owners' Action League of Massachusetts. She is a contributor to *Women and Guns*, an SAF publication geared toward increasing women's involvement in the gun culture.

McCarthy, Carolyn (1944–)

With no background in politics, New Yorker Carolyn McCarthy was elected to the U.S. House of Representatives in 1996. Personal tragedy motivated her to run for the office. On December 7, 1993, Colin Ferguson shot twenty-five people, killing six of them, on a Long Island commuter train in Garden City, New York. Carolyn McCarthy's husband was killed and her son seriously injured in the attack. It is thus not surprising that she was shocked when her congressional representative, Dan Frisa, voted to repeal the federal Assault Weapons Ban of 1994. The ban outlawed the kind of high-capacity ammunition magazine that Ferguson's gun used. Incensed, McCarthy decided to run against Frisa when he came up for reelection. Her campaign focused on one issue, gun control. She won and has been reelected every two years to represent New York's Fourth Congressional District ever since.

McCarthy has supported all major legislative efforts to strengthen federal gun control laws, even though most have not been successful. This failed legislation has included renewing the Assault Weapons Ban of 1994 and requiring background checks for *all* purchases at gun shows. She was part of a successful congressional effort to stop the passage of 2004 legislation that would have given "immunity" from civil lawsuits to gun manufacturers—but this success was temporary, as in the fall of 2005 immunity legislation in the form of the Protection of Lawful Commerce in Arms Act was passed in both Houses of Congress.

McDowall, David (1949–)

David McDowall is a professor at the School of Criminal Justice at the State University of New York (SUNY), Albany. He received a B.S. in sociology from Portland State University before receiving his M.A. and Ph.D. in sociology from Northwestern University. He is a coeditor of the *Statistical Handbook on Violence in America*.

McDowall has authored many articles on gun control that cover a broad range of topics. They include examining the effects of stiffening penalties for firearms-related crimes; of easing the restrictions to obtain a concealed-weapons permit; and of the Kennesaw, Georgia, law requiring household heads to own a firearm and ammunition. Because he and his colleagues found that Kennesaw's falling crime rate was unlikely due to the mandatory gun-ownership law, and because he and his coauthors found little benefit and possible negative consequences of Florida's relaxing restrictions on concealed-weapons permits, his research has been criticized by gun rights advocates. However, he has found that waiting periods for firearms do not have an effect on homicides and suicides, to the chagrin of gun control advocates.

Metaksa, Tanya K. (1936–)

Serving from 1994 to 1998, Tanya Metaksa was the first woman to become the executive director of the National Rifle Association's (NRA) Institute for Legislative Action (ILA), the political lobbying branch of the organization. She also headed CrimeStrike, the criminal justice reform and victims' rights unit of the ILA. As an avid shooter, certified firearms instructor, and a former major spokesperson for the NRA, Metaksa is against all forms of gun control, including all of those that have become popular since the 1990s—including assault-weapons bans, background checks at gun shows, and limiting an individual to buying no more than one gun per month. Metaksa espouses the NRA philosophy that the Second Amendment guarantees the right of the *individual* to keep and bear arms and that most forms of gun control infringe upon this right. She also extols the use of firearms by ordinary citizens to defend themselves against criminal attack. As ILA's executive director, she was a strong supporter of and spokesperson for the right of ordinary citizens to carry concealed weapons, and twelve states enacted right-to-carry laws while she was in office.

Metaksa's distrust of the governmental control of firearms is rooted in her upbringing. Her father had fled Bolshevik Russia. A graduate of Smith College, her battle against gun control began while she was a housewife in Connecticut during the late 1960s. She wrote to then Senator Thomas J. Dodd (himself a strong supporter of federal gun control legislation) to express her disapproval with his support for the Gun Control Act of 1968. Metaksa then helped to found the Connecticut Sportsmen's Alliance, a grassroots gun rights and hunter organization, before joining the NRA in 1975. She became a board member of the NRA in 1991, before becoming ILA's executive director.

Metaksa is the author of a guide for women on defensive gun use, *Safe, Not Sorry: Keeping Yourself and Your Family Safe in a Violent Age,* and was interviewed by Deborah Homsher (q.v.) for Homsher's popular book *Women and Guns: Politics and the Culture of Firearms in America.* Metaksa remains active in the gun rights movement and is a frequent contributor to online and print opinion pages.

Miller, Bryan (1951–)

Bryan Miller is the executive director of Ceasefire New Jersey, the largest gun control advocacy organization in the state. Tragedy motivated Miller to become active in the gun control movement: On November 22, 1994, his brother, Mike, was one of three murder victims of a street thug named Bennie Lawson. Lawson was seeking revenge on the chief of the Washington, D.C., Police Homicide Unit, but ended up in the wrong office and shot to death Mike Miller, an FBI special agent, and two others, with a MAC-10 semiautomatic pistol. The MAC-10 is a military-style assault weapon that is a favorite of street criminals and gang members.

Stunned by his brother's murder and angry that weapons like a MAC-10 were available to nonmilitary individuals, Bryan Miller left a successful career in business to join Ceasefire New Jersey, soon becoming its executive director. Ceasefire and other advocates of strong gun control have been successful in New Jersey, which has among the nation's strongest gun regulations— New Jersey earned the Brady Campaign's strongest grade in 2005 for strictness of gun laws, an A–. Miller is particularly questioning of the position of gun rights activists that handguns are good defenses against criminal assault and of the U.S.'s failure to ban assault weapons. He points out that his brother and the other two law enforcement agents that Lawson murdered were well armed, but were overwhelmed by the rapid-firing MAC-10.

Moore, Michael (1954–)

Writer and filmmaker Michael Moore has made his living as a social critic. Moore has become famous for his movies *Bowling for Columbine* and *Fahrenheit 9/11* and his books *Stupid White Men* and *Dude, Where's My Country?* The documentary *Bowling for Columbine* was a major commercial success and critically examined contemporary gun violence in the United States. The movie's central thesis is that the violence is, in large part, due to our lack of strong national gun control regulations. It also acknowledges that U.S. history and culture are so violence-filled that even with stronger gun control the United States would have a high murder rate compared with those of Canada, Australia, and other economically developed, democratic nations in Western Europe.

Orth, Franklin L. (1907–1970)

From 1959 to 1970, Franklin L. Orth was the executive vice president of the National Rifle Association (NRA). During his reign, the NRA was much less political than it is today, and Orth's views on gun control were quite moderate compared with the staunch and uncompromising anti-gun control stance of the current executive vice president, Wayne LaPierre Jr. (q.v.). Orth opposed firearm registration and licensing, but supported many parts of the Gun Control Act of 1968. He testified before Congress in support of banning cheaply made handguns (so-called Saturday night specials) and for the prohibition of mail-order gun purchases—observing that such a firearm was used to assassinate President Kennedy. Orth saw the NRA much less as a political lobbying organization and much more as the promoter of recreational shooting, hunting, and environmental protection. His views were to be all but eliminated after the infamous "Revolt at Cincinnati," whereby staunch gun rights activists took control of the organization at its 1977 national meeting.

Paul, Ron (1935–)

A member of the U.S. House of Representatives representing the Fourteenth Congressional District of Texas since 1997, Republican Ron Paul is a libertarian favoring limited government. A medical doctor and former U.S. Air Force flight surgeon, Paul was a member of Congress in the late 1970s before leaving the position voluntarily in 1984 as an expression of his belief in limited terms. After his return to Congress, Paul became a member of the House of Representatives Financial Services Committee and the International Relations Committee. On the Financial Services Committee, he serves as the vice chairman of the Oversight and Investigations subcommittee.

Paul believes that the Second Amendment grants *individuals* the right "to keep and bear Arms" and sees most forms of gun control as infringing upon this right. In 1997, he sponsored the Second Amendment Restoration Act to repeal federal bans on semiautomatic guns and large capacity ammunition clips. He also introduced the Second Amendment Protection Act, meant to rescind the 1993 Brady Handgun Violence Prevention Act and weaken the Gun Control Act of 1968. In recent years, Paul has been working on legislation that would give ordinary citizens the nationwide right to carry concealed weapons. He is also a strong supporter of the Protection of Lawful Commerce in Arms Act (H.R.800), which would prohibit "civil liability actions" against manufacturers, distributors, dealers, and importers of firearms and ammunition for any harm caused by the criminal or unlawful misuse of their firearms or ammunition. Gun control advocates see this legislation as a major setback in their attempts to promote reform in the gun industry. For example, a $2.5 million settlement against gun retailer Bulls Eye and gun manufacturer Bushmaster reached in 2004 for their responsibility in the 2002 Washington, D.C., sniper shootings motivated both the retailer and the manufacturer to revise their inventory-control procedures to reduce the probability of the theft of their guns and to let law enforcement know immediately if a theft actually occurs.

Pierce, Glenn (1945–)

Glenn Pierce is the Principal Research Scientist at the Center for Criminal Justice Research as well as the acting director of the Institute for Security and Public Policy, at Northeastern University. He received his Ph.D. from Northeastern University in 1989 and has been the director of the Division of Academic Computing and codirector of the Center for Criminal Justice Policy Research. His specialties include criminal justice information systems, gun control, and the death penalty. Early in his career, he and William Bowers assessed the impact of the Bartley-Fox Law in Massachusetts, which requires licenses for carrying handguns in public and mandatory prison sentences for violations. They found a significant drop in homicides and robberies after passage of this law.

Pierce is one of a small number of researchers that have been given access to the Bureau of Alcohol, Tobacco, Firearms and Explosives (ATF) gun-tracing data. His analyses reveal that three-quarters of all trace requests involve handguns and that very few of them are possessed by the original purchaser. He concludes that this is strong evidence of illegal gun trafficking. Other evidence supporting illegal trafficking is that only about 1 percent of the tens of thousands of federally licensed firearms dealers account for more than half of the successfully traced crime guns. His findings have led many gun control advocates to emphasize close scrutiny of licensed gun dealers and to root out that small minority who are corrupt.

Pratt, Larry (1942–)

Larry Pratt is the executive director of the Gun Owners of America (GOA), a staunch gun rights advocacy organization. GOA is well known on Capitol Hill and many state legislatures for its strong pro-gun lobbying efforts. The organization provides legal assistance to those involved in lawsuits with the Bureau of Alcohol, Tobacco, Firearms and Explosives.

Pratt is against all forms of gun control, seeing them as ineffective and in violation of the constitutional rights of legal gun owners. Consequently, he fought against the 1988 prohibition against plastic guns (the Undetectable Firearms Act); the 1993 Brady Handgun Violence Prevention Act; the 1996 Lautenberg Amendment (which barred those convicted of a domestic violence misdemeanor or under a domestic-violence related restraining order from possessing a gun); and even the National Instant Background Check System, which federally licensed firearms retailers are required to use to do criminal background checks on prospective gun buyers. Like most strong advocates of the rights of gun owners, he sees firearms as offering ordinary citizens protection against criminal attack and against a government that might someday fall into tyranny. His philosophy is detailed in his books *Armed People Victorious, Safeguarding Liberty: The Constitution and Militias,* and *On the Firing Line: Essays in the Defense of Liberty.*

Reagan, Ronald Wilson (1911–2004)

Democrat-turned-Republican Ronald Wilson Reagan was a film and television actor for three decades before becoming governor of California in 1966. Elected the fortieth U.S. president in 1980 and winning reelection in 1984, Reagan was the endorsed candidate of the National Rifle Association (NRA). He generally opposed gun control, but was not a member of the extreme gunrights camp. Despite being seriously wounded when John Hinckley Jr. tried to assassinate him with a cheap handgun (an attack that left White House Press Secretary James S. Brady [q.v.] partially paralyzed), Reagan maintained his pro-gun-rights platform when he ran for reelection in 1984. He believed that "gun control" is best brought about by stiff penalties for those using guns to commit crimes. To this end, he signed the Armed Career Criminal Act in 1986, which increased the penalties for possession of firearms by those prohibited from doing so by federal law (including convicted felons).

Congress passed the Firearms Owners' Protection Act (FOPA) during Reagan's administration. The act was seen by gun control advocates as a huge setback to the progress in regulating guns that had been made with the passage of the Gun Control Act (GCA) of 1968. Among many other modifications, it prohibited punishment of unintentional violations of the GCA (by requiring that the government prove that the violation was willful or knowing)—thus encouraging no serious effort on the part of federally licensed retail gun dealers to do any background checking on prospective gun buyers (this problem was short-lived, though, as the 1993 Brady Handgun Violence Prevention Act *required* a comprehensive criminal background check of all prospective buyers).

FOPA also allows a federally licensed gun retailer to sell guns away from their principal place of business, as long as the sales comply with all relevant laws (thus allowing FFL holders to sell their firearms at gun shows); and it prohibits BATF from creating a national gun registry.

Despite his popularity with the NRA, Reagan was willing to back some limited forms of gun control. For example, as governor of California, he supported the 1967 Mulford Act that prohibited carrying guns in public, and he signed legislation requiring a fifteen-day waiting period on handgun purchases. As president, Reagan signed the Law Enforcement Officers Protection Act, which banned so-called cop killer handgun bullets—or more accurately, bullets with very dense cores—that were capable of piercing bulletproof vests. He also signed the Undetectable Firearms Act (Terrorist Firearms Detection), banning the manufacture, importation, possession, receipt, and transfer of "plastic" guns—those that substituted part of the metal in a normal gun with plastic polymers. Notably, after leaving office, Reagan supported the Brady Handgun Violence Protection Act, which was eventually passed in 1993 and required background checks and waiting periods for handgun purchases.

Robbins, Michael A. (1951–)

As a member of the Gang Crimes Unit for the Chicago Police Department, Michael A. Robbins's job included taking guns off the streets. His police career was to end, however, on September 10, 1994, when a street criminal shot Robbins thirteen times, including twice in the chest and once in the stomach. A slow, painful recovery left his left arm an inch shorter than his right and three of the bullets buried so deeply in his body that they could not be safely removed. Forced to retire from the police force, he found a new career as a gun control activist. He involved himself with several youth gun-violence prevention programs and eventually became the executive director of HELP for Survivors, part of the Chicago based-educational and advocacy group Hands Without Guns.

Robbins supports gun control measures that would help the Bureau of Alcohol, Tobacco, Firearms and Explosives increase its ability to trace crime guns, and he is a proponent of a waiting period. The original 1993 Brady Handgun Prevention Act required a five-day waiting period for the purchase of a handgun, but beginning in 1998, the waiting period was dropped and replaced by the National Instant Background Check System. Robbins believes the waiting period should be reinstated. Like all of those in the gun control camp, he believes that gun shows—and other parts of the secondary market whereby firearms sales are transacted between private individuals—should not be exempt from the Brady Act, as they currently are in most states (the so-called gun show loophole).

Schumer, Charles E. "Chuck" (1950–)

Elected to the U.S. House of Representatives in 1980, where he served the Ninth Congressional District of New York until 1998, and then to the U.S. Senate in 1998, Democrat Charles E. "Chuck" Schumer has been one of the country's most high-profile and effective political advocates for the strict federal regulation of firearms. He was a sponsor of the 1993 Brady Handgun Violence Prevention Act and cowrote the Assault Weapons Ban of 1994.

Schumer has been a part of all federal gun control legislation since arriving on Capitol Hill. As such, he is a favorite target of criticism of the National Rifle Association (NRA) and other gun rights organizations—and is often excoriated on their Web pages with one or more of a long list of epithets (e.g., he has been labeled a whiner, ignorant self-serving politician, and prevaricator). His only common ground with gun-rights activists is that both are strong supporters of using the federal government to help local communities catch and prosecute violators of gun laws—the most publicized example being Richmond, Virginia's Project Exile. Project Exile is aimed at deterring illegal gun use by diverting weapons-related offenses from the state to the federal court system—with the expected benefits of higher conviction rates and stiffer prison sentences. Begun in February 1997, the project provides training to law enforcement agents on federal gun laws and proper procedures for search and seizure, and it funds an advertising campaign telling would-be criminals that any gun offense will be dealt with swiftly and sternly by the judicial system. Firearm-related murders dropped 40 percent during the project's first year alone.

Schumer's current agenda includes closing the "gun show loophole"—which means subjecting *all* gun purchasers to a criminal background check, not just those buying a gun from a federally licensed firearms retailer. He and fellow congressional leaders favoring strong gun control were frustrated in their attempts to get the Assault Weapons Ban of 1994 renewed; it expired in September 2004 without ever coming up for a renewal vote in the Republican-dominated Congress. Similarly, Schumer and his like-minded colleagues lost in their efforts to stop the Protection of Lawful Commerce in Arms Act, a gun-industry "immunity" proposal—sponsored by NRA board member and Republican Idaho Senator Larry Craig (q.v.)—that passed both Houses of Congress in the fall of 2005; this act protects gun manufacturers from civil lawsuits related to the misuse of their guns (e.g., a community or individual could not sue a manufacturer if one of its guns were used in a violent crime).

Shields, Nelson T. "Pete" (1924–1993)

Nelson T. "Pete" Shields was a founder of the modern gun control movement. His motivation was born in the tragedy of his teenage son's murder with a handgun as part of infamous Zebra Killings in the San Francisco area. From October 1973 through April 1974, the Zebra Killings received huge media coverage and focused national attention on gun control. The label was given to the killings because the killers were black and the victims mostly white. Fourteen people were murdered and seven wounded during the five-month spree of violence. Four members of a Black Muslim cult called the "Death Angels" were eventually convicted and given life sentences. Their motive was to incite a race war.

His son's murder prompted Shields to leave the corporate world and join the newly founded National Council to Control Handguns (NCCH) in Washington, D.C. His organizational talents were quickly acclaimed, and he soon became its executive director, then its chair. In 1981, Shields changed the name of NCCH to Handgun Control Inc. (HCI) to avoid confusion with the National Coalition to Ban Handguns (now the Coalition to Stop Gun Violence). Shields recognized that U.S. public opinion was overwhelmingly against the banning of handguns, so HCI sought more modest aims—strict gun control (without banning) achieved through lobbying, education, legal advocacy, and grassroots organizing. During Shield's years of leadership, HCI became *the* lobbying voice for gun control on Capitol Hill, the counterbalance to the growing power of the National Rifle Association. After being diagnosed with cancer in 1989, Shields resigned his chairmanship, succumbing to the disease in 1993. In 2001, HCI renamed itself the Brady Campaign to Prevent Gun Violence; and HCI's legal advocacy and research group, the Center to Prevent Handgun Violence, was renamed The Brady Center to Prevent Gun Violence.

Soto, Andrés (1955–)

Andrés Soto is a role model for many gun control activists. He has been instrumental in the passage of gun control laws in his hometown of Richmond, California, and the surrounding East Bay area. While working for the Contra Costa County Health Services Department, Soto fought for legislation that banned gun dealers working out of their homes. This led to the elimination of 80 percent of the firearms dealers in the county and all of the gun dealers in Richmond. The success of this legislation started a movement throughout California to crack down on residential gun dealers. Gun control advocates link the decline in gun deaths in the state to the near elimination of such dealers. Soto moved on to help write state legislation imposing stricter regulations at gun shows and banning the manufacture of cheaply made handguns (Saturday night specials)—an industry that southern California was famous for during the 1980s and 1990s. He has also worked on California's efforts to expand its assault weapons ban and to require gun owners to keep their weapons and ammunition locked up to prevent access by children.

Soto has been shot at himself after turning around in somebody's driveway in a neighborhood he was unfamiliar with, and he knows many victims of gun violence. He now serves as the policy director of the Pacific Center for Violence Prevention, a statewide youth violence prevention program that uses a public health approach. The center belongs to the Trauma Foundation, a private nonprofit group with a mission to prevent injury.

Spitzer, Robert J. (1953–)

Robert J. Spitzer is Distinguished Service Professor of Political Science at the State University of New York (SUNY), Cortland. He earned his B.A. from SUNY, Fredonia, and his M.A. and Ph.D. from Cornell University. Spitzer has criticized Gary Kleck's (q.v.) research on how often ordinary citizens use their guns each year to fend off criminal attacks, and his research is touted by gun control activists as evidence of the effectiveness of gun control laws.

Spitzer is the author of *The Right to Bear Arms: Rights and Liberties under the Law,* a comprehensive examination of the Second Amendment. It examines the legal, political, and historical aspects of the debate over the amendment, concluding that it provides the citizens of a state the *collective* right to organize and maintain a militia, and that no *personal* right "to keep and bear Arms" was intended. Spitzer is also the author of *The Politics of Gun Control,* a thorough analysis of the gun debate in U.S. society. It has gone through three editions and features analyses of the Second Amendment and the politics underlying key gun control legislation—including the Gun Control Act of 1968, the Firearms Owners Protection Act of 1986, the Brady Handgun Violence Prevention Act of 1993, and the Assault Weapons Ban of 1994. The book examines liability lawsuits against gun manufacturers, political campaign funds coming from gun-rights and gun control advocacy groups, and the crime-reducing effects of the spate of concealed-carry laws that were passed in many states during the 1990s. It also applies international relations theory to the domestic gun debate as a framework of how the gun debate's continued political gridlock might be broken.

Sugarmann, Josh (1960–)

As the executive director of the Violence Policy Center, a non-profit organization researching firearms-related violence and advocating for gun control, Josh Sugarmann is one of the strongest proponents of the strict regulation of firearms in the United States. Indeed, he is one of a minority of gun control advocates believing that the United States should outlaw handguns. In his book, *Every Handgun Is Aimed at You: The Case for Banning Handguns,* he makes the argument that simply *controlling* handguns, for example by doing background checks on prospective purchasers, is not enough to keep them out of the hands of dangerous people; as such, these weapons should be *banned* outright. Sugarmann has also assailed the NRA in his highly publicized book *National Rifle Association: Money, Firepower and Fear.* He sees the organization as having influence in Washington, D.C., far beyond what its membership size should warrant. Its power has corrupted the national debate over gun control, in Sugarmann's view, because the NRA will not compromise; its leadership sees all forms of gun control as infringing upon the rights of legitimate gun owners, pure and simple.

Tartaro, Joseph P. (1931–)

Joseph P. Tartaro serves as the president of the Second Amendment Foundation (SAF), a gun rights advocacy group, and is the executive editor of *The New Gun Week,* one of SAF's publications. He also works with Alan Merril Gottlieb (q.v.) to produce the monthly SAF newsletter, *The Gottlieb-Tartaro Report.* During the 1970s, he played a central role in converting the National Rifle Association from a mostly apolitical organization for hunters and recreational shooters into *the* lobby for rights of gun owners.

Tartaro believes that the rights of gun owners are best supported through grassroots organizations, and he sees most forms of gun control as ineffective and as infringements upon the Second Amendment rights of ordinary citizens. He is sensitive to media portrayals of the national debate over gun control and believes that far too often newspapers and the major networks paint guns as intrinsically evil. Like most gun rights activists, Tartaro believes better enforcement of selected gun laws—those meant to punish gun-toting criminals—is a better use of the nation's resources than trying to enact more gun control laws.

Tartaro, Patricia Margaret "Peggy" (1955–)

The daughter of Joseph P. Tartaro (q.v.), Patricia Margaret "Peggy" Tartaro is the executive editor of *Women and Guns*, a publication of the Second Amendment Foundation. The magazine emphasizes the role of firearms in women's defense against criminal attack. She is a strong spokesperson for the rights of gun owners. She espouses the gun rights agenda at meetings and expositions, including the annual Gun Rights Policy Conference, and appears frequently in print media and on radio talk shows.

Like her father, Tartaro believes in working from the ground up. She feels that only when ordinary individuals understand the positive impacts of guns on their everyday lives will they be willing to involve themselves in the national debate over gun control. To this end, she has helped train gun rights activists through the Leadership Training Conference program, which is operated by the SAF and Citizens Committee for the Right to Keep and Bear Arms (CCRKBA). She is a trustee and the treasurer of the CCRKBA. In addition to being a life member of the National Rifle Association (NRA), she has been a member of the NRA's Women's Policies Committee. In honor of her work, Tartaro was the runner up in 2005 for the NRA's Sybil Ludington Women's Freedom Award.

Webster, Daniel W. (1960–)

Daniel W. Webster is codirector of the Center for Gun Policy and Research and associate professor in the Department of Health Policy and Management at the Johns Hopkins Bloomberg School of Public Health. He earned his M.P.H. from the University of Michigan and his Sc.D. from Johns Hopkins University. Webster has authored and coauthored many studies on youth access to firearms, the role of firearms in violence, and the effectiveness of various gun policies. His research has appeared in *Guns in American Society: An Encyclopedia of History, Politics, Culture, and the Law*, the *American Journal of Epidemiology*, the public health journal *Injury Prevention*, the *Journal of the American Medical Association*, and in various publications put out by the Center for Gun Policy and Research at Johns Hopkins University. His research is often cited by gun control advocates as evidence that strong firearms regulations can reduce gun violence.

Wintemute, Garen J. (1951–)

Dr. Garen J. Wintemute is the director of the Violence Prevention Research Program (VPRP) at the University of California, Davis, which researches and examines violence in the United States, especially pertaining to firearms. Wintemute graduated from Yale University and earned his M.D. from the University of California before going on to obtain a M.P.H. at Johns Hopkins University School of Public Health. In addition to being the director of the VPRP, he is an emergency medicine physician at the UC Davis Medial Center and a professor of emergency medicine at the UC Davis School of Medicine.

Wintemute has done extensive studies on firearm violence, especially relating to suicides, hospital costs, child accidents, and law enforcement officer murders. His most notable research has been on cheaply made handguns (Saturday night specials) produced in Southern California. His research indicates that buyers with a criminal past are more likely to acquire such guns and that these guns are disproportionately used in crimes. His best-known and most widely cited publication in this area is *Ring of Fire: The Handgun Makers of Southern California.*

Wright, James D. (1947–)

James D. Wright is the Provost Distinguished Research Professor at the University of Central Florida and editor in chief of *Social Science Research.* He previously taught at the University of Massachusetts, Amherst, and was the Charles A. and Leo M. Favrot Professor of Human Relations at Tulane University.

Wright was one of the first scholars to bring sophisticated social science research methodologies to the study of guns in the contemporary United States. His most important work—coauthored with Peter Rossi and Kathleen Daly—is *Under the Gun: Weapons, Crime, and Violence in America.* The work is among the most-cited in academic and government publications on gun violence. Wright and his coauthors conclude that there is no persuasive evidence that gun control laws work to reduce criminal violence. Wright and Rossi also wrote *Armed and Considered Dangerous: A Survey of Felons and Their Firearms,* another often-cited study, in which they found that gun control laws have little or no impact on criminals getting their hands on guns. Most criminals get their guns through theft or by way of straw purchasers (e.g., a girlfriend with no criminal record buying a gun for a convicted felon). With Joseph F. Sheley, Wright wrote *In the Line of Fire: Youths, Guns, and Violence in Urban America*, which closely examines the use of guns among high-risk youths—including street gang members, inner-city high school students, and juveniles serving time in various correctional facilities. Wright's research has led him to the conclusion that gun control, per se, is ineffective. What will reduce the gun violence that has plagued the nation for decades, in his opinion, are broader social measures to reduce poverty and the tensions inherent in a culturally heterogeneous society such as exists in the United States today.

Zimring, Franklin E. (1942–)

Franklin E. Zimring is the William F. Simon Professor of Law and Director of the Earl Warren Legal Institute at the University of California at Berkeley. He earned his B.A. from Wayne State University and his J.D. from the University of Chicago Law School. Zimring joined the University of California, Berkeley, in 1985, and is currently a member of the American Academy of Arts and Sciences and a fellow of the American Society of Criminology. He has studied gun control and crime extensively. Among his most-cited writings are those on the "instrumentality effect"—assessing the weapon used in an assault as it relates to the seriousness of any resulting injury. Zimring concludes that the lethality of a confrontation does in fact depend on the weapon used, with a gun inflicting much greater harm than any other weapon, including a knife. Before his research, many criminologists and others had thought that if someone were intent on killing another person that they would substitute another means—and the choice of weapon, per se, had little consequence.

Zimring and coauthor Gordon Hawkins wrote *Crime Is Not the Problem: Lethal Violence in America*, a book that transformed the way many social scientists now think about the gun violence problem in the United States. Its main thesis is that what distinguishes the United States from its peer nations (other economically developed democracies) is not its crime rate, but its rate of deadly violence. This deadly violence is a product, in part, of the volatile combination of having so many firearms in circulation (more than 200 million) with comparatively lax laws controlling them. Zimring and Hawkins zero in on the high positive correlation between handgun availability and lethal violence and ultimately conclude that the United States will have to ban handguns if it is to bring its rate of lethal violence in line with the very low rates of its peer nations (other economically developed democracies, e.g., Australia, Canada, and the nations of Western Europe).

8

Directory of Organizations, Associations, and Agencies

The number of groups concerned with the gun debate in the United States is immense. The groups listed in this chapter represent some of the better-known and more influential of those groups. Almost all of them are readily classifiable as either advocating a "gun control" or a "gun rights" position. Thus, for organizational purposes, the groups are divided according to which side of the debate they fall, as well as whether they operate more on a national versus a state or local level. During the 1970s and 1980s, gun rights organizations were generally quicker to form and become actively involved in state and local politics, but gun control organizations have been catching up and closing the gap in recent years. Currently, there are thirty-three states with at least one gun control group that is well organized enough to maintain a regularly updated World Wide Web address, and thirty-six states fall in this category for the gun rights side of the debate.

For those wanting to involve themselves directly in the political debate over gun control, the two most important organizations to contact are the Brady Campaign (http://www.bradycenter .org; for those wanting to work for stronger gun control) and the National Rifle Association (http://www.nra.org; for those wanting to protect the rights of gun owners).

Selected government agencies are listed separately at the end of this chapter. Note that even though they purportedly represent all of the people, these agencies are, in fact, largely allies of gun control groups.

Pro-Gun Control, National Groups

AFL-CIO
815 16th Street NW
Washington, DC 20006
(202) 637–5000
http://www.aflcio.org/

African Methodist Episcopal Church
700 Martin Luther King SW
Atlanta, GA 30314
(404) 522–0800
http://www.amecnet.org/

Alliance for Justice
11 Dupont Circle NW, 2nd floor
Washington, DC 20036
(202) 822–6070
http://www.allianceforjustice.org

American Academy of Pediatrics
141 Northwest Point Boulevard
Elk Grove Village, IL 60007–1098
(847) 434–4000
http://www.aap.org

**American Academy of Physical Medicine and
    Rehabilitation**
One IBM Plaza, Suite 2500
Chicago, IL 60611–3604
(312) 464–9700
http://www.aapmr.org/

American Association of Retired Persons
601 East Street NW
Washington, DC 20049
(888) 687–2277
http://www.aarp.org/

American Association of Suicidology
5221 Wisconsin Avenue NW

Washington, DC 20015
(202) 237–2280
http://www.suicidology.org

American Bar Association
321 North Clark Street
Chicago, IL 60610
(312) 988–5000
http://www.abanet.org

American Civil Liberties Union
125 Broad Street, 18th Floor
New York, NY 10004
(212) 549–2585
http://www.aclu.org/

American College of Emergency Physicians
2121 K Street NW, Suite 325
Washington, DC 20037
(202) 728–0610
http://www.acep.org/

American Ethical Union
2 West 64th Street
New York, NY 10023
(212) 873–6500
http://www.aeu.org/

American Federation of Teachers
555 New Jersey Avenue NW
Washington, DC 20001
(202) 879–4400
http://www.aft.org/

American Humanist Association
1777 T Street NW
Washington, DC 20009–7125
(800) 837–3792
http://www.americanhumanist.org

American Jewish Committee
P.O. Box 705
New York, NY 10150
(212) 891–1492
http://www.ajc.org/

American Jewish Congress
825 3rd Avenue, 18th Floor
New York, NY 10022
(212) 879–4500
http://www.ajcongress.org/

American Medical Association
515 N. State Street
Chicago, IL 60610
(800) 621–8335
http://www.ama-assn.org

American Medical Student Association
1902 Association Drive
Reston, VA 20191
(703) 620–6600
http://www.amsa.org

American Psychiatric Association
1000 Wilson Boulevard, Suite 1825
Arlington, VA 22209–3901
(703) 907–7300
http://www.psych.org/

American Public Health Association
800 I Street NW
Washington, DC 20001–3710
(202) 777–APHA
http://www.apha.org/

Americans for Democratic Action
1625 K Street NW, Suite 210
Washington, DC 20006
(202) 785–5980
http://www.adaction.org

Americans for Gun Safety
200 L Street
Washington, DC 20036
(202) 775–0300
http://ww2.americansforgunsafety.com

Anti-Defamation League of B'nai B'rith
823 United Nations Plaza
New York, NY 10017
(212) 490–2525
http://www.adl.org

Baptist Peace Fellowship of North America
4800 Wedgewood Drive
Charlotte, NC 28210
(704) 521–6051
http://www.bpfna.org

B'nai B'rith International
2020 K Street NW, 7th Floor
Washington, DC 20006
(202) 857–6600
http://bnaibrith.org/index.cfm

Brady Campaign to Prevent Gun Violence
1225 Eye Street NW, Suite 1100
Washington, DC 20005
(202) 289–7319
http://www.bradycampaign.org

Brady Center to Prevent Gun Violence
1225 Eye Street NW, Suite 1100
Washington, DC 20005
(202) 289–7319
http://www.bradycenter.org

Center for Science in the Public Interest
1875 Connecticut Avenue NW, Suite 300
Washington, DC 20009
(202) 332–9110
http://www.cspinet.org/

Center for the Study and Prevention of Violence
Institute of Behavioral Science
University of Colorado at Boulder
439 UCB
Boulder, CO 80309–0439
(303) 492–8465
http://www.colorado.edu/cspv/

Centers for Disease Control and Prevention
1600 Clifton Road
Atlanta, GA 30333
(404) 639–3311
http://www.cdc.gov/

Central Conference of American Rabbis
355 Lexington Avenue
New York, NY 10017
(212) 972–3636
http://ccarnet.org

Child Welfare League of America
440 First Street NW, 3rd Floor
Washington, DC 20001–2085
(202) 638–2952
http://www.cwla.org

Children's Defense Fund
25 E. Street NW
Washington, DC 20001
(202) 628–8787
http://www.childrensdefense.org

Church of the Brethren General Board
1451 Dundee Avenue
Elgin, IL 60120–1694
(800) 323–8039
http://www.brethren.org

Church Women United
The Interchurch Center
475 Riverside Drive, Room 1626
New York, NY 10115

(800) 298–5551
http://www.churchwomen.org

Coalition for Gun Control
P.O. Box 90062
1448 Queen Street W.
Toronto, ON M6K 3K3
Fax: (414) 604–0209
http://www.guncontrol.ca/Content/default-english.htm

Coalition to Stop Gun Violence
1023 15th Street NW, Suite 301
Washington, DC 20005
(202) 408–0061
http://www.csgv.org

Common Cause
1250 Connecticut Avenue NW, Suite 600
Washington, DC 20036
(202) 833–1200
http://www.commoncause.org

Common Sense about Kids and Guns
1225 I Street NW, Suite 1100
Washington, DC 20005–3914
(877) 955-KIDS
(202) 546–0200
http://www.kidsandguns.org

Communitarian Network
2130 H Street NW, Suite 703
Washington DC 20052
(202) 994–7997
http://www.gwu.edu/~ccps/

Co/Motion
Alliance for Justice
11 Dupont Circle NW, 2nd Floor
Washington, DC 20036
(202) 822–6070
http://www.allianceforjustice.org/student/co_motion
    /index.html

Consumer Federation of America
1424 16th Street NW, Suite 604
Washington, DC 20036
(202) 387–6121
http://www.consumerfed.org

Council of the Great City Schools
1301 Pennsylvania Avenue NW, Suite 702
Washington, DC 20004
(202) 393–2427
http://www.cgcs.org

DISARM Education Fund
113 University Place, 8th Floor
New York, NY 10003
(212) 353–9800
http://www.disarm.org

Disciples Justice Action Network
1040 Harbor Drive
Annapolis, MD 21403
(410) 212–7964
http://www.djan.net

Doctors Against Handgun Injury
1216 Fifth Avenue
New York, NY 10029
(212) 822-7287
http://www.doctorsagainsthandguninjury.org

Educational Fund to Stop Gun Violence
1023 15th Street NW, Suite 301
Washington, DC 20005
(202) 408–0061
http://www.csgv.org

Emergency Nurses Association
915 Lee Street
Des Plaines, IL 60016–6569
(800) 900–9659
http://www.ena.org

Evangelical Lutheran Church in America
8765 W. Higgins Road
Chicago, IL 60631
(800) 638–3522
http://www.elca.org

Federal Law Enforcement Officers Association
P.O. Box 326
Lewisberry, PA 17339
(717) 938–2300
http://www.fleoa.org

Fellowship of Reconciliation
P.O. Box 271
Nyack, NY 10960
(914) 358–4601
http://www.forusa.org

Firearms Litigation Clearinghouse
1023 15th Street NW, Suite 301
Washington, DC 20005
(202) 408–0061
http://www.csgv.org/issues/litigation/index.cfm

Firearms Research and Identification Association
5800 Acorn Drive
P.O. Box 620
Wrightwood, CA 92397–0620
(760) 249–1098
http://www.jacaudron.com

Follow the Money
833 N. Main, 2nd Floor
Helena, MT 59601
(406) 449–2480
http://www.followthemoney.org/

Fraternal Order of Police
1410 Donelson Pike A-17
Nashville, TN 37217
(615) 399–0900
http://www.grandlodgefop.org

Friends Committee on National Legislation
245 Second Street NE
Washington, DC 20002–5795
(202) 547–6000
http://www.fcnl.org

General Board of Church and Society (GBCS)
United Methodist Church
100 Maryland NE
Washington, DC 20002
(202) 488–5600
http://www.umc-gbcs.org/site/pp.asp?
    c=fsJNK0PKJrH&b=849409

Get Unloaded Gun Safety and Education Campaign
15 West Strong Street, Suite 10-A
Pensacola, FL 32501
(850) 434–0500
http://www.getunloaded.org

Handgun-Free America
1600 Wilson Boulevard, Suite 800
Arlington, VA 22209
(703) 465–0474
http://www.handgunfreedc.org

Harborview Injury Prevention and Research Center
325 Ninth Avenue, Box 359960
Seattle, WA 98104
(206) 744–9430
http://depts.washington.edu/hiprc

Harvard Injury Control Research Center
Harvard School of Public Health
Kresge Building 3rd Floor
677 Huntington Avenue
Boston, MA 02115
(617) 432–3420
http://www.hsph.harvard.edu/hicrc/

HELP Network
Children's Memorial Hospital

2300 Children's Plaza #88
Chicago, IL 60614
(773) 880–3826
http://www.helpnetwork.org

International Association of Chiefs of Police
515 North Washington Street
Alexandria, VA 22314
(703) 836–6767
http://www.theiacp.org

Jewish Community Center Association
15 E 26th Street
New York, NY 10010–1579
(212) 532–4949
http://www.jcca.org

Jewish Women International
2000 M Street NW, Suite 720
Washington, DC 20036
(202) 857–1300
http://www.jewishwomen.org

Johns Hopkins Center for Gun Policy and Research
Bloomberg School of Public Health
624 N. Broadway
Baltimore, MD 21205
(410) 614–3243
http://www.jhsph.edu/gunpolicy

Join Together Online
One Appleton Street, 4th floor
Boston, MA 02116–5223
(617) 437–1500
http://www.jointogether.org

League of Women Voters
1730 M Street NW, Suite 1000
Washington, DC 20036–4508
(202) 429–1965
http://www.lwv.org

The Legal Action Project of the Brady Center to Prevent Gun Violence
1225 Eye Street NW, Suite 1100
Washington, DC 20005
(202) 289–7319
http://www.gunlawsuits.org

Legal Community Against Violence
268 Bush Street, Suite 555
San Francisco, CA 94104
(415) 433–2062
http://www.lcav.org

Mennonite Central Committee
21 South 12th Street
P.O. Box 500
Akron, PA 17501–0500
(717) 859–1151 *or* (888) 563–4676
http://www.mcc.org

Million Mom March
Brady Campaign to Prevent Gun Violence
1225 Eye Street NW, Suite 1100
Washington, DC 20005
(202) 898–0792
http://www.millionmommarch.com

Mothers Against Guns
P.O. Box 230332
Hollis, NY 11423
(718) 276–5802
http://www.mothersagainstguns.org

Mothers Against Teen Violence
P.O. Box 150055
Dallas, TX 75315
(214) 565–0422
http://www.matvinc.org/index.asp

Ms. Foundation for Women
120 Wall Street, 33rd Floor
New York, NY 10005

(212) 742–2300
http://www.ms.foundation.org

NAACP
4805 Mt Hope Drive
Baltimore, MD 21215
(877) NAACP-98
http://www.naacp.org

National Association of Counties
440 State Street NW
Washington, DC 20001
(202) 393–6226
http://www.naco.org

Society for Advancement of Violence and Injury
Research, SAVIR
SAVIR Admin Offices
305 W. Magnolia 183
Fort Collins, CO 80521
(970) 231–0251
http://www.naicrc.org/index.html

National Association of Police Organizations
750 First Street NE, Suite 920
Washington, DC 20002–4241
(202) 842–3560
http://www.napo.org

National Association of SAVE (Students Against
Violence Everywhere)
322 Chapanoke Road, Suite 110
Raleigh, NC 27603
(866) 343–7283
http://www.nationalsave.org/

National Association of School Psychologists
4340 East-West Highway, #402
Bethesda, MD 20814
(301) 657–0270
http://www.nasponline.org/index.html

National Association of Social Workers
750 First Street NE, Suite 700
Washington, DC 20002–4241
(202) 408–8600
http://www.naswdc.org

National Coalition Against Domestic Violence
P.O. Box 18749
Denver, CO 80218
(303) 839–1852
http://www.ncadv.org

National Council of Jewish Women
53 West 23rd Street, 6th Floor
New York, NY 10010–4204
(212) 645–4048
http://www.ncjw.org

National Council of Negro Women
633 Pennsylvania Avenue NW
Washington, DC 20004
(202) 737–0120
http://www.ncnw.org

National Council of Women's Organization
1050 17th Street NW, Suite 250
Washington, DC 20036
(202) 293–4505
http://www.womensorganizations.org

National Crime Prevention Council
1000 Connecticut Avenue NW, 13th Floor
Washington, DC 20036
(202) 466–6272
http://www.ncpc.org

National Criminal Justice Reference Service (NCJRS)
P.O. Box 6000
Rockville, MD 20849–6000
(800) 851–3420
http://www.ncjrs.org/

National Education Association
1201 16th Street NW
Washington, DC 20036–3290
(202) 833–4000
http://www.nea.org/index.html

National Institutes of Health
9000 Rockville Pike
Bethesda, MD 20892
(301) 496–4000
http://www.nih.gov

National League of Cities
1301 Pennsylvania Avenue NW, Suite 550
Washington, DC 20004
(202) 626–3000
http://www.nlc.org/home/

National Network for Youth
1319 F Street NW, Suite 401
Washington, DC 20004
(202) 783–7949
http://www.nn4youth.org

National Organization for Women
P.O. Box 1848
Merrifield, VA 22116–8048
(202) 628–8669
http://www.now.org

**National Organization of Black Law Enforcement
   Executives**
4609 Pinecrest Office Park Drive, Suite F
Alexandria, VA 22312–1442
(703) 658–1529
http://www.noblenatl.org

National Parent Teacher Association
541 N. Fairbanks Court, Suite 1300
Chicago, IL 60611–3396

(312) 670–6782
http://www.pta.org

National Research Center for Women & Families
1701 K Street NW, Suite 700
Washington, DC 20006
(202) 223–4000
http://www.center4research.org

National School Safety Center
141 Duesenberg Drive, Suite 11
Westlake Village, CA 91362
(805) 373–9977
http://www.nssc1.org

National Sheriffs' Association
1450 Duke Street
Alexandria, VA 22314–3490
(703) 836–7827
http://www.sheriffs.org

National Urban League
120 Wall Street, 8th Floor
New York, NY 10005
(212) 558–5300
http://www.nul.org

North American Federation of Temple Youth
633 3rd Avenue, 7th Floor
New York, NY 10017
(212) 650–4070
http://www.nfty.org

Office of Juvenile Justice and Delinquency Prevention
810 Seventh Street NW
Washington, DC 20531
(202) 307–5911
http://www.ojjdp.ncjrs.org

Open Society Institute
400 West 59th Street
New York, NY 10019

(212) 548–0600
http://www.soros.org/crime/guncontrol.htm

Partnerships Against Violence Network
c/o John Gladstone
10301 Baltimore Avenue
Beltsville, MD 20705
(800) 851–3420
http://www.pavnet.org

PAX
801 Second Avenue, Suite 1400
New York, NY 10017
(212) 269–5100
http://www.paxusa.org

Peace Action
1100 Wayne Avenue, Suite 1020
Silver Spring, MD 20910
(301) 565–4050
http://www.peace-action.org

Physicians for Social Responsibility
1875 Connecticut Avenue NW, Suite 1012
Washington, DC 20009
(202) 667–4260
http://www.psr.org

Police Executive Research Forum
1120 Connecticut Avenue NW, Suite 930
Washington, DC 20036
(202) 466–7820
http://www.policeforum.org

Police Foundation
1201 Connecticut Avenue NW
Washington, DC 20036
(202) 833–1460
http://www.policefoundation.org

Presbyterian Church (U.S.A.)
100 Witherspoon Street

Louisville, KY 40202–1396
(800) 872–3283
http://www.pcusa.org

Public Citizen
1600 20th Street NW
Washington, DC 20009
(202) 588–1000
http://www.citizen.org/

Rainbow/Push Coalition (RPC)
930 East 50th Street
Chicago, IL 60615–2702
(773) 373–3366
http://www.rainbowpush.org

Religious Action Center of Reform Judaism (RAC/RJ)
2027 Massachusetts Avenue NW
Washington, DC 20036
(202) 387–2800
http://www.rac.org

Safe Kids Worldwide
1301 Pennsylvania Avenue, Suite 1000
Washington, DC 20004–1707
(202) 662–0600
http://www.safekids.org

Society for Public Health Education (SOPHE)
750 First Street NE, Suite 910
Washington, DC 20002–4242
(202) 408–9804
http://www.sophe.org

Southern Christian Leadership Conference
P.O. Box 89128
Atlanta, GA 30312
(404) 522–1420
http://www.sclcnational.org

Southern Poverty Law Center
400 Washington Avenue

Montgomery, AL 36104
(334) 956–8200
http://www.splcenter.org

Stop Handgun Violence
One Bridge Street
Newton, MA 02458
(877) SAFEARMS
http://www.stophandgunviolence.com

Student Pledge Against Gun Violence
112 Nevada Street
Northfield, MN 55057
(507) 645–5378
http://www.pledge.org

Religious Action Center of Reformed Judaism
Arthur and Sara Jo Kobacker Building
2027 Massachusetts Avenue NW
Washington, DC 20036
(202) 387–2800
http://rac.org/

Unitarian Universalist Association
25 Beacon Street
Boston, MA 02108
(617) 742–2100
http://www.uua.org/index.html

UNITE HERE Headquarters
275 Seventh Avenue
New York, NY 10001
(212) 265–7000
http://www.unitehere.org

United Church of Christ Justice and Peace Ministries
700 Prospect Avenue
Cleveland, OH 44115
(866) 822–8224
http://www.ucc.org/justice/index.html

United Federation of Teachers
52 Broadway
New York, NY 10004
(212) 777–7500
http://www.uft.org

United States Conference of Catholic Bishops
3211 Fourth Street NE
Washington, DC 20017
(202) 541–3000
http://www.usccb.org

United States Student Association
1413 K Street NW, 19th Floor
Washington, DC 20005
(202) 347–8772
http://www.usstudents.org

United Synagogue of Conservative Judaism
155 Fifth Avenue
New York, NY 10010–6802
(212) 533–7800
http://www.uscj.org

U.S. Conference of Mayors
1620 Eye Street NW
Washington, DC 20006
(202) 293–7330
http://www.mayors.org

U.S. Jesuit Conference
1616 P Street NW, Suite 300
Washington, DC 20036–1420
(202) 462–0400
http://www.jesuit.org

Veteran Feminists of America
220 Doucet Road, 225-D
Lafayette, LA 70503
(337) 984–3599
http://www.vfa.us

Violence Policy Center
1730 Rhode Island Avenue NW, Suite 1014
Washington, DC 20036
(202) 822–8200
http://www.vpc.org

Violence Prevention Research Program
Western Fairs Building
University of California, Davis
2315 Stockton Boulevard
Sacramento, CA 95817
(916) 734–3539
http://www.ucdmc.ucdavis.edu/vprp/

Voices for America's Children
1522 K Street NW, Suite 600
Washington, DC 20005–1202
(202) 289–0777
http://www.childadvocacy.org

Women's Institute for Freedom of the Press
1940 Calvert Street
Washington, DC 20009–1502
(202) 265–6707
http://www.wifp.org/

Women's League for Conservative Judaism
475 Riverside Drive, Suite 820
New York, NY 10115
(212) 870–1260
http://www.wlcj.org

Women's National Democratic Club
1526 New Hampshire Avenue NW
Washington, DC 20036
(202) 232–7363
http://www.democraticwoman.org

YMCA of U.S.A.
c/o Association Advancement
101 N. Wacker Drive

Chicago, IL 60606
(312) 977–0031
(800) 872–9622
http://www.ymca.net

Pro-Gun Control, State and Local Groups

Alaska

Alaska Public Interest Research Group
P.O. Box 101093
Anchorage, AK 99510
(907) 278–3661
http://www.akpirg.org/

Arizona

Arizona Consumers Council
P.O. Box 1288
Phoenix, AZ 85001
(602) 265–9625 or (602) 266–3913
http://azconsumerscouncil.org/

Arizonans for Gun Safety Phoenix
P.O. Box 11552
Glendale, AZ 85318
(602) 547–0976
http://www.azgs.org

Volunteer Center of Southern Arizona
924 N. Alvernon Way
Tucson, AZ 85711
(520) 881–3300
http://www.volunteertucson.org/

Arkansas

Arkansas Public Policy Panel
1308 W. Second Street
Little Rock, AR 72201

(501) 376–7913
http://www.arpanel.org

California

California Federation of Teachers
2550 N. Hollywood Way, Suite 400
Burbank, CA 91505
(818) 843–8226
http://www.cft.org

California Licensed Vocational Nurses' Association
(CLVNA)
620 Sunbeam Avenue
Sacramento, CA 95814
(800) 411–6901
http://www.clvna.org

Consumer Attorneys of California
770 L Street, Suite 1200
Sacramento, CA 95814
(916) 442–6902
http://www.caoc.com

Consumer Federation of California
P.O. Box 1340
Millbrae, CA 94030
(650) 589–3135
http://www.consumerfedofca.org

Sacramento Central Labor Council
2840 El Centro Road, Suite 111
Sacramento, CA 95833
(916) 927–9772
http://www.sacramentolabor.org

Stop Gun Violence: Orange County Citizens for the
Prevention of Gun Violence
25225 Cabot Road, Suite 215
Laguna Hills, CA 92653
(949) 206–9676
http://www.stopgunviolence.org

Stop Our Shootings
3972 Barranca Parkway, Suite J609
Irvine, CA 92606
(949) 733–8136
http://stopourshootings.org

Violence Prevention Coalition of Greater Los Angeles
3530 Wilshire Boulevard, Suite 800
Los Angeles, CA 90010
(213) 351–7888
http://www.vpcla.org

Youth Alive
3300 Elm Street
Oakland, CA 94609
(510) 594–2588
http://www.youthalive.org/

Colorado

Colorado Ceasefire
P.O. Box 7501
Denver, CO 80207–0501
(303) 380–6711
http://www.coloradoceasefire.org/

Million Mom March—Denver Chapter
P.O. Box 100432
Denver, CO 80250–0432
(303) 302–3300
http://www.mmmdenver.org/

Connecticut

Connecticut Against Gun Violence
P.O. Box 523
Southport, CT 06890–0523
(203) 268–3050
http://www.cagv.org

Florida

Florida Coalition Against Domestic Violence
425 Office Plaza
Tallahassee, FL 32301
(850) 425–2749
http://www.fcadv.org/

Florida Coalition to Stop Gun Violence, Inc.
P.O. Box 7238
Wesley Chapel, FL 33543
(813) 991–9584
http://www.floridaguncontrol.org

Florida Consumer Action Network
2005 Pan Am Circle, Suite 200
Tampa, FL 33607
(813) 877–6712
http://www.fcan.org

Florida National Organization for Women, Inc.
c/o Chris Schilling, Exec. Officer
1710 W. Colonial Drive
Orlando, FL 32804
(888) 5-FLA-NOW
http://www.flnow.org

Pinnelas County NOW
P.O. Box 40612
St. Petersburg, FL 33743–3281
(727) 823–3281
http://erights4all.com/now/pinellas

South Florida Urban Ministries
2850 SW 27th Avenue
Miami, FL 33133
(305) 442–8306
http://www.sflum.org/

Georgia

Georgians for Gun Safety
100 Edgewood Avenue NE, Suite 1008
Atlanta, GA 30303
(404) 527–7426
http://www.georgiansforgunsafety.org/

Illinois

Champaign County Health Care Consumers
Gun Regulation Project
44 E. Main Street, Suite 208
Champaign, IL 61821
(217) 352–6533
http://www.healthcareconsumers.org

El Centro por los Trabajadores
4 Buena Vista Court
Urbana, IL 61803
(217) 328–0718
http://www.prairienet.org/elcentro

Illinois Council Against Handgun Violence
223 W. Jackson Boulevard, Suite 1106
Chicago, IL 60606
(312) 341–0939
http://www.ichv.org

Illinois Disciples Foundation
610 E. Springfield Avenue
Champaign, IL 61820–1601
(217) 352–8721
http://www.prairienet.org/idf

Progressive Resource/Action Cooperative
610 E. Springfield
Champaign, IL 61820
(217) 352–8721
http://www.prairienet.org/prc

Spinal Cord Injury Association of Illinois
1032 S. LaGrange Road
LaGrange, IL 60525
(708) 352–6223
http://www.sci-illinois.org/

Uhlich Children's Advantage Network
3737 N. Hozart Street
Chicago, IL 60618
(773) 588–0180
http://www.ucanchicago.org/

University Place Christian Church
403 S. Wright Street
Champaign, IL 61820
(217) 352–5118
http://www.uniplace.org/

Voices for Illinois Children
208 S. LaSalle Street, Suite 1490
Chicago, IL 60604–1120
(312) 456–0600
http://www.voices4kids.org/

Women's Direct Action Collective
c/o the Illinois Disciples Foundation (IDF)
610 E. Springfield Avenue
Champaign, IL 61820
(217) 352–8721
http://www.prairienet.org/tbtn/

Indiana

Hoosiers Concerned About Gun Violence
2511 E. 46th Street, Suite A-6
Indianapolis, IN 46205
(317) 377–0700
http://www.hcgv.org

Iowa

Iowa Coalition Against Domestic Violence
515 28th Street
Des Moines, IA 50312
(515) 244–8028
http://www.icadv.org/Default.htm

Iowans for the Prevention of Gun Violence
4403 First Avenue SE, Suite 113
Cedar Rapids, IA 52402–3221
(319) 743–7823
http://www.ipgv.org

Kansas

Safe State Kansas
829 N. Market
Wichita, KS 67214
(316) 264–9303
http://www.safestatekansas.org

Kentucky

Just Solutions
410 W. Chestnut Street, Suite 628
Louisville, KY 40202
(502) 581–1961
http://www.just-solutions.org

Maine

Maine Citizens Against Handgun Violence
P.O. Box 92
Portland, ME 04112
(207) 780–0501
http://www.mcahv.org

Maryland

Baltimore Jewish Council
5750 Park Heights Avenue

Baltimore, MD 21215
(410) 542–4850
http://www.baltjc.org/

Ceasefire Maryland
3000 Chestnut Avenue, Suite 203
Baltimore, MD 21211
(410) 889–1477
http://www.ceasefiremd.org/

Greater Washington Area Chapter of Hadassah
1220 East West Highway, Suite 120
Silver Spring, MD 20910
(301) 585–7772
http://www.hadassahdc.org/index.asp

Maryland Consumer Rights Coalition, Inc.
The Mill Centre
3000 Chestnut Avenue, Suite 203
Baltimore, MD 21211
(410) 366–1965
http://www.mdconsumers.org/

NAACP, Baltimore Branch
8 W. 26th Street
Baltimore, MD 21218
(410) 366–3300
http://www.naacpbaltimore.org/

Women's Law Center of Maryland, Inc.
305 West Chesapeake Avenue, Suite 201
Towson, MD 21204
(410) 321–8761
http://www.wlcmd.org/

Massachusetts

Massachusetts Consumer's Coalition
831 Massachusetts Avenue
Cambridge, MA 02139–3068
(617) 349–6152
http://www.massconsumers.org/

Million Mom March—Massachusetts Chapter
P.O. Box 862
Natick, MA 01760
(508) 655–9724
http://www.greaterbostonmmm.com/

Michigan

Public Interest Research Group in Michigan
103 E. Liberty, Suite 202
Ann Arbor, MI 48104
(734) 662–6597
http://www.pirgim.org/

Michigan Partnership to Prevent Gun Violence
P.O. Box 14307
Lansing, MI 48901–4307
(517) 321–0195
http://www.mppgv.org

Neighborhood Service Organization
5470 Chene Street
Detroit, MI 48211
(313) 579–0610
http://www.nso-mi.org/Default.asp

Minnesota

Citizens for a Safer Minnesota (Working to End Gun
    Violence)
2395 University Avenue W, Suite 300E
St. Paul, MN 55114
(651) 645–3271
http://www.endgunviolence.com

Initiative for Violence-Free Families
4123 E. Lake Street
Minneapolis, MN 55406
(612) 728–2094
http://www.ivff.org/ivff/index.html

Million Mom March—Minnesota Chapter
P.O. Box 390623
Edina, MN 55439
(612) 202–8177
http://www.millionmommarchmn.com/

Missouri

Missourians Against Handgun Violence
8420 Delmar Street, Suite 300
St. Louis, MO 63124–2178
(314) 997–6301
http://mahv.moaction.com/default.asp

New Jersey

Ceasefire New Jersey
1995 E. Marlton Pike
Cherry Hill, NJ 08003
(856) 489–5960
http://www.Ceasefirenj.org

Consumers League of New Jersey
155 McCosh Road
Upper Montclair, NJ 07043
(973) 744–6449
http://www.clnj.org/

Million Mom March—NJ State Council
P.O. Box 77333
Ewing, NJ 08628
(609) 882–3711
http://mmmnj.bizland.com/

New Mexico

New Mexico Voices for Children
2340 Alamo SE, Suite 120
Albuquerque, NM 87106
(505) 244–9505
http://www.nmvoices.org/

New York

The CityKids Foundation
57 Leonard Street
New York, NY 10013
(212) 925–3320
http://www.citykids.com/main.html

Fresh Youth Initiatives
Storefront South
2201 Amsterdam Avenue
New York, NY 10032
(212) 781–1113
http://www.freshyouth.org/

New York PIRG
9 Murray Street, Floor 3
New York, NY 10007–2223
(212) 349–6460
http://www.nypirg.org

New Yorkers Against Gun Violence
332 Bleecker Street, Box E-9
New York, NY 10014
(212) 674–3710
http://www.nyagv.org

North Carolina

North Carolina Consumers Council, Inc.
3725 National Drive, Suite 115
Raleigh, NC 27612–4879
(919) 781–8654
http://www.ncconsumer.org/

North Carolinians Against Gun Violence Education Fund
P.O. Box 9204
Chapel Hill, NC 27515
(919) 403–7665
http://www.ncgv.org

Ohio

Ohio Coalition Against Gun Violence
P.O. Box 1078
Toledo, OH 43697
(419) 244–7440
http://www.ocagv.org

Oregon

Ceasefire Oregon/Ceasefire Oregon Education Fund
7327 SW Barnes Road, #316
Portland, OR 97225
(503) 220–1669
http://www.ceasefireoregon.org

First Unitarian Church, Peace Action Committee
1011 SW 12th Avenue
Portland, OR 97205
(503) 228–6389
http://www.firstunitarianportland.org/

Jewish Federation of Portland, Community Relations
Committee
6680 SW Capitol Highway
Portland, OR 97219
(503) 245–6219
http://www.jewishportland.org/

Oregon Consumer League
P.O. Box 10281
Portland, OR 97296–0281
(503) 227–3882
http://www.orconsumer.org/

Oregon Student Public Interest Research Group
1536 SE 11th Avenue
Portland, OR 97214
(503) 231–4181
http://www.ospirgstudents.org/

Pennsylvania

Ceasefire Pennsylvania
111 S. Independence Mall E, Suite 572
Philadelphia, PA 19106
(215) 923–3151
http://www.CeaseFirePA.org

Goods for Guns
801 Union Place, Suite 420
Pittsburgh, PA 15212
(412) 322–1330
http://goodsforguns.org

**Pennsylvanians Against Handgun Violence/Safe
    Pennsylvania**
5125 Penn Avenue, Suite 300
Pittsburgh, PA 15224
(888) 444-PAHV
http://www.pahv.org

Rhode Island

Institute for the Study and Practice of Nonviolence
239 Oxford Street
Providence, RI 02905
(401) 781–7210
http://www.nonviolenceinstitute.org

Texas

National Domestic Violence Hotline
P.O. Box 161810
Austin, TX 78716
(800) 799-SAFE (7233)
http://www.ndvh.org/

Texans for Gun Safety
1302 Waugh Drive, PMB 498
Houston, TX 77019–4944
(832) 250–6360
http://www.texansforgunsafety.org

Texas Council on Family Violence
P.O. Box 161810
Austin, TX 78716
(800) 799-SAFE
http://www.tcfv.org/

Texas Fund for Energy and Environmental Education (TFE3)
611 S. Congress, 200
Austin, TX 78704
(512) 479–7744
http://www.undueinfluence.com/tfeee.htm

Utah

Gun Violence Prevention Center of Utah
406 E. 300 Street, Suite 115
Salt Lake City, UT 84111
(801) 487–5987
http://www.gvpc.org

Vermont

Vermont Public Interest Research Group
141 Main Street, Suite 6
Montpelier, VT 05602
(802) 223–5221
http://www.vpirg.org/

Virginia

Feminist Majority Foundation
1600 Wilson Boulevard, Suite 801
Arlington, VA 22209
(703) 522–2214
http://www.feminist.org/

Virginians Against Handgun Violence
Hampton Roads Chapter
P.O. Box 271
Norfolk, VA 23501
(757) 423–8801
http://www.vahv.org

Voices for Virginia's Children
701 E. Franklin Street
Richmond, VA 23219
(804) 649–0184
http://www.vakids.org/

Washington

Trauma Nurses Talk Tough
400 S. 43rd Street
P.O. Box 50010
Renton, WA 98058–5010
(503) 231–4181
http://www.valleymed.org/community
/talk_tough.asp

Washington Ceasefire
P.O. Box 20246
Seattle, WA 98102
(206) 322–1236
http://www.washingtonceasefire.org

Wisconsin

Firearm Injury Center
Department of Emergency Medicine
Medical College of Wisconsin
8701 Watertown Plank Road
Milwaukee, WI 53226
(414) 456–8296
http://www.mcw.edu/fic/

Peace Action Wisconsin
1001 E. Keefe Avenue
Milwaukee, WI 53212
(414) 964–5158
http://www.peaceactionwi.org/

Wisconsin Anti-Violence Effort (WAVE)
P.O. Box 170393

Milwaukee, WI 53217
(414) 351–9283
http://www.waveedfund.org

Pro-Gun Rights, National Groups

Amateur Trapshooting Association
601 W. National Road
Vandalia, OH 45377–1096
(937) 898–4638
http://www.shootata.com/ATAHome.cfm

American Custom Gunmakers Guild
22 Vista View Lane
Cody, WY 82414–9606
(307) 587–4297
http://www.acgg.org/

American Firearms Industry
150 SE 12th Street, Suite 200
Ft Lauderdale, FL 33316
(954) 467–9994
http://www.amfire.com/php/container.php

American Legislative Exchange Council
1129 20th Street NW, Suite 500
Washington, DC 20036
(202) 466–3800
http://www.alec.org

American Single Shot Rifle Association
15770 Road, 1037
Oakwood, OH 45833
(419) 692–3866
http://www.assra.com/

American Society of Law Enforcement Trainers
7611-B Willow Road
Frederick, MD 21702
(301) 668–9466
http://www.aslet.org/i4a/pages/index.cfm?pageid=1

American Women's Self-Defense Association
713 N. Wellwood Avenue
Lindenhurst NY 11757
(631) 225–6262
http://www.awsda.org/

Armed Females of America
2702 E. University, Suite 103, PMB 213
Mesa, AZ 85213
(480) 924–8202
http://www.armedfemalesofamerica.com

Arming Women Against Rape and Endangerment (AWARE)
P.O. Box 242
Bedford, MA 01730–0242
(781) 893–0500
http://www.aware.org

Association of American Physicians and Surgeons, Inc.
1601 N. Tucson Boulevard, Suite 9
Tucson, AZ 85716–3450
(800) 635–1196
http://www.aapsonline.org

Browning Collectors Association
5603-B W. Friendly Avenue, Suite 166
Greensboro, NC 27410
(402) 694–6602
http://www.browningcollectors.com/

Cast Bullet Association, Inc.
1 Nantucket Lane
St. Louis, MO 63132
(314) 425–2466
http://www.castbulletassoc.org/

Cato Institute
1000 Massachusetts Avenue NW
Washington, DC 20001–5403
(202) 842–0200
http://www.cato.org/

Citizens Committee for the Right to Keep and Bear Arms
Liberty Park
12500 NE 10th Place
Bellevue, WA 98005
(425) 454–4911
http://www.ccrkba.org

Concerned Women for America (CWA)
1015 15th NW, Suite 1100
Washington, DC 20005
(202) 488–7000
http://www.cwfa.org

Congress of Racial Equality
817 Broadway, Third Floor
New York, NY 10003
(212) 598–4000
http://www.core-online.org/

Doctors for Responsible Gun Ownership
Claremont Institute
250 W. First Street, Suite 330
Claremont, CA 91711
(909) 621–6825
http://www.claremont.org/projects/doctors/index.html

Ducks Unlimited
1 Waterfowl Way
Memphis, TN 38120
(901) 758–3825
http://www.ducks.org

Fifty Caliber Shooters Association
P.O. Box 111
Monroe, UT 84754–0111
(435) 527–9245
http://www.fcsa.org/

Firearms Coalition
P.O. Box 3313
Manassas, VA 20108

(703) 753–0424
http://www.nealknox.com

Firearms Owners Against Crime
P.O. Box 75
Presto, PA 15142
(412) 221–4595
http://www.foac-pac.org

Gun Owners of America
8001 Forbes Place, Suite 102
Springfield, VA 22151
(703) 321–8585
http://www.gunowners.org

Heartland Institute
19 South LaSalle Street, #903
Chicago, IL 60603
(312) 377–4000
http://www.heartland.org

Heritage Foundation
214 Massachusetts Avenue NE
Washington, DC 20002–4999
(202) 546–4400
http://www.heritage.org/

Hunting & Shooting Sports Heritage Foundation
Flintlock Ridge Office Center
11 Mile Hill Road
Newtown, CT 06470–2359
(203) 426–1320
http://www.hsshf.org

Independence Institute
13952 Denver West Parkway, Suite 400
Golden, CO 80401
(303) 279–6536
http://i2i.org/index.aspx

Independent Women's Forum
1726 M Street NW, Tenth Floor

Washington, DC 20036
(202) 419–1820
http://www.iwf.org

International Association of Fish and Wildlife Agencies
444 N. Capitol Street NW, Suite 725
Washington, DC 20001
(202) 624–7890
http://www.iafwa.org

International Association of Law Enforcement Firearms
  Instructors
25 Country Club Road, Suite 707
Gilford, NH 03249
(603) 524–8787
http://www.ialefi.com/

International Benchrest Shooters
RR1 Box 250BB
Springville, PA 18844
(570) 965–2505
http://www.international-benchrest.com/

International Brotherhood of Police Officers
159 Burgin Parkway
Quincy, MA 02169
(617) 376–0220
http://www.ibpo.org

International Defensive Pistol Association
2232 CR 719
Berryville, AR 72616
(870) 545–3886
http://www.idpa.com

International Handgun Metallic Silhouette Association
P.O. Box 901120
Sandy, UT 84090–1120
(801) 733–8423
http://www.ihmsa.org/

International Hunters Association
P.O. Box 820
Knightdale, NC 27545
(919) 365–7157
http://internationalhunters.homestead.com/

International Hunter Education Association
P.O. Box 490
3725 Cleveland Avenue
Wellington, CO 80549
(970) 568–7954
http://www.ihea.com/

Izaak Walton League of America
707 Conservation Lane
Gaithersburg, MD 20878
(301) 548–0150
http://www.iwla.org

Jews for the Preservation of Firearms Ownership
P.O. Box 270143
Hartford, WI 53027
(262) 673–9745
http://www.jpfo.org

John Birch Society
P.O. Box 8040
Appleton, WI 54913
(920) 749–3780
http://www.jbs.org

Keep and Bear Arms
Liberty Park
12500 NE Tenth Place
Bellevue, WA 98005
(425) 454–7012
http://www.keepandbeararms.com

Law Enforcement Alliance of America
7700 Leesburg Pike, Suite 421
Falls Church, VA 22043

(800) 766–8578 *or* (703) 847-COPS
http://www.leaa.org

Libertarian Party
2600 Virginia Avenue NW, Suite 100
Washington, DC 20037
(202) 333–0008
http://www.lp.org

Madison Society Foundation, Inc.
P.O. Box 577101
Modesto, CA 95357–7101
(800) 446–4499
http://www.madison-society.org

Mothers Arms
Safely in Mothers Arms, Inc.
4757 E. Greenway Road, 107B #124
Phoenix, AZ 85032
(800) 464–4840 or (602) 493–1348
http://www.mothersarms.org

National Association of Firearm Instructors
10299 Johnstown Road
New Albany, OH 43054
(614) 939–1285
http://www.usnafi.org/

National Association of Firearms Retailers
11 Mile Hill Road
Newtown, CT 06470
(203) 426–1320
http://www.nafr.org/

National Bench Rest Shooters Association
2835 Guilford Lane
Oklahoma City, OK 73120–4404
(405) 842–9585
http://nbrsa.benchrest.com/

National Center for Policy Analysis
12770 Coit Road, Suite 800
Dallas, TX 75251
(972) 386–6272
http://www.ncpa.org

National Hunters Association
P.O. Box 820
Knightdale, NC 27545
(919) 365–7157
http://www.nationalhunters.com

National Mossberg Collectors Association
P.O. Box 487
Festus, MO 63028
(636) 937–6401
http://www.mossbergcollectors.org/

National Muzzle Loading Rifle Association
P.O. Box 67
Friendship, IN 47021
(812) 667–5131
http://www.nmlra.org

National Reloading Manufacturers Association
1 Centerpointe Drive, Suite 300
Lake Oswego, OR 97035
(503) 639–9190
http://www.reload-nrma.com/

National Rifle Association
11250 Waples Mill Road
Fairfax, VA 22030
(800) 421–4NRA
http://www.nra.org

National Skeet Shooting Association
5931 Roft Road
San Antonio, TX 78253–9261
(800) 877–5538
http://www.mynssa.com/

North American Hunting Club
12301 Whitewater Drive
P.O. Box 3401
Minnetonka, MN 55343
(612) 936–9333
http://www.huntingclub.com/

North-South Skirmish Association, Inc.
507 N. Brighton Court
Sterling, VA 20164–3919
(804) 266–0898
http://www.n-ssa.org/

Pacific International Trapshooting Association
P.O. Box 770
Lebanon, OR 97355
(541) 258–8766
http://www.shootpita.com/

Pacific Research Institute
755 Sansone Street, Suite 450
San Francisco, CA 94111
(415) 989–0833
http://www.pacificresearch.org/

Peoples Rights Organization
3953 Indianola Avenue
Columbus, OH 43214
(614) 268–0122
http://www.peoplesrights.org

Pink Pistols
P.O. Box 60342
King of Prussia, PA 19406
(267) 386–8907
http://www.pinkpistols.org

Safari Club International
4800 W. Gates Pass Road
Tucson, AZ 85745–9490
(520) 620–1220
http://www.safariclub.org/

Second Amendment Club
P.O. Box 1661
Land O Lakes, FL 34639
(813) 973–8918
http://www.secondamendmentclub.org

Second Amendment Committee
P.O. Box 1776
Hanford, CA 93232
(209) 584–5209
http://www.libertygunrights.com

Second Amendment Foundation
James Madison Building
12500 NE Tenth Place
Bellevue, WA 98005
(425) 454–7012
http://www.saf.org

Second Amendment Sisters
900 RR 620 S, Suite C-101 Box 228
Lakeway, TX 78734
(877) 271–6216
http://www.2asisters.org/

Shooting for Women Alliance
P.O. Box 2167
Knoxville, TN 37901
(865) 686–3098
http://www.shootingforwomenalliance.com/

Southern States Police Benevolent Association
1900 Brannan Road
McDonough, GA 30253–4310
(800) 233–3506
http://www.sspba.org

**Sporting Arms and Ammunition Manufacturers'
Institute**
11 Mile Hill Road
Newtown, CT 06470

(203) 426–1320
http://www.saami.org

Students for the Second Amendment
12911 Vidorra Circle
San Antonio, TX 78245
(210) 674–5559
http://www.sf2a.org/

Ted Nugent United Sportsmen of America
4008 W. Michigan Avenue
Jackson, MI 49202
(517) 750–3640
http://tnugent.com/about_tnusa/

United States Concealed Carry Association
4466 Highway P, Suite 204
Jackson, WI 53037
(877) 677–1919
http://www.uscca.us/

United States Practical Shooting Association
P.O. Box 811
Sedro Woolley, WA 98284
(306) 855–2245
http://www.uspsa.org

United States Sportsmen's Alliance
801 Kingsmill Parkway
Columbus, OH 43229
(614) 888–4868
http://www.ussportsmen.org

Women Against Gun Control
P.O. Box 95357
South Jordan, UT 84095
(801) 328–9660
http://www.wagc.com

Women's Firearm Network
P.O. Box 990

One Court Street
Exeter, NH 03833
(603) 778–4720
http://www.womenshooters.com/wfn/index.html

World Fast-Draw Association
7708 Bethalto Road
Bethalto, IL 62010
(618) 377–5629
http://www.fastdraw.org/wfda/

Pro-Gun Rights, State and Local Groups

Alaska

Alaska Outdoor Council
P.O. Box 73902
Fairbanks, AK 99707–3902
(907) 455–4262
http://www.alaskaoutdoorcouncil.org/

Arizona

Arizona Arms Association, Inc.
c/o Cindy Hale—Secretary
P.O. Box 11057
Glendale, AZ 85318–1057
(623) 210–3959
http://www.azarms.com

Arizona State Rifle and Pistol Association
P.O. Box 40962
Mesa, AZ 85274
(480) 838–6064
http://www.asrpa.com/

Arkansas

Central Arkansas Shooters Association
P.O. Box 190701

Little Rock, AR 72219–0701
(501) 681–4321
http://www.casarange.com/

California

California Rifle and Pistol Association, Inc.
271 E. Imperial Highway, Suite 620
Fullerton, CA 92835
(714) 992–2772
http://www.crpa.org

Golden Gate United NRA Members' Council
3739 Balboa Street, Suite 147
San Francisco, CA 94121
(415) 221–9333
http://www.ggnra.org

Gun Owners of California
7996 California Avenue, Suite F
Fair Oaks, CA 95628
(916) 967–4970
http://www.gunownersca.com

NRA Members' Councils of California
3565 La Ciotat Way
Riverside, CA 92501
(951) 683–4NRA (4672)
http://www.nramemberscouncils.com

Colorado

Clear Creek County Sportsman's Club
P.O. Box 1145
Idaho Springs, CO 80452
(303) 567–4033
http://www.cccsclub.com/

Colorado State Shooting Association
609 W. Littleton Boulevard
Littleton, CO 80210–2368

(720) 283–1376
http://www.cssa.org

Liberty Day
2275 E. Arapahoe Road, Suite 218
Centennial, CO 80122
(303) 333–3434
http://www.libertyday.org/

Pikes Peak Firearms Coalition, Inc.
P.O. Box 17253
Colorado Springs, CO 80935–7253
(719) 590–8663
http://www.ppfc.org

Rocky Mountain Gun Owners
P.O. Box 3006
Brush, CO 80723
(970) 842–3006
http://www.rmgo.org

Connecticut

Coalition of Connecticut Sportsmen
P.O. Box 2506
Hartford, CT 06146
(203) 245–8076
http://www.ctsportsmen.com/

Florida

The James Madison Institute
P.O. Box 37460
Tallahassee, FL 32315
(850) 386–3131
http://jamesmadison.org/

North Central Florida Sportsman Association
P.O. Box 23642
Gainesville, FL 32601
(352) 378–2222
http://www.afn.org/~ncfsa/

Second Amendment Coalition of Florida, Inc.
P.O. Box 17335
West Palm Beach, FL 33416
(561) 697–0818
http://www.sacfla.org

Seminole Country Gun & Archery Association, Inc.
P.O. Box 6565
Tallahassee, FL 32314–6565
(850) 222–9518
http://www.scgaa.org

South Florida Firearm Owners
P.O. Box 523476
Miami, FL 33152–3976
(305) 460–2261
http://www.smartcarry.com/sffo.htm

Georgia

Georgia Firearm Owners Defense League
P.O. Box 1391
Smyrna, GA 30081
(770) 815–7480
http://www.gfodl.org

Georgia Sport Shooting Association
P.O. Box 1882
Blairsville, GA 30514
(706) 722–1326
http://www.gssa.com

Hawaii Rifle Association
P.O. Box 543
Kailua, HA 96734
(808) 261–2754
http://www.hawaiirifleassn.org/

Illinois

Concealed Carry, Inc.
P.O. Box 4597

Oak Brook, IL 60522–4597
(630) 660–3935
http://www.concealcarry.org

Guns Save Life
Champaign County Rifle Association
P.O. Box 51
Savoy, IL 61874
(217) 384–7302
http://www.gunssavelife.com

Illinois State Rifle Association
P.O. Box 637
Chatsworth, IL 60921
(815) 635–3198
http://www.isra.org

Iowa

Iowa State Rifle and Pistol Association
713 Second Avenue
Evansdale, IA 50707–2001
(319) 233–1587
http://www.iowastateriflepistol.org/

Kansas

Kansas State Rifle Association
KSRA Headquarters
P.O. Box 212
Norton, KS 67654–0212
(875) 877–2750
http://www.ksraweb.net

Missouri Valley Arms Collectors Association
P.O. Box 6013
Leawood, KS 66206
(816) 339–2631
http://www.mvacagunshow.com

Kentucky

Jefferson Gun Club
660 Gun Club Road
Brooks, KY 40109
(502) 957–4661
http://www.jeffersongunclub.org

Kentucky Coalition to Carry Concealed
P.O. Box 1269
Frankfort, KY 40602
(502) 223–8360
http://www.kc3.com

Kentucky Firearms Foundation, Inc.
P.O. Box 1249
Owingsville, KY 40360–1249
(866) 674–9193
http://www.kyfirearms.org

Louisiana

Louisiana Shooting Association
821 McCall Street
Lake Charles, LA 70607
(337) 477–5277
http://www.lsa1.org

Maine

Pine Tree State Rifle and Pistol Association
73 Sunset Strip
Brewer, ME 04412
(207) 989–7304
http://www.mainerpa.org

Maryland

Associated Gun Clubs of Baltimore, Inc.
11518 Marriotsville Road
Marriotsville, MD 21104–1220

(410) 461–8532
http://www.associatedgunclubs.org

Berwyn Rod & Gun Club, Inc.
8311 Laurel-Bowie Road
P.O. Box 666
Bowie, MD 20718–0666
(301) 464–9830
http://www.berwyn.org/

Maryland Sportsmen's Association
P.O. Box 649
White Marsh, MD 21162
(410) 392–6776
http://www.marylandsportsmen.org/

Maryland State Rifle and Pistol Association, Inc.
c/o Bethesda Business Service Spring Center
P.O. Box 224
Chase, MD 21027
(410) 335–7758
http://www.msrpa.org

Montgomery Citizens for a Safer Maryland
P.O. Box 2563
Silver Spring, MD 20915
(301) 776–4488
http://www.mcsm.org

Massachusetts

Braintree Rifle and Pistol Club, Inc.
P.O. Box 850024
Braintree, MA 02184–0024
(781) 848–3377
http://www.brp.org

GOAL: Gun Owners' Action League
P.O. Box 567
Northboro, MA 01532
(508) 393–5333
http://www.goal.org

Michigan

Great Lakes Shooting Sports Association
P.O. Box 81166
Lansing, MI 48908
(517) 886–4572
http://www.glssa.org/

Michigan Coalition for Responsible Gun Owners
P.O. Box 14014
Lansing, MI 48901
(517) 484–2746
http://www.mcrgo.org

Michigan Rifle and Pistol Association
P.O. Box 71
Marshall, MI 49068–0071
(888) 655-MRPA
http://www.michrpa.com

Minnesota

Minnesota Concealed Carry Reform
P.O. Box 131254
Saint Paul, MN 55113
(651) 636–4465
http://www.mnccrn.org

Missouri

Gateway Civil Liberties Alliance
P.O. Box 19739
Brentwood, MO 63144
(314) 385–4867
http://www.gclastl.org

Missourians for Personal Safety
2000 E. Broadway, PMB-120
Columbia, MO 65201–6091
(417) 257–7457
http://www.moccw.org

Second Amendment Coalition of Missouri
517 Connie Lane
Manchester, MO 63021
(636) 230–2399
http://www.sacmo.org

Western Missouri Shooters Alliance
1551 SW 25th Road
Kingsville, MO 64061
(816) 333-WMSA
http://www.wmsa.net/

Nebraska

BBC Birds
2348 220 Avenue
Albion, NE 68620
(402) 395–6131
http://www.bbcbirds.com/

Hunt Nebraska Inc.
P.O. Box 328
Arapahoe, NE 68922
(800) HUNT NEB
http://www.huntnebraskainc.com/

New Hampshire

Gun Owners of New Hampshire, Inc
P.O. Box 847
Concord, NH 03302–0847
(603) 225-GONH
http://www.gonh.org

New Jersey

**Association of New Jersey Rifle & Pistol Clubs
(ANJRPC)**
President—Robert Esch
825 Stonewall Court
Franklin Lakes, NJ 07417
(631) 462–9260

http://www.anjrpc.org

New Jersey Coalition for Self Defense
P.O. Box 2166
Brick, NJ 08723
(732) 247–2282
http://www.njcsd.org

**New Jersey State Federation of Sportsmen's
   Clubs**
P.O. Box 742
Newfoundland, NJ 07435
(973) 208–7779
http://www.njsfsc.org/

New Mexico
New Mexico Shooting Sports Association
1049 Alamo Road
Los Alamos, NM 87544
(505) 672–9180
http://www.nmssa.org/

New York
New York State Rifle & Pistol Association
P.O. Box 1023
Troy, NY 12181–1023
(518) 272–2654
http://www.nysrpa.org/

Sportsmen's Association for Firearms Education, Inc.
P.O. Box 343
Commack, NY 11725
(631) 957–7527
http://www.nysafe.org

Tyranny Response Team (TRTNY)
259 Route 146
Altamont, NY 12009
(877) 590–6703
http://www.trt-ny.org/index.htm

North Carolina

Grass Roots North Carolina
P.O. Box 10684
Raleigh, NC 27604
(919) 664–8565
http://www.grnc.org

North Carolina Rifle & Pistol Association
P.O. Box 4116
Pinehurst, NC 28374
(910) 295–2480
http://www.ncrpa.org/

North Dakota

North Dakota Shooting Sports Association, Inc.
P.O. Box 9242
Fargo, ND 58106–9242
(701) 282–1133
http://www.ndssa.org/

Ohio

Ohio Gun Collectors Association
P.O. Box 670406
Sagamore Hills, OH 44067–0406
(330) 467–5733
http://www.ogca.com

Peoples Rights Organization
4444 Indianola Avenue
Columbus, OH 43214
(614) 268–0122
http://www.peoplesrights.org

Oklahoma

Oklahoma Rifle Association
P.O. Box 850602
Yukon, OK 73085–0602
(405) 324–8498
http://www.oklarifle.org

Oregon

Oregon Firearms Federation
P.O. Box 556
Canby, OR 97013
(503) 263–5830
oregonfirearms.org

Oregon Gun Owners
P.O. Box 2839
Portland, OR 97283
(503) 286–3206
http://www.ogo.org/index1.htm

Oregon State Shooting Association
P.O. Box 66481
Portland, OR 97290
(503) 775–4057
http://www.ossa.org

Pennsylvania

Allegheny County Sportsmen's League
1028 Hulton Road
Pittsburgh, PA 15147
(412) 714–0395
http://www.acslpa.org/

Pennsylvania Federation of Sportsmen's Clubs
2426 N. 2nd Street
Harrisburg, PA 17110
(717) 232–3480
http://www.pfsc.org

Pennsylvania Rifle & Pistol Association
P.O. Box 216
Sand Lake, PA 16145–0216
(724) 376–3251
http://www.pennarifleandpistol.org

Texas

Dallas Arms Collectors Association, Inc.
P.O. Box 170415
Irving, TX 75017
(972) 255–5280
http://www.dallasarms.com

Houston Gun Collectors Association
P.O. Box 741429
Houston, TX 77274–1429
(713) 981–6463
http://www.hgca.org

Peaceable Texans for Firearms Rights
1122 Colorado Street Suite, 2320
Austin, TX 78702
(512) 476–2299
http://www.io.com/~velte/pt.htm

Texas Concealed Handgun Instructor Association
P.O. Box 1762
Uvalde, TX 78802–1762
(830) 278–2815
http://www.txchia.org

Justice Foundation
8122 Datapoint, Suite 812
San Antonio, TX 78229
(210) 614–7157
http://www.txjf.org

Texas State Rifle Association
4570 Westgrove Drive, Suite 200
Addison, TX 75001–3222
(972) 889–8772
http://www.tsra.com

Utah

Utah Precision Marksmanship Society
1884 Yale Avenue

Salt Lake City, UT 84108
(801) 278–6335
http://www.upms.org

Utah State Rifle and Pistol Association
110 South 650 East
Bountiful, UT 84010
(801) 825–6631
http://www.usrpa.org/index.html

Virginia

Virginia Citizens Defense League, Inc.
P.O. Box 513
Newington, VA 22122
(804) 639–0600
http://www.vcdl.org

Virginia Shooting Sports Association
P.O. Box 1258
Orange, VA 22960
(540) 672–5848
http://www.myvssa.org

Washington

Washington Arms Collectors
P.O. Box 389
Renton, WA 98057–0389
(425) 255–8410
http://www.washingtonarmscollectors.org

Wisconsin

Wisconsin Concealed Carry Association
3263 S. 45th Street
Milwaukee, WI 53219
(414) 543–1916
http://www.wisconsinconcealedcarry.com

Wisconsin Rifle and Pistol Association
Secretary—Bill King

P.O. Box 922
Wisconsin Rapids, WI 54494
(715) 423–7454
http://www.wrpa.com/

Government Agencies

Bureau of Alcohol, Tobacco, Firearms and Explosives
Office of Liaison and Public Information
650 Massachusetts Avenue NW, Room 8290
Washington, DC 20226
(202) 927–8500
http://www.atf.treas.gov

Bureau of Justice Statistics
810 Seventh Street NW
Washington, DC 20531
(202) 307–0765
http://www.ojp.usdoj.gov/bjs/

Centers for Disease Control and Prevention
1600 Clifton Road
Atlanta, GA 30333
Tel: (404) 639–3311
Public Inquiries: (404) 639–3534 / (800) 311–3435
http://www.cdc.gov/

Civilian Marksmanship Program
P.O. Box 576
Port Clinton, OH 43452
(419) 635–2141 *or* (888) 267–0796
http://www.odcmp.com

Federal Bureau of Investigation
J. Edgar Hoover Building
935 Pennsylvania Avenue NW
Washington, DC 20535–0001
(202) 324–3000
http://www.fbi.gov/

National Center for Health Statistics
3311 Toledo Road
Hyattsville, MD 20782
(301) 458–4000
http://www.cdc.gov/nchs/

National Center for Injury Prevention and Control
4770 Buford Highway NE
Atlanta, GA 30341–3724
(770) 488–1506
http://www.cdc.gov/ncipc

National Institute of Justice
810 Seventh Street NW
Washington, DC 20531
(202) 307–2942
http://www.ojp.usdoj.gov/nij/

Office of Safe and Drug-Free Schools
400 Maryland Avenue SW, Room 3E300
Washington, DC 20202–6450
(202) 260–3954
http://www.ed.gov/about/offices/list/osdfs
  /index.html?src=oc

United States Department of Justice
950 Pennsylvania Avenue NW
Washington, DC 20530–0001
(202) 514–2000
http://www.usdoj.gov/

9

Selected Print and Nonprint Resources

The literature on guns in American society is enormous. The print and nonprint sources listed in this chapter represent some of the better known and more influential in the field. They are slanted toward peer-reviewed academic journals, scholarly presses, and the Web sites of government agencies and larger advocacy organizations. It is important to keep in mind that even "dispassionate" scholars often find it hard to conceal their predispositions; as such, the reader should stay alert to their pro- or anti-gun inclinations and biases. Academicians, government researchers, and popular writers alike generally begin their studies with either a pro- or anti-gun perspective and then proceed to line up the evidence correspondingly—ignoring or discounting or minimizing any findings that do not fit the given perspective.

Sources are categorized by topic, for each of which a relatively small number of sources is given. Scholars and general readers alike can easily become overwhelmed by the volume of studies available in print and on the Web, and each topical list could have easily extended into the dozens, if not the hundreds. However, the law of diminishing returns applies, and the number and importance of fresh ideas and data shrinks quickly as one moves beyond the top handful of sources.

Gun Violence, the United States versus Other Economically Developed Nations

Criminologist Gary Kleck and legal scholars David B. Kopel and Don B. Kates Jr. are well-known authors associated with the gun rights side of the contemporary debate over gun control. All three are highly critical of cross-national comparisons of gun availability, gun control laws, and the prevalence of gun violence, which usually reveal the United States as an outcast nation. Compared with other economically developed democracies, the United States has very high rates of gun ownership and gun violence. Gun control advocates see these rates as causally connected, but Kopel's comparative analysis of gun violence in the United States, Great Britain, Canada, and Japan leads him to conclude that the key explanation of a nation's violence should be sought in culture, not gun availability; see his *Gun Control in Great Britain: Saving Lives or Constricting Liberty?* (Chicago: Office of International Criminal Justice, University of Illinois, 1992) and his *The Samurai, the Mountie, and the Cowboy: Should America Adopt the Gun Controls of Other Democracies?* (Buffalo, NY: Prometheus Books, 1992). Kopel's similarly pro-gun rights anthology, *Guns: Who Should Have Them?* (Amherst, NY: Prometheus Books, 1995) contains U.S. and cross-national analyses contending that only a weak link—at best—exists between gun prevalence and crime/violence/suicide/accidents. Similar conclusions are drawn in Gary Kleck and Don B. Kates, *Armed: New Perspectives on Gun Control* (Amherst, NY: Prometheus Books, 2001) and Gary Kleck, *Targeting Guns: Firearms and Their Control* (Hawthorne, NY: Aldine de Gruyter, 1997).

In contrast, Martin Killias argues for strong links between cross-national homicide/suicide rates and gun availability in his "International Correlations between Gun Ownership and Rates of Homicide and Suicide" (*Canadian Medical Association Journal,* Vol. 148, 1993). Killias's gun data are taken from one of the best known and most often used sources of cross-national crime data, *Experiences of Crime across the World: Key Findings from the 1989 International Crime Survey* (Boston: Kluwer Law and Taxation Publishers, 1991)—authored by Jan J. M. van Dijk, Pat Mayhew, and Killias himself. More recently, Etienne G. Krug and his colleagues Kenneth E. Powell and Linda Dahlberg show a strong connection between cross-national firearms availability and gun violence in

their "Firearm-Related Deaths in the United States and 35 Other
High- and Upper-Middle-Income Countries" (*International Journal of Epidemiology*, Vol. 27, 1998), as do David Hemenway and
Matthew Miller in their "Firearm Availability and Homicide
Rates across 26 High-Income Countries" (*Journal of Trauma*, Vol.
49, 2000). Franklin E. Zimring and Gordin Hawkins acknowledge
that many developed nations have serious crime problems, but
they conclude that the United States stands out regarding its high
murder rate, which they attribute to its high prevalence of handguns. Handgun ownership is rare in all other nations—save for
Switzerland (due to near universal membership in the militia);
see their *Crime Is Not the Problem: Lethal Violence in America* (New
York: Oxford University Press, 1997).

Anyone doing serious research in the area of cross-national
gun violence and gun control laws today will draw much of their
data from the *United Nations International Study on Firearm Regulation* (Vienna, Austria: Crime Prevention and Criminal Justice Division, United Nations Office, 1999). The U.S. Department of Justice's Bureau of Justice Statistics provides much of the
cross-national gun violence data from this and other sources online at http://www.ojp.usdoj.gov/bjs/ijs.htm.

The Second Amendment

Virtually all recent scholarly analyses of the Second Amendment
have been motivated by the gun control debate. Pro-gun rights authors argue that the framers of the Bill of Rights intended the Second Amendment to guarantee an *individual*—and not just a collective (state)—right. Among the most readable of these are Clayton
E. Cramer, *For the Defense of Themselves: The Original Intent and Judicial Interpretation of the Right to Keep and Bear Arms* (Westport, CT:
Praeger, 1994); Stephen P. Halbrook, *A Right to Bear Arms: State and
Federal Bills of Rights and Constitutional Guarantees* (Westport, CT:
Greenwood Press, 1989); David T. Hardy, *Origins and Development
of the Second Amendment* (Chino Valley, AZ: Blacksmith Publishers,
1986); Joyce Lee Malcolm, *To Keep and Bear Arms: The Origins of an
Anglo-American Right* (Cambridge, MA: Harvard University Press,
1994); the various authors in the *Tennessee Law Review: A Second
Amendment Symposium Issue* (Vol. 62, #3, Spring 1995); and the
reprints published in recent issues of the *Journal on Firearms Research* (http://www.saf.org/default.asp?p=jfpp). Hardy's work

contains mainly original sources and has the least amount of interpretation.

While authors most often cited by gun control advocates emphasize the first half of the Second Amendment ("*A well regulated Militia, being necessary to the security of a free State*"), authors extolled by gun rights advocates tend to emphasize its second half ("*the right of the people to keep and bear Arms, shall not be infringed*"). In other words, authors seeing no constitutional problems associated with gun control emphasize that the original aim of the Second Amendment was to guarantee the right of the states to form their own militias and that no personal right to keep and bear arms was intended. Further, these authors argue that even if the original aim were to guarantee the rights of individuals, the courts and legislatures of the states and of the federal government have never felt the need to be in lockstep with such an interpretation. Indeed, they have regularly "infringed" upon the right "to keep and bear Arms" by way of a host of gun regulations and rulings. Among the most readable books in this camp are Dennis A. Henigan, E. Bruce Nicholson, and David Hemenway, *Guns and the Constitution: The Myth of the Second Amendment Protection for Firearms in America* (Northampton, MA: Aletheia Press, 1995); Warren Freedman, *The Privilege to Keep and Bear Arms: The Second Amendment and Its Interpretation* (New York: Quorum Books, 1990); and Robert J. Spitzer, *The Right to Bear Arms: Rights and Liberties under the Law* (Santa Barbara, CA: ABC-CLIO, 2001). Also popular with gun control advocates are H. Richard Uviller and William G. Merkel, *The Militia and the Right to Arms, Or, How the Second Amendment Fell Silent* (Durham, NC: Duke University Press, 2003); and the recent writings of Saul Cornell ("A New Paradigm for the Second Amendment," *Law and History Review*, Vol. 161, 2004; "A Well Regulated Right: The Early American Origins of Gun Control," *Fordham Law Review*, Vol. 73, 2005, coauthored with Nathan DeDino; also see Cornell's forthcoming *A Well Regulated Militia: The Founding Fathers and the Origins of Gun Control in America*, Oxford University Press, 2006).

Uviller, Merkel, and Cornell emphasize that the contemporary debate over gun control has ignored the language and culture of the founding fathers, and that when these are taken into account both the "individual-right" and the "collective-right" interpretations are found wanting. The founders, according to these scholars, viewed the Second Amendment as giving individuals—

or rather *selected* individuals (able-bodied, free white men)—the right to bear arms, but only to fulfill their duty of serving in the state militia. Because state militias have long since disappeared (their modern-day equivalent would be the National Guards of the individual states), the amendment is, at worst, irrelevant to the modern debate and, at best, no barrier to the enactment of strict gun regulations. When a 2003 Gallup poll asked a national probability sample of U.S. adults if the amendment "was intended to give Americans the right to keep and bear arms for their own defense, (or) was only intended to preserve the existence of citizen-militias," 68 percent responded that it "gives the right to keep and bear arms"; however, of those respondents saying that the Second Amendment was so intended, 82 percent responded that "the government can impose some restrictions on gun ownership without violating the [amendment]" ("Guns," http://www.gallup.com/poll/, 2004).

Public Opinion

The Gallup poll regularly asks a random sample of U.S. adults their opinions about guns and gun control. Over the years, there has been a strong pattern of support for almost all forms of gun control, save the banning of handguns (for a small annual fee, subscribers can see these polls online at: http://www.gallup.com /poll/). The General Social Survey also regularly asks the U.S. public whether it would "favor or oppose a law which would require a person to obtain a police permit before he or she could buy a gun," and the results consistently show three-quarters responding with "favor" (http://webapp.icpsr.umich.edu/GSS/). Tom W. Smith intensively examines public opinion about gun control and finds strong support for strict gun regulation in his *2001 National Gun Policy Survey of the National Opinion Research Center: Research Findings* (Chicago: National Opinion Research Center, 2001; http://www.norc.uchicago.edu/online/guns01 .pdf). Gun rights advocates emphasize the research of Gary Kleck and James D. Wright. In his *Point Blank: Guns and Violence in America* (New York: Aldine de Gruyter, 1991), Kleck stresses that public opinion studies tell us little about the actual feelings of people. Wright reaches a similar conclusion in his "Public Opinion and Gun Control" (*Annals of the American Academy of Political and Social Science*, Vol. 453, 1981).

The Role of Politics

For generally balanced analyses of the gun control debate as it is played out in American society and politics, see John M. Bruce and Clyde Wilcox, eds., *The Changing Politics of Gun Control* (Lanham, MD: Rowman & Littlefield, 1998); Gregg Lee Carter, *The Gun Control Movement* (New York: Twayne Publishers, 1997); Alexander DeConde *Gun Violence in America: The Struggle for Control* (Boston: Northeastern University Press, 2001); Wilbur Edel, *Gun Control: Threat to Liberty or Defense against Anarchy?* (Westport, CT: Praeger, 1995); Gerald D. Robin, *Violent Crime and Gun Control* (Cincinnati, OH: Anderson Publishing Co., 1991); and William J. Vizzard, *Shots in the Dark: The Politics, Policy, and Symbolism of Gun Control* (Lanham, MD: Rowman & Littlefield, 2000). Vizzard is a former agent of the Bureau of Alcohol, Tobacco, Firearms and Explosives, the key federal agency charged with enforcing national firearms laws.

For pro-gun rights descriptions of how the NRA and its allies work the political system to achieve their aims, see Edward F. Leddy, *Magnum Force Lobby: The National Rifle Association Fights Gun Control* (Lanham, MD: University Press of America, 1987); Wayne R. LaPierre, *Guns, Crime, and Freedom* (Washington, DC: Regnery Publishing, 1994); and almost any issue of the NRA's monthly publication *American Rifleman*. LaPierre is the NRA's chief national spokesperson.

For pro-gun control analyses of the same topic, see Peter Harry Brown and Daniel G. Abel, *Outgunned: Up against the NRA—The First Complete Insider Account of the Battle over Gun Control* (New York: Free Press, 2003); Osha Gray Davidson, *Under Fire: The NRA and the Battle for Gun Control* (New York: Henry Holt, 1993); Robert Sherrill, *The Saturday Night Special* (New York: Charterhouse, 1972); Pete Shields, *Guns Don't Die—People Do* (New York: Arbor House, 1981); Robert J. Spitzer, *The Politics of Gun Control* 3rd ed. (Washington, DC: Congressional Quarterly Press, 2004); and Josh Sugarmann, *NRA: Money, Firepower, Fear* (Washington, DC: National Press Books, 1992). Shields (deceased in 1993) was chair of Handgun Control Inc. (now the Brady Campaign to Prevent Gun Violence), and Sugarmann is executive director of a Washington, D.C., gun-control advocacy group, the Violence Policy Center.

For more objective analyses on how pressure groups influence Congress and the political process more generally, see Jeffrey

H. Birnbaum, *The Lobbyists: How Influence Peddlers Get Their Way in Washington* (Three Rivers, MI: Three Rivers Press, 1993); Kenneth M. Goldstein, *Interest Groups, Lobbying, and Participation in America* (New York: Cambridge University Press, 1999); Leroy N. Rieselbach, *Congressional Politics: The Evolving Legislative System*, 2nd ed. (Boulder, CO: Westview Press, 1995); Bruce C. Wolpe, *Lobbying Congress: How the System Works* (Washington, DC: Congressional Quarterly, 1990); and the various articles—including a detailed one on the NRA—in Allan J. Cigler and Burdett A. Loomis, eds., *Interest Group Politics*, 6th ed. (Washington, DC: Congressional Quarterly, 2002).

Gun Control, the Public Health Approach

The best single source detailing the public health approach to gun violence, which includes the national and cross-national evidence for the efficacy of this approach, is David Hemenway, *Private Guns, Public Health* (Ann Arbor: University of Michigan Press, 2004). Hemenway is a professor of health policy at Harvard University, where he has worked closely with his colleagues at the Harvard Injury Control Research Center to amass many useful links to articles and data analyzing gun control and gun violence from the public health perspective (see http://www.hsph .harvard.edu/hicrc/). Similarly well known public health research centers making a wide range of gun-related research readily available on the Web are the Center for Gun Policy and Research at Johns Hopkins University Bloomberg School of Public Health (http://www.jhsph.edu/gunpolicy/) and the Violence Prevention Research Program at the University of California, Davis (http://www.ucdmc.ucdavis.edu/vprp/). The public health approach emphasizes the huge economic cost of gun violence to the United States, which Philip J. Cook and Jens Ludwig estimate at $100 billion per year in their *Gun Violence: The Real Costs* (New York: Oxford University Press).

Gun rights advocates are very critical of the public health approach, and they praise the criticisms of this approach found in Don B. Kates Jr., John K. Lattimer, and James Boen, "Sagecraft: Bias and Mendacity in the Public Health Literature (Chapter 5 in Don B. Kates Jr. and Gary Kleck, *The Great American Gun Debate: Essays on Firearms and Violence,* San Francisco: Pacific Research Institute for Public Policy). Gun rights advocates are particularly upset that public health estimates of the costs of gun violence to the United State ignore the *savings* incurred from the *defensive* use of guns by law-abiding citizens to fend off criminal attacks. These advocates point to the findings of John R. Lott Jr. that "more guns" in the hands of ordinary citizens translates into "less crime," and less of all its associated costs to the judicial and health-care systems (see Lott's *More Guns, Less Crime: Understanding Crime and Gun-Control Law*, 2nd ed., Chicago: University of Chicago Press, 2000; and *The Bias against Guns: Why Almost Everything You've Heard about Gun Control is Wrong*, Washington, DC: Regnery Publishing, 2003). Lott's research coheres with the findings of Gary Kleck and Marc Gertz in their national survey showing that the defensive use of guns is quite common (an estimated 2.5 million such uses per year); see their "Armed Resistance to Crime: The Prevalence and Nature of Self-Defense with a Gun" (*Journal of Criminal Law and Criminology*, Vol. 86, 1995). The highly publicized research of Lott, Kleck, and Gertz spawned a huge backlash of public health research—much touted by gun control advocates—showing that "more guns," in actuality, translates into "more crime"; see Ian Ayres and John J. Donohue III, "Shooting Down the 'More Guns, Less Crime' Hypothesis" (*Stanford Law Review*, Vol. 55, 2003); Mark Duggan, "More Guns More Crime" (*Journal of Political Economy*, Vol. 99, 2001); and Tim Lambert, *Do More Guns Cause Less Crime?* (http://timlambert.org/guns /lott/onepage.html).

The National Center for Injury Prevention and Control—of the Centers for Disease Control and Prevention of the U.S. Department of Health and Human Service—publishes historical and recent data on firearms fatalities, injuries, and accidents. Its data extraction program, known as "WISQERS" (*Web-Based Injury Statistics Query and Reporting System*), takes only a few minutes to learn, and ordinary users can generate sophisticated reports with very little practice (see http://webappa.cdc.gov/sasweb /ncipc/mortrate10_sy.html).

Gun Control, the Law Enforcement Approach

Both sides of the gun debate contend that better law enforcement can reduce gun violence. The National Research Council's intensive review of the relevant research found that community-oriented policing combined with stiff sentences of gun-law violators can reduce gun violence. Community-oriented policing focuses police work in neighborhoods where gun violence is high. The police crack down hard on gun-law violators and process them through the federal court system whenever possible (punishments are generally stiffer in federal courts than in state courts); see National Research Council, *Firearms and Violence: A Critical Review* (Washington, DC: National Academies Press, 2004). The Bureau of Alcohol, Tobacco, Firearms and Explosives found that the unregulated market in firearms at gun shows ends up supplying many street criminals with their weapons; see its *Gun Shows: Brady Checks and Crime Traces.* http://www.atf.treas.gov/pub /treas_pub/gun_show.pdf. It also found that a relatively few guns are involved in large number crimes, and, likewise, a relatively few gun retail dealers sell a large proportion of guns used in crimes; see *Crime Gun Trace Reports (2000) National Report* (http://www.atf.gov/firearms/ycgii/2000/index.htm). Glenn L. Pierce and his colleagues conclude from their analyses of crime-gun trace data that cracking down on corrupt gun dealers can reduce gun violence by cutting the supply of new guns ending up in the hands of street criminals. Each new generation of felons must be armed, and many of their guns actually come from federally licensed firearms dealers; see Glenn L. Pierce, Anthony A. Braga, Raymond Hyatt Jr., and Christopher S. Koper, "Characteristics and Dynamics of Illegal Firearms Markets: Implications for a Supply-Side Enforcement Strategy" (*Justice Quarterly*, Vol. 21, 2004).

The U.S. Department of Justice has published two comprehensive assessments of dozens of law-enforcement and community-oriented strategies to reduce gun violence, both available on the Web: *Gun Violence Reduction: National Integrated Firearms Violence Reduction Strategy* (http://www.usdoj.gov/archive/opd /gunviolence.htm) and *Promising Strategies to Reduce Gun Violence* (http://ojjdp.ncjrs.org/pubs/gun_violence/contents.html).

Gun Control, the Lawsuit Approach

Over the past decade, gun control advocates have lost many more battles than they have won in various state legislatures, as well as in both Houses of the U.S. Congress. As such, gun control advocates have increasingly turned to the courts to press for more gun regulations, especially those aimed at the gun industry. In particular, gun control advocates want the industry to produce guns with more safety features (e.g., trigger locks; chamber-loaded indicators; magazine-disconnect safeties) and to increase its monitoring of the gun wholesalers and retailers (e.g., stop supplying those with poor recordkeeping; train retailers to recognize "straw purchasers"—those with no criminal record who are simply buying guns for prohibited persons, such as convicted felons or minors). The lawsuit strategy is detailed in the various articles in Timothy Lytton, ed., *Suing the Gun Industry: A Battle at the Crossroads of Gun Control and Mass Torts* (Ann Arbor: University of Michigan Press, 2005). The gun rights versus gun control perspectives on using the courts to pursue gun regulations are succinctly put forth in the legal analyses of David B. Kopel ("Product Liability Lawsuits"), whose writings are often upheld by gun rights advocates, and Dennis A. Henigan ("Lawsuits against Gun Manufacturers," "Nuisance Law and Gun Suits," and "Smith & Wesson Settlement Agreement"), director of the Legal Action Project for the Brady Center to Prevent Gun Violence, in Gregg Lee Carter, ed., *Guns in American Society: An Encyclopedia of History, Politics, Culture, and the Law*, Vols. 1 and 2 (Santa Barbara, CA: ABC-CLIO, 2002).

Current civil lawsuits against the gun industry are monitored at the Firearms Litigation Clearing House (http://www.csgv.org/issues/litigation/index.cfm), an affiliate of the Educational Fund to Stop Gun Violence and the Coalition to Stop Gun Violence. Various advocacy organizations also keep their Web sites up to date with the latest news on these lawsuits; in particular, see the relevant URLs of the largest gun rights advocacy group, the National Rifle Association (http://www.nraila.org/Issues/Filter.aspx?ID=022) and of the largest gun control group, the Brady Campaign to Prevent Gun Violence (http://www.gunlawsuits.org/). Civil actions against the gun industry will all but cease beginning in 2006, as Congress passed the Protection of Lawful Commerce in Arms Act (S.397; H.R.800) in the late fall of 2005. The act will prohibit "civil liability actions" against firearms manufacturers and dealers for any harm caused by the criminal or unlawful misuse of the guns or ammunition they sell.

Glossary

AK-47 A military rifle that can be fired in both automatic (continuous fire) or semiautomatic modes, it is one of the most widely used guns in the world. AK-47 is an abbreviation of "Avtomat Kalashnikova obrazets 1947g"—which translates from Russian as "Automatic Kalashnikov model 1947." Since the late 1950s, it has seen many derivatives that shoot only as semiautomatics, even though they have the look and feel of the original AK-47, including having a high-capacity ammunition clip that can hold up to 30 rounds. Although these derivatives are characterized by gun control advocates as "assault rifles," the usual definition of this term only includes guns that can be fired in a fully automatic mode.

American Rifleman The principle magazine published by the National Rifle Association. Started in 1995, it is the oldest firearms magazine in the U.S. and has the largest circulation. Its articles strongly support the rights of gun owners. Among its most popular regular features is "The Armed Citizen," which reports on recent instances in which ordinary citizens have defended themselves with firearms from criminal attack.

ammunition A combination of a projectile or projectiles (bullet in the case of rifles and handguns; pellets in the case of shotguns), powder, and an igniter into a single unit—called a *cartridge* for rifle and handgun ammunition, and a *shell* for shotguns. The modern cartridge uses a brass case with the projectile held by friction at one end and the ignition system mounted at the other. Brass is used because of its flexibility—it expands when the powder ignited, providing a tight seal within the barrel of the gun, but returns to its original size allowing the fired cartridge to be readily removed. A shotgun shell has a plastic cartridge case on which a brass base and rim are mounted. After powder, a plastic wad, and the pellets (also called "shot") are loaded, the open end of the cartridge is sealed by crimping it inward.

amnesty program Gun amnesty programs—usually accompanying *gun buyback programs*—are one means by which law enforcement agencies remove firearms from circulation. In such programs, weapons that are turned in (often for cash or some other material inducement) are accepted with "no questions asked." Also, those turning in illegal guns are

359

not prosecuted for illegal possession of a firearm. Typically, no background checks or criminal investigations of participants are conducted.

antique gun Usually considered a gun over 100 years old for which ammunition is no longer commercially manufactured.

armor-piercing ammunition A cartridge with an armor-piercing capacity (the ability to penetrate a bullet-proof vest) has a bullet (projectile) with a large, pointed core made of steel or other dense metals (e.g., tungsten alloys, iron, bronze). In the 1980s, a national debate arose over armor-piercing handgun ammunition. Critics charged that these projectiles could pierce body armor and labeled them "cop-killer bullets." The U.S. Congress ultimately outlawed civilian production of handgun ammunition made with very dense cores capable of piercing bullet-resistant vests and other body armor (Public Law 99-308, the Law Enforcement Officers Protection Act of 1986).

assault rifle The Department of Defense defines an assault rifle as a military rifle capable of "selective fire." That is, it is capable of being fired semiautomatically or fully automatically. Journalists during the 1980s and 1990s changed the definition to mean firearms that can be fired in an automatic mode alone, thus seriously misleading the public.

assault weapon A firearm developed for military use as a light machine gun, but capable of firing in semi-automatic or fully automatic mode. The most common assault firearm is a rifle, but there are also shotgun and handgun forms. Assault weapons first came into the civilian population in large quantities during the 1960s with the sale of surplus U.S. military M1 rifles; AK-47-type rifles proliferated in the 1980s, most imported from China. Semi-automatic pistols — which could illegally but easily be made to fire automatically — also became popular during the 1980s and early 1990s (the most famous models were the MAC-10 and the Tec-9). A semi-automatic fires one bullet with each trigger pull, while a fully automatic weapon fires continuously when the trigger is pulled and not released. Assault weapons were subject to strict federal controls between September of 1994 and September of 2004.

automatic weapon A fully automatic weapon fires continuously when the trigger is pulled and not released. Automatic weapons may be handguns, shotguns, rifles, or machine guns. In 1986, federal law banned the civilian sale, transfer, or possession of automatic weapons. However, those automatic weapons legally possessed before 1986 may be sold by a federally licensed firearms dealer if the buyer passes a background check and pays a special federal tax. Approximately 120,000 automatic weapons are currently legally possessed by private individuals, while about the same number are in the hands of various law enforcement agencies.

background check An inspection of criminal and mental-health history of a prospective purchaser of a firearm. The 1993 federal Brady

Handgun Violence Prevention Act required a five-business-day waiting period for purchase of a handgun, for the purpose of conducting a background check on the prospective buyer. Amendments were eventually added requiring the same check for the buyers of rifles and shotguns. Five years after enactment of the law, the five-day waiting period was eliminated and replaced by a computerized instant background check system. Firearm purchases are to be rejected if the applicant has been convicted of a crime that carries a sentence of at least a year (not including misdemeanors); if there is a violence-based restraining order against the applicant; if the person has been convicted of domestic abuse, arrested for using or selling drugs, is a fugitive from justice, is certified as mentally unstable or is in a mental institution, or is an illegal alien or has renounced U.S. citizenship. Brady law supporters complain that the background check provision only applied to licensed dealers. At gun shows and flea markets in most states, guns can be bought and sold by unlicensed individuals. National legislative efforts to close this so-called "gun-show loophole" failed in 1999 and 2000. However, eleven states required background checks even for unlicensed sellers.

black market The U.S. black market for firearms involves transactions in which stolen or purchased firearms (including both new and secondhand guns) are illegally transferred between buyers and sellers. Individuals diverting firearms from the legal to the illegal market are labeled "gun traffickers." Gun trafficking is a primary source of the firearms used in crime. The Bureau of Alcohol, Tobacco, Firearms and Explosives is responsible for preventing and combating the black market and gun trafficking.

Black Talon A hollow-point handgun bullet manufactured by Winchester designed to mushroom on impact to produce a larger wound. In July 1993, Gian Luigi Ferri fired Black Talons to kill six people in a San Francisco office building. The Black Talon was strongly criticized both for its lethality and the potential of the mushroom shape it took on after impact for penetrating surgical gloves during emergency surgery. Winchester responded by renaming the bullet the "Ranger Talon" and restricting sales to law enforcement agencies.

Brady Campaign to Prevent Gun Violence Formerly known as Handgun Control Inc., the Brady Campaign is the largest and best-known nonprofit organization working for stronger gun laws in the United States. The Campaign believes gun violence can be reduced by strong gun laws, and to this end it supports political candidates with similar beliefs, and it organizes and mobilizes grassroots organizations to work for such candidates and to increase public awareness of the gun control issue. The organization's biggest successes were the 1993 enactment of legislation to require background checks on gun purchasers—the Brady Handgun Violence Prevention Act—and the 1994 federal ban on assault weapons (which expired in 2004).

breech The rear of the barrel of a firearm, which in modern guns is the point of entry for a cartridge when a gun is being loaded.

Bureau of Alcohol, Tobacco, Firearms, and Explosives Known as the ATF or BATF, it is the federal law enforcement agency responsible for administering federal laws regulating alcohol, tobacco, firearms, and explosives. ATF also conducts arson investigations when called upon to assist a local, state, or national law enforcement agency. ATF is headquartered in Washington, D.C., with field offices located in various states as well as in a few other countries. The enforcement of federal firearms regulations dominates ATF's expenditures and activities. It is responsible for licensing and monitoring gun manufacturers and dealers. The Brady Handgun Violence Prevention Act requires dealers to obtain a criminal background check on a prospective buyer prior to making a sale. They do so through the FBI's National Instant Criminal Background Check System (NICS). Even though ATF does not operate the NICS, it is responsible for insuring dealer compliance with this provision of the Brady Act. ATF is also responsible for the National Tracing Center, which traces the ownership of guns recovered from criminal investigations.

caliber The diameter of a bullet (the projectile portion of a cartridge) of a rifle or handgun. Depending on which country a gun and its ammunition are manufactured in, the diameter is expressed in hundredths (in the U.S.) or thousandths (U.K.) of an inch, or in millimeters (Europe, Asia, and elsewhere). Thus, for example, a U.S.-made .50 caliber handgun shoots ammunition with a bullet diameter of $1/2$ inch.

cartridge A single round of rifle or handgun ammunition that combines a projectile (bullet), powder, and an igniter into a single unit.

case, or casing The container used for the powder, igniter, and a portion of the projectile (bullet) of a cartridge. The casings for handguns and rifles are usually brass, while the casing (or "shell") for shotguns are paper or plastic.

concealed weapons laws Laws adopted by most states in the 1800s and early 1900s banning the carrying of concealed weapons, including handguns and other firearms. Such laws became an important part of the gun control debate in the late 1980s and throughout the 1990s when gun rights proponents pushed to remove permit-granting discretion from local police chiefs and sheriffs and to allow issuance of permits to those passing a criminal background check (and in some cases, a gun safety course). Before 1987, only Georgia, Indiana, Maine, New Hampshire, North Dakota, South Dakota, Vermont, and Washington had "shall issue" laws, requiring law enforcement officials to issue concealed weapons permits to ordinary citizens. In 1987, Florida enacted a "shall issue" right-to-carry law that eventually served as the framework for more than two dozen other states that passed similar laws in the late 1980s and 1990s. At present, 37 states have such laws.

clip   A container for the cartridges of a handgun or rifle that usually uses a metal spring to load each cartridge into the firing chamber; it is often used synonymously with the term *magazine*. High-capacity ammunition clips (or magazines) hold ten or more cartridges and are a controversial part of the modern gun control debate. Traditionally (and by law in many jurisdictions), hunters' ammunition clips hold no more than 5 cartridges. Gun control advocates point out that high-capacity clips are a favorite of gang members and street criminals and have no legitimate purposes.

collective right interpretation (Second Amendment)   Gun control proponents generally hold that the Second Amendment refers to a *collective* right that guarantees *states*, not individuals, the right to form armed militias for protection in case the democracy of the fledgling nation failed. Thus the amendment does not guarantee the right of the *individual* to keep and bear firearms. Both state and federal courts have favored the collective right interpretation, and thus the challenges to gun control regulations based on the Second Amendment have generally been unsuccessful.

cooling-off period   A legally mandated delay between the time a gun is purchased and the time the purchaser may take possession of it. Although the primary purpose for this delay is to allow for a "cooling-off" period in case the individual is buying the gun on impulse (to commit a crime or suicide), it also provides authorities with the opportunity to conduct a criminal and mental competency background check of the prospective buyer. The 1993 Brady Handgun Violence Prevention Act imposed a five-business-day waiting period for handgun purchases, but was replaced by a computerized "instant" background checking system in 1998. However, 18 states still mandate a waiting period of anywhere from 3 to 180 days, especially for the purchase of handguns.

defensive gun use   Considered by gun rights activists to be one of the major "good" effects of gun possession—that is, its usefulness in defending against criminal attack.

derringer   A small pistol, usually firing only one or two shots (single or double barreled), designed to be carried in a pocket. The first derringer was developed by Henry Deringer (one "r") in Philadelphia in the 1850s. Copycat models were soon developed and used the double "r" to avoid trademark violations. Most derringers are small caliber, generally .22s or .25s.

dime novel   A fiction form popular in the mid- to late 19th century meant to excite the reading public with violent plots—often extolling the Western gunfighter. Technological advances allowed for cheap printing and books were priced between 5 and 10 cents. The dime novel made guns a cultural icon, as the chief tool by which the "Wild West" was conquered and the nation's borders expanded.

domestic violence   Violence between spouses or intimate partners or between these individuals and children in the home. A major effort of the gun control movement was to mandate that those convicted of domestic violence or under a court-ordered domestic violence restraining order (e.g., dictating that a husband cannot come within 500 feet of his wife) could not buy or possess firearms. This goal was achieved with the 1996 passage of the Lautenberg Amendment to the Gun Control Act of 1968.

drive-by shooting   A shooting associated with gang violence that occurs when a firearm is fired from a vehicle (usually slow-moving). Drive-by shootings became popular with the rise of street gangs and their drug trafficking during the 1980s and 1990s. They gained infamy because of their high likelihood of injuring or killing innocent bystanders.

Eddie Eagle   A gun safety program that the National Rifle Association (NRA) began in 1988 to teach children how to prevent gun accidents. Lauded by gun rights activists, many gun control proponents criticize the program as a backdoor method for recruiting children into gun use.

expanding bullet   A bullet that expands upon impact. Such bullets are required by most state game laws, as the expanded bullet creates a more severe wound and is thus more lethal—which is considered more humane. On the other hand, these bullets were banned for wartime use by the Hague Declaration of 1899 because of the very severity of the wounds they incur in humans.

Federal Bureau of Investigation (FBI)   The federal law enforcement agency in charge of the National Instant Criminal Background Check System (NICS), a critical part of the gun control efforts of the U.S. government. Federal law requires that the prospective purchaser of a firearm be subjected to a NICS background check to determine that he or she is in compliance with the laws that limit which persons may or may not purchase firearms—the most important of which include age (at least 18), lack of a felony conviction, and lack of any domestic violence offense (misdemeanor or felony) or restraining order.

Federal Firearms Licensee (FFL)   All civilian sales of new firearms in the United States are made through federally licensed firearms licensees (FFLs), regulated by the federal Gun Control Act of 1968. Retail licensees range from individuals selling guns from their homes to large chain stores such as Wal-Mart. Retailers get most of their guns from wholesale distributors, who are also federally licensed. Nevertheless, a large percentage of all gun sales each year are bought in the so-called "secondary market"—such as flea markets, gun shows, and private transactions between individuals—which allow for the easy evasion of federal gun control laws. For example, FFLs must request a computerized background check on prospective buyers to prevent felons, juveniles (under 18), and those with a domestic violence conviction (misdemeanor or felony) from acquiring guns. FFLs must also do their best to prevent so-called "straw purchases"—whereby a person barred from purchasing a firearm uses a legal purchaser (the classic example would be the girlfriend with no criminal record buying a gun for her convicted felon boyfriend). FFLs must also be alert to "gun traffickers"—individuals buying a large number of guns with the intention of selling them on the street to persons otherwise barred from buying guns, or, for example, buying a large number of guns in a state with lax gun control regulations with the intention of selling them on the street in a state with strict gun regulations.

The Bureau of Alcohol, Tobacco, Firearms and Explosives (ATF) issues 11 types of licenses, depending on the nature of the licensee's activity. The most common, Type 01, is issued to retail dealers (70 percent), but some other common licenses include Type 02 for pawnbrokers (10 percent), Type 06 for ammunition manufacturers (two percent), Type 07 for firearms manufacturers (two percent), and Type 08 for importers (less than one percent). FFLs are required to maintain detailed records of firearms transactions, and are subject to periodic inspection by the ATF. (Note that some states impose their own licensing requirements on gun dealers.)

firearm   A rifle, shotgun, or handgun; BB guns and pellet guns are not considered firearms, even though gas fired models are extremely powerful.

firearm injury statistical system   Comprehensive, national information about firearm injuries does not exist, so most policy questions in the firearm area are currently unanswerable. Initial steps toward the creation of a national firearm injury data system are underway at the Harvard Injury Control Research Center and the national Centers for Disease Control (CDC). Such a system would record more than 100 variables related to each firearm incident involving injury or death (e.g., the age, sex, and race of the victim and of the shooter; the type of gun used, and so on). The Harvard project has worked with sites around the country to pilot-test a model reporting system. Data focus not only on gun injuries (both fatal and non-fatal), but homicides and suicides by all weapon types. The CDC is developing a National Violent Death Reporting System (NVDRS) based on the Harvard project. A long-term goal is to expand the system to cover all injury deaths, including unintentional injuries due to falls, fires, drownings, and other causes. The NVDRS has been endorsed by a wide variety of organizations and its implementation is recommended by the Surgeon General's 2001 National Strategy for Suicide Prevention. Data collection has proven crucial in tracking and eliminating contagious disease epidemics and was an important tool in reducing motor vehicle injuries and fatalities in recent decades. Many public health officials now argue that the U.S. needs equivalent data to help reduce the tens of thousands of firearms-related deaths and injuries.

firearm sentence enhancement laws Criminal laws imposing stiffer penalties if a gun was used in the commission of a crime—typically longer prison terms.

flash suppressor A device attached to the muzzle of a firearm that minimizes and redirects the flash occurring when it is fired. The redirection is from the top of the barrel to its sides—thus preventing the shooter from suffering temporary blindness that occurs when the eyes are subject to a sudden, bright light. Flash suppressors are controversial in that they appear mainly on firearms deemed "assault weapons"—which gun control advocates argue have no legitimate civilian gun use such as hunting or target shooting.

gauge The size of the bore of a shotgun barrel. The gauge is defined as the number of round lead balls of the bore diameter's equal to a pound. The smaller the gauge, the more powerful the shotgun. The most common gauge is 12; other popular gauges include 10, 16, and 20. The one exception is the ".410"; a .410 shotgun refers to the gun's barrel diameter (0.410 inch). If the .410 used the definition of other shotguns, it would be a 68 gauge.

General Social Survey Since 1972, the National Opinion Research Center (NORC) at the University of Chicago has polled a random sample of adult Americans on a variety of social issues (almost annually until 1994, with samples of approximately 1,600; and bi-annually since then, with samples of approximately 3,000). NORC's *General Social Survey* (GSS) provides one of the best data sources currently available on U.S. social structure, as well as on the attitudes and self-reported behaviors of the population. Because it asks the same question concerning gun control on all of its surveys, the GSS provides one of the most important over-time data sources available on this issue: *Would you favor or oppose a law which would require a person to obtain a police permit before he or she could buy a gun?* (in 2002, 80.5 % of respondents said that they would "favor" such a law). The GSS is also an important measure of the percentage of households with guns (in 2002, 33.9 % responded "yes" to the question: *Do you happen to have in your home [or garage] any guns or revolvers?)*

gun buyback program Programs sponsored by local governments that encourage residents to turn in firearms by offering cash or some other form of remuneration, e.g., gift certificates or merchandise. The programs first became popular during the 1990s and are intended to reduce gun violence by reducing the number of guns circulating in the community. However, there is little evidence supporting their effectiveness.

gun control Government regulations meant to influence the availability and use of firearms in the civilian populations. Common forms of gun control include child access protection laws that require gun owners to keep their guns and ammunition in locked cabinets or safes; laws requiring that guns be transported safely (e.g., be unloaded and locked in the trunk of a car); the banning of cheaply-made handguns; regulations aimed at controlling the trafficking of guns between states with lax gun regulations and states with stricter regulations (e.g., by limiting a purchaser to only one gun per month); banning military-style "assault weapons"; mandatory firearms registration with local or state law enforcement authorities; mandatory licensing of gun owners; mandatory training in gun safety; and criminal and mental competency background checks of prospective gun buyers. The most important federal gun control legislation includes the 1934 National Firearms Act, the 1938 Federal Firearms Act, the 1968 Gun Control Act, the 1986 Firearm Owners' Protection Act, and the 1993 Brady Handgun Violence Prevention Act. In most states, towns and cities are "preempted" from enacting gun control laws stricter than those of the state.

gun culture   The values, viewpoints, and gun-related activities of those having a longstanding, personal attachment to guns, gun ownership, and gun-related activities—including hunting, target shooting, or membership in a gun club. Because gun ownership is so widespread, there are a number of subcultures with the general gun culture; they include Civil War re-enactors, hunters, collectors, and target shooters. However, much of the ideology of these groups is overlapping. The role of women and minorities in the gun culture has, until recently, been insignificant. Gun culture adherents tend to be politically conservative and are more often found in smaller communities and rural areas. Hunting and shooting magazines help keep the gun culture alive, as do local gun clubs and national groups such as the National Rifle Association.

gun rights advocate/proponent   Individuals believing that the Second Amendment guarantees the right of the individual to keep and bear firearms. Gun rights proponents tend to find themselves at odds with the proponents of gun control. Their major concern is that gun control regulations will snowball to the point where gun ownership is banned outright. Although many gun rights proponents agree with certain limited forms of gun control, the major organizations representing the "rights of gun owners" in the political area—such as the National Rifle Association and the Gun Owners of America—resist almost all forms of gun control, no matter how much they are supported by public opinion.

gunshot detection technologies   Technologies designed to detect the sound of gun fire within seconds of the firing and then pinpoint its location for the police. Gunshot detection technologies (GDT) identify the location of gunfire in a given zone through one or more acoustic sensors. The sensors transmit data within seconds—either via radio waves or over telephone lines—to the nearest police station. GDT technology has been found to identify three times as many gunshot incidents as what is typically reported to the police by citizens.

gun show   An exposition where an organizer rents a facility and sells booth or table space to people selling guns. Gun shows appeal to hunters, target shooters, collectors, and those interested in self-defense. Many of the dealers at gun shows are licensed by the federal government and thus submit all prospective purchasers to a computerized background check to make sure they are legal buyers (e.g., do not have a felony conviction). However, many other dealers are licensed and do not conduct any background checking. Gun control proponents have labeled the latter situation the "gun show loophole," and closing this loophole has become one of their major aims. Although federal legislation has been proposed many times to close this loophole, none has been passed into law. Gun rights advocates contend that such legislation would increase costs for law-abiding citizens and do little to prevent criminals and others barred from possession (such as minors) from acquiring guns.

handgun   A short firearm that can be held and fired with one hand. The two main types are revolvers and semi-automatic pistols. Handguns make up about one third of the privately owned firearms in the United States and are present in about one quarter of households. Most owners cite self-defense as their primary reason for owning a handgun. Other reasons for handgun ownership include target shooting and job-related needs. A relatively small number of people also collect handguns or hunt with them.

The distinctive feature of handguns is their small size, which makes them handy, concealable, and portable. Compared to rifles, handguns gain the advantages associated with small size at the expense of range, accuracy, and lethality. Although many rifles are accurate to ranges of 300 yards or more, it is difficult to hit targets with even the most accurate handguns beyond about 50 yards. Also, even though all handgun cartridges have the potential to cause lethal injury, handgun rounds tend to cause less damage than their rifle counterparts.

The same features that make handguns useful for self-defense make them useful in criminal acts. About two-thirds of murders in the U.S. are committed with firearms, and approximately 80% of those (or half the total number of murders) are committed with handguns.

The three main varieties of modern handguns are single-shot pistols, revolvers, and semi-automatic pistols. Single shot pistols find specialized use in target shooting, hunting, and as very small self-defense weapons ("derringers"), and are much less common than revolvers or semi-automatics. Revolvers hold several rounds—usually six—in chambers bored in a rotating cylinder located at the breech of the barrel. Before each shot is fired, the cylinder is rotated to bring the next chamber in line with the barrel for firing. Cylinder rotation is accomplished by cocking the hammer. This can be done manually or, in double action revolvers, merely by pulling the trigger. Semi-automatic pistols hold rounds in a magazine inside the butt or handle. Magazine capacities vary, but most hold between seven and seventeen rounds. When the pistol's slide is pulled back and allowed to move forward under spring pressure, the action advances a round from the magazine into the firing chamber and the pistol is ready to fire. When a round is fired, energy from the shot pushes the slide back, ejecting the empty cartridge that was just fired; the spring then pushes the slide forward again and loads the next cartridge.

high-capacity magazine   An ammunition clip that holds ten or more cartridges. High-capacity magazines are a controversial part of the modern gun control debate. Traditionally (and by law in many jurisdictions), hunters' ammunition clips hold no more than 5 or 6 cartridges. Gun control advocates contend that high-capacity magazines are a favorite of gang members and street criminals and have no legitimate purposes. On the other hand, gun rights proponents maintain that such magazines are legitimate for sporting purposes other than hunting, as well as for self-defense.

hollow-point bullet   A bullet with a concave nose designed to expand upon impact.

individual right interpretation (Second Amendment)   Gun rights proponents generally hold that the Second Amendment refers to an *individual* right to keep and bear firearms, not a *collective* right that guaranteed *states* the right to form armed militias for protection in case the democracy of the fledgling nation failed. Both state and federal courts have favored the collective right interpretation, and thus the challenges to gun control regulations based on the Second Amendment have generally been unsuccessful.

instant background check   When the Brady Handgun Violence Prevention Act was signed into law in November 1993, it required that a National Instant Criminal Background Check System (NICS) be established by November 30, 1998. The NICS enables Federal Firearms Licensees (FFLs) to contact the system to obtain information on whether a person attempting to purchase a firearm is disqualified under federal or state law from owning a firearm (such as convicted felons). The FBI maintains the NICS, a computerized system designed to respond almost immediately to most requests for information. Ninety-five percent of all NICS background checks are completed within two hours.

lethality effect   The comparative deadliness of different weapons used in criminal assault. The concept has been part of the gun control debate since the late 1960s, when criminologist Franklin Zimring found that gunshot wounds are five times more lethal than knife wounds (the second most deadly weapon used by criminal attackers). Gun control advocates contend that if we can reduce the number of guns in criminal hands, we can reduce the gun homicide rate. On the other hand, gun rights advocates sometimes counter that this reasoning is flawed because attackers would substitute guns with large, dangerous knives. Zimring's study did not focus on large knives, but rather on all kinds of knives, from sharpened finger files to paring knives to larger hunting knives. One study of victims hospitalized with abdominal wounds revealed

16.8% of those shot with handguns died, while nearly the same percentage died when stabbed with large knives (13.3%).

licensing   A method that governments use to regulate behavior by the granting of permission (i.e., licensing) to engage in a particular activity. Gun licensing applies to gun manufacturers, gun dealers, and gun owners. Proponents of licensing justify it on the basis that it can help to prevent selected categories of individuals from obtaining guns—including criminals, children, and those considered mentally incompetent. It is also justified as a means to promote competency in gun use and safety on the part of gun owners.

Retail and wholesale gun dealers, as well as gun and ammunition manufacturers, are required to have a federal license. The enactment of a national system of licensing for gun owners is a critical goal of gun control advocates, but all of their attempts to bring this about have failed. However, 13 states require gun owners to be licensed.

long gun   A gun that is normally fired from the shoulder. Rifles and shotguns are the two primary types of long guns. About 70 million rifles and 49 million shotguns are owned by civilians in the United States. Most owners are hunters and target shooters, though many also cite self-defense as a reason for owning a long gun.

Compared to handguns, rifles have longer barrels and use more powerful ammunition—making them more accurate and more deadly at greater distances. Handguns are rarely accurate at 50 yards, while most rifles can maintain accuracy at 300 yards or more.

magazine   A spring-loaded cartridge container that may be either built into a firearm or detachable. High-capacity magazines hold ten or more cartridges and are a controversial part of the modern gun control debate.

Magna-Trigger   A safety device preventing a handgun from firing unless the shooter wears a special magnetic ring. Tarnhelm Supply Company manufactures the device and holds its trademark. Gun control advocates view that device as critical for police officers and security guards—who might find themselves being overpowered by a criminal. These advocates also see the device as useful for gun owners with small children, who can inadvertently come across a gun and try to play with it. Critics, however, fear that the device could fail during a self-defense situation.

magnum   A cartridge or shotgun shell with an extra amount of gun powder and the weapon used to fire it. A magnum version of a particular weapon is more powerful than its nonmagnum counterpart; thus, for example, a .22 magnum has greater penetrating and knock-down force than an ordinary .22.

militia   A citizens group organized to defend the community or state, whether against outside attack, rebellion, or the threats of a tyrannical government. All 13 of the original colonies had a colony-wide militia, in addition to many local militias within each colony. In the modern era, militia groups have most often been associated with strong sentiments against the federal government, which is perceived as a tyranny. In the first years of the nation, militias were seen as critical to national defense—from both internal and external threats—and to keeping the national government in check. This view of the importance of militias motivated the Second Amendment to our Constitution (*"A well regulated Militia, being necessary to the security of a free State, the right of the people to keep and bear Arms, shall not be infringed."*).

By the early twentieth century, state and local militias were replaced by the U.S. military and the National Guard. The National Guard units of the 50 states were created by the Dick Act of 1903. This legislation, however, recognized two branches of the militia, the organized and the unorganized. The National Guard became the organized militia, while the "unorganized militia" was left empty for several decades. The term "unorganized militia" was adopted by dozens of right-wing groups during the 1970s and 1980s. They blamed the federal government for the economic and political problems of the nation (from recession to urban rioting) and viewed their mission as resisting the tyrannies of the government. The FBI keeps tabs on these groups. Such scrutiny has been partly responsible for their decline over the past decade—from the hundreds to the dozens.

Million Mom March   A grassroots women's movement supporting stronger gun regulations. It drew national attention to the issue when it held a rally of 700,000 women in Washington, D.C. on Mother's Day, 2000. The rally was the largest ever held on behalf of stronger gun control. In 2001, the organization merged with the Brady Campaign to Prevent Gun Violence.

muzzle   The end of the barrel of a firearm.

National Crime Victimization Survey   The National Crime Victimization Survey (NCVS) is one of the two major sources of data on crime in the United States, the other being the Uniform Crime Reports. Collected from a representative sample of the nation's residents, the NCVS provides detailed information on incidences of rape, robbery, assault, burglary, larceny, and motor vehicle theft. It gathers detailed victim and offender data—including age, sex, and race—as well as detailed data about the nature of the crime, e.g., location, weapon use, and injury. Its major advantage over the Uniform Crime Reports is its inclusion of crimes that victims often do not report to the police. The NCVS is a major resource that researchers use to understand gun-related crime.

The NCVS relies upon a random sample of households and gathers interviews from about 100,000 individuals. The U.S. Bureau of Justice Statistics publishes the findings of the NCVS annually.

National Guard   The reserve fighting force of the U.S. military establishment, which is controlled by both the federal and state governments. Its key divisions are the Army National Guard, the Air Guard, and the Naval Reserve. The National Guard marks its founding as 1636, when the Massachusetts Bay Colony formed a militia.

In 1903 Congress passed the Militia Act (the "Dick Act") and reaffirmed its power to call up the Guard in national emergencies. The Act instituted the uniform federal funding of the 50 state National Guard units. Strong federal control of the Guard was further increased with the 1916 National Defense Act, which placed Guard units under national military rules, organization, and authority. While a state governor may call the state National Guard unit to assist in state emergencies, the governor cannot contravene its deployment by the federal government.

National Instant Check System   The 1993 Brady Handgun Violence Prevention Act required that the FBI set up a National Instant Criminal Background Check System (NICS) by November 30, 1998. The NICS enables Federal Firearms Licensees (FFLs) to contact the system to obtain information on whether a person attempting to purchase a firearm is disqualified from owning one under federal or state law. A typical NICS check takes less than two hours. Those prohibited from possessing a firearm include: (1) convicted felons or those under indictment for a felony; (2) fugitives from justice; (3) unlawful drug users or drug addicts; (4) individuals who have been involuntarily committed to a mental institution or determined to be mentally incompetent; (5) illegal aliens and legal aliens admitted under non-immigrant visas; (6) individuals who have been dishonorably discharged from the military; (7) persons who have renounced their citizenship; (8) persons subject to certain domestic violence restraining orders; and (9) persons convicted of misdemeanor crimes of domestic violence.

Sixteen states contact the NICS on behalf of firearms dealers (the dealer calls a state telephone number to initiate the check). Ten states contact NICS for handgun purchases, but not for the purchase of rifles or shotguns; the FBI processes the checks for long gun purchases in those states. In all states, FFLs contact the FBI directly for an NICS check.

National Rifle Association (NRA)   The nation's largest and most politically powerful organization in support of the rights of gun owners. With few exceptions, it opposes the regulation of firearms—viewing such regulation as a violation of the intent of the Second Amendment to the U.S. Constitution and as having no effect on the criminal use of firearms. Its most powerful division is the Institute for Legislative Action, which is involved in fighting gun control and promoting the rights of gun owners in all 50 states' capitals, as well as in the U.S. Congress. The NRA also promotes gun safety programs, and provides information and services for hunters, target shooters, and gun collectors.

National Tracing Center (NTC)   A division of the Bureau of Alcohol, Tobacco, Firearms and Explosives, the NTC traces the origins and ownership of recovered guns used in crimes. Its goal is to follow a gun from its origin at the manufacturer or importer, through its distribution at the wholesale and retail levels, to the initial retail purchaser. It handles over 200,000 trace requests annually. Law enforcement officials use the tracing data to investigate specific crimes, as well as to establish patterns of gun sales that can identify gun trafficking rings.

one-gun-per-month laws   Laws restricting individuals from buying more than a single gun in any 30-day period. Eliminating multiple gun sales is a central aim of gun control advocates as a means to reduce the trafficking of firearms from states with lax gun regulations to states with strict regulations. For example, Virginia enacted the first one-gun-per-month law in June of 1993, after realizing that many of the guns sold in its state ended up as crime guns in New York, New Jersey and several New England states. Crime guns recovered in New York, New Jersey, and southern New England (CT, MA, and RI) that originated in Virginia dropped from 1 in 3 between September of 1989 and June of 1993, to 1 in 6 between July of 1993 and March of 1995.

California and Maryland, as well as many municipalities, have used the success of the Virginia law to justify enacting their own one-gun-per-month laws.

personalized (or "smart") guns   Guns that use a microchip that biologically identifies the guns owner or authorized user. For example, Oxford Micro Devices is developing a grip with a microchip that stores the thermal imprint of several different fingerprints. If the user's print matches one stored in memory, the gun can be fired, otherwise it can't. Another biometric technology currently under development at the New Jersey Institute of Technology, employs "dynamic grip" technology. A handgun fitted with this technology can recognize the grip pattern and pressure of an authorized user and prevent its firing by anyone else. Dynamic grip technology is expected to be ready for production by the end of 2006. Gun control advocates applaud a New Jersey initiative that will require that all guns sold in the state be "smart guns" within three years after "dynamic grip" technology is perfected.

Gun rights advocates are generally opposed to personalized gun technologies. They contend that such technologies will lead to more accidents because many gun owners will become complacent if they have a "smart gun" and thus will be more likely to leave it around unlocked and loaded; when the smart-gun technology fails, as do all mechanical and electronic devices, an accident will be waiting to happen. A smart-gun failure would also be disastrous for a police officer if it occurred when the officer needed to use his or her weapon.

pistol grip   A pistol grip refers to the handle of a handgun. However, the term most commonly comes up when gun control advocates try to define what constitutes an "assault rifle," as this type of grip has been incorporated into many military-style assault rifles (other characteristics that gun control advocates use in defining this kind of weapon include a barrel less than twenty inches, a barrel shroud, and a threaded barrel for adding a silencer or flash suppressor).

preemption laws Laws passed in 42 states, mainly during the 1990s, that prevent local communities from passing firearms laws stricter than those of the state. The passage and maintenance of preemption laws is a major goal of the NRA and gun rights activists.

purchase permit The requirement that an individual obtain a permit (or license) before purchasing a firearm. A license is only granted after a criminal background check and a specified waiting period (ranging from 3 to 180 days). Gun control advocates defend licensing because it can prevent (at least some) criminals, children, and those considered mentally incompetent from gaining easy access to guns. A Johns Hopkins University study found that states requiring licenses had two and a half times fewer crime guns traceable back to an in-state dealer compared to states not requiring licenses.

The United States is the only developed country that does not have a national purchase permit law. However, 13 U.S. states currently require a prospective gun buyer to obtain a license for buying a handgun (CA, CT, HI, IL, IA, MA, MI, MN, MO, NB, NJ, NY, and NC) and 4 for the purchase of a "long gun" (rifle or shotgun; CA, HI, MA, and NJ).

registration laws Registration laws require that individuals possessing a firearm record that fact with law enforcement officials (at the local, state, or national level). Registration laws also cover the transfer of a firearm from one person to another (e.g., through purchase). U.S. law requires that a dealer must fill out a form that discloses the identity of the purchaser of a new gun, as well as the gun's serial number. The dealer must keep this form available for inspection by the Bureau of Alcohol, Tobacco, Firearms and Explosives (ATF). If a dealer closes shop, he or she must turn all such forms over to the ATF. However, guns bought in the so-called "secondary market" (e.g., at gun shows or flea markets) are not required to be registered. The one exception is that several states require that all handguns be registered, no matter how acquired. New York City and the District of Columbia require not only all handguns to be registered, but also all rifles and shotguns (DC only allows the possession of handguns acquired before September 24, 1976, and outlaws the possession of all other handguns). Federal law also requires all automatic firearms (machine guns) to be registered (such guns must have been acquired before the enactment of the law in 1986; future sales and transfers were outlawed).

revolver A handgun holding 5–9 rounds (usually 6) in chambers bored in a rotating cylinder located at the breech of the barrel. Before each shot is fired the cylinder is rotated to bring the next chamber in line with the barrel for firing. Cylinder rotation is accomplished by cocking the hammer. This can be done manually or, in double action revolvers, merely by pulling the trigger.

rifle   A shoulder-fired gun with a long barrel. It differs from shotguns and muskets in that the inside of the barrel has spiral shaped grooves (usually three) running the length of the barrel. The grooves or rifling in the barrel impart a spin on the bullet which keeps it moving on a straighter path for longer distances compared to being shot from a smoothed bore gun (such as a musket or shotgun).

rifling   In modern handguns and rifles, a cartridge (which consists of a bullet mounted in a brass case with gunpowder and a primer) is inserted in the firing chamber at the breech, or rear end of the barrel. When the trigger is pulled, the firing pin is allowed to strike the primer, igniting the powder, which propels the bullet down the barrel. The barrel is "rifled" with spiral grooves running its entire length to make the bullet spin. This prevents the bullet from tumbling in flight, increasing accuracy over longer distances.

right-to-carry laws   Laws allowing for the average citizen to acquire, relatively easily, a concealed weapons permit to carry a handgun. The usual requirements are a background check revealing no felony convictions or domestic violence abuse incidents and a training course in gun safety and operation.

During the first third of the 20th century, 44 states banned most private citizens from carrying concealed firearms (with special exceptions being made for occupational purposes, e.g., private security). These bans received little public resistance, even from gun enthusiasts. However, beginning with the state of Florida in 1987, more than two dozen states enacted "shall issue" laws allowing for the average citizen to readily obtain a permit to carry a concealed handgun. Currently, there are 34 states with a right-to-carry law.

Saturday Night Special   A cheap handgun that is often of poor quality. Gun control advocates note that they are a favorite of street criminals and would thus like to see them banned. However, gun rights advocates believe that such a ban would discriminate against the poor—who would be priced out of buying a gun for self-defense.

Six states currently have laws placing restrictions on the manufacture and sale of cheaply made handguns (CA, HI, IL, MD, MN, and SC).

sawed-off shotgun   To help conceal a shotgun intended for criminal use, the barrel may be shortened by sawing off 12 or more inches; at the same time, the handle is often sawed down so that the weapon is transformed from one that is normally fired from the shoulder to one that can be fired from the hand. The National Firearms Act of 1934 mandates that all persons selling or owning such a gun register it with the Internal Revenue and pay applicable taxes, the effect of which is to make them all but illegal (save for a few collectors). Federal law defines a sawed-off shot-gun as a conventional shotgun that has had its barrel reduced to 18 inches or less.

Second Amendment   The Second Amendment to the U.S. Constitution reads: "A well regulated Militia, being necessary to the security of a free State, the right of the people to keep and bear Arms, shall not be in-fringed." The amendment defies easy interpretation, and its true mean-ing is a central aspect of the contemporary gun control debate. The pro-ponents of "gun rights" would have the public, lawmakers, and judges believe that the amendment guarantees the *individual* the right to own and use arms for protection—protection of one's person, home, or prop-erty, as well as against a government that might descend from democ-racy into tyranny. On the other hand, the proponents of gun control would have everyone believe that the Second Amendment is a *collective* right that guaranteed *states*, not individuals, the right to form armed militias for protection in case the democracy of the fledgling nation failed. Both state and federal courts (including the U.S. Supreme Court) have generally held that the amendment does not prevent government from strictly regulating guns and gun ownership.

Second Amendment Sisters (SAS)   A gun rights group formed to counter the rallies sponsored by the Million Mom March (MMM). The group's position on gun control is identical to that of the National Rifle Association (there is no such thing as "good gun control"). SAS contends that strong gun laws would make it more difficult for a woman to obtain and carry a gun, and thus would reduce the probability that she could defend herself from criminal attack. When MMM brought out 700,000 women at a rally in support of stronger national gun regulations on Mother's Day in 2000, the SAS counter-rally attracted about 2,000 women.

semiautomatic   A gun that fires with each pull of the trigger without the shooter having to manually insert a cartridge into the chamber. After each shot, the spent shell is automatically ejected and a new cartridge is automatically loaded into the chamber for immediate firing. Rifles, shot-guns, and handguns all have semi-automatic versions. Semi-automatics increase the firing rate compared to their bolt action, lever action, and re-volver counterparts.

shall-issue law   The definition of "shall-issue law" is the same as "right-to-carry law." "Shall-issue" implies that local or state law enforce-ment agencies do not have the *discretion* to issue a concealed weapons permit for an ordinary citizen to carry a handgun. If a citizen passes a criminal background check and, in some cases, a firearms safety course, the relevant agency *must* issue a permit. Thirty-four states currently have a shall-issue law.

shotgun   A long gun developed for bird hunting. Unlike the other type of long gun, the rifle, the inside of a shotgun barrel is smooth—and thus incapable of throwing projects very far (targets are usually less than 100 yards away) or very accurate. The loss of accuracy is made up for by the large number of pellets contained in a shotgun shell. The pellets spray out in a large circular pattern (up to 3 feet in diameter; note that many birds can be taken down when hit by only a few pellets). Shotguns are a preferred weapon for self-defense, as the shooter does not have to aim that well to hit an attacker.

silencer   An illegal device attached to the muzzle of a handgun or rifle to reduce its sound when fired.

straw purchaser   An acquaintance or relative without a criminal record purchasing a gun on behalf of someone barred from possessing a firearm—such as a juvenile or convicted felon.

trafficking   The purchase of guns, often in the dozens or even hundreds, from a dealer in a state with few gun regulations and then transporting and selling them in a state with strict gun regulations. Gun control advocates point out that the U.S. needs national-level gun regulations because state-level regulations can easily be avoided through gun trafficking.

trigger lock   A device designed to prevent the accidental discharge of a firearm. The simplest of these is a combination or key lock that fits over the trigger area (called a "clamshell" lock); a related type is the cable lock, which is strung through the barrel or trigger guard. Since 1999, the U.S. Department of Justice, in conjunction with the National Shooting Sports Foundation, has funded the distribution of millions of cable and related trigger locks through their Project HomeSafe/ChildSafe programs. More sophisticated trigger locks use "smart gun" technology that makes the weapon inoperable until the lock is released by a signal from a special ring or bracelet worn by the owner, or until the owner's finger or palm print is matched.

   Gun control advocates argue that trigger locks can prevent accidental shootings and injuries, especially of children. Gun rights advocates counter that the locks serve to reduce the usefulness of a gun for self-defense (critical seconds can be lost as an owner attempts to remove or disengage the trigger lock); they argue further that locks may actually increase the likelihood of an accidental shooting, as a gun owner may rely upon a lock at the expense of careful storage and monitoring.

Uniform Crime Reports **(UCR)**   Crime data published annually by the Federal Bureau of Investigation (FBI) based on information provided voluntarily by police departments throughout the United States. UCR data are of several types, but the most important are known as "Part I" offenses—that is, arrests for homicide, rape, robbery, aggravated assault, burglary, larceny-theft, motor vehicle theft, and arson. The data are often reported as rates; a rate is the number of arrests occurring in a given area for every 100,000 residents in that area. Rates allow for comparison of crime data from city to city and state to state, as well as across time.

Because many crimes are not reported to police, UCR data underestimate the true number of crimes committed. Thus, many social scientists and law enforcement agencies believe that victimization data—especially the National Crime Victimization Survey—provide a more accurate measure of crime.

waiting periods   A legally mandated delay between the time a gun is purchased and the time the purchaser may take possession of it. Waiting periods provide authorities with the opportunity to conduct a criminal and mental competency background check of the prospective purchaser and allow for a cooling-off period—in case the individual is buying the gun on impulse (to commit a crime or suicide). The 1993 Brady Handgun Violence Prevention Act imposed a five-business-day waiting period for handgun purchases, but was replaced by a computerized "instant" background checking system in 1998. However, 18 states maintain waiting periods, ranging from 3 to 180 days, especially for the purchase of handguns.

Index

About the Author

Gregg Lee Carter is professor of sociology at Bryant University in Smithfield, Rhode Island, where he is chair of the department of history and social sciences. He earned his Ph.D. degree in sociology at Columbia University. He has authored or edited 19 books, including *Guns in American Society: An Encyclopedia of History, Politics, Culture, and the Law* (ABC-CLIO, 2002) and *The Gun Control Movement* (Twayne Publishers, 1997).

His writings on gun control and contemporary social issues have also appeared in more than a dozen academic journals.